CONNECTED COMMUNITIES
Creating a new knowledge landscape

THE CREATIVE CITIZEN UNBOUND

How social media and DIY culture contribute to democracy, communities and the creative economy

Edited by
Ian Hargreaves and John Hartley

D1614681

P

First published in Great Britain in 2016 by

Policy Press
University of Bristol
1-9 Old Park Hill
Bristol
BS2 8BB
UK
t: +44 (0)117 954 5940
pp-info@bristol.ac.uk
www.policypress.co.uk

North America office:
Policy Press
c/o The University of Chicago Press
1427 East 60th Street
Chicago, IL 60637, USA
t: +1 773 702 7700
f: +1 773-702-9756
sales@press.uchicago.edu
www.press.uchicago.edu

© Policy Press 2016

British Library Cataloguing in Publication Data
A catalogue record for this book is available from the British Library

Library of Congress Cataloging-in-Publication Data
A catalog record for this book has been requested

ISBN 978-1-4473-2495-9 paperback
ISBN 978-1-4473-2494-2 hardback
ISBN 978-1-4473-2498-0 ePub
ISBN 978-1-4473-2499-7 Mobi

The right of Ian Hargreaves and John Hartley to be identified as editors of this work has been asserted by them in accordance with the Copyright, Designs and Patents Act 1988.

Every reasonable effort has been made to obtain permission to reproduce copyrighted material. If, however, anyone knows of an oversight, please contact the publisher.

The statements and opinions contained within this publication are solely those of the contributors and editors and not of the University of Bristol or Policy Press. The University of Bristol and Policy Press disclaim responsibility for any injury to persons or property resulting from any material published in this publication.

Policy Press works to counter discrimination on grounds of gender, race, disability, age and sexuality.

Cover design by Hayes Design
Front cover image: Getty
Printed and bound in Great Britain by CPI Group (UK) Ltd, Croydon, CR0 4YY
Policy Press uses environmentally responsible print partners

We dedicate this book to the children born to members of our research team during the Creative Citizenship project – next generation creative citizens:

Dimitris Dylan Alexiou Zamenopoulos
Kaspar Williams Schuffenhauer
Dylan James Harrison
Thea May Harrison
William Ramster
Ephrem Tettey James Animley

Contents

Acknowledgements

With thanks to our partners, without whom the Creative Citizen project and this book could not have been undertaken: *Connect Cannock*, Goldsmiths Community Centre, Kentish Town Neighbourhood Forum, Moseley Community Development Trust, Nesta, Ofcom, South Blessed, Talk About Local, The Glass-House Community Led Design, The Mill, *Tyburn Mail* and Wards Corner Community Coalition. More detail about the role of these partners is given in the main text of the book.

Thanks also to our funders, the Arts and Humanities Research Council and the Engineering and Physical Sciences Research Council, and especially to those who had the vision to create the Connected Communities programme.

List of illustrations

Chapter 5

Chapter 6

Chapter 7

Chapter 8

Chapter 9

Chapter 10

Notes on contributors

Ian Hargreaves, CBE, is Professor of Digital Economy at Cardiff University. He spent most of his working life in journalism, serving as Deputy Editor of the *Financial Times*, Editor of *The Independent*, Editor of the *New Statesman* and Director of BBC News and Current Affairs. In 2010/11 he authored a review of intellectual property issues and their effect upon growth and innovation for the UK government (*Digital Opportunity,* IPO, 2011*)*. In 2013, he co-authored a *Manifesto for the Creative Economy* for Nesta. He is a member of boards for a number of civic organisations, including National Theatre Wales, the Alacrity Foundation, the Wincott Trust, the Reuters Institute for the Study of Journalism, the European Observatory for Intellectual Property (OHIM) and the Wales Millennium Centre. He was appointed CBE in the Queen's Diamond Jubilee Honours List in 2012 for services to the creative economy and higher education.

John Hartley, AM, is John Curtin Distinguished Professor and Professor of Cultural Science at Curtin University, Australia. His research interests cross communication, cultural, media and journalism studies, the creative industries and cultural science – the attempt to reconfigure the study of culture using evolutionary and complexity approaches. Recent books include: *Creative Economy and Culture* (with Wen Wen and Henry Siling Li, Sage, 2015); *Cultural Science: A Natural History of Stories, Demes, Knowledge and Innovation* (with Jason Potts, Bloomsbury, 2014), *A Companion to New Media Dynamics* (edited with Jean Burgess and Axel Bruns, Wiley-Blackwell, 2013) and *Digital Futures for Cultural and Media Studies* (Wiley-Blackwell, 2012). Hartley is a Fellow of the Australian Academy of the Humanities, International Communication Association and Royal Society of Arts. He was awarded the Order of Australia (AM) for service to education.

Emma Agusita is Senior Lecturer in Cultural Industries and a research fellow in creative businesses at the University of the West of England, Bristol. Her work is clustered around media, arts and education, specialising in digital cultures and communications (particularly youth media), informal media education, use of creative technologies and development of creative entrepreneurship education. Emma's background is in community and participatory media production as practitioner and researcher.

Katerina Alexiou is a lecturer in design at the Open University. Her academic research falls in the area of design theory and methods and she has published articles on design cognition, collaborative design, learning, creativity and social aspects of design. She also has a special interest in complexity science. Her most recent activity is focused on co-design and co-production with civil society organisations and communities engaged in place-making and creative civic action.

Giota Alevizou is currently a research fellow in digital cultures and connected communities at the Open University. She has published on the cultural politics of technology in education, online communities and information systems. Her current research explores the intersections of media, civic culture and urban politics. She leads an AHRC-funded project comparing approaches to asset mapping and exploring methods for public engagement and community capacity building.

Caroline Chapain is a lecturer at the Business School, University of Birmingham. She has been researching creative industries in UK and European cities and regions on behalf of organisations such as local authorities, Nesta and the British Council. Recently, she has explored links between creative practices and online media and the development of creative systems as part of the Arts and Humanities Research Council Connected Communities Programme. Caroline co-chairs the Regional Studies Association Network on Creative Regions in Europe.

Jon Dovey is Professor of Screen Media at the University of the West of England, Bristol. In 2008 he launched the Digital Cultures Research Centre, which he directed until 2012. He was a knowledge transfer fellow at Bristol's Pervasive Media Studio from 2010–12, co-authoring the *Pervasive Media Cookbook*. In 2012 he became Director of REACT (Research and Enterprise for Arts and Creative Technologies), one of four Hubs for the Creative Economy funded by the AHRC. He is co-author of *Game Cultures* (Open University Press, 2006) and *New Media – A Critical Introduction* (Routledge, 2009.)

Catherine Greene graduated from the Royal College of Art in 2007 and joined the Helen Hamlyn Centre for Design. Her research focuses on community, workplace design and the influence of new technologies on the way people live and work. Catherine's interest in people-centred design and design research methods have led her to work on a variety of academic and commercially partnered projects.

In her current role as Senior Associate, Catherine plays a lead role in the centre's Work & City Research Lab.

David Harte is Senior Lecturer in Media and Communications at Birmingham City University where he has led the Masters in Social Media since 2009. His main research interests are on the role that community news websites play in fostering citizenship. He has an extensive background in working with regional policy makers on developing the creative economy and has managed projects with a focus on supporting creative businesses. He edits the hyperlocal news website for Bournville in Birmingham, UK.

Dan Lockton is Visiting Research Tutor in Innovation Design Engineering at the Royal College of Art. From 2013–15 he was a senior associate at the Helen Hamlyn Centre for Design, working on the Creative Citizen project, alongside a range of other aspects of design, energy in everyday life and community innovation. As a researcher, Dan specialises in design for behaviour change and people's understanding of complex everyday systems, particularly around social and environmental impacts of technology.

Gail Ramster is Senior Research Associate, Royal College of Art, The Helen Hamlyn Centre for Design. She is a design researcher in the Work & City Research Lab at the Helen Hamlyn Centre for Design. Her research takes a people-centred design approach to everyday challenges with interests in civic technology, community engagement and open data. Gail also manages the website 'The Great British Public Toilet Map'.

Shawn Sobers is Senior Lecturer in Photography and Media, University of the West of England, Bristol. His research is primarily concerned with the use of media and arts in participatory education, community media, advocacy, marginalised voices and untold history. Topics have included the use of youth media in informal education, and using media as an ethnographic research tool, exploring subjects such as the legacy of the transatlantic slave trade, disability issues and walking.

Jerome Turner is a research assistant at Birmingham Centre for Media and Cultural Research at Birmingham City University. He worked on the hyperlocal strand of the Creative Citizen project. He has research interests in social media and web cultures, and is currently completing an ethnographic PhD study of hyperlocal media audiences in the West Midlands.

Andy Williams is a lecturer and researches news and journalism at Cardiff University's School of Journalism, Media and Cultural Studies. His current major research interests relate to the decline of mainstream local newspaper journalism and the rise of citizen-produced community digital news, news sources and the influence of public relations on the UK news media and in the areas of environment, science, and health news in particular.

Theo Zamenopoulos is a senior lecturer in design at the Open University. He is a professional architect with expertise in design cognition, community-led design practices and complexity research. His research focuses on the conditions that make people and communities able to design and develop approaches that foster design thinking in everyday life. He has been involved in a number of research projects around the themes of civic engagement in design and the empowerment of people through design.

Series editors' foreword

Around the globe, communities of all shapes and sizes are increasingly seeking an active role in producing knowledge about how to understand, represent and shape their world for the better. At the same time, academic research is increasingly realising the critical importance of community knowledge in producing robust insights into contemporary change in all fields. New collaborations, networks, relationships and dialogues are being formed between academic and community partners, characterised by a radical intermingling of disciplinary traditions and by creative methodological experimentation.

There is a groundswell of research practice that aims to build new knowledge, address longstanding silences and exclusions, and pluralise the forms of knowledge used to inform common-sense understandings of the world.

The aim of this book series is to act as a magnet and focus for the research that emerges from this work. Originating from the UK Arts and Humanities Research Council's Connected Communities programme (www.connected-communities.org), the series showcases critical discussion of the latest methods and theoretical resources for combining academic and public knowledge via high-quality, creative, engaged research. It connects the emergent practice happening around the world with the longstanding and highly diverse traditions of engaged and collaborative practice from which that practice draws.

This series seeks to engage a wide audience of academic and community researchers, policy-makers and others with an interest in how to combine academic and public expertise. The wide range of publications in the series demonstrate that this field of work is helping to reshape the knowledge landscape as a site of democratic dialogue and collaborative practice, as well as contestation and imagination. The series editors welcome approaches from academic and community researchers working in this field who have a distinctive contribution to make to these debates and practices today.

Keri Facer, Professor of Educational and Social Futures,
University of Bristol

George McKay, Professor of Media Studies,
University of East Anglia

ONE

Are you a creative citizen?

Ian Hargreaves

There are several explanations for this book, but only one for its title. Before we get to that, let me sketch out the circumstances that have led to this point.

Connected Communities

The book itself would not exist but for the Creative Citizen research project, which took place in various locations across the United Kingdom between 2011 and 2014. *The Creative Citizen Unbound* represents the research team's overarching reflection upon this ambitious and experimental collaboration between scholars of numerous disciplines, backgrounds and ages from half a dozen very different British universities, working within the framework of the UK Research Councils' Connected Communities programme.[1] That wave of community-focused research activities, involving over 300 projects, emerged in 2010 in the wake of the formation of the Conservative-Liberal Democrat government led by Prime Minister David Cameron. The Connected Communities programme's stated intention was to motivate understanding of the nature and potential of communities, in terms of 'their changing place in our lives, their role in encouraging health, economic prosperity and creativity, their history and their future'.[2]

Our own polydisciplinary research team (economics, journalism, business, cultural studies, design, architecture and community media) was formed at a Connected Communities 'sandpit' event held at Birmingham University in late 2010. In this period, the word 'sand' was popular across the public and private sectors among event organisers who wished to indicate their commitment to the value of playfulness in bringing new ideas to bear upon serious concerns. Our sandpit gathered UK academics and community-based practitioners to generate ideas, partnerships and potential bids for Connected Communities funding. From this process, the Creative Citizens pitch emerged, with a research theme labelled and carefully punctuated: *Media, Community and the Creative Citizen.* By the time we reached this stage, we had also recruited an overseas academic partner in the person of John Hartley, Professor of Cultural Science at Curtin University in Perth, Western Australia. Hartley brought welcome international experience, a high profile and feisty career in cultural studies and a strong personal link with myself, based upon our previous collaborations at Cardiff University's School of Journalism, Media and Cultural Studies, which Hartley founded. For me, the opportunity to reconnect with John was a big attraction, celebrated in our joint presentation 'Creative Citizenship: Two Journeys, One Destination', at the Creative Citizens Conference in September 2014 (see Hargreaves and Hartley, 2015 for an edited version).

The project's central research question, intensively cross-examined within the team, asked this: how does creative citizenship generate value for communities within a changing media landscape; and how can this pursuit of value be intensified, propagated and sustained?

Our funding was fittingly transdisciplinary, coming chiefly from the Arts and Humanities Research Council (AHRC), but with a contribution from the Engineering and Physical Science Research Council (EPSRC), which was at the time rolling out its own cross-disciplinary 'digital economy' research theme and thereby taking an unprecedented interest in cultural and humanities questions. In all of these programmes, digital communications technologies were identified as important crossover points and drivers.

Our research team was also diverse. Some members were career academics, but others had more complex backgrounds. One designer had spent time working on user-tested solutions for Blackberry mobile phones. Another had been deeply immersed in the practice of community media. As leader of the project, I had spent almost 30 years in professional journalism, before expanding my horizons into other areas, including politics, business and academia. At the time of the Connected Communities award I had just been appointed professor of digital economy at Cardiff University, with a base in the university's Business School as well as the School of Journalism, Media and Cultural Studies.

Our aim, in the midst of this melting pot of ideas and circumstance, was to make sense of the implications for Creative Citizenship of pervasive and global digital communications technologies. By the time of our project, these technologies, centred on the internet, were in their third decade and so no longer a wellspring of unchecked optimism about their implications for democracy and human wellbeing, but nonetheless a still formidable source of disruption, innovation and novel collaborations.

The research team also shared another pivotal commitment: that we would work closely with community practitioners and other partners beyond the academy, in order to share existing knowledge in both directions, thus enabling us to co-create new knowledge in ways that would take account of a genuine diversity of perspectives and interests. Executed successfully, this offered hope that our work would generate what the university research funding system termed 'impact' in the world beyond universities. This co-creative ethos has its roots in deep experience among arts and humanities and social science researchers, alive to the dangers of treating complex human subjects like laboratory rats or worse, as lifeless matter. Co-creation takes into account ethical and cultural sensitivities, exposing inequalities built into the researcher–subject relationship. For us, co-creation also meant learning from the user-testing practices of digital product and service design, where customers and users have become increasingly involved in design development and the iterative modification of prototypes, as expressed abundantly in the strongly collaborative culture of the emergent 'maker' movement (Anderson, 2012).

With this in mind, we recruited two groups of partners. The first, taking a somewhat strategic role, included Ofcom, the UK Communications regulator; Nesta, the UK's increasingly internationally-minded innovation agency; Talk About Local, an advocacy body for the then newish, digital wave of 'hyperlocal' journalism; and the Glass-House Community Led Design, a charity whose goals are captured in its name. In addition, we formed close working links with small community groups in Birmingham, London, South Wales and Bristol, with whom we intended directly and co-creatively to explore matters of mutual interest. We did not set out primarily to do research *on* or *into* these partners; we worked *with* them, investing shared time, knowledge and other resources. As well as thinking together, we also tried to make things together; but we, the academic researchers, also constructed conceptual models and methodological frameworks, surveyed a voluminous but barely overlapping literature on both creativity and citizenship, did media discourse analysis, conducted interviews, ran surveys and analysed data. From this experience, we now offer this book.

Converging on creative citizens as a hybrid concept

The outputs achieved were inevitably diverse. They included at one end of the spectrum a graphic novel, *Indigo Babies*, created with South Blessed, a small network of young musicians, writers, video makers and activists based in the St Pauls area of Bristol. This publication tells the story of a group of tech-aware young people responding to a protest movement against plans for a supermarket in their neighbourhood: a morality tale of creative citizenship. At the other end of the spectrum, our research team delivered an unprecedentedly comprehensive survey of the UK's hyperlocal journalists, exploring their motivations and ambitions. It was clear from an early stage that this work had immediate value to Ofcom, charged with understanding the emerging shape of a news industry battered by the turbulence of the internet, as part of the regulator's annual communications market reports.[3] But the same research also had great value for the community bloggers with whom we worked, enabling them to learn from others, to see a bigger picture and to join with us (for example) in reverse engineering experiments to extend online-only services to newsprint: what we called the 'printervention'. The experience of our team members with a design background, who had already worked with users and makers to enhance and modify physical products and services, turned out to be highly relevant to our work with activists seeking to counter a London local authority's neighbourhood redevelopment plan. Our design researchers grappled with the challenge of working with whole communities, as well as with individual users, finding that apps and other software solutions were mostly designed with the latter rather than the former in mind. Elsewhere, in partnership with the provider of a co-working space for entrepreneurs in Birmingham, we used digital storytelling and media analysis to test ways of extending the community's reach and engagement, reliving stories through old photographs, such as the one surrounding a visit to Moseley in 1984 of Muhammad Ali, heavyweight boxing champion of the world (see Figure 1.1).

This 'mixed methods' or, more accurately, 'very mixed methods' approach to our research enabled us to remain open to ideas from our partners throughout, whilst also seeking to ensure that some methods, such as community 'asset mapping,' were deployed across all research sites, in the interests of generating strands of comparable data.

The approach also required that we remain open-minded throughout the project at a conceptual level. We did not set out with a fixed definition of creative citizenship and an intent to exemplify, taxonomise and evaluate what we observed in the field. In 2010, the term 'creative

Figure 1.1

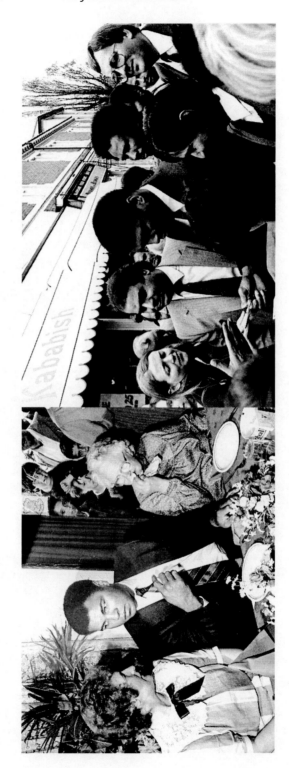

Heavyweight Boxing Champion of the World Muhammad Ali visits Moseley, Birmingham, in 1984. Ali's visit was captured for a community photo archive by Fiona Adams, who can claim to be an early pioneer of creative citizenship. The Moseley Exchange was a partner case study for the Creative Citizen project. (© The Moseley Society)

citizenship' was not exactly unknown, but nor was it established. It had featured fleetingly in the work of one of this volume's co-editors in the 1990s, as well as in differently labelled discussions, such as *DIY Citizenship* (Ratto and Boler, 2014). Hartley toyed with a number of other technologically augmented civic constructs, including 'silly citizenship' (2010), whilst others had explored 'cultural citizenship' (Miller, 2006). In an early literature review to support our practical work, Hartley argued that we were engaged in making new knowledge, so that empirical attempts to find, observe and analyse acts of creative citizenship were premature. Stretching our canvass to include these and other considerations, alongside the intense nitty-gritty of working with varied, straight talking and passionate community groups, themselves motivated by a fluid mix of sociability and civic purpose, generated energy, ideas and sometimes tensions. At an early stage, Hartley advised us to 'enjoy the tensions and learn from them.'

The basic notion of creative citizenship had appealed instinctively to the research team from our earliest conversations and did so more thoughtfully as we made our way through the research programme. Even without systematic and detailed definition, the term creative citizenship wore a good deal of meaning on its sleeve. Both words, creative and citizenship, are in ready circulation day to day; they are not technical terms or neologisms. When we set out to assemble a photographic gallery of creative citizenship for exhibition, we asked our subjects whether they considered themselves to be creative citizens. This invariably led to a conversation rather than a short answer or a blank stare (see Greene and Lindsey, 2015). When I was asked myself: but what is creative citizenship? I would reply that it is the application of creativity to civic purpose or civic effect, intending to indicate that creativity might well have considerable civic value, even where it does not have consciously civic intent. It seemed to me obvious on a practical level that creative, civic acts were both multitudinous and growing, as I said in straightforward terms for the soundtrack for an early video for the project in 2011:

> They are everywhere and they do just about everything, from knitting and bird-watching to book clubs and public safety. We call them creative citizens. You probably call them friends and neighbours and though there's nothing new about most of these activities, there is something new about the tools available to the people involved. Today, half of the adult population uses Facebook, increasingly on their mobile phones as well as on computers.

Twitter is smaller but growing faster. There have been 65 million downloads of current WordPress open access blogging software. And though much social media use is simply for fun, it's also big businesses, a route to stardom and, more routinely, a way of responding to unmet civic and cultural need.

In effect, we pursued a deliberate strategy of avoiding any firm *ex ante* definition of the term, so that we would sense its auto-generative potential, for individuals and for communities. Or, put another way, we co-created the theoretical approach to the research's key terminology as we went along. This felt right because we were not spreading a religion or conducting a campaign. We were not even testing a theory with hypotheses built upon known methodology; we were inviting individuals, groups and communities to collaborate with us in search of meaning and action which made sense to, and could be trusted by all the parties involved.

This provisional and probing approach led to an interesting engagement with the political mainstream. Towards the end of our work, we held a conference at the Royal College of Art in London and invited a group of London political think tank leaders to debate with us. Stephen Lee, Chief Executive of Centre Forum, one of the think tanks, produced a short discussion paper, which identified a paradox. Creative Citizenship, he said, drawing upon lyrics from *The Sound of Music*, had the feel of a 'a will-o'-the-wisp, a flibbertigibbet, a clown' – because even those who were studying it (namely ourselves) had offered 'no succinct definition of the term; it points to a myriad of alternate forms and expressions whose informality of cohesion and depth of complexity appear to defy classification and/or structural confinement' (Lee, 2015: 3). This was, he observed, the sort of 'Big Idea' all too likely to attract the professional politician. Such 'Big Ideas', in Lee's view, should be classified as 'one of those Loch Ness Monsters of British politics: everyone's heard of them, there are occasional sightings, but no one is sure the beast really exists.' In order to pin us and the concept down, Lee proposed a nine-point manifesto (for which, check out Chapter 11), rooted in what he saw as the concept's greatest strength; namely its commitment to the ground-up principle of voluntary co-creation. Here, Lee argued, you could already point to successful exemplars in areas such as the community delivery of social care, education, mental health, community journalism and digital access programmes. In short, 'not one big idea'. Rather the development of tangible initiatives delivering measurable outcomes' or an aggregation of smaller ideas. We attempt to summarise the potential political and policy implications of our work, in the final chapter of this book.

But who wants to be a citizen anyway?

It is also important to place our Creative Citizenship project temporally and culturally. It belongs to the period of global political insurgency, which followed the banking crisis of 2008. This calamity of the financial system, fuelled by the networked adrenaline of social media and the growing, high-speed 'fin-tech' platforms of the global banking industry, threatened to destroy the European Union's currency system and gave birth to or strengthened numerous insurgencies or movements from below. These included the 'Occupy' movement and its offshoots, which targeted growing polarities of wealth and wellbeing; Tea Party politics in the US and the rise of new or young political parties across Europe, from the anti-EU, anti-immigration UK Independence Party, UKIP (born 1993) to its older French counterpart the Front National (born 1972), both of which outpolled major parties in the 2014 European Parliament elections. These dynamics were even more important for political newcomers such as Syriza of Greece, which won a snap general election in 2015 on an anti-austerity ticket, and Podemos in Spain, which set its sights on following suit. All of this occurred against a background of falling membership of political parties generally across Europe (Van Biezen et al, 2012), with the UK a standout poor performer. New downward thresholds have been crossed in voter turnout at elections in many countries in recent years, including in the 2014 US mid-term elections (36.4%). During the 2005–15 decade, no UK election at the local or European level has attracted the involvement of more than half the electorate and today fewer than one per cent of citizens are members of the UK's so-called 'Big Three' parties, Conservative, Labour and Liberal Democrat.[4]

It was also striking during the three years of our Creative Citizenship research that many significant organisations outside politics also found themselves struggling to save their own reputations. These so-called 'cultural' crises have been identified within UK institutions as diverse as the police, the newspaper industry, banking, the health service, the entertainment industry and in social care for the elderly and for children. The failure to expose these crises in a timely manner (for example a string of historical revelations concerning unprosecuted child abuse by the television celebrity Jimmy Savile) is frequently said to have arisen from the erosion of shared values and goals; an indicator, you might think, of civic decline. What precipitated the string of crises?

Arguably, intensified exposure from new networks of communication that have strengthened the hand of whistleblowers and victims at a time of growing scepticism about the values and contribution of elite groups, including elected politicians and the officials who support them.[5] Was it possible that a more creative, innovative and collaborative approach to definition and delivery of community needs would be part of the solution here? That creative citizenship might provide both a warning mechanism against corruption – or in John Keane's phrase part of a 'monitory democracy' (Keane, 2010) – as well as a response to exhausted models of service provision? Not one Big Idea, but an ecology of specifically targeted interventions based upon collaborative analysis, delivery and evaluation?

Big ideas – Big Society, or big mistake?

Mainstream politicians have, naturally, sought to understand and harness the forces of social media and community building themselves, making their own responses to the new localist or community 'agenda' in terms of campaigning style and priorities. In his two victorious presidential campaigns (2008 and 2012), US President Obama appeared to connect successfully with an interlocking set of online communities, not least among black and Hispanic citizens, mobilised using social media techniques and agile organisations such moveon.org, which itself morphed into upwardly.com – both entrepreneurially communitarian institutions of the social media age (Pew, 2012).

The UK Conservative Party Manifesto for the 2010 general election, which indirectly triggered the Research Councils' Connected Communities programme, gave top billing to the then current UK version of a mainstream communitarian pitch, in this case labelled 'the Big Society'. The manifesto called for 'a society with much higher levels of personal, professional, civic and corporate responsibility: a society where people come together to solve problems and improve life for themselves and their communities: a society where the leading force for progress is social responsibility, not state control'.[6] This Big Society thinking, the manifesto added, 'runs consistently through our policy programme'.

When the electoral arithmetic in 2010 pointed to a hung parliament, the Big Society's community spirit and proclaimed 'green' dimension provided a feasible mooring point for the smaller Liberal Democrat party, itself the UK's most longstanding party of community politics. In government, the two parties consciously, though not often explicitly, reached back to the three-term success of 'New Labour' Prime Minister

Tony Blair (modelled on Bill Clinton's 'New Democrats'), with a centre-ground appeal 'beyond left and right' (Giddens, 1994) and addressing a communitarian-flavoured 'third way' (Giddens, 1998). The coalition gestured towards a new generation of 'active citizens', proposing enhanced roles for charities, social enterprise, cooperatives and mutuals in the delivery of public services. The government proposed, and carried through parliament, a 'Localism Act', which created a framework to encourage the construction of 'neighbourhood plans'.

When it came under attack, intellectually aware ministers defended the 'Big Society' with reference to the goal of boosting 'social capital' (Putnam, 2001).[7] Numerous critics, however, attacked both Blair's Third Way and Cameron's Big Society as cynical covers for cuts in public spending, which became draconian and long-lasting in the 'age of austerity' which followed the 2008 banking crisis.[8] The Big Society was dismissed as yet more window dressing for an even more aggressive version of the global capitalism frequently labelled by its many academic enemies as 'neo-liberal' (Flew, 2014). Within two years of Cameron taking office as prime minister, the term Big Society had been dropped and its principal author, Cameron's policy adviser Steve Hilton, had moved from Westminster to a post at Stanford University in California. Worth noting, however, that the term Big Society still found its way into the Conservative Party's 2015 election manifesto, itself the prelude to an outright election victory for David Cameron and shortly afterwards the publication of Hilton's book, *More Human: Designing a world where people come first.* (Hilton et al, 2015)

On a more momentous scale, social media were seen to be playing a global role in the democratically aspirational insurrections of the briefly mislabelled 'Arab Spring,' which ignited in 2010 and informed popular protest in places as widely spread as Tunisia, Cairo, Istanbul, Morocco, Kiev, Libya and Hong Kong. All too quickly these events gave way to less wholesome outcomes, from anarchy (Libya) to resumed military determination of politics (Egypt) and invasion (Ukraine), helping, as a by-product, to create space in the Middle East for the social media fuelled rise of the brutal Islamic State. By November 2014, the incoming head of the UK intelligence centre, GCHQ, putting pressure on internet platforms to make their encrypted traffic visible to the intelligence authorities in the wake of the Edward Snowden security leaks, made the argument that Islamic State relied upon Facebook, Google and Twitter as their 'command and control networks of choice'.[9] For all the flourishing of 'spreadable media' (Jenkins et al, 2013) and its expression in countless book clubs, quilter groups, choirs, 'craftivist' knitting circles, allotment gardening combines and fan networks (including those capable of generating blockbuster successes like *Fifty Shades of Grey*),[10] social media's glad confident morning was well and truly passed, rhetorically if not in point of fact among millions of citizens internationally who continued to mediate among themselves socially, and boost the global reach of Facebook and Twitter. Dystopian analyses of social media in particular, and digital communications in general, now proliferated, portraying social media users as exploited consumers and algorithmically controlled beings (for example, Lanier, 2010; 2013; Morozov, 2011; 2013).

Enter the creative

As we designed our work plan, we sought to put ourselves in a position to understand how these dynamics were working not at the level of 'causes celebres' but in everyday situations. So we studied community blogs, neighbourhood planning and a local music scene, seeking to understand motivations, value and potential in a creative, economic and political context.

Our goal was to uncover and describe both a contemporary perspective on citizenship and a civic perspective on creativity in the age of the internet. We wanted to understand in as much detail as we could, and without distracting hyperbole, the effects or 'affordances' for community creatives of digital communications technologies and the burgeoning 'social media' which began to emerge in the first decade of the new millennium and which by the time of our project were in active use by roughly 60 per cent of the UK adult population and still growing. We also recognised that as university-based researchers, we were engaged in an experiment on the edge of changes which were in the process of imagining a restructured and more 'porous' university system, committed to a wider range of mechanisms for the pursuit of useful knowledge (see, for examples, Stewart, 2013). In this and many other respects, we enjoyed our interactions with other projects from the Connected Communities stable, where other interrelated missions were in play.

In this same period, during which the internet has placed itself at the centre of our lives, economically, socially and culturally, it is not coincidental to observe that the subject of creativity has also achieved a new salience in discussions about the economy, business and even sport, as well as in discussions about the arts and culture. The Creative Commons came into being in 2001 as a standard bearer for open source approaches to software and online culture more generally; a

Silicon Valley ethos, which predated the growth to global dominance of its corporate flag carriers. Whilst some educationists and many politicians have continued, with good reason, to emphasise core literacy and numeracy attainments in the curriculum of schools and others have prioritised higher education funding of STEM subjects (science, technology, engineering and maths), a growing number of voices have made creativity their focal point. Ken Robinson's landmark report for the UK Government, *All Our Futures* (1999), urged that creativity be placed at the centre of the UK schools curriculum, a call subsequently re-echoed in many places on many occasions. During the late 1990s, the idea of the 'creative industries' as an important and growing business sector in advanced, knowledge economies was established (DCMS, 1998), followed a decade later by the emergence of the still more ambitious idea of the 'creative economy' where creativity is seen as fundamental to innovation and economic success across all sectors of business, as well as in the public sector and in non-profit organisations (for a summary, see Bakhshi et al, 2013; and Chapter 3 of this volume). Howkins (2001; new edition, 2013) defined the creative economy as 'creativity plus electronics', whilst others focused upon the emergence of a 'creative class' (Florida, 2002), 'creative cities' (Hartley et al, 2012) and creative 'complex systems' (Hartley and Potts, 2014). A series of United Nations interventions also tackled these themes, whilst arguments to protect or enhance funding for the arts increasingly referenced their spillover value across the creative economy (Warwick Commission, 2015).

This was by no means only or mainly an American, British, Anglophone, European or Western phenomenon. Visitors to China in the second decade of this century came home struck by the persistence with which they had been told that 'made in China' would now be superseded by 'created in China' (see Keane, 2006). Singapore and Korea established themselves as pacesetters and small countries such as Israel, Estonia and Iceland made distinctive contributions. Among scholars, John Hartley established a path-breaking Centre for Creative Industries and Innovation at Queensland University of Technology in Australia. In a 2009 book, he wrote that 'reflexive creativity is what enables human culture to adapt and change … with the growing ubiquity of digital media these are becoming a more dynamic source of productivity than industrial innovation … The social network 'swarm' outperforms the IP-protected lab, and at twice the speed' (Hartley, 2009: 216).

Whilst working on the Creative Citizen project, I myself undertook two other pieces of work that contributed to the evolution of my own thinking on creative citizenship and social media. For the UK government I carried out an independent review of intellectual property law (Hargreaves, 2011). This involved grappling with the highly contentious issue of copyright law in the digital age – itself an increasingly vital question in shaping the legal and cultural framework for creative citizenship, determining as it does the terms on which the citizen may consume, borrow, adapt, parody or 'remix' (Lessig, 2008) the digital versions of other people's music, words or visual outputs, and the relationship between the citizen/consumer, on the one hand, and the corporate supplier on the other. This is a front line in the creative struggle between the user as 'produser' (Bruns, 2008) and established business and professional interests. I proposed significant adjustments in the balance between producers and consumers, designed to make copyright law simpler, more plausible, less aggressive in unconstructive situations, and so more effective and supportive of the innovation-boosting properties of the internet. I also urged copyright-based businesses to do a better job of making their repertoire available through simple digital transactions via a new 'copyright hub' www.copyrighthub.org. Eventually, in 2014/15, the reforms proposed in my 2011 review made their way into UK law. By this time, I was working on related themes in the context of the European Union, which had previously talked itself into stalemate on a similar range of issues – a situation indicative of the continent's simultaneous and prolonged crisis of stalled productivity growth (Hargreaves et al, 2015).

A further piece of work, a *Manifesto for the Creative Economy* (Bakhshi et al, 2013), arose from a blend of the concerns raised in the IP review and our Creative Citizen research work. This manifesto examines the history of creative industries and the creative economy and advocates a range of measures in education, competition policy, intellectual property reform, R&D, arts funding and public service broadcasting to support the growth of the UK creative economy, which the manifesto calculates to account for 2.5 million jobs and roughly 10 per cent of UK economic gross value added. The manifesto also acknowledges that these numbers do not include or account for the economic value of the activities of creative citizens, most of which are voluntary and operating below the radar of official statistics on economic output and labour markets. Since in politics, what goes uncounted tends to go unheeded and neglected, the conclusions of this book include some thoughts on mapping, counting and evaluating civic creativity.

Unbound

None of what has been said so far, however, explains the title of this book – *The Creative Citizen Unbound*. For that, I bear sole responsibility. The thought or instinct simply came to me one day, sitting in front of my computer, finishing off the presentation we would use to pitch our final research bid. It was that most rewarding of human pleasures: an idea, apparently from nowhere, but in reality, quarried from memory and half hidden association; a flaring of the taper Thomas Jefferson saw affording a cost free spread of the benefits of human knowledge. At this stage of our bid, the ideas of creativity and citizenship were already well baked into our thinking, but the title? Why would we be drawn to imagine the creative citizen 'unbound'?

The link, of course, is with Shelley's 'lyrical drama in four acts', *Prometheus Unbound*. I had come across this extraordinary piece 40 years earlier, during my undergraduate English literature studies when its contemporary appeal as an antidote to the schematic and mechanical literary criticism methods of the schools of I.A. Richards and F.R Leavis commended it to the would-be unbiddable teenage undergraduate.

Published in 1820, Shelley's poem was a response to two decades of political frustration, as the French Revolution turned into Napoleonic dictatorship and a global contest for imperial power with the United Kingdom. World events had disappointed internationalist dreamers like Shelley, perhaps even shown them to be fools. Matthew Arnold, who considered himself very much the grown-up's grown-up, patronisingly called the young poet 'an ineffectual angel'. Among Shelley's responses was to take the Greek legend of Prometheus, the god who brought fire and other illuminations to mankind, and to retell the story of his battle with Jupiter, the mightiest but not the most far-seeing of the gods, who first bound but then found it necessary to liberate the troublesome but determined freethinker. This was Shelley's evangelical and self-motivating way of toughing it out himself, ending his epic work with this obdurately practical restatement of vision:

> To suffer woes which Hope thinks infinite;
>> To forgive wrongs darker than death or night;
>> To defy power, which seems omnipotent;
>> To love, and bear; to hope till Hope creates
>> From its own wreck the thing it contemplates.

This scale of moral defiance or faith, arising from an experimental and imaginative vision not contingent upon any expectation of success or any campaign to enhance its chances of success, is perhaps the quality Yeats had in mind when he placed *Prometheus Unbound* 'among the sacred books of the world'. At roughly the same time, Shelley also cranked up the political rhetoric in a more polemical, street-smart manner. His sonnet 'England in 1819' savages a ruling class who 'leech-like to their fainting country cling'. And in *The Mask of Anarchy* of the same year, he addresses the workers slaughtered by soldiers in Manchester's Peterloo Massacre. Shelley's call for mass civil disobedience, not published until 1832, a decade after his death in a boating accident in Italy, would resonate into the next century in the thinking of community-based non-violent resistance championed by Mahatma Gandhi and Martin Luther King. The closing lines of *The Mask of Anarchy* have been much anthologised. When I mentioned them in a talk at a music festival during our Creative Citizen work, a young man from Manchester came to me at the close and promised that he would immediately incorporate them into a car bumper sticker – just one more act of creative citizenship.

> Rise like Lions after slumber
> In unvanquishable number –
> Shake your chains to earth like dew
> Which in sleep had fallen on you –
> Ye are many – they are few.

This rabble rousing was consistent with Shelley's declaration that poets (and philosophers) are 'the unacknowledged legislators of the world', a thought so radical that it still startles, in a world of Isis, drone strikes, global warming and crisis in the Crimea. Viewed from one direction it is the original clarion call for the place of arts and humanities in the world's knowledge and innovation systems. Here is a force whose *unbinding* might indeed imply serious 'impact' and that is why I proposed it for a book concerned with the potentially transformative impact of creative citizenship, arising from its own imaginative civic commitment. In Creative Citizenship, the unwritten rules say that anyone can join in and that no one has the right to exclude anyone else. The primary goal may be economic, cohesive, revolutionary, aesthetic, routine, hermetic or even banal, but the culture of participation and collaboration holds true whatever the purpose. Or, as Hartley has put it, we are motivated to explore 'the generative potential of new forms of productivity based on individual agency, technological affordances, global interconnectedness and rapid social change' (2009: 201).

The term 'creative citizenship' itself is somewhere between recent and novel, but its component parts are obviously ancient: citizenship (Latin *civitas*, via Anglo-French) and creativity (inter alia, the Book of Genesis and the Gospel of Saint John: 'in the beginning was the word'). These are concepts rich and strong enough to have endured dispute, reinvention and redefinition through time. The ideas they represent can be traced to the beginning of human civilisation and it is impossible to imagine any habitable future for planet earth in their absence.

Another way of outlining this vast stretch of history is to think of it in terms of the evolution of systems of knowledge (Hartley and Potts, 2014). These systems arise from humankind's transition through prehistoric processes of 'association among strangers' (cooperation among non-kin is rare in nature) in the form of 'we' groups or demes. These themselves are capable of evolution through language and culture into what we experience as a demos, with potential for both adversarial ('we' know who we are because we are opposed to 'they', Cold War style) and universalist formations (*'Alle Menschen werden Brüder'* [all men are brothers], as Schiller's 'Ode to Joy' put it, with a Romantic abandon matching Shelley's).

By drawing together the sociopolitical with the cultural possibility of imaginative self or community-actualising potential of creativity, we establish the prospect of a creative citizenship which speaks to the emergence of new and diverse forms of creative collaboration, innovation and civic expression in our age of digital communicative abundance. For this prospect, we argue that the time is ripe.

We also note the undeniably relevant context of the much discussed 'crisis' in representative democracy and, by extension, in civics: a sense of malaise not only among the agencies traditionally responsible for civic and political leadership but of leaders more generally, in once highly respected activities such as banking and religion, for example. A UK poll run annually since 1993 asking people who they trust to tell the truth,[11] suggests consistently that politicians and journalists enjoy the trust of roughly one in five or less, worse even than bankers and business leaders, who do not score much better. The most trusted figures, according to these data, are doctors, suggesting that the highest degrees of trust are associated with human experience at its most vulnerable.

The technologies with which we have been blessed, or in some accounts cursed, will continue to raise difficult questions and force controversial choices. At the time of writing, the internet and the World Wide Web are a generation old (by some accounts the internet is over 40, while Tim Berners-Lee invented WWW in 1989). The highest profile landmarks in that breathless period have been the overheating of technology stocks in world markets (the 'dot com bubble') around the turn of the millennium, followed by the emergence of a group of dominant American technology companies: Apple Phase Two (with its iPod of 2001 and its first iPhone in 2007); Amazon (launch 1995); Google (1998); Facebook (2004); and Twitter (2006). This dominance of the by now fully developed commercial models of all of these Silicon Valley companies has raised difficult questions about the respect they show (or don't) for their customers' data privacy or the legal and tax-collecting regimes (and so, implicitly, the civic cultures) of the countries within which they operate.

Today, half the world's adult population owns a smartphone, a figure forecast to rise to 80 per cent by 2020,[12] making the internet itself accessible to most human beings for the first time in this coming period and indicating that the 'mobile internet' is now the location of choice for most forms of digital communication, especially among younger users. In 2015, Facebook had 1.39 billion regular users and Google was providing over 90 per cent of Europe's web searches. Both had taken steps to adapt their services to the preference for mobile devices. At this point, Apple was the most valuable brand on earth and Amazon the largest online retailer. Europe's digital economy was, meanwhile, in danger of stagnation, diminished by the continent's inward-facing concerns in the wake of the Eurozone crisis. In so far as competition at scale with the big American digital companies looked feasible, the focus was upon China, where Alibaba was chasing Amazon; where Google and Facebook were heavily restricted on Chinese sovereign territory, and where a number of Chinese manufacturers were growing fast in the mobile device market, Huawei being the best known internationally. A group of three internet giants known as BAT (Baidu, Alibaba and Tencent) held centre stage in China. In the meantime, perhaps China's most distinctive contribution to the internet, at least in western commentary, was to demonstrate that behind 'the Great Chinese Firewall', its operations could be subject to forms of surveillance and control that its inventors thought impossible as well as undesirable (Qiu, 1999/2000; King et al, 2013). Chinese scholars identified room to manoeuvre for its creative citizens in the study and discussion of entertainment media where 'fans not only discuss the aesthetics of the show but also express concerns and opinions on broader social issues, develop civic values and practice civic engagement' (Chen, 2015, citing Wu, 2015). Europe, looking east to a newly aggressive Russia and an assertive and self-confident China, and west to the land of the First Amendment, where a federal constitution puts free expression at its core and offers 'fair use' as a routine defence to charges of breach of copyright, found itself struggling to balance its own claims of free expression and rights to privacy set out within its own framework of human rights law.

Our investigation into creative citizenship has, however, taken place in the UK, a country within a continent that increasingly appears to view the digital prospect with anxiety, whilst embracing with enthusiasm the internet as a place for commercial transactions (online shopping is more popular in the UK than anywhere in the world). The idea of creative citizenship belongs in this period, in the years that followed the 2008 banking 'bust' and its nervous aftermath, not in the long 'boom' which preceded it. A time of digital unease has replaced the Pentecostal years of early digital superabundance. The Shelleyite romantics, the hopers and dreamers, are out of favour; it is the prophets of pessimism who are in vogue.

Our social network

As we embarked upon our studies, it seemed to our research group that whilst the mood had darkened sufficiently to obscure utopian visions, there was still enough richness and flexibility in 'social network markets' (Potts et al, 2008) to make a new wave of civic collaboration and enterprise feasible and sustainable. We were even prepared to consider the possibility that these activities would indeed play an important part in the further evolution of democracy, perhaps in the direction of a multilayered and network-like 'monitory democracy' imagined by John Keane (2010) based upon a 'monitorial citizenship' (Schudson, 1999) rather than one overdependent upon the more rigid and centralised structures of the industrial era. Whenever we returned to our research question, with its focus upon the affordances of 'a changing media landscape' for the needs and aspirations of communities, we felt that we were working on ground rich in potential, as well as cunning in complexity. As we rolled out our fieldwork and built our case studies, we sought to discover value and ways in which this might be 'intensified, propagated and sustained'. In our imaginations at least, we wished to hypothesise the potential not only of the creative citizen but also of the creative citizen *unbound*.

Let me now say something about the structure of this book and the way that it arises from the structure of the Creative Citizen research programme. Throughout the project's life, a cast of about 20 academic researchers took part directly. Some made their contribution and moved on before the entire work programme was complete. Others were involved on a short-term basis in a particular element of the work. Of this group of 20, 14 names appear in this book as authors.

Our field work was divided into three strands and in summarising these, I will mention our community partners, each of which engaged with a specific strand of work, though all contributed in various ways to the thinking of the project as a whole, through regular team meetings and at presentations we made at festivals and conferences throughout the project's life. The details of each strand of work are set out below:

- **Hyperlocal news** brought together two research groups, one based at Birmingham City University and one at Cardiff University. Dave Harte, of BCU and Dr Andy Williams of Cardiff University were this strand's co-investigators, supported for a time by Glyn Mottershead. Jerome Turner contributed throughout to the research in both locations. This team formed partnerships with Ofcom and with Talk About Local, a hyperlocal advocacy group led very effectively by Will Perrin, and we drew deeply upon TAL's data, insights and encouragement, taking part in its bustling 'unconferences'. On the ground, the research team worked closely with hyperlocal practitioners in Birmingham and South Wales (*Tyburn Mail*, *Connect Cannock*, B31, *Port Talbot Magnet*, *Pobl Caerdydd*). The Centre for Community Journalism, born at Cardiff University in 2013, during the life of the Creative Citizen project, provided assistance in various ways during our research, along with offering a legacy for its insights. Damian Radcliffe, based during our project chiefly in Qatar, and a noted contributor to the study of hyperlocals, contributed consistently to our thinking.
- **Community-led design** involved research teams from the Open University and the Helen Hamlyn Centre for Design, which is itself part of the Royal College of Art in London. The OU's Katerina Alexiou and Theo Zamenopoulos, along with Catherine Greene of the Helen Hamlyn Centre, were the project's co-investigators, supported by Dr Panagiota Alevizou from the OU's Department of Engineering and Innovation. Gail Ramster, Dr Dan Lockton and Dr Alan Outten, all of the Helen Hamlyn Centre, worked on the project at different stages. Our strategic research partners in community-led design were The Glass-House Community Led Design, a national UK charity which supports public participation and leadership in design of the built environment; and Nesta, the UK's leading innovation practice body, which is also a charity. This strand's community partners were: Wards Corner Community Coalition, a grassroots organisation working to stop the demolition

of the homes, businesses and indoor market above Seven Sisters Tube Station in North London; the Mill, a volunteer-run community centre in Walthamstow, East London, which helps local people to design and run new services or activities within its space; Goldsmiths Community Centre in Lewisham, South London, which has served local people for over 70 years; and the Kentish Town Neighbourhood Forum, a community in North London working to develop a neighbourhood plan.

- **Creative networks:** this strand had two points of geographic focus, one in Bristol, the second in Birmingham. The strand's three co-investigators were Jon Dovey, Professor of Screen Media at the University of the West of England (Bristol) and Director of REACT, a Bristol-centred creative economy knowledge exchange hub, Dr Caroline Chapain, from Birmingham University's Business School, and Dr Shawn Sobers, from the Faculty of Creative Arts, Humanities and Education at University of West of England. They were supported by Dr Tamara West, University of Birmingham, and Dr Emma Agusita, University of the West of England. There were two research partners in this strand, both major contributors to our detailed co-creative work: South Blessed, a highly informal but innovative, self-funded and self-generating video channel, based in Bristol; and the Moseley Community Development Trust, a charity which leads regeneration of its neighbourhood through social, economic and environmental projects. Its work includes the creation and running of the Moseley Exchange, a co-working space.

These interdisciplinary teams of researchers deployed a range of methods, including asset mapping, interviews, surveys, observation, and co-created media interventions, designed to discover new solutions to old problems.

In this book, our aim is to enable the reader to consider our general thinking about creative citizenship and its potential to the case studies undertaken. With that in mind, we have structured the book to offer three opening chapters, which deal with the political and scholarly context for this work, followed by seven chapters, which from different angles, draw upon the case studies. Each of these seven chapters has its own theme – these were selected through discussion within the research team and with our partners, to include aspects such as value, networks, place and technology. Inevitably, this approach involves some repetition of information about our community partners and the case studies, though we have tried to minimise this. The advantage is that the reader has access to a common set of case studies from a variety of intellectual and 'domain' perspectives; offering an interdisciplinary perspective. The final chapter draws together some conclusions and looks ahead.

The outcome, we intend, is that the reader experiences access to a single stage, lit from a multiplicity of angles. This should enable the reader to consider the aggregation of perspectives presented by the book as a whole, or to dip into individual chapters where these are of particular interest to, for example, students of planning, urban studies, journalism or community media.

Book structure

Chapter 1 sets the political and intellectual context for the concept of creative citizenship and explains the Creative Citizen project's motivation, goals, structure and working methods.

Chapter 2 reviews relevant scholarship, including cultural studies, economics, innovation science, complexity theory and the emerging field of 'cultural science'. In noting the disciplinary tension between the location of citizenship theory in social and political science and the location of creativity in arts and humanities, this chapter considers the resultant 'problem of knowledge' and asks what it would involve to 'unbind' this knowledge amid unavoidable disciplinary friction.

Chapter 3 considers creative citizenship from the perspective of the creative economy – the now clearly defined construct which accounts for 2.5 million UK jobs and 10 per cent of UK economic gross value added. We ask what contribution creative citizens do and might make to this creative economy, formal and informal, and how this can be both measured and enhanced.

Chapter 4 poses a series of wider questions about the value contributed by acts of creative citizenship. Observing that most creative citizenship undertaken in the communities we have studied occurs without remuneration and with little reference to monetary reward, we seek to establish the nature and scale of the non-monetary value involved in creative citizenship, in terms of a 'contribution economy' which delivers substantial benefits and results in enhanced social capital in areas such as education, training, public safety and general wellbeing. The benefits to the individual creative citizen are also considered, in terms of personal growth and 'self-actualisation'.'

Chapter 5 addresses 'varieties' of creative citizenship, exploring in greater detail the relationship between creativity and civic contribution and investigating the challenges involved in group or community-based forms of creativity, as opposed to creativity of the individual.

Chapter 6 looks at the effective and increasingly complex and distributed networks that are a feature of contemporary creative citizenship, providing connectivity among fellow creatives; between creators and their audiences; and in specifically civic forms of creativity. Focusing upon two case studies, we explore the relevance of a movement from network theory to complexity theory, noting the way that even highly localised creative activities can have system-wide and global inputs and consequences in a complex system.

Chapter 7 considers the 'co-creative' practices that have been at the heart of all of our research within communities. We play back conversations between researchers and creative citizens within communities and ask questions about this approach to research and its value to our own community partners.

Chapter 8 discusses the technique of 'asset mapping' and how it can be used to evaluate the resources available to creative citizens in a community setting in order to build strategies, deploy tactics and evaluate strengths and weaknesses. Advances in the use of this technique in the Creative Citizen project point the way forward for other community-based applications.

Chapter 9 deals with three case studies and the role of physical place in creative citizenship. We suggest that place operates as a focus for identity, spurring civic engagement and social activism, but resulting in articulations of civic value that both transcend and renew local and 'glocal' geographies.

Chapter 10 draws together our thinking about the place of the online communications technologies, which are now in such very wide use within communities, making possible previously unprecedented levels of discussion, activism, collaboration and creativity – globally, as well as within geographically bound territories. Here we offer judgments on the utopian versus dystopian argument about social media, arguing that citizen-led social media are both important and continuingly promising, yet also constrained by their emerging corporate and political context. We show how creative citizens frequently adapt these platforms and software to their own needs in an improvised creative commons within specific communities.

Chapter 11 lays out some concluding thoughts from the Creative Citizen project. We set out ways in which government and other agents might support creative citizenship and the conditions under which such interventions are most likely to thrive. We also reflect upon the implications of the insight that co-creative activity within communities will not progress where it is subject to authority that lacks legitimacy in the eyes of the citizen. This requires a high quality of understanding about the relationship between formal tiers of government and informal, community structures. In spite of these challenges, we argue that creative citizenship offers a potentially valuable way of framing policy thinking, which addresses community wellbeing, consistent with wider policy goals addressing the needs of the creative economy. We entertain the following possibilities for creative citizenship:

- Politically, can it provide motivation to draw individual citizens more closely and imaginatively into the life of the places to which they belong, offering the potential of more vibrant and entrepreneurial communities and more inclusive decision taking?
- Culturally, can creative citizenship support the perspective of the user/creator; the phenomenon of the 'amateur' in tension with the 'professional'; the contribution of the networked 'crowd' to communal achievement and ambition; the enhanced accessibility of the 'user' perspective in art, design and 'making'.
- Economically, creative citizens provide services and goods to each other, which represent, in aggregate, an uncounted contribution to economic output and specifically to the output per head of those who work in the economy, contributing their 'microproductivity'. This demands attention so that policy makers can take it into account when they think about matters such as education, skills, benefit systems and investment.

To the question that sits at the top of this chapter, 'Are You a Creative Citizen?', you will answer as you see fit. Our aim is that this book will persuade you that the question is, at least, relevant to you on a personal level as well as to any professional or work interest that has directed you to this text. The unwritten first rule of creative citizenship states that if you want to be in, you're in.

Notes

[1] www.connected-communities.org
[2] www.ahrc.ac.uk, accessed 30/12/14
[3] Communications Market Report. 2012; 2013; 2014. Available at: www.ofcom. org.uk
[4] See: www.parliament.uk/business/publications/research/briefing-papers/ SN05125/membership-of-uk-political-parties.
[5] These events included unexplained mortality levels in a UK National Health Trust; the exposure of the Jimmy Savile sexual abuse history, much of it located within the BBC and the NHS; as well as the dimensions of the banking crisis which were rooted in dishonest activity in high-speed electronic markets, such as the one which sets the international benchmark LIBOR interest rate.

6   *Invitation to Join the Government of Britain*. The Conservative Manifesto 2010, page 37.

7   In answer to a question from Hargreaves about Connected Communities and the Big Society, the UK Universities Minister David Willetts pointed to a series of studies indicating the importance of social capital in community wellbeing in many settings. Connected Communities London showcase 2012.

8   The think tank Demos, which for a time I chaired, made many interventions in this territory. In one publication (Hargreaves, 1998), I note the emerging importance of digital communications as a community enhancing technology and suggest that if New Labour's communitarian instincts proved insufficiently hardy in terms of political action, as opposed to rhetoric, the effect would open up an opportunity for their political opponents.

9   Robert Hannigan, Director of GCHQ in *The Guardian*. See: www.theguardian.com/uk-news/2014/nov/03/privacy-gchq-spying-robert-hannigan

10 *Fifty Shades of Grey* (2011) is a best-selling novel by E.L. James, which arose from fictional prototypes published on a fan fiction website connected to the *Twilight* series of stories.

11 Ipsos-Mori 'Veracity Index': www.ipsos-mori.com; and see: www.ipsos-mori.com/researchpublications/researcharchive/poll.aspx?oItcmId=15&view=wide

12 'Planet of the Phones', *Economist* 28/2 – 6/3, 2015.

TWO

A problem of knowledge – solved?

John Hartley

The experience of citizenship may seem very far removed from both creativity and the economy, especially from the 'community' perspective of the AHRC's 'Connected Communities' scheme under which our project, *Media, Community and the Creative Citizen*, was funded. In a time when so much political discourse is focused upon economic competitiveness, it is striking that economists continue to struggle to include in their calculations of economic importance the outputs of acts of citizenship, especially where these are voluntary or nonprofessional in character. Where concessions are made, the tendency has been to add matters such as 'wellbeing' or 'happiness' to economic models (Layard, 2006; Frey and Stutzer, 2013). The economics of happiness, however, is based on psychology (how do I feel and what do I want more of?), not citizenship (how do I decide and act in concert with others, as part of our group?). As yet, economics based on cost benefit frameworks has not developed an 'economics of citizenship'.[1] Such a move conflicts with the discipline's commitment to individual motivation (or 'rational choice theory', where 'rational' means 'wanting more of a given good'). Citizenship is a property of groups. It cannot be understood within the framework of methodological individualism. Thus, it remains the case, even when it is possible to speak of a creative *economy* (albeit as a contested term), that creative *citizenship* seems to be going too far.

Indeed, within the bounds of formal, disciplinary knowledge, the concepts of creativity, citizenship and economics all belong to different domains. The absence of a ready-made discipline is a disadvantage, in the sense that there's no body of knowledge or method to which our research is a further contribution. On the other hand it is an advantage in the sense that the field is open to new ways of understanding both economics and citizenship. That makes our research project itself a creative and civic act, even as it strives to describe something real, which in turn may serve to modernise interdisciplinary scholarship about both citizenship and creativity in the context of economic and cultural development. Not only is the work of research creative, it is also civic. The research team, together with community partners and interlocutors such as policy makers, activists and 'ordinary' citizens, as they congregate and self-organise around the problem of knowledge that is posed by trying to join creativity and citizenship together, make this kind of future-facing research an example of what it seeks to analyse: a contribution to creative citizenship.

Citizenship studies

In order to make a leap into the interdisciplinary unknown, it is necessary to start from the known. I will sketch some of the established approaches to citizenship, to trace where and how creativity comes into the literature.

Social sciences

The *behavioural* sciences have not had much to say about citizenship, or indeed any concept that requires analysis of groups rather than agents. This includes both psychology and economics, the success of which in the US especially has influenced other disciplines, such as political science, with the idea that group level 'behaviour' can – and should – be studied on the assumption that whatever is observed can be explained by individual actions (and motivations), so there's no need for group level or institutional analysis (for example, they apply Occam's Razor to groups). For true behaviourists, there's not much interest in citizenship, which in any case describes a kind of 'good' that the individual cannot improve, or trade, or be cured of, so there's no point in economists and psychologists studying it.

Such methodological individualism has not entirely captured sociology (which, however, is no longer the ascendant discipline that it was in the 1960s and 70s). Here is where the most familiar scholarship related to citizenship may be found. Sociology has had a particular interest in the relations between the individual and the *state* (as well as in other high-level abstractions such as class, gender and ethnicity), and in *modernity*, which is the period when citizenship evolved from previous conceptualisations that were based on monarchical or religious subjection to a higher power. As a result, citizenship studies have been preoccupied with identifying the rights, obligations and power asymmetries that characterise the relations between citizens and state agencies in modernising societies.

They have not been so interested in how such relations are *mediated*, at individual (sense-making or semiotic) level, or at 'mass' scale, where media agencies take on some of the functions of states, especially in relation to the characterisation of national identity, propaganda about who 'we' are and what should be done to protect, extend or defend 'our' values, and so forth. It is here that creativity enters the picture, for citizenship needs not only to be made but also to be made sense of. That work goes on in civic action among citizens but also, more spectacularly, in the productions of giant sociocultural agencies such as media (propaganda, ideology and civic pedagogy), social networks (connectivity and association among strangers) and culture (subjectivity, including national identity).

The concept of citizenship is also historical, both in scholarship and in society. Citizens were once the (free, male, native, adult, property-owning, uncriminalised) inhabitants of a city. The American and French Revolutions vastly inflated that notion to make citizenship a national project. In Britain, the slow advance of democratic representation meant that citizenship was not granted to British 'subjects' until 1983. By then, citizenship was not understood merely as civic and political rights (personal freedom, security of property and contract, right to vote), but had already extended into the social realm with rights to education, health, welfare and certain types of information. Obligations to the state have meanwhile weakened, for instance with the abolition of conscription, and the slow withdrawal of the state from private life (for example, in relation to given names, marriage, sexual conduct and privacy). Thus, citizenship studies have tended to focus on the twists and turns, successes and failures, of the endless pressure required to establish citizens' rights in the 'public' domain.

Hence citizenship is regarded as part of public life, which has brought this branch of scholarship into close contact with the idea of the public sphere, public sector and public *as opposed to* private interests, where 'public' is code for state subsidy or state provision and 'private' is code for commercial exploitation and markets. Locating citizenship on one side of this divide (on the other is found only the behaviour of the consumer or audience) means that the concept has been caught up in partisan politics, where one side seeks to maximise state support (funding) for civic community and creative activities, and the other prefers to satisfy citizens' 'needs' via the market.

The politics of all this was intensified through the Reagan–Thatcher doctrines of deregulation, privatisation, and disinvestment by the state in relation to the provision of social, community, educational, health, welfare and cultural services to their own populations. A high-water mark of this turn to privatisation was reached in Margaret Thatcher's celebrated claim that there is 'no such thing as society', only 'individuals and families', so that using 'taxpayers' money' to assist any one citizen or group is tantamount to theft from their 'neighbours'.[2] This attempt to drive 'social responsibility' down to individual level, and to make (civic) 'entitlements' depend on the fulfilment of 'obligations', was widely seen at the time as ideological cover for an attempt to cut benefits. Although a later UK Conservative led government sought to replace 'there's no such thing as society' with 'the Big Society' (see Chapter 1), the suspicion remained that this too was cover for cuts – get people to volunteer, and you can cut back state-based social services.

Unfortunately, such febrile politics has left its mark on citizenship studies, where suspicion of the market and defensiveness about the welfare state have made observers suspicious of any work that investigates how citizenship has extended into private and commercial contexts, as indeed it has in relation to media representations (where 'we the citizens' become 'me the audience'), social networks (how can they be civic when they are on proprietorial platforms?), and the voluntaristic, playful, informal 'citizenship' that links celebrity and pop culture with civic identity and activism (Hartley, 2010). In a mediated, celebrity-orientated commercial democracy, the boundaries between private and public life, individual and social action, commercial and public domains – and thus between creative and civic values – have blurred beyond recognition. The place of citizenship in society, and with that its connection with creativity, needs a radical rethink.

There are three established social-science approaches to the concept of citizenship:

1. *The 'civil' or 'liberal' approach*, where the state exists to help citizens and to protect rights (weak state, individual freedom).

2. *The active, or 'enterprise' approach* (Oakeshott, 1975), where a state exists to universalise the 'rights of man' (French Revolution) or universal rights (American Revolution), sometimes imposing democracy by force (for example, WW2 and the Vietnam War), where the citizen has no option but to participate in the state's 'enterprise'.

3. *The 'critical' or 'ideological' approach*, which analyses modern citizenship in the name of identities or groups that it fails to emancipate or accommodate, especially those based on religion (for example, Islam), class (Marxism), gender (feminism) and race (the colonial, ethnic, migrant or multicultural subject).

Citizenship, even of an avowed liberal democracy, is not equal for all subjects. Or, as Nelson Mandela put it, 'We were taught – and believed

– that the best ideas were English ideas, the best government was English government and the best men were Englishmen' (*Long Walk to Freedom* 1995: 35–6). Here, the very concept of citizenship entails its own opposite for 'others' who are denied entry – subordination to inequality, 'subaltern' status, or abjection. Versions of the dilemmas resulting from that history emerge frequently in contemporary events. When, during the time of assembling this book, 'Islamist' fighters murdered journalists from the Parisian satirical magazine *Charlie Hebdo*, they provoked a debate not only about religion and civic culture, but about the tensions between the French Republic's values of 'liberty, equality and fraternity', illustrating the many different gradations of view among those willing to see liberty of expression qualified in some measure by the demands of equality and fraternity, exposing an unforeseen tension between three words that have been engraved on the stone porticos of French town halls for two and a half centuries. Such complexities and tensions are not, of course, a European or Judeo-Christian preserve: citizenship claims among Islamic communities around the world are no less intense or diverse.

This project seeks to add to these approaches, not simply to 'apply' one or more of them. Thus, in line with media and communication studies more generally, we are moving towards a fourth approach, derived not from social science directly ('citizenship studies') but from the humanities and creative arts ('creativity studies'):

4. The *creative, cultural or DIY approach*, which has developed within cultural, communication and media studies (that is, not in sociology or social science directly), not least in my own work over a series of publications from the 1990s onwards. Here, citizens create their own forms of 'association among strangers' using the affordances of digital and interactive *media*, social *networks*, and their experiences and practices as *audiences* and *consumers*. All this activity occurs within a *market* environment and in what would previously have been understood as *private* life, where 'private' signifies personal, domestic, family and lifestyle affiliations, not just commercial enterprise.

Nowhere is 'all market' or 'all state', of course. The distinctions between private life and private enterprise on one side, and the public sphere and public sector on the other, are neither clear nor absolute (except where political preference and critical analysis hold fast to one side only). But cultural, media and communication studies have been innovative over a long period in finding 'the politics of the personal' within previously neglected parameters of private life, where the market rules the roost but self-organised citizenship practices nevertheless emerge in DIY form (Ratto and Boler, 2014) and express themselves in the emergence of communitarian phenomena such as the Creative Commons.

The mixture of 'public' (civic) with 'private' (personal) interests has been well mapped in the domain of identity politics, from feminism onwards, and it has been boosted in the online era because people can organise their lives around affiliations (such as fanship, minority identity, or taste) that entail association, obligations and actions indistinguishable from civic ones (Baym, 2010; Papacharissi 2010a; 2010b; 2015). But such 'mixture' in citizenship *theory* will swiftly attract criticism (of playing into the hands of neo-liberalism), leaving the very real observations of those interested in identity, creativity, culture and media out in the cold. Thus, at the risk of attracting adverse attention from the defenders of public culture (for example, Oakley, 2009; Lee et al, 2011), in this volume we seek to advance citizenship studies by adding cultural, mediated, DIY and creative citizenship to the conceptual mix.

Historical approaches

In addition to these categorical approaches, there are important historical treatments of citizenship (especially Western, European/US versions) showing how it emerged in the process of contextual struggle and institutional change. Prominent among these are:

- T.H. Marshall's (1963) now classic periodisation of citizenship across three successive phases, beginning with the Enlightenment or modern state:
    - *Civic rights* (freedom of person, contract, access to justice);
    - *Political rights* (the vote, representative bodies and the right to be elected to them);
    - *Social rights* (welfare, education).

- In the US context, Michael Schudson (1999) suggested four periods:
    - *Patrician* citizenship ('Founding fathers'): rights held by male heads of leading white households – the only voters – post-1783;
    - *Partisan* citizenship (19th century) mass political parties, public rallies;
    - The *informed* citizen (1880s–1920s), closely connected to the rise of mass communication and the press;
    - Citizenship of *rights* (1960s on): civil rights movement, new social movements.

Schudson argues that the contemporary citizen is *'monitorial'*, keeping a watching brief on matters of personal interest but not necessarily active in traditional civic practices, 'defensive' rather than proactive. In the British context, John Keane (2010) also advances the notion of a 'monitory democracy', which differs from Schudson's by locating scrutiny in monitory *bodies*: 'many different kinds of extra-parliamentary, power-scrutinising mechanisms' (Keane, 2010: 169). Keane identifies the importance of associations – groups – in the maintenance of democracy, and thus locates effective citizenship at the level of institutions rather than that of individuals. Keane also takes, on balance, a positive view about the role of the superabundant communicative media of the digital age in this evolution of democratic texture.

Theoretical approaches

There is an extensive scholarly literature on citizenship from different disciplinary perspectives, notably political science, sociology, history and political communications. The concept has become a major issue within philosophy since the 1990s (Leydet, 2011). Studies are mostly concerned with the civic, political, and other legal rights and obligations of citizens. Topics include race, gender, border control, federalism and so forth, which are often used as the basis for critiques of contemporary liberal (or neo-liberal) citizenship. Thus has arisen a distinct field of citizenship studies, associated with scholars such as Bryan Turner (1993), Will Kimlicka (1995) and others (Isin and Turner 2002; Isin and Nielsen 2008). This field considers the tensions between citizenship and contemporary problems, including migration (Soysal, 1994), globalisation (Urry, 1998), and ecology (Steenbergen, 1994). As Soysal argues, legitimising a *globalised* discourse of human rights has the counterintuitive effect of hollowing out the substance of *national* citizenship, by decoupling rights from national belonging.

Theorists of the 'network society', notably Manuel Castells, have increased sociological *knowledge* of networks, and they have also begun to show how such knowledge can and should inform policy, including citizenship policy. The point, of course, is that information and communications networks are beginning to have a transformative impact on the state, not just on the 'behaviour' of individuals or the growth of markets. Because of their new mix of global and proprietorial properties combined with users' own use of them for democratic, deliberative, advocacy and activist association, social networks have a major impact on citizenship and its conduct (Castells and Cardoso,

2005; Mulgan, 2005). This is a step forward from classic sociological accounts of the 'information society' (for example, Webster 2006), which still prioritise class and embedded power structures over knowledge and information networks. Rather than reinstating an opposition between social class and knowledge societies, as Webster does in his critique of Castells and others (for example. Daniel Bell), it is better to investigate the network society and knowledge economy with such power structures in mind (as Castells does). The creative citizen idea is especially useful in this respect, because it encourages granular analysis of how these forces are navigated at the local level.

There are also theoretical approaches to the historical and political production and administration of identity (subjectivity), principally in the context of the asymmetry between the individual subject's freedom of action and the legal and coercive powers of the expanding nation state. Here, Michel Foucault was the thought leader. Others theorised the contradiction between the claims of universal citizenship (Young, 1989) and the experience of many groups, especially those marked by ethnic, gender, class and cultural difference, as well as indigenous peoples, aliens, refugees and children, who still struggle to achieve and exercise civil rights equally with the Enlightenment subject. Approaches include Marxism and post-Marxism (for example, Laclau and Mouffe, 1985), feminism (for example, Fraser, 1989), Foucauldian (Miller, 2006), and postcolonial approaches (Ong, 1999; Saada, 2012), which critique the concept of citizenship, arguing that the state (or social order) and the 'free' citizen are mutually incommensurable. Habermas (1998, ch 4; 2001) has sought to reconcile the tensions with his notion of 'liberal nationalism' or 'constitutional patriotism'.

Humanities approaches

This rather copious social-science scholarship is however marked by a notable *lack* of attention to the role of creativity in acts of civic association. Such scholarship proceeds quickly to institutional analysis, rather than to the 'content' of what ordinary citizens may do, say, make or produce for themselves. We are more familiar with media 'barons', who, like their imaginary apotheosis, *Citizen Kane*, present an uncertain vision of democratic accountability, than we are with expressions of 'journalism as a human right' (Hartley, 2008), where the much vaunted freedoms of expression, association and communication are taken into their own hands by citizens at large, who cannot avoid finding creative ways to secure, share and enjoy those rights. The concept of street theatre – and its use in demonstrations – shows how advocacy and political opposition may take extremely creative forms. It shows too how such antics may reprise much older civic customs, such as the use of games, carnival, pageants and festivals, even Halloween parties, which show how 'social inversion and youthful exuberance' may nevertheless express community identity, especially in experimental settler-societies like the USA (Rogers, 2002: 56-70). Thus, the Bakhtinian 'carnivalesque' is part of civic life. It may even be said that the sober, obligation-based side of citizenship is a social science, while carnivalesque exuberance belongs to the humanities. But – as Bakhtin argued, when introducing the idea in the first place – these are but two aspects of every citizen's life, and have been since medieval times if not longer:

> It could be said (with certain reservations, of course) that a person of the Middle Ages lived, as it were, two lives: one that was the official life, monolithically serious and gloomy, subjugated to a strict hierarchical order, full of terror, dogmatism, reverence and piety; the other was the life of the carnival square, free and unrestricted, full of ambivalent laughter, blasphemy, the profanation of everything sacred, full of debasing and obscenities, familiar contact with everyone and everything. Both these lives were legitimate, but separated by strict temporal boundaries. (Bakhtin, 1984: 129–30)

The aspects were separated by strict *disciplinary* boundaries too, it seems. It's clearly well past time when these two 'legitimate' aspects of citizenship – obligatory and playful, straight version and inversion – are brought together in one knowledge system, even though they remain apart from one another in scholarly traditions. We think 'creative citizenship' can do that job.

Creativity has been a dominant trope in humanities-based approaches to communal life, but the concept of *citizenship* is much weaker in this domain. Thus, the 19th-century founders of the concept of culture – John Ruskin, Matthew Arnold and Walter Pater – all worked to a 'civic' sense of creativity. A flavour of it may be gained from John Ruskin's distinction between 'political economy' (pertaining to citizens) and 'mercantile economy' (pertaining to 'power over labour'), in *Unto This Last* (1862):

> Political economy (the economy of a State, or of citizens) consists simply in the production, preservation, and

distribution, at fittest time and place, of useful or pleasurable things. The farmer who cuts his hay at the right time; the shipwright who drives his bolts well home in sound wood; the builder who lays good bricks in well-tempered mortar; the housewife who takes care of her furniture in the parlour, and guards against all waste in her kitchen; and the singer who rightly disciplines, and never overstrains her voice, are all political economists in the true and final sense: adding continually to the riches and well-being of the nation to which they belong. But mercantile economy, the economy of 'merces' or of 'pay,' signifies the accumulation, in the hands of individuals, of legal or moral claim upon, or power over, the labour of others; every such claim implying precisely as much poverty or debt on one side, as it implies riches or right on the other. (Essay II: 'The Veins of Wealth').

This preoccupation with the 'fittest' artisanship and 'disciplined' creative expression, as the foundation of the 'riches and well-being of the nation', has lasted well beyond Ruskin's own era, just as Matthew Arnold's prescription about culture as the pursuit of perfection has long outlived the contemporary fears (occasioned by the extension of the franchise to working men) that inspired it. Both writers were influential in literary culture, their ideas being taken up and modified among influential literary critics down to T.S. Eliot, F.R. Leavis and Richard Hoggart, and thence to contemporary cultural studies, for whom Ruskin's notion of a 'political economy' based on the what we might call the creative industriousness of the citizenry has morphed into a demand for 'critical literacy'. F.R. Leavis famously distinguished between 'culture' and 'civilisation' (as Ruskin had between 'political' and 'mercantile' economy), concluding that in the face of burgeoning 'civilisation' (that is, industrial mass modernity), 'the citizen … must be trained … to resist' (Leavis and Thompson, 1933: 3–4).

The instrument of that training was a literary education, which was duly enforced in British schools, just as these expanded to a universal, compulsory experience for all citizens after the 1944 Education Act. Training in discrimination, critical literacy and 'resistance' to the blandishments of commercial mass culture implies – and acquired – a strong sense of moral purpose, such that a literary education was soon construed as a training in *criticism* rather than *creation*, the idea being to turn out good citizens not good poets, artists or singers, much less farmers, shipwrights or builders. Notably, the BBC arises from this rather lofty perspective: using popular broadcasting for 'education by stealth', in an approach known as Reithianism, after the BBC's first director general. But Reithianism was constantly challenged by the emergence of things more vernacular, especially after the establishment of commercial television in 1955. Long dominant in the arts, the BBC is now being challenged by commercial providers such as Sky, Netflix and HBO, who are beating it at its own 'quality' game. It is also challenged by digital developments, despite its own early leadership in that field. Thus, the link identified by the Victorian inventors of 'culture', between quality of expression and quality of citizenship, remains as a force in media policy to this day, prodding major players to recognise a responsibility towards 'critical' citizenship based on exposure to 'the best that has been thought and said', as Arnold had put it.

Communication and media studies approaches

Clearly, from the late 19th century onwards – with the increasing ubiquity of the popular press, publishing, cinema and broadcasting – citizenship and consumption, commercial marketing and political propaganda, information and ideology, were increasingly hard to tell apart, especially as states and political parties as well as news media and entertainment networks were all using the same persuasive techniques to reach the same population. As Scammell puts it:

> The act of consumption is becoming increasingly suffused with citizenship characteristics and considerations… It is no longer possible to cut the deck neatly between citizenship and civic duty, on one side, and consumption and self interest, on the other. (Scammell, 2000: 351–2)

A clear example of this arose when UK politicians debated in 2003 the need for a 'converged' regulator of communications, attentive to both citizenship and consumer issues. The resultant offspring, Ofcom, concluded that it had a mission to serve the 'citizen–consumer' (Livingstone and Lunt, 2007).

It began to seem, even among critics, that democracy and markets needed each other (are co-constituted). And among those who had not experienced totalitarianism, world wars or the Cold War, that is 'Gen X' and its 'media native' successors, the categorical suspicion of commercial media was not 'hard wired', as it were. They could see no need to 'resist' Leavis's 'civilisation' root and branch, but were drawn instead to seek employment and artistic fulfilment in a media-rich economy.

In countries where authoritarianism was of more recent memory or still present, from Germany in Europe, across South American ex-dictatorships, to China and the former Soviet bloc, commercialism and media were seen in the post-Cold War environment not as a threat to liberty but as its guarantor, essential to civic development.

Those ordinary people ('consumers') who did not aspire to professional media careers were nevertheless able to improve their own 'public' performances owing to continuous improvements in technological affordances, and concomitant practical competence. Skills that were once confined to professions and artisans (for example, in writing, graphics, audiovisual production and editing) were 'democratised' across whole populations (Bruns, 2008; Cheshire, 2013; Flowers, 2008; Rose, 2012). Pretty soon, astute observers noted that audiences who participated in forms of association via entertainment formats were not only 'media-savvy' but also more civic-minded than the experts: they could teach those who insisted on political or critical purity a thing or two about civic values (Coleman, 2003; 2005). Similarly, 'pro-ams' and 'makers' (Leadbeater and Miller, 2004) were the 'new innovators'. A high level of expertise may be discovered among a distributed citizenry. When combined into groups, this is the source of crowdsourcing, which can be observed across multitudinous activities from astronomical observation to city renewal campaigns.

Technological and economic approaches

Technological and economic trends constantly transform the media landscape as a whole (Hartley et al, 2013), and at an accelerating rate with the emergence of digital technologies (Bollier, 2008), the internet (Zittrain, 2006), interactive and mobile media (Goggin, 2008; Goggin and Clark, 2009), and social network markets (Potts et al, 2008). At the same time, media and communication studies matured, absorbing 'critical' citizenship from literary studies, 'political' citizenship from social sciences, and 'creative production' from vocational training. Gradually new approaches to the concept of citizenship were clarified and established in which such terms – 'critical', 'political', 'creative' and 'production' – were not seen as being in opposition but as orchestrated and mutually constitutive. Although the 'critical' (literary) and 'media effects' (social science) traditions were slow to decay in educational settings, dissatisfaction with their presumption of a 'command-and-control' model of centralised mass communication that manipulates individual (behavioural) consumers has increased with the emergence of interactive, participatory, digital media, and the concomitant spread of the notion of the *user*, who is among other things an *information-user* (Gans, 2012), a maker (Anderson, 2012) and a creative consumer (Jenkins et al, 2013).

Cultural, media and DIY citizenship

It is from the humanistic tradition that the concept of the *creative citizen* has developed, not directly from citizenship studies, nor from political communication or the social sciences, which sometimes remain sceptical about user agency (O'Connor, 2010). Even so, some leading political scientists such as Lance Bennett (2008) have increasingly included aspects of creativity in their models of political communication:

> Many observers properly note that there are impressive signs of youth civic engagement in these nongovernmental areas, including increases in community volunteer work, high levels of consumer activism, and impressive involvement in social causes from the environment to economic injustice in local and global arenas. Some even ascribe civic engagement qualities to many activities that occur in online social networking and entertainment communities. (Bennett, 2008: 2)

Chris Bilton (2007) extends creativity to management studies. He observes that complexity and contradiction in the domain of business makes novel but feasible demands upon managers and workers:

> Creative management requires a similar split focus, between present realities and future possibilities, between individuals and teams, between organisations and systems. Nobody should pretend that this dualism is easy – it is much more difficult than mere innovation, which may plunge us into the unexpected and unpredictable but does not require us to make sense of what we find there. (Bilton, 2007: 173)

Toby Miller (2006) proposes that cultural citizenship ('the right to know and speak') should be added to political citizenship ('the right to reside and vote') and economic citizenship ('the right to work and prosper'). In my own work (1996a; 1996b; 2010) I have proposed 'media citizenship', based on a combination of audiencehood practices (including fandom) and identity politics in commercial and mediated democracies.

From there, attention readily shifts across to 'new media,' where the *use* of mediated representations, including user-created content and socially networked association, leads to consideration of 'DIY citizenship', and to what may be termed, channelling the pioneering ideas of William Stephenson (1967), a 'play theory of citizenship' (Gray et al, 2009; Hartley, 2010), where user citizens make their own forms of association and civic meaningfulness out of the resources of entertainment media, private life and consumption, often even while disengaging from formal civic participation (for example, not registering to vote), and from consumption of erstwhile 'organs of enlightenment' (the press) that had constructed and instructed the 'informed' citizen. Thus, observers from many disciplinary backgrounds have noted simultaneous disengagement from the industrial-era technologies of democracy (voting, party membership), and rapid uptake of 'new' digital, mobile and social media, such that accusations of 'civic apathy' coincide with exponential growth of user interactivity (see Harris et al, 2010).

Creative cities and other novelties

Creative citizenship as a field of research has by now also intersected with 'creative economy' research and policymaking. There are different strands to such work.

Creative cities

An important strand is where the emphasis is on the 'city' part of creative citizenship – in cultural geography, urban planning and design, and the sociology of occupations. Classic accounts of the city abound (see in particular Jane Jacobs (1969); Saxenian (1994); Holston and Appadurai (1996) and Ladd (2000)), where a 'bottom-up', citizen-centric approach predominates. Australian-born American visionary architect William J. Mitchell combined urban planning and the internet in his smart city concept (Mitchell, 1999). See Florida (2002 and other publications) for the geographical pull of competition for creative occupations; and see Oakley (2011) for a contrary view. Elizabeth Currid (2007) reconfigures New York City as a complex system of systems that generates the 'Warhol economy'. De Propris et al (2009) use the geographical approach to 'map' creativity in the UK (as do other Nesta and Demos reports). Further dimensions of creative citizenship, such as creative activism generally and co-creative planning and design interventions, form a running theme in the chapters which follow. Hartley et al (2012) produce a new comparative *Creative City Index* based on eight dimensions (with over 250 indicator measures) that include citizen creativity as well as economic activity. I have also contributed to the city-economy-policy complex with the notion of 'urban semiosis' (Hartley et al, 2015). Media are essential to civic life, playing a coordinating role for cities (urban culture) as a 'system of systems', where tensions and clashes among incommensurate but proximate complex systems of meaning, institutional organisation and society-scale action are worked through at the discursive level.

Creative design

The concept of design has emerged as a master metaphor, replacing the 'engineer' of the 19th and 20th centuries, as the sign of professional expertise in a growth economy. Where engineers make things work, designers make things desirable. Increasingly, these two value systems have been integrated in the creative industries, where the design aspects of corporations like Apple (and previously Nokia) were given much of the credit for the commercial success of their products (in contrast to engineer-led corporations such as Erikson). This 'alpha' version of design did not leave much room for users, beyond their role as feedback-providing consumers (often avid ones). Design became a costly signal that consumers could send to demonstrate their astute status (Hartley, 2012). However, the systems in which devices operated were often *designed* to *restrict* users' room for independent, creative, civic or collective-action manoeuvre. The rights that were most strongly enforced were the proprietary rights of the corporation, not the creative (design) rights of the community.

On the other hand, the variety and innovation shown in the things that ordinary people, singly or in association, using proprietary devices, have made, shared, and caused to change, thereby contributing their 'microproductivity' to the growth of knowledge, is remarkable, to say the least. Maiden (2013) celebrates citizens' participation in design practices. Wright et al (2013) seek to bridge the gap between design professionals and users with design education. Carvalho (2011) studies arts in the community (in Boston, US neighbourhoods) to suggest a new approach to the realisation of citizenship, where artistic practice and the development of cultural awareness combine to produce the creative citizen.

Creative policy

Another important strand is the 'policy response' literature. This includes attention to what regulators are doing (Gibbs, 2004; Hargreaves, 2011); reports on sectors of the creative economy (Chapain et al, 2010; Bakhshi et al, 2013); as well as specific material relating to citizenship (Hoskins et al, 2012). The 'policy response' environment is governed by growth economics (not non-linear or evolutionary economics), and by restricting agency to the level of the firm (and larger), rather than incorporating the 'digital dark matter' of user-created content and social interaction beyond the firm, which is now the source of much of the productivity of the creative economy (see Hartley et al, 2012). Where macroeconomics does take an interest in the individual worker, for example, to explain the relation between wages and prices, the focus of attention is on '*Homo* œconomicus', not on creative productivity in the community as an autonomous source of value. One potential next stage contribution to the consideration of creative citizenship might include a more developed appreciation of its contribution to the currently prevalent problem in advanced economies of stagnant productivity.

Participation – another problem of knowledge

The foregoing literature review demonstrates clearly why and how the concept of the 'creative citizen' presents itself as a problem of knowledge. As we've seen, the terms 'creative' and 'citizen' don't readily fit together as concepts, except creatively of course. Further, the methods of inquiry into them are poles apart. What should a research project do about that? Looking for 'real world' evidence on the ground may be premature, for the 'creative citizen' may not exist 'on the ground', at least in 'significant' numbers (that is, numbers that might compel policy attention).

Can such a creature be discovered by empirical research? Not yet, seems to be the answer. In a recent critique of British arts and culture policy, the historian Robert Hewison (2014) has commented on official figures released in a survey called *Taking Part*, which track participation or engagement in 'the arts' and 'culture' over the previous decade. Essentially, these figures measure consumption not creation – visits to cultural institutions, and so on.[3] That's a pretty attenuated notion of 'participation'. Even so, since the surveys began in 2005, according to Hewison, the UK's Department of Culture Media and Sport (DCMS), has 'directed more than £15 billion of grant-in-aid and National

Lottery funds towards the cultural sector, yet audience numbers and their social make-up remain scarcely altered'. He summarises the figures:

> The number of adults who have 'engaged' with the arts just once a year has increased by 0.7% between 2005/6 and the first quarter of 2014/15 (77%). The number of adults engaging with the arts three or more times in a year has fallen by 0.5% (62.5%). Single museum and gallery visits have increased, from 48.2% in 2005/6 to 51.8%, and visits to heritage sites from 69.9% to 72.4%, but public library visits have fallen by 11.8% to 34.9%, and visits to archives have halved to 2.9%.[4]

Hewison comments, 'The DCMS set these relatively modest targets – is participation just once a year really "taking part"? – in order to increase access to the arts and heritage, but the figures are flat lining. Now that cultural funding is falling off a cliff, whatever government is elected in 2015 will have to have a radical rethink of cultural policy.'

The problem with Hewison's analysis is that he restricts 'participation' to individual consumption (following behavioural approaches), and he reduces creative culture to the subsidised arts (following Arnoldian notions). It's an easy step from there to the conclusion that 'citizens' (now reduced to 'adults') aren't very participatory at all, and stubbornly refuse to improve themselves. In other words, here is a clear example of how putting the wrong questions into the research will result in the wrong answers coming out.

Creative citizens? Not likely, is Hewison's foregone conclusion. He notes that the population is still sorted by class: 'taking part' (as defined by the figures) is strongly asymmetrical (class divided). Those in what the DCMS calls 'the upper socio-economic group' consistently 'take part' more than 'black and minority ethnic groups'. His verdict: 'culture cannot escape class' (which is where cultural studies came in, back in the 1960s). It *seems* not only that government investment has failed to change cultural participation, but also that more than half a century of critique and scholarship have failed to solve the problem that was posed by Richard Hoggart in 1957: how can class-based citizens of commercial democracies use the affordances of consumer and media culture to express their own civic, community and creative realities?

Thus, political and ideological questions cannot be avoided, still. But conceptual issues demand attention too: it is no good leaving the inherited concepts of 'the arts' and 'culture' in place, no good defining 'participation' in terms of consumption or audiencehood, and no good judging 'engagement' on a (class) model that seems to require a 'redistribution of culture' policy response. The fault does not lie with Hewison, who's only pursuing the logic of the figures, nor does it lie with a government department that cannot find a way to account for its expenditure other than by traditional economic measures of traditional cultural categories. The problem lies in knowledge itself. 'Government figures' don't actually tell us anything useful about the relationships among creativity, culture and citizenship. 'Visits to cultural institutions' is a very poor proxy for a digitally equipped population's creativity and its interconnected (socially networked) collective action.

Here is where a new concept of cultural participation is needed, one where culture is not confined to what the educated elites like, and participation includes doing and making as well as consuming. Conceptualising creative citizenship needs to be alive to how consumption, plus 'microproductive' DIY creation, plus mediated association (doing it with others – DIWO) via digital and social networks, are mutually emergent, working together.

The thing about ordinary citizens is that they are never only one thing: they are not only classed, raced, and sexual subjects, resistant or otherwise, but also audiences and consumers, and simultaneously citizens and members of the public, who may (from time to time) get together for associative or activist purposes. These social categories cohabit in the same biological specimens; and the sphere of meanings – language, media, culture, communications – is where all possible permutations of these different identities, subjectivities and relational associations are 'in play', to uncertain effect. 'Individuals' are not pre-given; identity is the outcome of these cultural and collective processes and is thus a product of culture – group-made or demic knowledge (Hartley and Potts, 2014).

The tense of research

Given that existing disciplinary approaches, in both economics and cultural criticism, seem to have trouble identifying creative citizenship, even when creative citizens are readily observable on the street, as it were, one important preliminary move in the search for a more adequate methodological framework is to begin by changing the *tense* of research. We can shift the analytical question from 'space' (is there anyone out there?) to 'time' (is something changing?). In any given project, the use of statistics that are drawn from people's activities means that we are investigating the past (essentially completed actions), rather than the future (emergent trends). Raymond Williams (1977) sorted culture into three forms that he dubbed 'dominant' (present powers), 'residual' (declining past) and 'emergent' (future patterns already in formation). Such approaches need to be revived, not necessarily to favour one form over another (Williams preferred 'emergent' over 'dominant' for political reasons), but simply to understand why something that is currently statistically insignificant may turn out later on to be historically important.

This question of tense relates back to the whole problem of evidence. 'Evidence-based research' is much in demand in policy circles, especially in the health and medical fields, and for good reason. But in the development of public policy about citizens (effectively everyone), it is inevitably orientated to the past – only completed actions or objects leave 'evidence' or traces behind them. To understand 'creative citizens' we need to conduct research that can help to reveal not only the sources of creative and civic action (the past), but also changes in how such actions are organised and scaled up in the digital age (the present), and what that might mean for the future of the creative economy, or of public policy and civic contribution in a given country. In this context, the concept of the 'creative citizen' is in the future tense: it remains a possibility space rather than an achieved category of knowledge. No matter what is actually happening on the ground, it won't show in official figures until suitable models for it, or proxy indicators, can be found, tested and accepted by statistical bureaux.

Fiction as ultimate truth (for group survival)

Seeking to research something that may not (yet) exist may sound suspiciously like fictional thinking, which the humanities are often said to be good at, without that being meant as a compliment. But this is not just a joke at non-scientists' expense. Historian Yuval Noah Harari (2014) thinks that what distinguishes the human species – '*Sapiens*' as he calls it – is our evolved ability to create fictions that bind a group together, enabling collective action. The 'fictions' or myths he mentions include religion, the nation, the law (and human rights), the economy (including both money and the firm) – all based on *stories* that we tell one another, with no existence beyond human communication:

> How did *Homo sapiens* come to dominate the planet? The secret was a very peculiar characteristic of our unique *Sapiens* language. Our language, alone of all the animals, enables us to talk about things that do not exist at all.

...Only *Sapiens* can believe such fictions. ...Fiction is
nevertheless of immense importance, because it enabled
us to imagine things collectively... It is these myths that
enable *Sapiens* alone to cooperate flexibly with thousands
and even millions of complete strangers. Yet none of these
things exists outside the stories that people invent and tell
one another. There are no gods, no nations, no money
and no human rights, except in our collective imagination.
(Harari, 2014: ch 2)[5]

This is a compelling view. It draws attention to the 'reality' of things
that 'don't exist' – the importance of stories in binding groups to
cooperate and take collective action, the (often devastating) effects of
which Harari goes on to enumerate (in an extrapolated argument that
may not be so compelling as its founding proposition). Thus, we may
conclude that imagining a story or myth that binds people together
may be just as important as the resultant crowd. Here is where the
idea of the creative citizen gains further force if it is attracting to itself
a community of those who believe the story and act accordingly,
collectively or cooperatively.

This kind of 'human fiction' research is not as easy to do as empirical
research, at least the kind that counts the frequency of narrowly
defined objects in a specified context to produce certainty (as closely
as possible). In conditions of *uncertainty* and dynamic change that
involves whole systems (not just individual agents within them), we
are dealing in probabilities, not certainties. The value of 'fictional' (or
'playful' or 'systems') thinking here is that it can imagine scenarios,
characters and conflicting actions, which may then be assessed using
more formal methods to come to a more accurate view of future
possibilities. Such 'gaming' methods are now familiar in the sciences
and in economics, where game theory is influential, for instance
in evolutionary economics (Beinhocker, 2006), while probability
approaches are becoming more familiar in business studies and the
social sciences (Bayesian statistics, for instance). Thus, the problem
of knowledge that needs to be decided for the 'creative citizen' to
be analysed is the question of *when* it is. In fact, it's all around us (as
successive chapters in this book attest); in knowledge systems, it is *next*.

Creative systems: the Three Bigs!

On this near horizon – one that many of the papers in this collection
have glimpsed and in part described – is a new and different way of

accounting for creativity in both economic and cultural contexts, and that is to ascribe it not to persons (or firms), but to *groups*. Such an approach, based on evolutionary and complex systems theory, explains why the very idea of the citizen *should* become much more prominent in creativity research and policy. 'Citizens' occur at whole-of-population level; they cannot be reduced to individual creativity alone. This kind of thinking redirects our attention towards much larger 'objects' of study.

In another book, working with two colleagues, I have tried to follow that logic (Hartley et al, 2015). The rationale in this case applies directly to the arguments of this chapter, so it is in order to reprise it here.[6] To make a start towards a systems approach to the creative industries and economy, we have identified what we call the 'Three Bigs':

- *Everyone* – A population approach, not a behavioural one. The latter focuses on the study either of trained artists and creative professionals in expert situations, or of creative firms, which are said to create value by producing intellectual property (itself anchored on individual invention). 'Everyone' challenges this approach by locating creativity at *population* level (as is required in evolutionary approaches). Thus 'property' is not the exclusive or even the main basis for value creation, but something more like a 'commons'. Creativity, not IP, is an output of groups.

- *Everything* – Here, the source of creativity and innovation is understood to lie beyond firms and beyond 'the' economy. 'Everything' designates not just extension of creativity from a specialised industry sector to 'all of the economy' (although that is worth the effort), but also an extension of 'the' economy to encompass all of the productivity of the cultural-knowledge creative systems and their interactions. This is because innovation is an output of social networks, which are made of interconnected citizens.

- *Everywhere* – A planetary approach. The creative industries are most intensively *studied* in the Anglosphere and in the EU, but they are *practised* across the globe in a coherent system of interconnected domains, often in competition with each other, such that emergent or developing economies (for example, Indonesia) may display more sophisticated creative economy policies than advanced ones (for example, the US). It is misleading to confine any notion of creativity and innovation to just one jurisdiction or region, because they are interlinked globally. The same goes for scholarship. There's an international community of interest around the creative economy; good ideas can come from 'anywhere'.

Here's the challenge. Evolutionary theory does not deal in persons, but in populations. Evolutionary change does not occur to favoured, trained or talented individuals, but to entire species. Complex systems are not an aggregate of individual actions and decisions, but a structure of dynamic relations among all, sometimes unthinkably large numbers of agents, relations, and energies or forces. Systems thinking does not analyse creativity in a linear way, by following causation through a kind of telegraph-wire model of information transference, from sender-artist-entrepreneur, via their creative work or text or firm, to receiver-consumer. Instead, creativity is the product of the interactions of all the agents in a given system, mutually influencing one another, such that creative causation is diffused throughout the system, and creative action is an output of it. This approach means that policy should stop trying to *manage* citizens through various strong or weak command and control mechanisms, from surveillance and data mining to physical controls when things get feisty on the street. Instead, policy needs to create or at least assist *relations* with citizen groups and associations that are engaged in concerted, purposeful action, as a wellspring of democratic governance.

Because groups (or demes) are made by culture in a process of adaptation to circumstances and environments, it is impossible to define a group in advance, beyond the basic requirement that it comprises numbers of *non-kin* humans bonded/bounded by communication, knowledge and purpose, from which identity, sociality, meaningfulness and a sense of bounded externality are derived and 'stored' in the group's self-made knowledge. Indeed, groups are scale free – cultural demes may be as small as a hunting party or as large as a nation, even a species. Demes may be 'real' (tribes) or 'virtual' (fans), they may be concrete (all speakers of a given language) or abstract ('citizens', 'audiences', 'the public', 'consumers'). Demes or groups are not only organised in shifting *opposition* to other groups (our nation vs. theirs), but also in overlapping and elaborate *complexity*, such that individuals belong to multiple demes, simultaneously or successively, and collaboration or cooperation is as important as competition or conflict (the latter may in fact be strong expressions of the former).[7] This is where the notion of citizenship is helpful, since it describes individuals (citizens), but only in relation to a population of others with a shared identity, within a particular (historically and geopolitically contingent) system (citizenship), which may also be conceived *adversarially*, in opposition to outsider or 'they' groups. Within a given citizen population, creativity, action and thus the advancement of causes is achieved via *groups* and their interactions (Leadbeater, 2014).

Because this refers to populations, not persons, the traditional 'uses' of culture and knowledge – to confirm identity, place and meaningfulness in a slow changing and relatively isolated small world – give way to new understandings of culture and knowledge. Now the imperative is *reflexivity under uncertainty*: learning to process difference (*translate*) and to navigate change (*trajectory*) across multiple cultural/knowledge boundaries, differences, conflicts and clashes. The opportunity for creativity and innovation at these boundaries is radically increased, because 'everyone', 'everywhere' is a potential source of new ideas, which may then be tested through social networks. This is an evolutionary view, because it posits random *variation* (new ideas from whole populations), but selected *adoption* (via meso-level institutions), and cultural *replication* – it is the culture/knowledge 'organism' as a whole (the system) that survives, not the individual.

The take-out lesson to be drawn from this logic is that if you are interested in creativity and innovation, then you need to take account of the extension of the potential for creativity and innovation across whole populations, and you need to note that more people are more reflexively linked to multiple, multivalent groups or demes than ever before, aided and equipped by technologies and social networks that extend the here and now to global connectedness. In such a situation, where we're dealing with complex systems, interacting and shifting in relation to one another at planetary scale, the policy settings devoted to promoting creativity and innovation will look pretty paltry if they don't take account of a reflexive, productive population that is continuously creating new groups, which in turn generate the (often disruptive) interactions between them, creating newness and knowledge that may prove 'useful' much more widely. Hence, policy needs to move from a 'mechanical' approach (engineered innovation, in expert labs) to a 'probabilistic' approach (population-wide random variation, speeded up by institutionalised 'search' functions across cultural demes and knowledge domains), in which everyone, everywhere, across everything, is a participant, part of the overall productivity of the system. Policy settings need to shift from central control, 'picking winners' and high investment in firms, to distributed control (self-organising systems), trial and error and experimentation, and investment in populations (education, connectivity, nurturing associations). Some of that work is under way, and is reported in the following chapters.

Notes

[1] A branch of labour economics does include the 'economics of citizenship', referring to the costs and benefits of acquiring it, for migrants. See Bevelander and DeVoretz (2008).

[2] See Mrs Thatcher's interview with *Woman's Own*, 23 September 1987. Available at: www.margaretthatcher.org/document/106689

[3] See the DCMS official site: www.gov.uk/government/collections/sat--2

[4] Hewison (2014). His comments and the figures can also be found here: www. booktrade.info/index.php/showarticle/56618/

[5] See: www.ynharari.com/power-and-imagination/articles/the-most-important-things-in-the-world-exist-only-in-our-imagination/

[6] What follows relies on Hartley et al (2015), ch 14.

[7] One transnational entity that has to grapple with these complexities on a daily basis is the EU, whose recent troubled history is testament to how hard 'complex system' analysis and action can be.

THREE

Citizenship in the creative economy

Caroline Chapain and Ian Hargreaves

The creative economy (Howkins, 2001) emerged as a concept in the first decade of the 21st century, linking the earlier idea of 'creative industries' (DCMS, 1998) with the role of creative inputs to the whole economy. The debates accompanying these changes have been summarised from an international perspective by United Nations Conference on Trade and Development reports (UNCTAD, 2008; 2010), which provided assessments of the creative economy and the factors that underpin its growth at differing stages of economic development.

The third iteration of the United Nations report on the creative economy, this time produced by the United Nations Educational, Scientific and Cultural Organization (UNESCO, 2013), adopts a different definition and approach from those of UNCTAD and focuses on 'uncovering the economic and non-economic benefits' of the creative economy in order better to support local pathways to development. The perceived 'non-economic benefits' stem from the wider contribution of cultural development and 'can lead to transformative changes when individuals and communities are empowered to take ownership of their own development processes, including the use of local resources, skills and knowledge and diverse creative and cultural expressions' (UNESCO, 2013: 17). Such benefits have been discussed intensively in the cultural economics literature and stem from the particular characteristics associated with the production and consumption of cultural goods, today more often called 'creative' (Towse, 2003). While the initial creative rhetoric of the early 2000s may have left aside some of these points to focus on the economic contribution of many cultural or creative activities (Hartley, 2005; O'Connor, 2010), the 2013 UNESCO report calls for a return to a more complex understanding of cultural and creative dynamics and the linkages between economic and non-economic acts of creativity. Such a tilt in thinking is highly relevant to the proposition that creative citizenship offers a value-rich way of thinking about the application of creativity in a civic setting, operating at the frontier between the public and private spheres, offering a route for policy makers to consider interventions supportive of the growth of creative citizenship.

As earlier work from Markusen (2010a) pointed out, taking into account the non-economic aspects of the creative economy implies recognising the links between the commercial and not-for-profit components of what she calls the 'creative ecology'. This also directs attention to cultural participation and amateur practices in neighbourhoods and other bounded communities (Jackson, 2008; Evans, 2010) as well as through the 'vernacular creativity' of everyday life (Burgess, 2010; Edensor et al, 2010). This is particularly relevant with the disruption, transformation or change to models of creative production and diffusion created by the new affordances of digital communications technologies (Howard, 2008).

In the UK, highlighting deficiencies of the previous 15 years of creative industries policy, Bakhshi et al (2013) called for new definitions of the creative industries and the wider creative economy, recognising the central role of digital technologies as an engine of innovation and growth in a creative economy that extends well beyond the sectoral domains of the creative industries. In addition, they recommend a broader assessment of the contribution of the creative economy in terms of cultural and economic values. It is also important to recognise the role that the creative economy has played in specific neighbourhoods and local communities, as well as cities and regions, in supporting social, environmental and physical regeneration or other urban development goals. (Bianchini and Parkinson, 1993; Landry, 2000; Kay, 2000; Evans, 2001, 2010; Smith and Warfield, 2008).

Understanding and reconciling these many dimensions of the creative economy is the underlying objective of this chapter. From the point of view of creative citizenship, this is an essential task. If we define creative citizenship as the application of creativity in civic settings and so at the frontier between the public and private spheres, we start by recognising that its evaluation will be complex and multifaceted, involving social, cultural, environmental, personal and economic perspectives. In this chapter, we explore these perspectives and their linkages, offering a way to reconcile them. Our approach challenges a unidisciplinary approach based only upon 'classical' economics, proposing inputs from economic geography, cultural studies, sociology, complexity theory and urban planning.

After presenting conceptual perspectives on the creative economy, we discuss the literature on cultural participation in everyday creativity, amateur practices and informal arts, along with their linkages to formal creative production. Then we examine how participation in both informal and formal creative activities contributes positively to personal development and communities. Finally, we bring together the different dimensions and, building on recent contributions inspired from complexity theory, offer a model of a creative ecosystem, interlinking the notions of creative citizenship and the creative economy.

Boundaries of the creative economy

John Howkins (2001: 8) defines a creative product as 'an economic good or service that results from creativity and has economic value'. He operationalises this through the notion of intellectual property:

> The creative economy consists of transactions in these creative products. Each transaction may have two complementary values: the value of the intangible, intellectual property, and the value of the physical carrier or platform (if any). In some industries, such as digital software, the intellectual property value is higher. In others, such as art, the unit cost of the physical object is higher. (2001; 2013: xiv)

Based on this definition, Howkins links the creative economy to economic activities whose products are protected by patents, copyrights, trademarks, design rights and secrets. As such, the creative economy comprises 15 core activities: advertising, architecture, art, craft, design, fashion, film, music, performing arts, publishing, software, toys and games, TV and radio, video games and research and development (R&D).

Howkins' contribution is rooted in the 'creative debate' at the turn of the century, with the introduction of new concepts such as the creative industries (DCMS, 1998) and the creative class (Florida, 2002), aiming to frame the role of creativity and innovation in supporting economic growth in post-industrial societies (Flew and Cunningham, 2010; Moore, 2014). Shorn of his early inclusion of R&D (that is, science, patents and inventions), Howkins' notion of the creative economy is close to the 'creative industries' thinking adopted by the UK government in 1998 and defined as:

> Those that are based on individual creativity, skill and talent. They also have the potential to create wealth

and jobs through developing and exploiting intellectual property. The creative industries include: Advertising, Architecture, Arts and antique markets, Computer and video games, Crafts, Design, Designer , Film and video, Music, Performing arts, Publishing, and Television and Radio. (DCMS, 2001: 5)

This new term was much debated at the time. Some saw the change in terminology as a way for policy makers to take advantage of growth in the software and new media industries to shift their policies from supporting access to culture as a merit good, to supporting artists in their creative processes for economic purposes (Garnham, 2005). Others argued that it simply reflected a change in the way cultural products are now produced and reproduced through the impact of new technologies:

> The idea of the creative industries seeks to describe the conceptual and practical convergence of the creative arts (individual talent) with cultural industries (mass scale) in the context of new media technologies (ICTs) within a new knowledge economy for the use of newly interactive citizen-consumers. (Hartley, 2005: 21)

Traditionally, creativity can be defined as 'the ability to come up with ideas and artefacts that are new, surprising and valuable' (Boden, 2003: 1). This ability encompasses most economic sectors and different types of creativity can be identified across the economy. For example, the United Nations (UNCTAD, 2010: 9) distinguishes three types of creativity, all supported by new technologies:

- Artistic creativity: involves imagination and a capacity to generate original ideas and novel ways of interpreting the world, expressed in text, sound and image
- Scientific creativity: involves curiosity and a willingness to experiment and make new connections in problem solving
- Economic creativity: a dynamic process leading towards innovation in technology, business practices, marketing, etc., and is closely linked to gaining competitive advantages in the economy.

This broad spectrum of creativity types and their contribution to economic development is central to Richard Florida's concept of the 'creative class,' which includes people working in specific occupations such as engineers, university professors, doctors, artists, media workers, computer programmers, business professionals and architects 'whose economic function is to create new ideas, new technology and/or creative content' (Florida, 2002: 8). In doing so, Florida's concept goes beyond occupations from the creative industries 'sectors' to include numerous activities from across the range of the knowledge economy (OECD, 1996, 2005).[1] In addition, by concentrating on occupations, Florida shifts the analytic lens from industries to individuals, adopting a transversal approach to the economy with a view that creativity is embodied in people more than within industrial processes – a contention that has provoked continuous debate in the literature (KEA, 2006).

While acknowledging the various types of creativity and despite the popularity of Howkins' and Florida's contributions among local planning authorities, most of the international 'creative debate' has tended to associate the creative economy with artistic creativity and a set of industries bearing strong resemblance to the 1998 UK list of creative sectors (UNESCO, 2013).[2] This might be explained partly by the fact that there is already a prolific literature on the knowledge economy, whose definitions tend to exclude the creative sectors or do not study their specific dynamic. In addition, there is a growing recognition that the creative industries can be as innovative as some knowledge sectors (Chapain et al, 2010) and that these are driving innovation across the rest of the economy (UNESCO, 2013), for example through the role that design can play in 'non-creative' industries (HM Treasury, 2005; Tether, 2009) or through other knowledge, products or network spillovers that creative activities can generate for the rest of the economy (DCMS, 2007). Some argue that these direct and indirect contributions of the creative industries are what make the creative economy transformative (Potts and Cunningham, 2008: 238–239):

> The creative industries may not be well characterized as an industry per se, but rather as an element of the innovation system of the whole economy. …Change in the creative industries therefore produces structural and not just operational change in the economy.

In other words, the 'output' of the creative *economy* (as opposed to the creative 'sector' or creative industries) is *innovation*, transforming other economic sectors (Potts, 2009; Hartley et al, 2013). As such, while limiting the creative economy to a set of industries linked to artistic or cultural creativity may help to circumscribe its boundaries, there is still debate about what to measure and how to measure it. First, the various industrial lists used across the world, and their justification (UNESCO, 2013), demonstrate that there is no consensus on what business sectors constitute the creative industries. While some industries such as performing arts, film and television 'are part of all classifications, other activities such as heritage, sport and entertainment are much more debated as some question to what extent they involve industrial approaches or produce symbolic content (Markusen, 2010a; O'Connor, 2010).

Some authors have favoured an occupational approach over an industrial one or promoted the use of both approaches. They argue that focusing on what workers do rather than (or only on) what they make better renders the complexity of interrelationships among creative activities as well as the fact that creative workers may work across creative sectors or outside them (Markusen, 2010a). Indeed, many cultural and creative productions operate on a project basis, bringing together workers with diverse and specialised skills along the value chain for a specific amount of time (Caves, 2000; Hesmondalgh, 2007; Burgess and Pankratz, 2008). For example, the production of a film will require expertise in film production, post-production and distribution as well as expertise from other industries such as music, TV, advertising, publishing, digital media and performing arts. This also explains why self-employment among contracted creative workers is the norm in most creative industries. Some also work in not-for-profit organisations and/or for the community sector and/or for the public sector (Markusen, 2010a); others such as designers, advertising copywriters and media producers can readily work outside the creative industries – adding to the creative economy's spillover effects.

From creative industries to creative economy in the UK

The challenges and issues in defining and measuring the creative economy can be illustrated by changes in the way the UK government has measured the economic contribution of the creative industries over a 20-year period. While a list of creative occupations was identified early on (DCMS, 2004), it was not really used until 2010. This is illustrated in the various reports and statistical bulletins produced by and for the DCMS between 1998 and 2010, which provide economic indicators in terms of jobs, businesses, gross value added (GVA)and exports by industries (DCMS, 1998; 2001; 2007; 2009; 2010a; Frontier Economics, 2006; Work Foundation, 2007).

Nevertheless, the UK government has supported research into better understanding the indirect contribution of the creative industries to the UK economy, notably with the launch of the Creative Economy programme in 2005 (HM Treasury, 2005; DCMS, 2007; Hartley et al, 2013). In this vein, a report commissioned by Nesta in 2008 questioned the prevailing industrial methodology. Adopting both industrial and occupational approaches and using census data, this report showed that 54% of all creative occupations were actually embedded outside the cultural and creative industries in the UK in 2001 – highlighting that more people worked in creative occupations outside the creative industries than within them (Higgs et al, 2008). As a result, both approaches start being used after 2010, under the newly elected Conservative-Liberal Democrat coalition government. Indeed, in its creative industries economic estimates bulletin of December 2010, the DCMS presented 'experimental data' both on employment in the creative industries and on creative occupations outside of the creative industries (DCMS, 2010b). This exercise was repeated in 2011 (DCMS, 2011). The following three years witnessed a period of consultations and revisions about the list of creative industries and the best methodology to capture creative employment. These discussions were strongly influenced by Nesta, which advocated combining occupational and industrial approaches to evaluate the creative intensity of existing creative industries and the extent to which occupations seen as creative involve creative skills (Bakhshi et al, 2013).[3]

This methodological reflection also informed *A Manifesto for the Creative Economy,* whose first recommendation was that 'The Government should adopt our proposed new definitions of the creative industries and the wider creative economy' (Bakhshi et al, 2013: 8). The *Manifesto* re-emphasised a shift away from a pure creative industries rhetoric by advocating a broader approach – demonstrated by the use in the title of the term 'creative economy;' defined as 'those economic activities which involve the use of creative talent for commercial purposes' (2013: 34) – economic activities here are seen as belonging to the entire economy not only the creative industries. This definition differs from Howkins' (2001) conception of the creative economy, which focused on creative outputs (protected by intellectual property). Instead, the manifesto focuses upon creative people. The authors argue that this approach better captures the way digital technologies may change business models across the whole economy.

This suggested new approach has been adopted in subsequent creative industries economic estimates produced by the DCMS. Their statistics include data on the creative industries as previously understood, and also on the newly redefined creative economy, covering 'those who are in creative occupations outside the creative industries as well as all those employed in the creative industries.' (DCMS, 2014: 5). It is interesting to note that this methodology also includes the 'GLAM' sector. Galleries, libraries, archives, museums are classified as creative-intensive, according to Bakhshi, Freeman and Higgs (2013). This change is notable because, until this point, these sectors were excluded from the UK creative industries definition, in contrast with those of organisations such as the European Commission or UNESCO (KEA, 2006; UNESCO, 2013).

According to DCMS (2014), while the creative industries accounted for 1.68 million jobs in the UK (5.6% of all UK jobs), this figure rises to 2.55 million for the creative economy as a whole (8.3% of all UK jobs) in 2012. Figure 3.1 presents the distribution of creative employment within and outside the creative industries. Sectors such as advertising and marketing, design and IT, software and computer services – reliant chiefly on a business-to-business value chain (Work Foundation, 2007; Chapain and Comunian, 2011) – provide large

Figure 3.1: Employment in the creative economy in the UK, 2012

	Employment in creative industries not classified as creative*	Creative jobs in creative industries	Total employment in creative industries	Creative jobs outside of the creative industries	Employment in the creative economy
Advertising and marketing	15%	16%	31%	69%	100%
Architecture	28%	46%	74%	25%	100%
Craft	04%	03%	07%	93%	100%
Design: product, graphic and fashion design	26%	44%	70%	30%	100%
Film, TV, video, radio and photography	35%	55%	89%	11%	100%
IT, software and computer services	40%	31%	71%	29%	100%
Publishing	41%	47%	87%	13%	100%
Museums, galleries and libraries	63%	17%	79%	20%	100%
Music, performing and visual arts	24 %	57%	81%	19%	100%
Total	31%	35%	66%	34%	100%
Wider UK Economy Total	-	-	-	-	08%

Note: * Standard Occupation classification codes from 2010 not classified as creative

Source: DCMS (2014). Available at https://www.gov.uk/government/statistics/creative-industries-economic-estimates-january-2014 [Accessed 19 October 2014]

proportions of their employment outside of the creative industries. However, it is also interesting that almost all craft jobs are located within non-creative industries as well as a quarter of those involving architecture, suggesting more complex integration patterns in the rest of the economy. Finally, despite their belated inclusion in the creative industries and economy's definitions, the majority of employment in museums, galleries and libraries comprises non-creative occupations (63%). One-fifth of creative occupations in that sector are not classified as being part of the creative industries – indicating a notable creative transversal role. These observations confirm the high degree of integration of various creative sectors across the rest of the economy, commercial and non-commercial, and the importance of recognising these complex dynamics.

Everyday creativity and amateur arts

These recent trends in more thorough definitions of creative industries and the creative economy are welcome, but they still offer only a partial understanding of its dynamic. The focus on formal production leaves aside a wider spectrum of cultural participation in society. While cultural participation can consist in audience participation in cultural activities, that is, the reception of formal cultural production in a supposedly 'passive' way, it can also encompass further downstream action, including actively making art or informally contributing to creative and cultural expressions in a variety of settings, as summarised by Jackson and Herranz (2003: 18):

> Participation is not just attendance, observation, consumption, or even audience participation. It includes many other categories of action – making, doing, teaching, learning, presenting, promoting, judging, supporting – and spans many artistic disciplines. It can be amateur or professional, active or passive, individual or collective, continuous or episodic, public or private.

This can also include informal acts of artistic creativity that people perform in their everyday lives (Inglis, 2005; Edensor et al, 2010). Nevertheless, these various informal, everyday or amateur acts of creativity have tended to be defined and considered separately from formal cultural and creative production. This separation needs to be re-evaluated as more research shows that the boundaries between these informal and amateur practices and the creative economy are porous, especially with the creative affordances offered by digital technologies.

Everyday creativity

Since the 1960s, various authors have argued for a better understanding of acts of everyday creativity – or vernacular culture (Williams, 1958 'Culture is Ordinary' [2002]; Lantis, 1960) – and how this relates to formal cultural production. The emergence of the notion of vernacular culture is situated within the debate on what arts and culture are, which social classes produce and consume them and how they are evaluated. Since the 19th century, there has been a tension between 'high', 'popular' and 'low' cultures (Inglis, 2005; Hesmondalgh, 2010; Hartley et al, 2013). Overall, high culture is seen as transcending human experience and producing high cultural value and aesthetic – it has also been associated with the upper middle class or elites. In contrast, the concept of popular culture has involved products destined for commercial purposes and considered 'mass produced, thoughtless, unsophisticated and hollow' (Inglis, 2005: 80) or less innovative, generating entertainment for the 'masses' or the lower classes. However, research into high culture has rejoined that, like popular culture, 'high' art objects are also routinely produced, distributed and consumed and that their value is also socially constructed (Inglis, 2005; O'Connor, 2010). The creative industries concept, by bringing together under the same umbrella, activities from the high arts with activities from popular culture, has emphasised their similarities (Hartley et al, 2013). Moreover, many activities associated with popular culture can lay claim to being highly innovative (Chapain et al, 2010).

A characteristic associated with 'low culture' has been its association with creative acts from people in the lower reaches of the social hierarchy in their everyday lives (for example, decorating one's home) along with common cultural and social practices (traditions, festivals and community practices) (Inglis, 2005). The notion of low culture is situated within a non-elitist view of culture or the anthropological idea that 'Culture is Ordinary' (Williams, 1958 [2002]). In this context, 'vernacular creativity is ordinary, as in non-elite and grounded in the materiality and experiences of everyday life'. (Burgess, 2010: 117) and it 'focuses attention on the overt – on acts and artefacts – and on its cultural meaning' (Lantis, 1960: 213).

While the dialectic of opposition has been crucial in defining high, popular and low cultures, Williams (1958 [2002]: 93) highlighted their interdependence:

> A culture has two aspects: the known meanings and direction, which its members are trained to; the new observations and meanings, which are offered and tested. These are the ordinary processes of human societies and human minds, and we see through them the nature of a culture: that is always both traditional and creative; that it is both the most ordinary common meanings and the finest individual meanings.

Since then, the emphasis has shifted towards demonstrating how everyday culture can be strongly bonded to both popular cultural practices and high cultural standards at a particular time and in a particular place (Inglis, 2005; Burgess, 2010). Some authors also argue that with digital technologies and the shift towards an economic view of culture, the divisions among the three have vanished (Hartley et al, 2013: 76):

> People's relationships, identities and meanings are all immersed in and shaped through media to an extent that was once available only to the aristocracy. Culture is marketised, but the market has distributed culture universally, and cultural 'consumption' is now more participatory and productive than ever.

Amateur practices and arts

In addition to everyday acts of creativity, more organised active cultural participation constitutes an important part of informal creative production. A report on the voluntary and amateur arts sector in England (DCMS, 2008) estimated that there were a minimum of 49,140 voluntary and amateur arts groups in England in 2006–2007, with 5,922,000 members and 3.5 million helpers.[4] A total of 9.4 million people participated: about 16% of the UK population at the time. This figure equals more than three times the number of creative jobs in the UK economy in 2012.

There is no single definition of what constitutes amateur arts. In a review in Europe, Ramsden (2013: 2) highlights the variety of understandings reflected through the use of different terms across countries: 'amateur arts, grassroots arts, leisure arts, active cultural participation and voluntary arts, for example'. In contrast, terminology in the United States includes informal, amateur, community-based and unincorporated arts. Differences in terminology reflect the fact that some of these activities take place at the level of individuals, at home or in informal settings, not necessarily with an audience; whereas others are part of public-facing groups or community activities, some of them formally registered as organisations or associations and performing at times in front of an audience (Jackson, 2008; Ramsden, 2013). Peters and Cherbo (1998: 116) offer a useful definition:

> The unincorporated sector comprises participation (either casual or serious) in a wide range of arts activities, from folk and traditional to fine arts, utilitarian art forms, and popular culture. They can be engaged in on an individual basis, in small informal groups or within legally organised entity.

The notion of amateur has generated academic research in ethnography, sociology, cultural studies and sciences, as well as policy interests which aim to understand the motivations, practices and contributions of amateurs to their domains of activity, for example, arts, science and sport (Stebbins, 1977; 1992; Zimmerman, 1986; Finnegan, 1989; Fox, 2004; Meyer, 2008; DCMS, 2008a; Ramsden et al, 2011; Ramsden, 2013). This body of research highlights the lack of a unifying conceptualisation of terms, but in general, amateurism tends to be distinguished from professional activities based on dimensions such as monetary compensation, skills and training, quality of outputs and publics.

Amateurs engage in activities during their leisure time that for others would be work roles, and they are usually not remunerated for these activities or at least do not derive their main income from them (Finnegan, 1989; Stebbins, 1992; Fox, 2004; Meyer, 2008). Rather, they engage in these activities for the love of them and for reasons such as personal development, developing creative skills, socialising... (DCMS, 2008a; Ramsden et al, 2011). Amateurs, however, may display a widespread knowledge and considerable technical skills, leading to debate about the extent to which they can achieve 'professional' standards (Stebbins, 1992; Meyer, 2008). Finally, like professionals, many amateurs have an audience (Stebbins, 1992; DCMS, 2008a). However, one of the more pronounced distinctions between amateurs and professionals resides in the spatiality of their activities and their audience, with amateurs operating mostly within local and regional environments (Meyer, 2008; Stern and Seifert, 2010; Ramsden et al, 2011). Stebbins (1977; 1992) argues that amateurs score lower on a set of professional attitudes such as confidence, perseverance and commitment.

In recent years, some authors have pointed towards blurring boundaries between amateurs and professionals (Meyer, 2008), especially as at times, amateurism is seen as a pathway towards professionalism (Stebbins, 1977; 1992). In the arts, this blurring can be even more important as questions arise on how to define and characterise professional artists (Finnegan, 1989; Frey, 2003; Benamou, 2003; Cherbo, 2008).

Linkages between everyday creativity, amateur arts and the creative economy

Existing literature on vernacular creativity and amateur creative practices has touched upon four main avenues of cross-over and linkages with formal creative production:

- as generators of innovative and alternative content for mainstream creative production;
- as supporting the development of mainstream cultural consumption;
- as part of the pathway towards professionalisation of amateurs;
- as part of the portfolio of creative professionals' activities.

While some authors emphasise the naivety and low quality of amateur production, others demonstrate how amateur production has generated innovative and radical content and processes (Zimmerman, 1986; Fox, 2004; Shand, 2008) for example by allowing more diversity of voices in terms of race, gender, sexual orientation, ethnicity, religion... (Fox, 2004; Markusen, 2010b).

As an example, advances in photographic and video technologies in the last 50 years, with the advent of personal and later digital cameras, have democratised the means of production and post-production in photography and film (Zimmerman, 1986; Conway, 2004; Fox, 2004; Katelle, 2004). Some amateur movie productions are still focused within the home or family, but others have adopted a more deliberate and sometimes radical approach aimed at a local or specialised public (Shand, 2008). Despite the still important industry monopoly on film distribution, some non-commercial productions have reached wide audiences, using alternative distribution avenues such as film clubs, festivals, microcinema, and so on, and sometimes leading to direct incorporation into mainstream commercial TV channels or cinema (Fox, 2004; Conway, 2004). Fox (2004) discusses the success of amateur documentaries on alternative topics such as feminism and sexuality in the 1990s. Other amateur productions have been targeted by mainstream TV programmes (see Shand, 2008) or to support self-representation, participation and media democracy such as the BBC programme *Video Nation* (Carpentier, 2003) and its Digital Storytelling venture *Capture Wales* (Meadows and Kidd, 2009), or as a mode of entertainment from 'home movies' (for example, *You've Been Framed*) all the way to *GoPro Adventures* (GoPro's YouTube channel has over 2.6 million subscribers).[5]

Similar interlinkages can be documented between everyday amateur blogging and the mainstream publishing industry with content produced by amateurs and independent writers being reused by professional media or integrated into professional blogs – amateurs and professionals reusing each other's contents in interactive ways – leading to a much more complex production and distribution of news over the internet (Chamberlain, 2004). Bruns (2008) terms these co-production processes *produsage*. These examples show a clear link between amateur and professional production either through direct distribution or hybrid production. The latter demonstrates more subtle dynamics between them, often overlooked or simplified by a strictly commercial approach to creative production. Exploring various spaces of vernacular or 'non-commodifiable' creativity, Edensor et al (2010: 11) point towards the 'blurring between spheres, where, for example, the non-economic can produce an economic resource.'

The development of skills in cultural consumption, such as building an audience, may further blur the amateur/professional distinction. Researchers claim that 'appreciation of the more complex arts requires investment in "consumption skills", learning to understand, say, opera' (Gray, 2003: 359). Indeed, amateurs tend to be significant consumers of professional cultural and creative products (Stebbins, 1992; Taylor, 2006). A survey on the use of free time by the UK adult population in 2011/12 showed that a great majority of adults engaged in cultural activities such as watching TV, reading or listening to music. Between a third and a half of them also visited art galleries and museums, historic sites, attended theatres or music concerts or went to the cinema. A further fifth actively participated in arts and craft activities and a tenth played a musical instrument (see Figure 3.2). In addition, around 78% of the UK adult population had engaged at least once in the arts in the previous year, with 69% attending at least one event and 48.1% actively participating in at least one art activity (DCMS, 2012). Figure 3.3 demonstrates the strong overlap between 'active' and 'passive' cultural participation, with 39% of the UK adult population (or half of those who engage in the arts) both consuming commercial arts 'passively' as an audience as well as actively participating in amateur

Figure 3.2: Proportion of adult population spending free time on cultural and creative activities in the UK, 2011/12

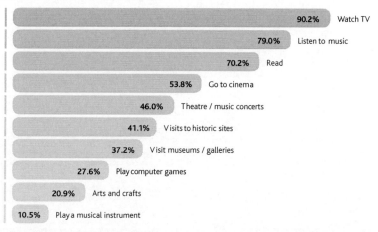

Source: Compiled with data from DCMS,2012) available at http://www.gov.uk/government/statistics/taking-part-the-national-survey-of-culture-leisure-and-sportadult-and-child-report-2011-12 [Accessed 17 October 2014]

Figure 3.3: Arts by attendance and participation in the UK, 2011/12

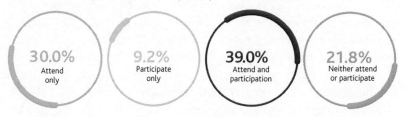

Source: Compiled with data from DCMS,2012) available at http://www.gov.uk/government/statistics/taking-part-the-national-survey-of-culture-leisure-and-sportadult-and-child-report-2011-12 [Accessed 17 October 2014]

arts. Most strikingly, 81% of people who participate in amateur arts are also consumers of mainstream cultural products.

Recent data on digital participation in arts and culture in England also illustrate how creative interests inform people's activities online (MTM, 2010). Around half (53%) of the online population had used the internet to engage with arts and culture in England in the previous 12 months in 2010. While many of these online activities related to finding information about artists or events (33%), about training (13%), on ways to engage (15%) or to purchase tickets (20%), some consisted in consuming formal creative production online such as viewing/listening to a clip (16%) or the full recording (8%) of an arts performance/exhibition (see Figure 3.4).

Figure 3.4: Online engagement with arts and culture in past 12 months in England, 2010

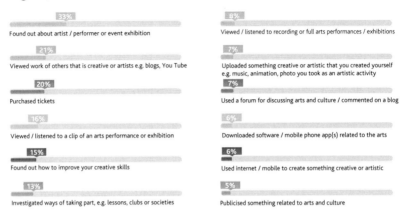

33% Found out about artist / performer or event exhibition	8% Viewed / listened to recording or full arts performances / exhibitions
21% Viewed work of others that is creative or artists e.g. blogs, You Tube	7% Uploaded something creative or artistic that you created yourself e.g. music, animation, photo you took as an artistic activity
20% Purchased tickets	7% Used a forum for discussing arts and culture / commented on a blog
16% Viewed / listened to a clip of an arts performance or exhibition	6% Downloaded software / mobile phone app(s) related to the arts
15% Found out how to improve your creative skills	6% Used internet / mobile to create something creative or artistic
13% Investigated ways of taking part, e.g. lessons, clubs or societies	5% Publicised something related to arts and culture

Source: MTM London (2010)

Interestingly, some of these activities also consist in viewing the artistic or creative work of others, for example, blogs or YouTube (21%), which may include less formal creative production. In addition, some online participation relates to being creatively active online (6%), to engaging in discussion on arts and culture (7%), or disseminating amateur creative production such as music, animation or artistic photos (7%). While the latter figures are still low in comparison to the overall figure on active participation, they evidence the new affordance offered by online technologies in terms of informal creative production, distribution and consumption. They may nevertheless overlook some online practices that people may not regard as formally 'creative' or 'artistic' and which belong to the domain of the everyday, for example in photography. Ramsden (2013) notes, for example, that 70% of the Belgian population practise photography and various researchers have demonstrated the emergence of online communities around these practices through sites such as Flickr (Burgess et al, 2006; Burgess, 2010) or other informal online and mobile platforms (Cooley, 2004), such as DeviantArt. These sharing platforms may support processes of play, reminiscence, community building or identity with place as well as direct artistic or creative endeavours.

For some, amateur practice can be a pathway to professionalism (Stebbins 1992), but a survey commissioned by the DCMS (2008) suggested that professional progression was not a strong motivation for participating in amateur groups. Nevertheless, in 2006, 34% of the amateur groups surveyed reported having seen members of their groups progress to become professionals in the previous five years – this proportion was particularly important for theatre groups (52%). However, these proportions are much lower if applied to members of these groups: only 4% of amateurs made this progression, ranging from 9% in dance to 3% in theatre. Reality TV shows such as *The X-Factor* and *Britain's Got Talent* have reinforced and popularised this phenomenon (Ramsden et al, 2011). It can be argued that participation in amateur creative practices supports the development of creative as well as other economically and socially valuable cognitive and transferable skills (Matarosso, 1997; Frey, 2003; Ramsden et al, 2011; Cebr, 2013).

Some linkages between amateur arts and professionals may generate direct economic benefits for both, as when amateur groups hire professionals for parts of their activities (for example, a professional soloist sings with an amateur choir). In 2006/07, amateur and voluntary arts groups generated income of £543,000 a year in the UK and 31% of their expenditures were spent on employing professionals (DCMS, 2008). Alternatively, creative professionals can participate in publicly funded programmes promoting amateur practices for community development (Matarosso, 1997; Markusen, 2010a). The work of choral *animateur* Gareth Malone, in promoting community development through choirs, has achieved international prominence following several successful documentary series about choirs in schools, unpromising districts or among unlikely groups, such as 'military wives' (Hogan and Warren, 2013: 3–5). Operating in the space between professional animateurism and popular TV documentary, one of his amateur choirs achieved the coveted number one slot on the UK Christmas pop music chart, generating half a million pounds for military charities.[6]

Cultural active participatory practices and amateur arts can also contribute to the economy through the outputs made by unpaid labour of participants, interns and volunteers (Matarosso, 1997; Ramsden et al, 2011).

A fuller understanding of informal arts practices and their linkages with formal creative production of a kind usable by policy makers may require examination not only of these practices in themselves but also measurement of opportunities for creative participation, the impacts of such participation and the relevance of infrastructure to support participation in various communities and places (Jackson and Herranz, 2003; Jackson et al, 2006). This approach recognises that creative participation tends to occur locally, not necessarily for economic reasons, and is embedded in local creative ecosystems, which influence participation. As a consequence:

> The boundaries between amateurs and professionals are not only negotiated in discourse. They are also revealed through temporal, spatial and material processes. There are, in fact, many places where boundary-work takes place; boundary-work is interconnected with objects, tools, bodies, and specific spaces and places. (Meyer, 2008: 48).

Participation and the creative ecosystem

There is widespread agreement among researchers that we need a more rounded understanding of the creative ecosystem (Evans, 2001; Hall, 2004; Taylor, 2006; 2008; Nowak, 2007; Cherbo et al, 2008; Chapain and Comunian, 2009; Chapple and Jackson, 2010; Stern and Seifert, 2007; 2010). Some authors show how cultural and creative participation can generate positive social and economic impacts on people and community development, potentially leading to regeneration. These might result from enhanced amenities (theatres, cinema, music shows …) and by improving the quality of the built environment.

Non-economic impacts of creative participation

Artistic creativity 'involves imagination and a capacity to generate original ideas and novel ways of interpreting the world, expressed in text, sound and image'. (UNCTAD, 2010: 9). This creativity generates cultural value or capital (Throsby, 2003) in the form of creative goods such as books, drawings, songs, heritage buildings … but also in the form of beliefs, values, attitudes, customs and practices which are associated with the production, use and interpretation of these goods either formally or informally. In addition to the cultural and associated economic values that the production and consumption of creative goods engender, it has been argued that participating in creative activities has inherently wider positive personal and social impacts. This is consistent with a view of culture as encompassing social relationships, meaningfulness and identities (Hartley et al, 2013). As a result, by participating in creative activities, people's cultural capital can be improved by purposeful intervention. (Throsby, 2003: 169).

The fact that creative participation can induce positive personal and social impacts has been widely acknowledged in the literature

(Matarosso, 1997; Lowe, 2000; Reeves, 2002; Wali et al, 2002; Evans and Shaw, 2004; Taylor, 2006; 2008; Arts Council, 2008; Dissanayake, 2008; Devlin, 2009; Chapple and Jackson, 2010; Stern and Seifert, 2010; Cebr, 2013). It follows that the arts can be used to support personal development, learning and skills as well as fostering social cohesion, pride and a sense of identity within communities. Matarosso (1997) identified 50 social impacts of the arts, grouped into six categories:

• personal development
• social cohesion
• community empowerment and self-determination
• local image and identity
• imagination and vision
• health and wellbeing.

This layering of beneficial impacts begins with the ways in which participation in the arts is shown to fulfil human needs with regards to exploiting cognitive and physical abilities, generating feelings of transcendence, providing playful experiences and entertainment, developing cultural and personal meanings, supporting a sense of belonging and identity through shared cultural experiences and leading to the adoption of particular cultural practices which help people cope in adverse circumstances (Dissanayake, 2008). Looking at adult active participation in the arts across various UK projects, Matorosso (1997) found that more than 80% of participants felt more confident, had tried things they had not done before and learnt new skills. Related to this, long-term engagement in arts and cultural participation can improve children's school performance (Cebr, 2013) as cultural participation also supports the development of critical thinking and the use of creativity to solve problems (Wali et al, 2002). Sheer enjoyment is also an important personal motivation to participate in the arts (DCMS, 2008) leading to a sense of fulfilment and helping people to keep in good health (Devlin, 2009). Matarosso (1997) found that 73% of those studied felt happier following their participation. Arts and cultural participation can help break social barriers in terms of gender, generation, authority and ethnicity, fostering acceptance of difference. Matarosso's UK survey (1997) showed that 49% of participants thought that taking part in the arts had changed their ideas, 54% had learnt about other people's culture, 84% had become interested in something new and 91% had made new friends.

Linked to this growth in 'social capital',[7] it has been demonstrated that arts and cultural participation can support a greater sense of community spirit and so enhance citizenship (Matarosso, 1997; Wali et al, 2002; Stern and Seifert, 2007; 2010). In their in-depth ethnographic study of informal arts participation across communities in Chicago, Wali et al (2002: xix) noted:

> Informal arts practice provides important sites for adult personal expression and creativity. In the process, it helps to build individual and community assets, by fostering social inclinations and skills critical to civic renewal. These include greater tolerance of difference, trust and consensus building, collaborative work habits, use of innovation and creativity to solve problems, the capacity to imagine change and the willingness to work for it.

This was confirmed by the Matarosso study (1997), which indicated that, among UK adults having participated in the arts and culture, 86% wanted to be involved in further projects. 63% were keen to help in local projects, 21% had a new sense of their rights and 40% felt more positive about where they live. The latter finding is reinforced by the positive impacts that some arts and cultural production can have in improving the quality of life by providing amenities and in the built environment (Reeves, 2002). Related to this, quantitative analyses have demonstrated positive correlations between participation in informal arts and improvement in social indicators such as levels of crime and poverty, along with increases in educational achievements (Taylor, 2006; Stern and Seifert, 2010).

In addition to the social impacts discussed above, the arts and creative activities can generate positive economic and environmental outcomes. Festivals, museums and strong performing arts contribute to tourism and frequently play a part in regenerating derelict buildings, leading to enhanced property values and intensified economic activity in creative quarters and clusters (Bianchini and Parkinson, 1993; Reeves, 2002; Florida, 2002; Evans and Shaw, 2004; Vickery, 2007; Galligan, 2008; Stewart, 2008; Legnér and Ponzini, 2009; Tallon, 2010, Cebr, 2013). Figure 3.5 from Cebr (2013) summarises the economic, social and environmental outcomes, which can be derived from investing in arts and culture. Increased recognition of these outcomes have led policy makers all over the world to invest in the creative economy in the past 30 years (Smith and Warfield, 2008; Chapain and Lee, 2009; Evans, 2009; Chapple and Jackson, 2010; Musterd and Murie, 2010).

Figure 3.5: Economic, social and environmental outcomes of investment in arts and culture

Economic Outcomes	Social Outcomes	Environmental Outcomes
Employment	Increased social capital	Re-use of redundant buildings
Inward investment	Change in perception of area	Increased sense of public safety
Attracting a skilled workforce	Volunteering	Reduced vandalism
Property values	Residents' confidence	Pride in place
Visitor and resident spending	Community cohesion	
	Educational achievement	
	Improved health and wellbeing	
	Crime reduction	

Source: Cebr (2013: 8).

Landry's book *The Creative City: A Toolkit for Urban Innovators* (2000) proposed a renewed approach to the development of cities by rendering the planning process itself more flexible, innovative, participative, collaborative and so creative. Activities like design and IT, software and information services have also played an increasing part in better engaging citizens in planning and developing cities in recent years (Foth et al, 2011; www.urbaninformatics.net).

It is important to note that investing in creative activities to foster non-economic outcomes is not without pitfalls (Chapple and Jackson, 2010). Some neighbourhood regeneration processes can lead to gentrification and displacement of communities. The instrumentalisation of creative activities for non-cultural goals can also counteract their creative power by undermining authenticity.

Creative places

Whereas consumption of both formal and informal creative activities can lead to positive impacts for communities, places are also crucial in supporting creative economy production processes. Research on the location of the creative industries in economic geography has shown that they tend to cluster in cities (Chapain et al, 2010; Power, 2011; Boix et al, 2014) to benefit from both economies of scale and agglomeration, that is, the various actors present at the different stages of the creative value chain from university graduates to creative workers, brokers, public institutions, arts galleries, theatres and creative associations.

Examples include the film cluster in Hollywood/Los Angeles (Scott, 2005), the new media cluster in San Francisco (Pratt, 2002), the jewellery quarter in Birmingham (Pollard, 2004) and the artistic district in Soho in New York City (Galligan, 2008). These clusters are characterised by particular creative milieux, that is, 'a shared space and tradition in which people can learn, compare, compete and collaborate and through which ideas can be proposed, developed, disseminated and rejected' (Leadbeater and Oakley, 1999: 31). These milieux or scenes offer a high level of interactions and information exchange among interdependent networks of producers with complementary skills and expertise (Scott, 1999; Hall, 2004). They may draw heavily on local cultural assets such as natural landscapes, way of life, street scenes and heritage as visual raw material and stimuli for creative inspiration (Scott, 1999; Drake, 2003). Such places experience perpetual movement of cultural influences between local producers and consumers – inducing a locally attractive 'buzz' and positive environment for creative producers both in their roles as workers and residents, leading to some overlaps between formal and informal creative acts (Lloyds, 2002; Chapain and Comunian, 2010). It is important to note that creative clusters have been shown to rely both on local buzz and global pipelines (transnational networks) (Bathelt et al, 2004). In addition, networks connecting producers and consumers have in the last quarter century been continuously reshaped by the spread of online technologies leading to more widely distributed consumption and collaboration patterns (Craig, 2013). Empirical research tends to demonstrate the importance of both place and local and international networks for successful creative clusters (see Chapain and Comunian, 2010 for a review)

In addition to being important sites of creative production and consumption, cities are also important meeting points for mainstream and amateur creative activities. This is illustrated by Cohendet et al, (2010: 95–7), who propose a model of the creative city constituted of three layers:

- the underground (the level of individuals)
- the upper ground (firms and institutions)
- the middle ground (the level of communities).

The upper ground firms and institutions have the financial capacity to test and launch new creative products by bringing together ideas and knowledge from various actors. The underground is inhabited by the 'creative, artistic and cultural activities taking place outside any formal organization or institution' such as graffiti artists. The middle ground then consists of informal groups and communities linking the upper ground with the underground by organising and codifying its content and favouring its transfer to the commercial sector.

Recognising these complex dynamics, Nowak (2007) suggests that the creative sector ecology in various communities includes a continuum of actors and places from media, arts and marketing departments of large corporations to small businesses, professional services companies, individual entrepreneurs and artists, non-profit corporations, schools, community centres and art studios.

Creative citizenship, creative economy and the creative ecosystem

According to theories of the creative economy, artistic creativity and its formal manifestations (that is, creative industries and occupations) play a transformative role in the entire economy (Potts and Cunningham, 2008; Potts, 2009) and so, by extension, in the whole of society. In recent years, complexity systems science has been used to develop a new analytical framework to explain the creative industries' dynamics (Comunian et al, 2012; Hartley et al, 2013; Hartley et al, 2015). This follows a trend to use complexity science to explain patterns of mutual adaptation and interaction within social, political and economic systems:

> What defines a complex system is distributed feedback and emergence. A complex system is composed of a set of elements and a set of connections, where connections carry information and feedback. Complex systems tend to form spontaneously, or to self-organise. Complex systems are usually the product of evolutionary process. (Hartley et al, 2013: 30)

Complex systems are sensitive to initial conditions and novel patterns can emerge which are not predictable (OECD, 2009). Relationships between constituent parts are thus non-linear.

Two tools from complexity science have been particularly useful to shed new light on social science processes: agent-based modelling and network analysis (OECD, 2009). Complexity economics relies on the assumption that the economy, as an open and non-linear system, is structured around a set of *adaptive agents* which interact within various networks (Beinhocker, 2006). In this vein, Potts et al (2008: 176) offer to redefine the creative industries as a 'set of economic activities that involve the creation and maintenance of social networks and the generation of value through production and consumption of network-valorised choices', building on the fact that many demand and supply dynamics operate within networks. Complex economic geographic models can help here as economic geographic systems are seen as 'interacting subsystems and hierarchical levels' (for example, Martin and Sunley, 2007). Building on this notion of multiscalar levels (Dopfer et al, 2004), Comunian et al (2012: 4) propose a representation of the creative economy based on three levels of analysis:

- micro-level i.e. idea generation, the role of individual creativity and the structures and processes that facilitate ideas flows and connections;
- meso-level i.e. the working of knowledge networks and communities and the location where these processes take place (e.g. creative clusters)
- macro level i.e. the creative economy, manifested in terms of geographical factors; the interaction between creative production and consumption and the role of policy.

Understanding and linking these levels of analysis requires a multidisciplinary approach. For example, Andres and Chapain (2015) combine cultural, economic and urban planning perspectives to examine the long-term development of the creative economy in different cities across the world. Their analysis demonstrates intricate overlaps between cultural, economic and planning dynamics.

A similar complexity -based approach can be used to illustrate how creative citizenship sits within a wider understanding of the creative economy. The notion of creative citizenship deployed in this book encompasses acts of creativity at the frontier between the public and private spheres. These are enacted in various every day, amateur and/or professional acts of creativity by individuals, groups and communities with a mix of cultural, civic, social, economic and environmental objectives. This overlap of objectives and mix of practices is inherent to the transformative role of artistic creativity, and the notion of creative citizenship helps to bridge that continuum. Thus, acts of creative citizenship can result in direct or indirect economic contributions but may or may not have economic objectives among their motivations. Building on models of the creative sector including informal acts of creative participation and adopting a complexity perspective, Figure 3.6

situates creative citizenship within four axes characterising the role and dynamic of the creative economy.

In Figure 3.6, different dimensions characterise the linkages between creative citizenship and the creative economy:

- acts of creativity: including everyday, amateur arts and formal production;
- actors and scales: individuals, groups, community, creative milieux and cities;
- places: home to cultural and community venues and professional spaces;
- objectives: personal expression and development; cultural, social, political, environmental and economic goals.

Figure 3.6: Creative citizenship and the creative economy

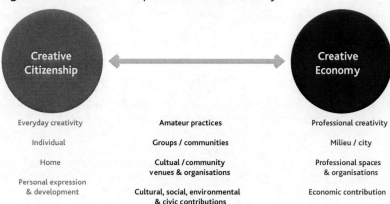

Everyday creativity	Amateur practices	Professional creativity
Individual	Groups / communities	Milieu / city
Home	Cultal / community venues & organisations	Professional spaces & organisations
Personal expression & development	Cultural, social, environmental & civic contributions	Economic contribution

Acts of creative citizenship can be situated at any point among these four dimensions. Over time, some practices will be reinforced, some will diminish, and others will emerge. Some practices will involve online media.

More research is necessary to develop empirical evidence capturing this more holistic understanding of the creative economy and its relationship with creative citizenship. Examples discussed elsewhere in this book stem from a range of disciplinary perspectives, which are by no means exhaustive. In dealing with a variety of case studies, we illustrate and to some extent test the confluence of dimensions presented in this model. This has been made possible by the multidisciplinary perspective adopted throughout our research. The focus of further research might usefully document the linkages between informal and formal creative production. Beyond individual research projects, this requires a systematic collection of data on everyday and amateur creative production across, as well as their points of encounter with formal production. Such an approach can challenge sectoral boundaries of existing policies and most statistical exercises. Without this knowledge it is difficult to see how either the creative economy or creative citizenship can fully achieve their potential.

Notes

[1] The knowledge economy is defined as 'directly based on the production, distribution and use of knowledge and information' (OECD, 1996: 7) and includes activities such as pharmaceutical, aerospace, computers, office machinery, electronic communications, scientific instruments, chemicals, non-electrical machinery, motors, other transport equipment, post and telecommunications, business services, finance and insurance, education and health (OECD, 2005).

[2] Even though some industrial classifications also include sectors such as heritage, tourism, sport and toys – see UNESCO (2013: 22–5).

[3] Defined as 'A role within the creative process that brings cognitive skills to bear to bring about differentiation to yield either novel, or significantly enhanced products whose final form is not fully specified in advance' and operationalised through five criteria (Bakhshi et al, 2013: 24).

[4] Voluntary and amateur groups that are governed or organised by those also participating in the activities, which members attend for reasons such as self-improvement, social networking or leisure, but primarily not for payment in craft, dance, festivals, literature, media, music, theatre and visual arts (DCMS, 2008: 12).

[5] See: www.youtube.com/user/GoProCamera/videos

[6] See: www.garethmalone.com/programmes/military-wives

[7] That is, 'the patterns and intensity of networks between people and their shared values'. See www.ons.gov.uk/ons/guide-method/user-guidance/social-capital-guide/the-social-capital-project/guide-to-social-capital.html

FOUR

Citizenship, value and digital culture

Jon Dovey, Giota Alevizou and Andy Williams

Introduction

This chapter sets out to illustrate how the many different notions of creative value among our research partners play out at the level of community practice. We work through a range of digitally enabled but locally determined amateur, semi-professional, informal and activist creative processes and attempt to articulate the nature and quality of the impact they create. It argues for the significance of these impacts on some of the infrastructures of citizenship: education, representation, communication, training, employment and environment, and thus supports the development of a new dimension to the concept of cultural value – one based on 'impact' rather than 'intrinsic merit'.

We begin with a brief overview of the analytical frameworks that have helped us position our evidence, namely digital gift economies, local public spheres and participatory cultures. We then move on to classifying the evidence. Our method here has been to examine the research evidence for value-making statements. These may be statements where value is understood from context as intrinsic (such as trust or confidence), or they may be more judgmental, where the statement clearly makes a positive or negative assessment of process or experience. The evidence has been drawn from interviews, focus groups and asset mapping workshops, conducted across all strands of the research project. The interviews have been coded and compared across the different sites of investigation in order to support this qualitative analysis with quantitative data. The evidence is supplemented by observation, participation in co-production and textual analysis of content produced by our project partners. All of our evidence is the outcome of co-creative processes: our time, expertise and resources have been invested in our community partners in order to strengthen their organisations and networks. We have worked with them to produce, for instance, hyperlocal newspapers, digital stories, a virtual environment for planning and a graphic novel. Our understanding of value in these processes is therefore profoundly inflected by the nature of the co-creative relationships we have enjoyed with partners whose voices we hope to represent fairly in what follows.

Framing value

The idea of value is in crisis. The 2008 banking crash re-exposed the boom and bust cycle of financial markets as a dangerous and expensive game played with imperfectly understood and poorly regulated algorithms. It provoked *Los Indignados* and the Occupy movements, among other international attempts to articulate new critical value systems. At the same time the 'web native' generation, coming to maturity during this 'age of austerity', has a historically unique experience of practices of co-creation and shared forms of socially mediated production. These events remind us that value is never stable; it forms on a permanently contested terrain.

Values and plural belief systems condense as commensurable value through complex discursive, cultural and political processes. We can, for instance, see motivation, beliefs, and attitude become value in the form of brands, where they produce private corporate wealth (Arviddson and Pietersen, 2013: 44), or in the form of politics where they drive the rise and fall of political parties. Values also play a key role in our sense of belonging, to the people, tribes, families, fandoms, geographical and mediated communities with whom we affiliate (Ostrom, 1990).

Our own approach to value in this chapter is that it is an enacted property of interactions between people in different domains. Value is relational, never absolute; it is created between agents in a network as they negotiate their different value systems, beliefs, motivations, rewards and behaviours (Sayer, 2003). Importantly, this approach recognises that different kinds of value can circulate within all kinds of living systems, and they can all play a part in maintaining the health and strength of the system itself (Bachman et al, 2012). More immediately, construing value as an enacted property in a pattern of relationships allows us to understand that the social value produced by creative citizens circulates as part of a 'value constellation' (Norman and Ramirez, 1993). The term 'value constellation' designates value as a co-production of many agents in a network, rather than being created (or consumed) in a linear value chain by individuals. Ramirez (1999) shows how the distinction between value 'chain' and value 'constellation' is appropriate to the logics of co-production, and through the collaborative mechanics of social media.

Importantly for our method, moreover, Ramirez's approach stresses the importance of the coordinating agent for any value constellation; these systems do not just evolve, they invite design and curation. We argue that they rely upon a particular kind of agency at their heart, where networked value creation is supported and directed by individuals, groups or organisations that mobilise creative citizens. This understanding allows the coordinator, the hyperlocal news producer, the community planning campaign, the informal creative network 'brand', the provider of the shared working environment, to articulate, to manage and maximise value creation.

The idea of value in relation to creativity has been the subject of intense scrutiny produced by the elevation of the cultural or creative industries from a domain of elites and 'bread and circuses' for the masses to a powerhouse of the UK economy. This decisive move characterised the cultural policy of New Labour governments 1997–2010 (tracked in greater detail in Chapter 3). Although some accounts record this as indicative of a point of decline, tracking 'the rise and fall of Creative Britain' (Hewison, 2014; see also Chapter 2 above), Government publications trumpeted the importance of the creative industries to the UK's global competitiveness, exemplified by Prime Minister Gordon Brown in 2008, looking forward to:

> ...a Britain in ten years' time where the local economies in our biggest cities are driven by creativity, where there is a much expanded range of creative job opportunities in every region with clear routes into creative careers from local schools and colleges, and where every young person believes they have a real choice to use their talents in a creative capacity. It is a vision of creativity as the engine of economic growth for towns, cities and regions. It's also a vision of dynamic, innovative, successful creative businesses providing prosperity and fulfilling job opportunities right across the country. (DCMS, 2008b: 1)

This identification of creativity at the level of school, college and career advice, as active regenerator of post-industrial cities, might be understood as one of the points of origin for the idea of creative citizenship. But whereas Brown's rallying cry points towards jobs and economic growth, our research seeks to articulate the impacts of digital creativity on communities across a broader evaluative framework. This approach aligns itself more closely with the UNESCO (2013) *Creative Economy Report: Widening Local Development Pathways*. Here creative economy is construed as a key sector for sustainable development:

> Unlocking the potential of the creative economy therefore involves promoting the overall creativity of societies, affirming the distinctive identity of the places where it flourishes and clusters, improving the quality of life where it exists, enhancing local image and prestige and strengthening the resources for imagining diverse new futures. In other words, the creative economy is the fount, metaphorically speaking, of a new 'economy of creativity', whose benefits go far beyond the economic realm alone. (UNESCO, 2013: 15)

Investigations of cultural value have continued in the UK throughout the period of our research. The Arts and Humanities Research Council (AHRC) simultaneously ran its Cultural Value Project, an ambitious attempt to produce a framework that would bring ways of articulating cultural value into a relational pattern across the very different processes through which culture is produced and consumed. This project sponsored a range of specific projects looking at different forms of value (Crossick and Kaszysnka, 2015). At the same time Warwick University Business School ran a commission on 'The Future of Cultural Value' (Warwick Commission, 2015). This report makes a broad-based argument for the continued investment of public money in the arts, on the basis of cross-fertilisation between cultural and economic outcomes. It also takes a strong position on inclusion and diversity: 'There are barriers and inequalities in Britain today that prevent this from being a universal human right. This is bad for business and bad for society' (Warwick Commission, 2015: 8). It recognises that creative work has a role to play in community development, urging cultural organisations to 'invest time, effort and self-criticism in a deeper understanding of the economic, social and environmental challenges facing their local communities so they are able to make an intelligent and realistic arts-based contribution to solving those problems' (Warwick Commission, 2015: 16).

Commons assets

The production of 'commons assets' through newly emergent modes of social production is a key feature of digital culture. Historically, practices of gifting and sharing were a fundamental process for open source computer software development; debugging a million lines of code is best managed by offering free beta software to 200 testers. Peer to peer, shareware and distributed learning structures are potentially more innovative and more efficient than hard-walled corporate IT and IP structures. The biggest cultural volunteering and sharing process in the history of humanity has substantially built the content and structure of the World Wide Web. Through the actions of those cybercitizens, we learnt that a new kind of digitally constituted 'collective intelligence' (Levy, 1997) could achieve new formations of knowledge, new co-created models of culture and new kinds of polity dominated by various constructions of the idea of *the commons* (Benkler, 2006; Lessig, 2001).

More recently social media have been part of a shift in the sites of productivity. Value is no longer produced solely in the workplace but also through life processes that we undertake, mostly without wage or salary. Our creative consumption, viewing, making, uploading, commenting, liking, tweeting, posting, and sharing all contribute to the creation of value (Arviddson and Colleoni, 2012) as well as to the emergence of new forms of citizenship (Hartley, 2010). Social media afford new ways of capitalising on the power of the collective. They increase the potential productivity and value generated by producers for networked user(s). This 'collective intelligence' is produced across both proprietary and non-proprietary spaces (Van Dijck, 2013), allowing critical and creative skills to develop.

These histories and practices have been mostly understood with reference to the operation of gift economies in digital cultures. This kind of argument can be found in numerous sites and traditions frequently derived from the work of Marcel Mauss (1925) (for example, Barbrook 1999; Hyde, 2007; Bruns, 2008; Henaff 2014: 36–40). This tradition argues for the importance of the exchange of symbolic goods and services as a way of enacting affiliation and obligation in producing communities. Symbolic goods, or creative products, become a *lingua franca* of everyday life, a vernacular that produces and shapes communities that can support or exclude civic essentials such as care, education, enterprise and empowerment.

However, the analysis of digital free labour has also emerged as an important critique of the commons position (Terranova, (2003). This account of participatory culture understands everyday creative work as a form of exploitation that creates value expropriated by brands typically associated with corporate enterprise (Andrejevic, 2008; 2009; Hesmondhalgh, 2010; Fuchs 2010). The value of this approach for us is to stress the actions of creative citizenship as a form of work. Building communities and networks is labour intensive, whether voluntary or paid. However, as we shall see, the evidence suggests that actions producing value for corporate interests (for example, Facebook or Wordpress) can at the same time generate assets available on a commons basis to communities of interest and of place. Just as self-interest and citizenship are often interwoven, so too are the actions of profit-seekers and non-profit-seekers.

Digital local

Our second approach draws on traditions of debate around the digital public sphere and applies them to place defined local communities. Whilst there is a well established research tradition looking at the web as a public sphere at national and global scales (for example, Poster, 1997; Kellner, 2001; Castells, 2012; Dahlgren, 2013) research at the local level is less developed. Previous research in the Connected Communities programme (Dovey et al, 2011) surveyed the aims of 100 community-based websites in the UK and categorised them as:

- promoting access and engagement with a specific sector or service, for example, health, education or social services;building people's digital skills through formal and informal training programmes;
- creating shared digital spaces for users to publish community information on the hyperlocal model;
- developing bespoke technologies to meet specific needs, where originality and innovation create new applications for specific community needs, for example, Homeless SMS in London, offering a text message service for finding hostel beds, food and healthcare at short notice.

We might understand these initiatives as being an extension of the local state or civic entity through new ways of linking services with new forms of social capital produced by digital communications platforms, exemplified by the work of hyperlocal activists. This distinction is typical of local digital initiatives as reported by De Cindio and Peraboni (2011) as part of their groundbreaking work in Milan. The Civic Informatics Laboratory at the University of Milan and its Milan Community Network are part of a long tradition of supporting access to a public sphere that is fundamentally focused on the process of deliberative democracy, getting more people involved in local decision-making processes. Its work has included the development of non-anonymous communication protocols and contractual agreements with local authorities to act on decisions made as part of network consultation processes. This emphasis on deliberation, decision making, consultation, access, and training for participation offers a formal approach to digital citizenship, using digital channels to widen participation in the local public sphere.

The domain of the creative citizen is not only defined by the process of deliberative democracy, it is also characterised by the unruly, affective, dynamic and disruptive processes of creativity, as a means of addressing audiences and enacting approaches to build communities, places and networks. Previous attempts to understand the social significance of creativity have focused on the impact of participation in arts processes (Matorosso, 1997) or the role of the amateur in the creative economy (DCMS, 2008). Whilst building on this tradition of research, our framing of creative citizens is explicitly grounded in digital cultural practices, where amateur/professional or creative/non-creative binary distinctions are challenged. Every digitally connected citizen has the potential to be publisher, editor and critic in any number of cultural fields. We are interested in how these potentials affect local networks. In this sense, Wittel's idea of 'networked sociality' may be of more use than the notion of the deliberative public sphere in understanding creative citizenship:

> Network sociality consists of fleeting and transient, yet iterative social relations; of ephemeral but intense encounters. Narrative sociality often takes place in bureaucratic organisations. In network sociality the social bond at work is not bureaucratic but informational; it is created on a project by project basis, by the movement of ideas, the establishment of solely temporary standards and protocols... *Network sociality is not characterised by a separation but by a combination of both work and play.* (Wittel, 2001, our emphasis)

Digital creativity and self-realisation

The third approach underpinning our evaluative framework derives from research into participatory culture (for example, Jenkins, 2006). It stresses the individual motivations and drives of the kinds of people involved in what we call creative citizenship. This echoes the approach underpinning the Nesta *Manifesto for the Creative Economy* (Bakhshi et al, 2013), arguing that the creative economy is best defined by the work of 'creative people' rather than the worth of creative 'sectors.' In that spirit, we have been attentive to the personal values of the people in the networks we have investigated and which drive and multiply involvement in creative citizenship. Whilst many of these values are familiar, even ancient, the context of digital culture offers a new inflection. Arviddson and Tjader (2009), for instance, in their research into what they called the 'underground' cultural scene in Copenhagen, argue that 'there is a direct relation between the reputation that a person has been able to accumulate and his (*sic*) ability to live off his activities. A lot of participants in free and open software publics build their reputation in those publics to find jobs and advance their corporate careers' (Arvidsson and Pietersen, 2013: 93).

Arviddson and Pieterson (2013: 105) draw on management studies literature into the performance of knowledge workers to argue that 'beyond a certain point values and an environment that encourages self-realisation count much more than money as a motivational force for many knowledge workers'. They argue that social production is frequently not motivated by money but has:

> A coherent logic that is visible in a multitude of manifestations of social production: from knowledge work, via peer production to the dynamics of brand communities and urban creative scenes. It is not a monetary logic, but what we call a logic of direct, unmediated social impact … what determines the value of a product, person or organization, is its ability to connect and organize social processes in productive ways. (Arviddson and Pieterson 2013: 13–14)

Creative activist or citizenship practices, supported through social media, offered our partners self-expression, self-improvement, reinvention, socialisation and the chance to make a different or a larger contribution; in short, the opportunity to feel like a valued and worthwhile member of a meaningful group.

Citizenship benefit

Following this framework we set out to investigate the values that are being enacted by the people we have been working with. The results of this investigation are then aggregated to offer a picture of the kinds of value that accrue from the acts of creative citizenship we have been considering. The evidence demonstrates that the values enacted through the creative engagements we examined can be understood as aggregated *citizen benefits*. That is to say, private and public motivations overlap and intertwine, at both individual and organisational levels. These public and private motivations produce benefits for individuals (for example, training, employment, personal development and wellbeing) as well as positive social impacts (for example, community cohesion, wealth creation, social mobility, safety and property regeneration). Understanding the way that these benefits are mutually co-constituted is key to understanding the potential in the idea of the creative citizen. In the evidence below we encounter new stories about the ways that social and creative media produce novel forms of social organisation with as yet barely articulated and poorly recognised positive citizenship impact.

Each one teach one – dynamic subjects

We begin with analysis of the personal value systems evidenced in the interview content, as we identify common sets of personal qualities, aspirations and beliefs in our participants. We find, for instance, a strong drive toward self-actualisation. By this we mean the idea that the individual person can define his or her own destiny through engaging with community organisation, creativity and social media. Our interviewees are engaged in acts of creative citizenship because they are motivated by a personal journey and a need for meaningful social engagement (see Greene and Lindsey, 2015).

South Blessed is an informal network of young people in Bristol that at the time of the research was centred on a website with over 1,000 music, comedy and news clips made in the south west of England. We worked with South Blessed to study informal creative economy networks, finding many comments speaking of a desire to take control of one's destiny:

> "So I have come to a point in my life now where I have said, 'I am 27 and I need to do something that I can be remembered for'. Or something that I can look back on and say that is how you actually did it, and things like that."

This motivation is frequently described in a language of self-actualisation and authenticity: "You are trying to tune into something. If you just manifest your radio station, your wavelength, whoever is tuned into that wavelength would naturally hear you." And:

> "People are happy to be themselves. They acknowledge who they are and they just want to manifest themselves. I

think that is what makes South Blessed interesting because you know you are seeing genuine people that are just manifesting themselves, rather than films that some people have probably done against their will … the unique selling point I suppose of South Blessed is the fact that these people are just being themselves, just spraying themselves all over a website."

In a far away cultural domain, the editor of a north east England hyperlocal news site was candid about the part played by her work in her own personal and professional development after a period of unemployment:

"I took to it like a duck to water, partly because I felt that I was making a positive contribution. And when you've been unemployed for a while, all those sorts of issues are really crammed in your head. You feel lost, you don't know who you are. …So when I realised that I could actually get involved and do something that I really felt was making a difference, where I was using my skills and I was learning, that's always important."

The editor of a Scottish environmentally focused hyperlocal news outlet expresses a similar urge towards learning and self-improvement:

"I was also very interested from a personal level from the outset, that I was always very explicit to the other people taking part that one of the reasons for my continued engagement in it was that I wanted to use it to gain extra skills and practical experience in setting up a social enterprise, and playing around with online community engagement tools."

The Wards Corner Community Coalition (WCC) offers different insights. An activist community organisation, formed in 2007, the group campaigned to halt the demolition of a city block which hosts a vibrant Latin American market in the Tottenham district of North London. Through persistent and extensive local consultations, they have produced an alternative planning application for the area. Personal affinity and the commitment to 'representation' and 'solidarity' mobilises the values of a group of people who are mostly both local residents and members of other local and volunteer groups concerned with planning, place making, activism, ecology and welfare. A member in her 50s is a local photographer, described by some as an outspoken vocaliser, a regular contributor to a local community forum and news hub, Haringey Online, and an instigator of local campaigns and petitions. For another three retired members, motivation comes from applying professional expertise (in the civil service, fundraising and social care) along with a continuous commitment to personal and political development.

For others the commitment to 'making a difference' is part of a process of self-actualisation and professional development in creative endeavours. A former member of WCC, whose work includes film and public policy advocacy, noted:

> "I want to make a participatory documentary that puts forward personal stories and reactions in the process of the campaign, with characters and developments, the council as adversary, the public hearings, the consultations; the key is to ensure continuity and communicating what's going on … it's part of a viral campaign."

For others, digital storytelling provides a medium through which community capacity building can be fostered, fusing personal narratives with a vision of the communal good. The observation of a key 'connector' and mobiliser at another research partner, Goldsmiths Community Centre in London, offers this insight into the identity of the creative citizen:

> "I am good at making connections too. I like making connections like a 'dating agency'… if I could find a way of making money out of it I would be a rich woman. I question everything. I never take anything at face value so I will always be asking the awkward questions."

Summing up, the characteristics of our creative citizens include a strong drive toward self-actualisation and self-improvement, being good communicators and 'connectors' and being invested in the values of self-determination within public democratic processes. Motivation and drive is here understood as a quality of both personal and community-level asset development. It comes together as a model of development where individual enterprise and community value overlap in a mutually co-productive manner.

Representation and participation: The Spurtle

Many of our research participants are committed to the value of increasing representation in order to produce more participation for people in the debates that affect the conditions in which they live. At one level this surfaces as a generalised intrinsic value – the more people can participate in local decisions, the better. This investment in the idea of a vibrant, local public sphere in which power is challenged and made accountable is a particularly strong value set among hyperlocal

Figure 4.1: Edinburgh's *Broughton Spurtle*: stirring things up with campaigning local news (broughtonspurtle.org.uk)

publishers. However, even here, it is combined with a commitment to the quieter virtues of civic life: mutual support, care for the vulnerable and conviviality.

Many community journalists talked of being motivated by sharing information about life in their communities, often with the hope that their news services would:

- enable local people to make better informed decisions locally;
- let people know what is going on where they live;
- support or initiate local campaigns;
- hold authorities to account;
- bring people in their communities together;
- represent their community in a positive light.

Some take an actively political and campaigning stance in their online news production, such as the producer of the *Broughton Spurtle* in North Edinburgh, who told us, when talking about the name of his hyperlocal news service:

> "Spurtle is the Scottish word for a wooden instrument which you stir porridge with, and the idea of Spurtle as a publication has always been to stir the neighbourhood up a little bit, to try and get people interested and proactive about issues such as politics, planning and the local environment."

Others do not campaign, but nonetheless take their role as enablers of local political participation very seriously. The editor of a North Wales hyperlocal told us he was motivated to start his site partly because of the potential citizenship benefits in new blogging software.

> "I suppose I could see there were tools out there, like Fix My Street, and I'm really interested in the idea of a democratic deficit, and accountability, and the citizens having a say in their local ... in how nice their local area is. So when I saw that there were these little tools ... and I was able to embed what my local MP or AM was saying as well, it was a case of trying to mix in the stuff that isn't often tackled in the media ... by putting a local context around it, suddenly you could present [this kind of political accountability information] alongside stories about potholes."

These sites then, as well as giving people information that could help them navigate local life, also often provide readers with tools that facilitate communication between citizens and local government.

Hyperlocal journalists in Wolverhampton have also covered and initiated their own campaigns on civic issues such as school closures and planning debates. They specialise in initiating appeals for local community solidarity with those in need, something they estimate they do at least once a month. Examples include setting up a school uniform exchange to help parents save money by recycling clothes and providing a focal point for neighbours who wanted to support a local family whose house had burned down while they were on holiday. They initially covered the latter story as breaking news, until the mother of the family got in touch to confirm the details of what had happened. After this they published an appeal to the community on the website and across their widely followed social media presence.

> "We were inundated with responses with people offering things. We were able to set up a drop off point at the local church where people dropped donations off and within 24 hours, we had over a dozen bags full of clothes, shoes, toys for the kids, even things like bedding. We had an offer from a local estate agent to try and help house them temporarily, deposit free, and we also had an offer from a couple of local businesses with offerings of furniture and stuff for when they got sorted. So it was a real example of how the online side of things, the website, can kind of galvanise people into acting offline."

Some interviewees talked about this motivation in terms of filling a gap in the local community. The founders of the hyperlocal news site, Kirkbymoorside.info, in Yorkshire told us that on moving to a new place:

> "We just found the town to be full of things happening, it's a very buzzy little town. It's an ordinary market town but we just found it great in terms of all the things that were going on that we could get involved in, that our children could get involved in, and so I didn't feel that there was kind of one place where all this information was kind of collated and people could find out about it."

This attention to defects in local information ecosystems was very common in our interviews with citizen journalists. However, it found expression most often in references to perceived problems with existing local newspaper publishers. The majority of our 36 interviewees talked of deficiencies in the coverage of their local community by the mainstream local and regional press, and many said they were motivated to produce community news at least in part because of these problems.

This 'representational deficit' also clearly motivates, but in a more instrumental way, the participants in our study who are active around planning issues in their communities. Here the value of participation through representation is a key to challenging certain values associated with much urban development. The values of self-representation and participation are understood as ways of challenging dominant interests in planning and development processes.

Our research with hyperlocal news producers highlighted much coverage of local planning issues. This ranged from gathering and circulating information to readers from diverse stakeholders about planning matters, hosting and facilitating debate and active participation in campaigns (Williams et al, 2014). Numerous campaigns have formed around the activities of local neighbourhood plans and neighbourhood forums, entities enabled under the UK's 2011 Localism Act and designed to enable more democratic control of planning issues. The presence of campaigns *against* these bodies, however, suggests concern in some communities about how democratic they actually are in practice.

One such campaign was initiated and fostered by the hyperlocal news site LoveWapping.org, and its publisher Mark Baynes. As part of a group of local bloggers, frustrated by a lack of mainstream media coverage of planning issues, he has covered scores of controversial developments. One involved an opaque neighbourhood plan from a group called Network Wapping:

> "For me it was the simple issue over democracy in that, as I've said in more than one post, anybody who wishes to represent people within our system in this country is open to scrutiny, full stop. ... We said to them, 'look, you're not open. You say you have these meetings that nobody knows about, and all sorts of stuff', and we've told them, 'you can't do this, it's wrong. Answer questions, you don't publish meeting minutes'. You name it, they didn't do it."

Figure 4.2: Love Wapping: independent investigative community news from East London (lovewapping.org)

Between April 2013 and January 2014 Baynes attended and covered meetings, researched and background checked key players, fostered, organised, and provided a media platform for local opposition groups (of which there were many) and promoted and facilitated widespread engagement with local council officials considering the validity of the plan. He was motivated in his coverage by the need to fill an information gap at a local level, but also by a desire to provide independent scrutiny and accountability lacking from local government and established media. He told us, "The scary thing is that anybody could do one of these applications and because there's nobody actually monitoring their process on the ground you can do what the hell you like, and say what the hell you like, and nobody's fact checking basically.

Which is what we were doing." Network Wapping submitted their (by now) contentious application twice and it was rejected or withdrawn both times largely because of the widespread local opposition to the plan in part facilitated by this citizen news service.

For Wards Corner Coalition (WCC), notions of local economy, solidarity and trust were mobilised as a way to address the perceived deficiencies in the planning consultation process. Social clusters and networks were proposed as processes for enhancing participation in existing and emerging networks of practice, interest and policy. The digital visualisation of the future and the current market building, produced through the research project's co-creation, offered a platform for debates about planning and to express tensions around the gentrification of Tottenham. For WCC, the launch of the community plan on the 'Stickyworld' platform was an opportunity to 'reconnect' with those directly affected by the future of the building – the traders. The vernacular and immersive qualities of the content (three-dimensional virtual tours to a futuristic yet inclusive vision of the space) and its interactive possibility for commentary provided an opportunity for the group to showcase its work as a catalyst for change, but also to operate beyond the means of mainstream representative consultation processes.

As one Colombian migrant and relative of a trader within the Wards Corner market noted, the Stickyworld plan offered them an opportunity to 'understand', to bear witness and also to speak against plans for eviction. He was able share his comment and a link to the WCC plan on Stickyworld and on the council's planning hub to his network in Whatsapp. His comment on Stickyworld was translated from Spanish to English by another WCC member:

> "What this new project proposes is a new landmark, a place with identity that people recognise, for people to find all different kinds of community. Additionally, it could be a place not only of commercial exchange, but also in which there is a strengthening of culture in which social cooperation can shine: family unity, recreation, and personal interrelationships. In conclusion, it will be an integrated space in which the people who work and those who visit it can relate like a family."

These values found expression not solely as a result of the digital platform intervention by the researchers. It also resulted from a concerted engagement effort by the WCC to explain the planning process to marginalised yet interested groups and involve them in expressing their views. The campaign strategy used face-to-face encounters, traditional booklets, the plan itself, and live events to celebrate the launch of the Stickyworld platform and the community plan. Exposure in blogs and social and local media was integrated into other live, face-to-face actions.

The informal creative networks studied in our research also showed interest in questions of representation and citizenship. The South Blessed website, although dominated by music videos, also supported a strong news and debate function. Of 201 video clips on the site made by South Blessed itself, 118 were music-related, but there were also 55 videos themed as 'journalism,' produced in documentary or current affairs style. A further 28 videos were personality-led polemics or contributions to debate. The music video component can also be understood to carry elements of 'public sphere' ambition, given hip-hop's explicit culture of urban messaging. One consequence of this creative citizen profile for South Blessed was the decision by the local police to recruit South Blessed's founder, Vince Baidoo, to the Bristol police liaison group. The local community beat officer told us:

"The police have got a website. I'm sure it costs a fortune. But the people I want to reach, the youngsters I want to reach, they're not going to read that. They're not going to go on that. If they do, they're going to say, 'That's the police, isn't it, police propaganda?' Whereas if they can tap into South Blessed, 'Right, okay, I know it's not a tool of government. He's not an arm of the establishment, or whatever. This person is speaking, and I can make up my mind'. So it should provide a neutral view to them."

The informal South Blessed network has also been recognised by mainstream regional news journalists as offering a way of providing reliable and inclusive information at a moment of high community tension. A reporter for ITV, the main commercial television presence in the area, commented:

"He struck me as well-connected, seemed to have quite a good knowledge of what was going on around him, because I'd witnessed some of the things he described. So I had a certain level of confidence in what he had to say. ...So from an information point of view, he was very useful when we're trying to build a picture of what was happening. Obviously, relevant video material in a TV world, that's incredibly important. So he had that to offer too."

A peer media producer in the South Blessed network offered a more expressive account of the representational significance of the website:

"I feel like it's a little bit like the Google of Bristol sometimes. If you want to know the real Bristol, none of this stuff that you see in tourist books, what's being recommended, if you just want to know what the people of Bristol are about, the youth of Bristol, everything Bristol really, I would just say go to South Blessed. They've got so many different videos, so many different bits of information."

There is then strong evidence from our research studies that creative citizens aspire to increase community engagement across a vast range of situations. Local representation, democratic consultation and dialogue were enacted as *intrinsic* values for the organisations and networks we investigated. Future policy aimed at supporting vibrant, inclusive, healthy and productive communities could clearly benefit from understanding better how creative citizens' commitment to local and regional representation produces value and how, through a carefully constructed and authentic process of co-creation, debate and negotiation can occur.

Education, training, employment and economic development

The people who choose to be creative citizens are also frequently part of a rich web of both resource and demand for informal education and training opportunities. These can have transformative impacts on confidence, aspiration and employment. The complexity of this web of activity makes assessment of its aggregate impact a methodological challenge. Transformative impacts are frequently experienced at a personal, emotional, level in the first instance, as this comment from a South Blessed peer producer illustrates: 'I think the point I am trying to make is that my confidence has definitely been built and has grown since working for him.' However these interactions may also have more formal outcomes:

"He has a couple of staff working for him now, and that boy who didn't have many opportunities or many options available to him. He's an insanely creative person but doesn't necessarily get to grips with mainstream culture and applying for jobs and filling out forms, all the rest of it. He's now completely motivated every morning to get up first thing and come and work there like a nine to five job, to do what he loves."

When there is a focus for creative talent it also has the effect of offering a bridge between less formal and more organised forms of creative production: 'Bristol subculture produces a lot of mainstream culture… South Blessed saw that there's an importance to highlight that subculture because it does produce and feed a lot of more mainstream culture'.

Many of the community news producers we interviewed were motivated by a wish to improve their own journalistic, technological, publishing, design, marketing, sales and online community management skills. The editor of a Scottish hyperlocal used the publishing, social enterprise and online engagement skills he honed on his blog to gain employment in the mainstream news industry. He told us, "My academic background isn't in journalism at all and so I've learned an incredible amount. Since I started work on *Greener Leith*, that led me to being hired as a professional journalist". Another hyperlocal journalist told us how he started blogging while unemployed and was at least in part motivated by a wish to maintain his employability and learn new skills. He said, "It was a way to keep my hand in, to learn a bit more about WordPress and about other social media things, which was all very new to me at the time". After a number of years covering community life in the town and running a number of successful local campaigns, he formed his own local media company and was employed as a freelance correspondent for a nearby local newspaper publisher.

However, the majority of hyperlocal journalists remain uninterested in making money from their news services, preferring to see their work as a hobby that benefits their local community. One of the Wolverhampton news site team told us, "We don't make any money whatsoever. We didn't start out with the aim of making money, we started out with this being of community benefit and us giving something back to the community". Nonetheless, their work on the site, and the skills they have fostered while doing it, have now begun to pay off in unexpected ways:

> "I'm beginning to get leads for work that have come out of things related to the website. That can be community groups that we're involved with through the site, people

who know we run the site and want a website or want training or consultancy on how they can do social media, that kind of thing. So whilst that wasn't one of the aims, over a number of years, we're now starting to see ... the result of running the site is that I'm getting job offers because of it, and because of the work I do there."

The same goes for his partner, who is now employed directly as a result of her current employers' familiarity with the skills she developed while working on the blog:

"The job that she actually has now, part of the reason she was offered the job was because of what we do with the website. It's a very similar area and she was seen by the person who now employs her as having the skills and the knowledge that she built up, that being an asset as an employee. So [the site] doesn't have an economic value in terms of it generates money itself, but it has definitely had an economic value to us personally in terms of the work we do, that it's helped us to gain work and to generate revenue."

This informal and opportunistic career development is typical of the emergent pathways produced through creative citizenship networks. They are precisely the kinds of economic benefit that remain invisible to macro analysis of the creative economy yet are palpable throughout our case study evidence.

Creative citizens in the hyperlocal news sector are also motivated by the opportunity to provide more informal training opportunities to others in their community. RoathCardiff.net is an urban hyperlocal site dedicated to news about the East Cardiff suburb of Roath. As well as producing local news and publishing events listings on their website and on Twitter, the team behind this service draw on the skills they have developed as community journalists and in their day jobs to run bimonthly social media surgeries where locals can get advice and learn better to use services like Facebook, Twitter, YouTube, and free blogging software. For instance, they worked with the Roath Local History Society, a local group about whom RoathCardiff.net contributors regularly write pieces:

"They didn't have a website, they didn't have anything, they just had these meetings and you could never find out when they were. Eventually we got them to come to a social media surgery and we just built them a website ... in one night, and then we gave them some special extra sessions as well, because they're things we really believe in and we want more people to know about them."

Other community news producers, especially those with more commercial ambitions, aim to provide formal employment opportunities for journalists. The *Port Talbot Magnet* is a South Wales local news website and newspaper run by a cooperative of local journalists made redundant from staff jobs in the local and regional news publishing industry. They started this news service shortly after the town lost its own weekly newspaper in one of its parent company's (*Trinity Mirror's*) numerous cost-cutting exercises. Creating jobs for themselves and other journalists was an explicit aim from the start for this social enterprise:

"There was an opportunity. There was a desire to do something to create jobs; that was the starting point. We wanted to create jobs for ourselves. We didn't want to just sit there and go, well, the old traditional paymasters are not providing us with jobs anymore, boo-hoo, let's all go and be press officers. We decided we wanted to do something proactive about that and try and maintain ourselves in journalism in a more entrepreneurial way, and to try out new ideas."

Their critical, trade union-informed, localist stance suggested that they could succeed where the mainstream local publishers were failing because their focus would be on sustaining journalism for the benefit of community rather than on generating unsustainably high profits:

"A lot of the arguments we were hearing were about the enormous profits that some of the newspaper groups were making from local news and thinking, well, we don't want to be in a position where we're trying to maintain a 30% profit margin in order to keep our local news service going. Actually what we want to do is just ensure there are jobs there for people like us in the future. It doesn't matter if we make a profit, a vast profit, as long as we can pay our bills and maintain journalism jobs."

The community centres in Lewisham and Walthamstow that were part of our research into design and planning also act as hubs of social activity for informal training, education and social entrepreneurship. A content analysis of the websites and social media of these two community centres revealed numerous examples that these spaces act as hubs for building networks among local voluntary groups and social enterprises. The role of digital media here is significant though not always dominant. Goldsmiths Community Centre, for instance, had developed a digital literacy/digital storytelling training programme in 2010–11, and a dedicated space within its website called *The Hubbub*:

> J. "*The Hubbub* has had about 15–20 participants; learning about, not necessarily using, but learning how to blog ..."

> T. "A few local residents have actually set up their own blogs and social media presence now."

> J. "So that is a really interesting way to tell your stories."

> S. "But others have wanted to know where they can find information out, about other organisations, or how to link up with other groups locally... Jane is the Google of Downham and South Lewisham."

> J. "I am actually the community, researcher, the roving reporter... I go and ask people around, source stories and then I tweet about it, or I post it on site."

> T. "We don't realise that we need to adopt, an 'integrated communications strategy': from the [garden] fence to Facebook."

Here there is a growing sense that connectivity through social media itself constitutes a form of cultural capital which can lead to the ability to 'tell your stories' as well as link up with other groups. This networked capital can be a social as well as a personal asset. Like other forms of cultural capital it may also become financial capital, not only by enhancing individuals' and organisations' capacity and capability, but also by its effect on neighbourhoods and property through reporting on and campaigning around planning processes.

A new commons – networked assets

It is clear that the cultural practices of social media and other digital communication technologies produce a value flow between individual, enterprise and community networks. The cultures of digital innovation and technology have had a particular resonance with questions of citizenship. Our case studies show us how values (for example, empowerment, self-development, teaching and learning, representation and accountability) enacted by agents in their networks are working with and through digital media platforms to create new kinds of commons assets. They are assets in so far as the creative work of individuals creates realisable value (attention, employment, communication, cohesion, training) and they are commons in so far as the values that underpin them aim towards the inclusive, the open and the public rather than the private, protected and commercial. So the Wards Corner Stickyworld site is a creative asset produced as a resource for the community to envisage potential futures for the place where they live or make their living. The hyperlocal news service involves much of the creative work of local journalism, from relationship building to reporting and design, deployed to produce assets available to the social media network, through tweeting or re-tweeting, sharing and posting on Facebook sites, linking to blogs and so on. The assets are designed to be networked. A Bristol poet and performer explains how South Blessed aggregates attention as an asset that can be shared by the whole of the creative community:

> "So if a rap group in Bristol just made a new video or just made a new track, they can promote it through their Facebook or their MySpace individually. So they're already limiting to only their fan or their social group to see it. Whereas if you have a slightly more independent objective forum to showcase all of it, then they're picking up new fans, new interest. ...I just think [South Blessed fills the] need for … a platform."

The website acts as a platform and a brand that aggregates attention in order to create value for the co-creators who post their music videos.

A clear example of how hyperlocal news uses digital communication platforms to create individual, community, and economic value can be found in the work of West Hampstead community journalist Jonathan Turton. A journalist by training, he had a range of personal and social motivations for starting out. He launched his service as an experiment in whether, and in what ways, Twitter might be used as a stand-alone local news platform. He started posting (necessarily) brief news updates about his area using his @WHampstead account, often with identifying hashtag #WestHampstead or #whamp. His motivation encompasses attention to traditional journalistic roles such as holding elites to account ("I like the journalism side of it a lot," he said, "I get to ask questions and I get to be nosy … I get to poke around a bit, and I get to challenge people, and find out what's really going on."), representing local life and people (particularly younger, what he terms less socially 'embedded', residents of West Hampstead) and passing on information that would be hard to get otherwise because of deficiencies in existing local media or local government communications. What started as a Twitter news service then led to the creation of a network of followers and readers which crossed over onto other new media platforms and into real world community life. He soon found out that not only could he 'do local news on Twitter', but that Twitter (where he has more than 11,100 followers) had allowed him to create further, innovative, community news-related commons assets such as a steady stream of original, often grassroots inflected, local news stories sourced directly from members of the network, a website-based 'digital newspaper' at Westhampsteadlife.com (with 15,000 monthly unique users and 52,000 page impressions), a well-subscribed monthly email newsletter (1,500 readers) and a series of regular real world social and cultural events, ranging from smaller restaurant meetings and cultural visits to large free parties in local pubs and clubs. These events allow him, and others in the community, the opportunity to socialise and have fun, as well as promoting community cohesion. Although the motivations for creating this service were never primarily financial, the site and email newsletter also carry advertising, which generates enough income to cover running costs and provide freelance employment to some contributors.

For Wards Corner the desire to build connections in social media is mobilised by the belief that using such networks will aid in the fostering and the strengthening of existing community ties:

> "Much of the work we do is about finding new and innovative ways to engage people in the planning and regeneration issues that directly affect them. This requires a lot of creativity and thinking beyond, often obtuse, plans and official policy documents. We try to use visual and social media and interactive platforms whenever possible, yet we

also really focus on talking to people about the things that matter to them."

'Talking to people' emphasises that building networked social assets is not just a matter of getting your digital communications strategy right. On the contrary, most of our partners also emphasised the importance of face-to-face communication, noticeboards, printed newsletters and meetings. Our respondents sought to establish networked connections of solidarity and trust with those directly engaged and directly affected by what they do, as well as those hard to reach through social media. Their communications ecology, involving numerous civic, ethnic and vernacular cultures, is necessarily mixed.

Conclusion

The values enacted in these accounts indicate that the fields of creative economy, local public sphere and social media are bought together in the idea of creative citizenship. This idea has a specific purchase because it recognises the importance of both the tangible and intangible assets of the knowledge economy for community development. Intangible assets, such as memories, skills, aspirations, and shared values for representation and solidarity, drive the production of mediated assets such as websites, hashtags, music videos and Facebook groups to build 'common knowledge' for the local networks of civic life. In our case studies, the value of this knowledge is realised in a local context, but where local geographic identity might be looser than in a more tightly knit traditional community, typical of the pre-social media age. The value we uncover in our study is not for a community in the traditional sense of a group of people with regular and longstanding face-to-face relationships of trust and shared histories. Though they share places, these creative citizens do not necessarily share lives. Sharing a particular geography does not automatically constitute community, but it does offer networked communications a potentially fertile territory. Creative citizens are mobilisers of the common resources that produce flexible, innovative and coherent community networks. The evidence from our case studies suggests that creative citizens enact values of self-actualisation, representation and participation, informal education and training. By enacting these values in their networks they produce significant assets and value.

This evidence confirms and builds upon research conclusions reviewed in Chapter 3, particularly research into the impacts of participation in cultural processes (for example, Stebbins, 1992; DCMS, 2008; Edensor et al, 2010; Ramsden, 2013). The authors are particularly struck by parallels in our findings with the work of François Matorosso (1997), which concluded that the social impacts of the arts could be classified as personal development, social cohesion, community empowerment and self-determination, local image and identity, imagination and vision, and health and wellbeing. This raises a key question for this research, since Matorosso's results were produced in the 1990s, way before the current near ubiquity of ICTs in every day life, and before social media. What is the difference now that those impacts are being produced to a considerable extent through digital mediation?

The first point to make is that the impacts noted in our work are not being produced *exclusively* through digital mediation. Rather we were struck time and again by the way that creative citizens interweave face-to-face events, physical media and physical gathering points with their online correlatives. Likewise, some of our hyperlocal research partners chose to follow a growing number of other UK community journalists into print formats of their services and South Blessed opted to write and publish a graphic novel to build the next phase of its community media network. Twitter and Facebook are a long way from being stand-alone community engagement tools. There is no single creative digital 'pill' for community engagement.

The second point is to consider more closely the dynamics, scale and range of the digital media processes used by our research partners. It is clear that the diffusion of the means of media production at an everyday level has powerful, if unevenly realised, potential for creative citizenship. We have seen how it plays a key role in strengthening informal creative economy networks and their processes of talent development, how hyperlocals are creating new information networks for neighbourhoods and how commons assets can create opportunities for dialogue, consultation, campaigning and cohesion. Because these effects can be achieved very rapidly, network building can be accomplished much more quickly than in the analogue world. We also know that because these effects can also scale from neighbourhood to region to nation to world, the potential of 'going viral' is an ever-present motivation for many with firm roots in defined physical and local communities. Like governments, public bodies and businesses, creative citizens understand that they need integrated communications strategies, 'from the fence to Facebook'. These differences of dynamics, scale and range mean that it is now possible (for those with the skills, the time and the equipment) to create a public around an interest or a challenge with a minimum of physical infrastructure. In short, creative citizenship practices predate the web, but in a digital world they can be scaled and distributed at much lower cost.

It has also become clear that the everyday work of 'affective labour' that citizens undertake in social media produces substantial economic value for a new hegemony of corporate giants. Social media and online data-scraping methods have harnessed co-creativity as a major producer of capital, such that the last great 'resource industry' is data mining, for which the raw materials are human interactions. Billions of dollars accumulated in tech takeovers and flotations represent a very significant investment in the affective attachments of users to Facebook, YouTube, Twitter or Instagram (Arvidsson and Colleoni, 2012). Our investigations into the digital dividends for citizenship of the co-productive practices of the internet are first steps in identifying what equivalent value is being created and circulated amongst UK communities. Our case studies suggest that creative citizens are creating *commons value* that can also be harnessed by communities of place and interest. Progress will depend on the development of policies and practices which support the role of creative citizens acting as agents in networks which consist in flows of information and affect, that are open, and that are aware of emergent possibilities. The challenge for research in the field is to develop methods that can evaluate these commons assets at regional, national and international scale in a way that policy makers and regulators can recognise.

FIVE

Varieties of creative citizenship

*Theodore Zamenopoulos, Katerina Alexiou, Giota Alevizou,
Caroline Chapain, Shawn Sobers and Andy Williams*

Introduction

In this chapter we identify some *varieties* of creative citizenship, not
with the expectation of achieving a comprehensive taxonomy, but
in order to test the scope, robustness and potential value of creative
citizenship, both as an idea and as a set of practices, with reference to
the case studies undertaken in the Creative Citizen project.

Creative citizenship as a concept can help us consider how 'everyday'
creative acts – such as cooking, dancing, knitting or debating – can
generate community engagement. It gives us a way of rendering
coherent an array of otherwise disparate phenomena: for example,
when pictures and messages in social media from the streets of a
turbulent neighbourhood become a catalyst for mobilising people
around an issue or cause; or when cultural or artistic activities transform
a planning consultation meeting into a creative experience, where
urban issues are deliberated upon in a more collaborative and dynamic
spirit. These are examples of creative citizenship in action.

'Creative citizenship' conceptualises the everyday creativity of
ordinary people (that is, not just creative professionals) as a core civic
resource, something that adds to the capacity of the community
and which harnesses their combined energy for change. Such
everyday creativity cannot be understood in isolation from the civic
networks within which it is situated. Creative citizenship does not
merely describe the acts of creative individuals. It depends upon and
contributes to the civic networks where it occurs, especially now that
the boundaries between producers and consumers are diminished by
digital abundance. It is more about the creativity of groups than the
creativity of individuals. This chapter explores a range of ways in which
acts of creativity occur within a civic and communicative context.

We test our theoretical approach by applying it to case studies in the Creative Citizen project, including examples of activism, community journalism, hyperlocal publishing, insurgent and formal community-led planning practices, and to informal and formal creative practices developed around music and media production.

Rage, renewal and everyday acts: initiation and purpose

Acts of citizenship can be considered creative in various ways. They may be creative in the same way that Schumpeterian 'creative destruction' is, where innovation is disruptive or a threat in circumstances where renewal is needed. Citizens may engage in protest, opposition or resistance, sometimes in highly controversial and divisive circumstances. Creativity here arises from the ways in which citizens are 'providing alternatives, possible sources for the development of new kinds of practices, narratives about belonging to and participating in society' (Holston, 1995: 48). Action for renewal, innovation and change, working against the grain of the formal procedures of the state, does not have to be seen in such stark oppositional terms, of course. Acts of citizenship may also be considered creative as part of a self-determination and engagement processes in a civic community's sense of being 'for itself' (Friedmann, 2011). Acts of creative citizenship for community self-representation can be observed, for instance, in the organisation of street parties, or sharing local news, especially where these activities inspire others to join in.

Acts of creative citizenship may be initiated in a number of ways. They may be *self-initiated acts*; that is spontaneous acts of people for themselves. This may include acts based on beliefs and desires, or reactions to contextual challenges. Examples of self-initiated acts include campaigning and advocacy practices in defence of disadvantaged communities such as those that arose in the context of the participatory design and planning movement in the USA during the late '60s and '70s (Davidoff, 1995); or practices that arise as part of the 'Do-it-Yourself' culture – one that is characterised by 'an increasing emphasis on self-determination as the foundation of citizenship' (Hartley, 1999: 178; Ratto and Boler, 2014). These ideas also find expression in what has been dubbed in recent years the 'social practices' movement in the arts. An example is the work of Theaster Gates, a Chicago-born 'social practices installation artist'. His work fuses concerns about poverty, urban planning and artistic practice with strategies that include the making of artefacts from raw materials found in a poor neighbourhood (South Chicago). Outputs are offered for profitable sale to those willing to pay for them in the art market, with a view to channelling investment back into the poor neighbourhood.[1] Much 'social practices art' defiantly operates entirely outside of the world of commercial art galleries, seeking to 'change the world, one row house at a time.' (Miranda, 2014).

At the other end of the spectrum, acts of citizenship may be *responsive acts*; that is, acts that are supported or even initiated by state-sponsored programmes, as political leaders seek to connect with the public in challenging circumstances and to make interventions that create an impact at the level of the community and the citizen. Examples of such responsive acts in the planning world are the self-help and self-build housing practices that arose in the '70s (for example, Turner, 1976; Ward, 1976); or more recently the community-led planning practices that support the development of neighbourhood development plans under the UK's Localism Act 2011, which was originally conceived as part of the UK government's 'Big Society' initiative (see Chapter 1).

When it comes to the *purposes* of different types of citizenship acts, Gallent and Ciaffi (2014) distinguish four major types:

- *reactive acts* to perceived threats or opportunities, including acts of protest, lobbying but also fundraising for campaigns;
- *community building acts* that intend to devise ways for creating social cohesion and identity;
- *self-help acts* that aim to respond to needs that neither the state nor private enterprise are ready to deliver;
- *taking control acts* that aim to control assets and develop plans that express opposition or alternatives.

From this discussion arises another foundational distinction between *collective* and *connective* acts of citizenship (for example, Bennett and Segerberg, 2012). Collective acts involve social groups that work towards a common goal (for example, neighbourhood forums) while connective acts arise from individually motivated actions that nevertheless depend or build on the interaction of others (for example, hyperlocal news, Wikipedia, Open Source Design).

Creative citizenship arises at a multitude of points across this wide spectrum of civic possibilities. It brings to the fore a new emphasis on the creative capacity of citizenship as a force for reflexive change. Creative citizenship acts make or produce something new, and in parallel induce a critical reflection on political, social or cultural issues.

Citizenship and creative acts

From a psychological perspective (for example, Sternberg, 1999), creative acts refer to the capacity of the mind to recognise or shape something *new* (for example, an unexpected image, a hidden association between ideas or a nonconformist view); but also something *valuable,* defined as something useful or appropriate for a specific context. Creative acts are therefore expressions of *originality* and *meaningfulness* within a certain context (for example, Richards, 2007).

One of the core challenges that emerges in any discussion that connects creative and civic acts is the commonplace assumption that creativity involves an *exceptional* product, process, or person. Indeed, research in creativity has predominantly focused on exceptional artists, scientists or engineers, the intelligence and thinking processes of those exceptional people, their characteristics or the characteristics of the period they belong to. But, creativity is also a general human capability. It underlies our everyday ability to respond to and change our environment according to our needs and aspirations (for example, Coyne, 1997; Richards, 2007). This is the field of *everyday creativity* where creative acts are 'commonplace' and part of everyday life. Burgess (2006) proposes the notion of 'vernacular creativity' to frame our understanding of the democratic potential arising from the accessibility of new media practices. In this context, creative acts are those that help to unearth a hidden potential in a given situation (Richards, 2007: 25–33). The agent may well be a group, social network, community or agency, not just a talented individual.

One way of looking at the varieties of everyday creative acts is to consider different types of practices of individuals, groups or networks. For instance, Sanders and Stappers (2008) identify four levels of creative practices in everyday life:

- *Doing:* This refers to acts with the purpose of 'getting something done' (to cite the authors' culinary example, this would be like 'organising one's herbs and spices').
- *Adaptation:* This refers to acts with the purpose of 'making things my own' (like making improvements to a 'ready meal' bought from the supermarket).
- *Making:* This refers to acts with the purpose of making things 'with my own hands' (such as cooking a recipe from scratch).
- *Creating:* This refers to acts with the purpose of 'expressing my creativity' (for example, coming up with an idea for a completely new dish).

Such types of creative practice take their specific meaning in relation to the *context* within which they are situated – the purpose that drives these acts and the space in which they are expressed (for example, online spaces for cultural activities or neighbourhood forums for urban regeneration). These practices depend on the capacities and capital of the social networks within which they are generated. This includes embedded human resources, such as the knowledge and skills of individuals, but also social relations, norms and shared ways of acting and collaborating. In short, creative acts, either collective or connective, depend on various types of human and social capital that enable them to take place (Rydin, 2014).

This brings us to White's (2008) philosophical argument about the relation between creative acts and civic action. For White, creative acts are those that unearth a hidden potential of a community and overcome predominant habits in order to produce a meaningful change. Such a process is more likely to involve a modest shift in behaviour or expression by a number of people in a community than to result from the 'Eureka moment' of the lone genius breakthrough. We need therefore to be able to capture the varieties of creative citizenship by looking at the purpose and context of their practices as well as the social capital involved in their creation (for a more detailed account of how creative acts depend on social networks and capital see Alexiou and Zamenopoulos, 2008; Alexiou, 2010).

The proposed approach: context, practices and social capital

Based upon the above theoretical analysis, we propose to explore different types of creativity in the Creative Citizen project's case studies by placing emphasis on three dimensions:

- *context:* the varieties of context in which creative citizenship arises; including individual and group motivations and the spaces in which creative acts take place;
- *practices:* the varieties of creative practice (that is, doing, adapting, making and creating) that arise within different contexts;
- *social capital:* the types of social capital that enable different creative citizenship acts to occur.

The first two dimensions will help us capture the 'structural complexity' of creative citizenship. That is the variation that arises by exploring a wide spectrum of practices (namely, doing, adapting, making and creating) across a wide range of contexts, including spaces for debate, cultural expression, information and sharing of resources. The third dimension will help us capture the 'effective complexity' of creative citizenship. That involves the types of social capital and intrinsic capacities of communities that make a variety of creative acts possible. While the notion of structural complexity refers here to the variety of practices and contexts, 'effective complexity' refers to the connectivity and coherence of the underlying social capital that enables those practices and contexts. (For more extended analysis of different types of complexity see Zamenopoulos and Alexiou, 2005.)

Varieties of context

Acts of creative citizenship arise in various spaces where some sort of 'open sharing' takes place within or between communities. This sets the context of creative citizenship. In order to illustrate the breadth of these spaces and the corresponding variation of creative citizenship let us briefly outline some examples derived from the Creative Citizen project case studies. We will classify them in the following spectrum of (sometimes overlapping) spaces: debate spaces, cultural spaces, information spaces and resource spaces.

Debate spaces

These are spaces where issues are shared and debated, such as cafes and restaurants or digital forums were people gather to discuss a shared concern. If creative citizenship is a form of critical change as discussed above, debate spaces are based on an explicit form of critical thinking and making. Creative exchange opens the way to social and political change.

Grassroots groups – such as the Wards Corner Community Coalition in London – are often created and developed out of debates that arise in the context of local businesses and markets. The Wards Corner Community Coalition present themselves in their website as 'a network of networks', predominantly created and nurtured out of public meetings and debates carried out in local cafes and other meeting places. Local businesses in the Wards Corner market have provided a debate space because of the lack of alternative public spaces and also because of the services they provide and their centrality to the cause of this group. Debate spaces can be places such as local libraries, community hubs, places of worship, or historic buildings, that are managed by local authorities or other organisations operating within civil society. They can also be online spaces. For example, the Wards Corner Community

Coalition uses a variety of online spaces for debate, including Facebook, email lists, local newspapers and an online consultation platform developed in collaboration with the Open University.

Examples of online spaces abound in the world of hyperlocal news. Many community news websites employ bulletin board technology as part of the services they offer to communities. Community publishers, such as London's well-established SE1.co.uk, not only furnish news but also provide spaces where people in their communities can discuss their area and what goes on in it. Others maintain active discussions on newer social media platforms such as Twitter or Facebook. For example, Jonathan Turton, editor and publisher of WestHampsteadLife.com, fosters discussion about the North London suburb among his more than 11,000 followers on Twitter. On Facebook, the journalism cooperative behind the *Port Talbot Magnet* posts links to its own blog's stories, and also provides a space where locals can and very often do create and publish their own news, starting discussions about issues that are important to them. The result is a more organic and participatory shaping of the community's news ecology from the bottom up, rather than one dominated by individual professional journalists and traditional one-to-many modes of publication. An analogous example in the realm of local history can be seen in the AHRC-funded initiative *Forgotten Abergavenny*. Here, a team of Cardiff University social scientists facilitate an active Facebook page centred on posting, sharing and discussing old photographs of a Welsh market town. The page has more than 3,400 Facebook 'likes', photographs are regularly viewed many thousands of times, prompting rich insights which, when viewed in the round, constitute a varied repository of democratic popular cultural history (Figure 5.1).

Figure 5.1: A photo from the Forgotten Abergavenny Facebook page, which provides space for debate around local history

Cultural spaces

These are spaces where cultural activities and creative expression are shared. They include social media platforms where communities of practice (for example, musicians, comedians, artists, and so forth share and disseminate their work). They also include physical/local spaces where cultural activities support the creation of identity, which itself fosters further participation and community engagement. An example of such a space is the South Blessed Facebook page, which is predominantly used by subscribers to post their own videos, news and events, and not by South Blessed administrators themselves, who post there only occasionally. Cultural spaces of this sort rely on the creation of a 'safe space' for expression for their growth and success. For instance, on the South Blessed Facebook page there is not much conversation or interaction on the page besides routine 'likes', but contributors know their posts will find an audience of interest, and not be met by unsolicited or gratuitously hostile feedback, such as might occur for example on an open Twitter platform.

Community centres such as The Mill and Goldsmiths Community Centre, both in outer London, provide facilities for education, recreation, leisure and health. Classes on dance, drama or music become the core mechanism for connecting a community but also a mechanism for promoting social change on issues related to health and wellbeing. These local spaces also host more implicit forms of critical reflection (as opposed to debate spaces) about political, social or cultural issues. The core emphasis is placed on the transformative nature of the cultural activities and their potential for creating identity and promoting engagement, alive to important considerations such as equality, diversity and wellbeing (Figure 5.2).

Information spaces

These are places where information is shared. They include spaces defined by technologies such as websites, social media and mobile applications where the production and consumption of information is exercised by the same group or individuals. As well as creating co-productive, collaborative spaces, where communities can discuss and achieve impact in debates about the areas in which they live, hyperlocal news producers also routinely provide online spaces for the one-way provision of local news. These websites (sometimes accompanied by print editions of newspapers) are often set up in places traditionally underserved by commercial local news media and they

Figure 5.2: The Goldsmiths Community Centre has been used as a space for social events, but also activities that promote health and wellbeing in the wider community

aim to combat perceived deficiencies in the provision and circulation of local information. In our quantitative work, we identified nearly 500 active hyperlocal websites in the UK in 2013, and our analysis of the content on such websites showed that they were producing local news rich in information about local civic and cultural life (including the activities of clubs, societies and community events) as well as providing high levels of coverage to local politics. We began our work sceptical about the capacity of hyperlocal news producers, most of whom lack a formal or professional background in journalism, to deliver the 'accountability journalism' imagined in journalism's mission to 'hold power to account'. We found that, in fact, more than half of those active in UK hyperlocals cover local campaigns, and almost half conduct their own critical investigations into perceived injustices or abuses of power. (A more detailed discussion of these issues can be found in Williams et al, 2015.)

Resource spaces

These are spaces where resources are shared. Examples in the Creative Citizen project include Creative Commons sites, open source design platforms and physical co-working spaces where people come to work individually or collaboratively using some shared resources. The co-working space run by the Moseley Exchange in Birmingham is a characteristic example of a resource space within which creative citizenship arises. Interviews carried out with the people who share this co-working space and those involved in the wider remit of the Moseley Community Development Trust which owns it, express enthusiasm about the possibilities afforded by the space. These include financial, social and professional collaborations. These potentialities are, according to the interviewees, the assets or resources that afford, support or drive their creative, entrepreneurial and social activities. However, the co-workers' social and economic values can also clash. In this atmosphere, network effects and creativity are stimulated.

Varieties of practice

A potentially infinite variety of practice of creative citizenship might feasibly arise in these different spaces or 'ecologies', to use a term preferred in the social media age (for example, Benkler, 2006). Here, we will explore the variety manifested in relation to everyday creative acts that underlie a critical change within a given space – namely acts that integrate creative action with an element (explicit or implicit) of critical thinking about political, social or cultural issues.

We consider acts of 'doing, adaptation, making and creating' (Sanders and Stappers, 2008) and explore how these elements become intermeshed in two examples from the Creative Citizen project:

- *hyperlocal news* – a core example within the context of *information and debate* spaces;
- *creative media networks* – an example of creative acts within *cultural and resource* spaces.

We go on to discuss the variety of motivations behind acts of creative citizenship, as a way of understanding how creative acts and citizenship acts interact to become a force for change.

Debate and information spaces

In hyperlocal news the act of *creating* is present in most of the daily routines of the community journalists with whom we worked, but it is also commonly found in the meta-level design, planning and maintenance work which goes into running a community news website. In the domain of hyperlocal news, this kind of work is done most often when dealing with the big picture. For instance, when building and maintaining the visual architecture of a site (for example, designing the look of its pages and the structure of its sections), when considering the overarching aims of a news service (what kinds of news will it publish, who is the target audience) and when deciding what tone to strike when producing news (editorial impartiality versus a more critical/campaigning stances).

These strategic expressions of creativity arise particularly at the beginning of projects when people set the overarching creative and ideological vision for their websites, but then continue on an ad hoc basis as hyperlocal journalists gain experience, confidence and skills, and as they react to unfolding events. An example can be found in the work of the *Port Talbot Magnet*. When this group of former journalists launched their cooperative news service they aimed to be a local news website for the people of this small industrial town on the South Wales coast. Not long after they began work on the site, however, they became aware of a number of local campaigns on a range of issues concerning council-imposed cuts to public services, notably a decision to renege on plans to rebuild a fire-damaged community resource and leisure centre. There was also evidence of local concern about a decision by Tata, owner of the local steelworks, to close public access to a beach. After many discussions about the value of objectivity in local news provision, the collective decision was taken to move the site in a new creative direction and to take an actively campaigning stance on some issues of local public concern. The decision was a good one for the *Magnet* news workers, campaigners, the readership of the website and arguably the community as a whole. The local journalists gained a reputation for supporting under-represented community voices, and holding local elites to account. They believe this was a factor in increasing their visibility among news audiences as well as building their credibility as a serious news outlet among official sources in local government and industry. Press officers and official spokespeople, who had previously not engaged with this nascent news start-up or had done so only sporadically, could no longer ignore them. Local civic activists gained an ally in their struggles, and access to new audiences in a sparse local news environment, under-served by mainstream news after the loss of its dedicated weekly newspaper in 2009. The *Magnet's* readers, for their part, learned about issues of concern to many in their community. They were exposed to a greater range of local perspectives in more depth than in other media coverage, and some were persuaded to participate in the campaigns or public debates about them, enriching the local public sphere. There is indicative further evidence to suggest the decision was good for the broader community of Port Talbot (even beyond the site's readership), because the increased presence of local journalists playing a monitorial, scrutinising role suggested to politicians and local business representatives that they could no longer make decisions without being held publicly to account, in what might be termed the 'scarecrow effect' of alert local journalism.

By contrast with such macro-level creative decisions, the day-to-day job of running a community news service comprises primarily micro-creative acts of *making*. This is where most hyperlocal news producers spend most of their time. The act of making something from scratch by asserting one's ability or skill is most commonly realised in this field by producing new posts for the website and associated social media outlets. Website posts can be very simple, composed of only a few lines of information, for instance when alerting readers to an upcoming event. Or they can be very complicated, requiring research, checking, and careful composition – for instance, publishing a news story about a complex or controversial planning issue including quotations from numerous parties, alongside background research into public documents and even investigative journalistic acts such as requests for private documents under Freedom of Information regulations.

As well as creating their own media, community news producers also routinely appropriate and adapt content created by others across the numerous communications platforms on which they operate. When producers are on social media platforms such as Facebook and Twitter, the act of *adaptation* is, of course, much more routine than on the news producer's website, partly because of the ease with which users are invited to 'share' and 'retweet' content among their networks.

When working on their own websites, common acts of adaptation include rewriting press releases from local public institutions or businesses. This is mostly done in order to simplify official messages, and to ensure they are communicated in a tone the audience is more likely to read and understand (as established in the outlet's house style). The use of press releases in this way is not universal. Some sites resist recycling such institutional material on the grounds of a strict approach to editorial independence. Others see it as unproblematic and a sensible way of sharing information, especially in relation to non-contentious local issues or events.

Another common act of aggregation found on such news sites involves using plugins to channel content from social media platforms, or other providers of local or regional news, such as newspapers or the BBC, based on keywords specific to one's location. So, for instance, the homepage of the North Wales hyperlocal Wrexham.com prominently displays the most recent tweets about the town, repurposing them as local news on this thriving, commercial hyperlocal outlet. The republished tweets get a new audience, and the editors ensure that their site remains regularly updated, even when longer posts are not being produced. Another related example comes from the Lichfieldlive.co.uk website, which (in common with many others) includes a plugin detailing recent requests for the local district council to improve amenities using My Society's FixMyStreet.com service.

Some hyperlocal journalists engage in much more time and labour intensive acts of creative adaptation. For example, it is becoming more common for critical and investigative community journalists to produce data journalism, which may require the transformation of dry tables full of figures into engaging visualisations. Some have taken figures from company or local government reports and used digital mapping services such as Open Street Map to lend new significance to the data, or to make them more accessible. An example of such adaptive UK hyperlocal data journalism can be found in the context of the harsh snowy weather Britain experienced in 2010. BournvilleVillage.com's mash up of online mapping software and inaccessible council data allowed residents to see clearly which streets would be treated with rock salt, and in what order, during a heavy snowfall (Figure 5.3).

The final category of creative act proposed by Sanders and Stappers (2008) relates to *doing* or *getting things done*. The acts of community news production best understood in this category relate to routine maintenance jobs such as upgrading software, keeping plugins up to date, managing databases of contacts and archiving site content. It should be noted, however, that we found a common tendency among hyperlocal news producers to neglect larger, overarching, tasks categorised as 'creating', along with the more routine jobs described here as 'doing'. Community news producers tend to be short of time and other resources, and so to prioritise the more immediately gratifying creative acts associated with producing or adapting content rather than devoting time to rethinking the philosophy of their services, redesigning the architecture of sites, or dealing with routine maintenance and technical issues (a more detailed discussion of

Figure 5.3: A screenshot of Bournville Village's website: online mapping software shows gritting routes in a time of heavy snow

hyperlocal time and resource poverty can be found in Williams et al, 2014).

Cultural and resource spaces

Similar practices, behaviours, patterns and examples can be observed in the apparently very different setting of South Blessed, a studio and web-based platform for music, video and news based in Bristol. Here we were able to see much evidence of practices categorised as *creating*, both new production structures and creative outputs. At an organisational level, this was the visioning and creation of an informal network of creative industry workers, such as filmmakers, rappers and graffiti artists. We describe them as dreamers, triers and doers, as they are driven by an energy for self-actualisation that enables them to take creative risks and try out idea after idea, continually urging each other collectively and independently to manifest further ideas.

One example of this was the creation of *The Shauna and Joe Show* on the South Blessed YouTube channel. Named after two South Blessed network members, the weekly programme addressed topical issues, such as, 'Why Are Young Parents Often Perceived as Bad Ones?' and 'Is Violence Amongst Youths in the Community Linked to Poor Parenting?'. These 20-minute programmes thus grappled with single issues in a manner rare in mainstream news media (Ananny, 2014: 362). The editorial challenge of *The Shauna and Joe Show*, and the element that made it so compelling, was that in each show, after about seven minutes of recorded clips, the show relied on Shauna and Joe in the studio teasing out the issue between themselves, relying on their own debating skills and insight to establish shared positions in an unedited studio discussion. Although it did not generate a large number of views, South Blessed used this test-bed experience to develop further factual packages for its channel.

Another major output of the Creative Citizen project's collaboration with South Blessed was the writing, illustration and production of a graphic novel, *Indigo Babies*. This is an example of a 'creating' output that aimed to produce a form of cultural expression new for the creator. Prior to this piece of work, Vince Baidoo, the founder of South Blessed, had been predominantly a filmmaker, but he took the opportunity of a new medium, personally scripting and overseeing the production of the book. *Indigo Babies* was based upon a locally set story about young people with extraordinary powers in relation to technology. Illustrations were created by Silent Hobo, a well-known graffiti writer, whose work Baidoo admired (more detail on the making of *Indigo Babies* can be found in Chapter 4). In this piece of work, we see a clear example of creativity, embedded in a robust physical and virtual network, emerging as a socially engaged platform for creative citizenship.

Creative acts are also related to *making*. South Blessed became known in the local hip-hop scene and further afield for their short freestyle rap films called *That Time* (Figure 5.4). Shot against a simple white background in the South Blessed studio, the films showcased the raw talent of artists by foregrounding their vocal skills in a single-shot clip without visual edits, counter-culturally to the distractions of mainstream music video. The message of *That Time* videos was very much the same as that of *The Shauna and Joe Show* – that citizens need only rely on their own talents on a self-built platform to provide meaning and entertainment. Use of a plain white background in unedited shots became symbolic of the uncompromising and confident challenge to the viewer, to 'accept me just as I am' (Macconville, 2007: 8).

Figure 5.4: The creative act of making is evident in the South Blessed YouTube channel and the 'That Time' music videos made by Vince Baidoo

A highly visible example of *adaptation* is in the South Blessed logo, which takes the form of the Union flag cast in a heart shape made up of the Jamaican national colours of black, green and yellow, rather than imperial red, white and blue. The name 'South Blessed' itself is an adaptation of 'South West', the region where the network is based (these examples are explored in detail in Chapter 9). Another aspect of South Blessed adaptation involved experimenting with traditional television formats in an online context. One such experiment was live streaming a series of studio discussions, hosted by a single presenter called Cyrus the Virus, for *The Cyrus Show*, utilising new live-streaming technology. Like *The Shauna and Joe Show*, Cyrus explored topical issues, but rather than taking a single issue, Cyrus would race through stories with a stream of consciousness discussion of related ideas. The adaptation element arose from references to traditional broadcast television and radio, inviting callers and tweeters to the studio to contribute to a live discussion. For a small media operation with only Facebook as its marketing platform, this was an ambitious enterprise.

It paved the way for even more ambitious forms of adaptation, when South Blessed live-streamed interviews with candidates in the election in 2012 of Bristol's first mayor. Outputs from mainstream television and radio were worked in, but adapted to ask different questions. This is what a local media producer said to us about Vince Baidoo and the South Blessed channel:

> "I think there are always people who distrust the mainstream media... Vince is quite critical, as an individual, of the quality or the content of a lot of the information that is in the mainstream media. I think what he is doing is actively creating an alternative channel. Credit to him that he has taken that step of putting it out there. He is not content to just complain about it, he has actually done something proactive about it."

Doing is central to the South Blessed enterprise of self-actualisation, and Vince Baidoo is the central energy. As Vince says of himself:

> "The first company I started up was when I was 15. And that started up with me and my two friends. That was just literally us picking up a camera. We messed about with it. So whilst everyone around us was being young and having fun, we knew that running this company would be fun for us. It's something that we wanted to do."

The confidence needed for many young people to 'try and do' is often underestimated, so for an operation such as South Blessed to provide a platform is a civic contribution to those in the network who seek to build that confidence in order to reach their aspirations.

Motivations

All these creative acts are also acts of citizenship, and vice versa. In some cases, individuals and communities that took part in the Creative Citizen project felt that their rights and aspirations as citizens were the main driver of their creative actions and ambitions. In other cases, they were driven by the desire and ability to act creatively in relation to civic action. In every community, both motivations were pursued simultaneously and often indistinguishably. Similarly, diverse motivations can be observed in the cases we studied in the community-led design strand of the Creative Citizen project. For example, the

Kentish Town Neighbourhood Forum saw the policy landscape as an opportunity in which creative acts could emerge and help address local issues more effectively. The starting point was an act of citizenship in the form of participation in public meetings. The process and outcomes were slowly shaped as creative acts (for example, the creation of a platform for public consultation, and the generation of new ideas for the neighbourhood). The activist group in Wards Corner was driven primarily by political purpose and a will to transform local planning, so in contrast to the Neighbourhood Forum, which operates within an established practice, its actions are contested. But the community was again starting with a stance rooted in citizenship, (the opposition to local government plans and protection of their cultural identity) deploying creative acts as an important vehicle of their practice.

By contrast, our study of a more mature community centre in Goldsmiths, South London, revealed a case where creative thinking and creative activities were necessary for its existence. In this case, creative acts, such as imaginative healthy food creations, became an important focal point. They enabled a stronger sense of identity, with the consequence that more people were engaged in a wider range of civic activities. This type of creative activity brings with it a sense of expression, whether of celebration or of satirical mischief, as we saw in the case of The Mill (a young community centre in North London), where novel forms of creative practice using storytelling, film and performance were deployed in order to connect local people and enhance social and cultural capital.

We were struck by the closeness in motivation for creativity and civic action. This is most obvious in the practice of producing local community news, which is at once an unequivocal act of citizenship, and clearly a creative productive practice. For example, whereas in the past, active UK citizens may have attended local council meetings in order to monitor proceedings and take a role in public debate, there were limited opportunities to extend the reach of political participation beyond the confines of the council chamber except by writing letters to the local newspaper. The job of telling people about what local government was doing fell principally to professional news journalists. The affordances of social media, which allow anyone with an internet connection and a computer to be a publisher, have in this case led to a merging of the roles of active, monitorial citizen and productive, creative, local journalist. This overlap of motivation is less obvious in the context of, say, a co-working space provided by a community development trust, but even here an intervention using digital storytelling was found to galvanise the community.

Varieties of social capital

Varieties of creative citizenship also depend on the capital of the social structures within which creative acts are generated. We have argued that creative citizenship is an opportunity for both individual and socially situated acts. It occurs as a collective or connective act among people who may well be active as both producers and consumers. Creative citizenship may arise in any type of community, including communities of practice, place or interest. For instance, community planning can be seen as a form of creative citizenship for communities of place (for example, Friedmann, 1987). In other cases it arises around a shared interest, for example, music, pictures, craft/making, local news and so forth, or around shared relationships, for example, friendships, work and affinity groups such as fan networks.

The soft infrastructure of these communities, their social capital, sets the enabling conditions for creative citizenship. We can identify three types of social capital of particular relevance to creative citizenship:

- *production capital* (the relationship between producers and consumers);
- *connective and collective capital* (the relationship between individual and collective goals and action);
- *expert capital* (the relationship between experts and non-experts).

Each part of this soft infrastructure is affected by changes in mediated social structures.

Production capital

Creative citizenship arises most abundantly within communities in which there is a blurred distinction between producers and consumers. In other words, creative citizenship assumes some form of reflexivity between communities of producers and those of consumers. Individuals or communities are performing creative acts (such as 'doing', 'adapting', 'making' or 'creating') and at the same time they are among the end users of the products resulting from these acts.

The clearest example is hyperlocal news, which exists in a liminal space between the positions of producer and consumer, journalist and audience member/reader. Around half of all UK hyperlocal news producers have some form of professional journalistic training or experience, more than half describe what they do as 'local journalism' and around 40% see themselves as 'citizen journalists' (Williams et al, 2014: 11). No matter what their professional backgrounds, or how they choose to self-identify, there is no doubt that the practice of hyperlocal news troubles traditional distinctions between news producer and news audience. In the UK, journalists working for the publishers of established newspapers and news websites were the sole producers of local news. However, since the emergence of simple-to-use free blogging software, these commercial players have suffered a crisis in their advertising-driven business model and a growing number of individuals have started to encroach on their territory as DIY journalists. UK hyperlocal news is produced, broadly speaking, by individuals who belong to three social groups:

- active citizens who take advantage of new opportunities to self-publish;
- trained local journalists (who have either been made redundant from the mainstream local press or are newly graduated from journalism school) and wish to set up on their own;
- paid community/charity workers whose job involves publishing local information.

The fact that the same creative work can be done by people in these different groups is testament to a radical blurring of the boundaries that used to demarcate journalism from citizenship. There are plusses and minuses in this shift. In the old regime, professional journalists could be relatively sure of their status, rights and accountabilities, but they suffered periodic crises of trust based upon perceptions of some journalistic behaviour. In the new regime, the newer, informal, de-professionalised journalists' motivations tend to be less commercial and their working method, of necessity, more collaborative, but they often lack the kind of institutional (and economic) support enjoyed by their mainstream professional counterparts, which may have implications for their ability to act as watchdogs (see Chapter 4 for a more extended discussion).

In the context of community architecture and planning, issues of professionalisation and expertise are also prominent. The distinction between producers and consumers needs to be understood in relation to the technical complexities and the scale of planning and building processes. In the context of design and planning, citizen participation – and thus creative citizenship – is on a spectrum, depending on the level and mode of citizens' involvement with the production process (for example, Arnstein, 1969; Toker, 2007). The lower level of participation is a consultation process, where citizens have space and time to express their views and debate problems or solutions identified by experts from local authorities or private companies. Higher levels of participation and empowerment arise when citizens are part of the production process. In this case, they may explore issues and opportunities for action, shape or reframe their own problems, seek ideas and solutions to these problems and even participate in a self-build process. In that context, individuals often come and go at different phases and times, but the relationship between production and consumption needs to be considered in relation to a broader notion of community.

Moreover, as the production of space is a complex and technical endeavour, the role of professionals is usually pivotal, whether they are local (for example, local architects or planning students) or independent ones (for example, universities). The role of design/planning experts in the process creates another point in the spectrum between the professional and the user (for example, Wulz, 1986).

Connective and collective capital

The core notion of creative citizenship suggests the existence of a 'creative citizen', which we have identified as a civically motivated individual who performs creative acts. But, we have also argued that creative citizenship can be either a collective or a connective act. Let us note three variations around this tension.

In community architecture and planning, creative citizenship is typically and predominantly a 'collective' act. It is organised as community building, collaborative rationality and collective action around a common purpose or issue (for example, Innes and Booher, 2010). These communities can be quite diverse, as observed in the Kentish Town Neighbourhood Forum and the Wards Corner Community Coalition case studies. They include residents, local entrepreneurs and professionals, but also people with a special interest in certain social, political or cultural issues.

The Wards Corner Community Coalition, in particular, was an interesting case of collaborative rationality because of their self-reflective and critical thinking about democratic processes in community action. The coalition holds regular and open meetings in local business premises and all decisions are taken only through a process of consensus building. There are no assigned leaders. People take different roles and responsibilities in meetings and in subsequent actions. But the meetings are not only about decision making. In some cases they also include creative brainstorming and ideas development. Acts of creative citizenship here are collective in that they go beyond the level of consultation or group decision making. One example was the idea of creating a 3D virtual online space to visualise the community plan for the area, and to invite further community engagement (Figure 5.5). Members of the Wards Corner Community Coalition then took different creative roles in the design of the space and its subsequent dissemination (see also Chapter 9). In this context, individual creativity is a core asset. People deploy their skills and knowledge in order to create outputs, such as booklets, leaflets or digital media. The community is the starting point and individual creative acts typically emerge within this space.

In hyperlocal news, on the other hand, creative citizenship is primarily an individual and connective action. Most sites are run by people producing news on their own or in very small teams, but they also act as nodes in extended community networks that enable the further production, adaptation, and dissemination of their work. Whilst responsibility for the production of hyperlocal news rests primarily with individual producers, many community outlets also publish collaboratively produced news. The publishers of these sites do most of the work themselves, but many have formed active networks of contributors among the communities they serve. Contributors produce guest posts or regular columns on issues that interest them, such as sport, gardening or politics. Crowdsourcing initiatives are used to gather and

Figure 5.5: Brainstorming session with members of Wards Corner Community Coalition to come up with ideas for media interventions

aggregate what is seen as newsworthy or otherwise valuable material from audiences. Examples we encountered include: asking community members for audio-visual material, or social media updates relevant to local news stories; asking for old photographs and accounts of community life for posts about local history; and prompting locals to take part in cultural events such as photography competitions. Because of the ways that digital news production practices have destabilised the relationship between producers and consumers of news, community journalism outlets can be seen as performative examples of creative citizenship in action, but also as enablers of such acts of citizenship for other members of the community.

Expert capital

Inevitably, processes of creative citizenship challenge hierarchies of expertise, raising the question of how projects ensure that they have the expertise to perform effectively. To some degree, social media and other online facilities permit unprecedented access to information and many types of data, along with the potential to crowdsource expertise online. In the case of design, how is a balance struck between wider participation and the need for expertise?

In our case studies we found professional designers taking different roles at different times in the co-design process:

- experts as *developers* – translating abstract ideas into detailed plans or objects;
- experts as *facilitators* – supporting and structuring the exploration of problems and conceptual development of ideas and solutions which is usually achieved by the use of specific techniques and methods. In the Creative Citizen project the role of facilitator was performed by academic partners but in other cases professional designers or planners may take that role;
- experts as *advocates* –supporting disadvantaged groups and/or promoting cross-sector collaboration between civil society groups and the public and private sectors.

For example, a local architect, who was paid a fee, drew up alternative plans for the contested market building at Wards Corner. She worked collaboratively with the community, playing a *developmental role*, translating ideas into plans that satisfied the requirements of the local council. The group also collaborated with a graphic designer to create a logo and produce branded merchandise, which they use to raise awareness and funds to support their campaign (Figure 5.6).

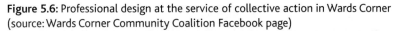

Figure 5.6: Professional design at the service of collective action in Wards Corner (source: Wards Corner Community Coalition Facebook page)

Across the case studies, designers from the research team often found themselves acting as facilitators to further creative processes in order to engage people, unearth needs and aspirations, communicate design problems and solutions and help evaluate outputs and outcomes. For example, in the Walthamstow community centre, residents were supported by research team designers and a local artist to invent, build and decorate a 'story machine' in order to help visitors create and record their own stories about the centre. The research team and the local artist had a *facilitation role*. The stories themselves are a manifestation of everyday creativity, which is constantly shared and built upon. In certain cases, the research team also played an *advocacy role* for promoting new collaborative practices.

Finally, we also found that volunteers with creative skills engage with community projects to give themselves an opportunity to gain practical experience and enhance those skills. These assets (see Chapter 8 on 'asset mapping' as a technique) increase in value as the level of expertise rises, and the awareness of the group about their salience grows. The most important insight, however, was the realisation that there is a necessary fluidity between informal and professional practice. In one direction, everyday creativity feeds into professional creativity, by either enhancing it or by transforming into creative outputs. But there is a flow in the other direction too. Within a community, the professional skills of individuals come to the service of everyday creativity. This is today's state of play: an ever-shifting set of tensions and balances through the structures of collective and connective relationships, expressed through a complex range of physical and virtual networks.

Multiple creative citizenships

This chapter has argued that creative citizenship is a useful idea. It helps us to explore and understand the variety of ways in which two seemingly disconnected categories of practices are increasingly intertwined.

From our theoretical investigation we saw that creative citizenship arises within a wide spectrum of civic acts but brings to the fore a new emphasis on the creative capacity of citizenship, foregrounding the role of *everyday* creativity. Creative acts release previously hidden potential in order to produce a critical change. Our theoretical investigation also pointed to a need to go beyond individualistic or psychological approaches to investigate the role and creative power of *connective* and *collective* acts. These are the components of 'the creative citizen unbound.'

We then explored variations in creative citizenship by focusing on three main dimensions:

- *the context:* the varieties of the context in which creative citizenship arises; including the purpose why and the spaces in which creative acts take place;
- *the practices:* the varieties of creative practices (that is doing, adapting, making and creating) that arise within different contexts;
- *the social capital:* the types of social capital that enable a variety of creative citizenship acts to take place.

We used these dimensions to look at various practices, drawing from the Creative Citizen project studies, around hyperlocal journalism, creative networks and community-led design and planning. Our investigation revealed multiple meanings and manifestations of creative citizenship. Creative citizenship is not a one-dimensional process happening in a single domain and with a specific type of social structure. Instead, it encompasses a great variety of making and producing, which in parallel induces critical reflection on political, social or cultural issues. These observations support the proposition that the 'unbound' creative citizen has the potential to make a very substantial and growing impact in many if not most areas of civic life. This involves, we are clear, a complex and constantly evolving civic system, which will be differentiated between different contexts and areas of practice. At its core, however, it invariably involves the unbinding of the everyday creative potential of the individual in a civic context.

Note

[1] Gates won the Cardiff-based Artes Mundi art prize in 2015 and expressed his convictions by sharing the proceeds of the prize with all of the shortlisted artists. His winning entry was entitled 'A complex relationship between heaven and earth' or 'When we believe'. It raised questions about non-Christian religious and cultural beliefs and the difficulties those outside these belief systems experience in interpreting their meanings.

SIX

From networks to complexity: two case studies

David Harte, Jon Dovey, Emma Agusita and Theodore Zamenopoulos

Introduction

From the noticeboard in the newsagent's window to multilayered online networks using social networking technologies, citizens access networks of support that uncover previously invisible opportunities. Such networks, online and offline, are facilitated by the use of social networking platforms but also through the everyday face-to-face interactions made possible by communities within localities. These overlapping networks are complex and dynamic and in this chapter we present two case studies where the micro-level actions of creative citizens generate impact within their communities and beyond. We consider how such actions, supported by and amplified by networks, often have wider impacts for the creative economy and for the relationship between citizens and those in power, taking us into territory illuminated by complexity theory.

In our first example we consider how a highly networked creative citizen has worked to fashion a 'milieu' to serve a community's creative needs and grow its cultural capital. We then turn to the way that citizen journalists, through a rejection of traditional journalistic practices and discourses, use networks to provide insight into everyday life, countering what Parker and Karner have described as externally-imposed 'negative reputational geographies' (2011: 309). In both cases these creative citizens enact a deft utilisation of their online and offline networks. Our intention here is to see beyond debates that tend to situate the affordances of networked technologies as the determining factor for success and instead ask how such technologies are put to use by creatives working in specific fields of cultural production. How do the networked actions of creative citizens create impact for themselves, their communities and for their practice? We begin by looking at debates about how the internet has by turns created and narrowed the opportunities for greater civic participation, before identifying useful frameworks to examine our case studies of networked creatives.

The civic potential of the internet

We might presume that in articulating a case for the importance of networks we take at face value the digitally enhanced role of technology as a transformative tool for positive change – a tool that seemingly allows those previously cut off from cultural or political participation to voice their concerns or engage in creative acts that will find global audiences. Dan Gillmor is one of those who has lauded the era of networked digital technologies, foreseeing an era of connected 'personal journalism' (2004: 1–22) with significant democratic benefits as a result of us all being 'active users of news, not mere consumers' (2004: 238). Likewise, Leah Lievrouw (2011) makes the point that the key characteristics of alternative media are 'connectivity, interactivity and community' (Lievrouw 2011: 121). danah boyd (2008) says that just as public spaces – such as the public park – play a connecting role in constituting new 'publics', so do technologies. An 'imagined community […] emerges as a result of the intersection of people, technology, and practice' (boyd, 2008: 15). Internet technologies, particularly social networking sites, have made the public into a 'networked public' (2008: 15).

Yet the notion that technology is playing a transformative role in networks has been met with some caution. The debates about its perceived value as a tool to encourage civic participation among citizens are well rehearsed, as Banaji and Buckingham (2013) remind us in their book *The Civic Web*:

> On the one hand are studies extolling the civic potential of the Internet and suggesting that it removes barriers to access, promotes participation, and creates new forms of civic community; on the other hand are studies that see it as merely confirming existing inequalities and making very little difference to people's inclination to participate in civic and political life. (2013: 9)

They go on to critique the way in which the utopian representation of the internet as a solution to democratic participation has prevailed at a time when longstanding civil liberties such as trade union membership and the right to protest in public spaces have been curtailed. Peter

Dahlgren (2001) makes the clearest of points that early positions on the internet by academics were naïve:

> A new medium is introduced, swathed in utopian rhetoric about how it will benefit society and enhance democracy. This cheery notion comes not only from those engaged in marketing it, but also from some voices within academia and other intellectual corners. (Dahlgren, 2001: 45)

Dahlgren does see the internet's potential in enhancing the public sphere but notes how its use seemed limited to those already interested in political discussion. To enrich the public sphere, he argues, participation must be expressly political in practice (for example, contributing to newsgroups, creating websites with political information from alternative viewpoints). He has reserved optimism for the internet's potential to allow 'new communicative spaces to develop – alternative public spheres – even if the paths to the centres of political decision making are far removed' (2001: 52). He later notes how early discussions about the role of the internet were framed by the feeling that 'democracy has hit upon hard times' (2005: 147) and laments that 'its development is quickly veering toward the intensified commercialisation that characterises the traditional media model' (2005: 151). Jose Van Dijck, adopting a cultural analysis perspective (2013), acknowledges that 'social media can be both intensely empowering and disturbingly exploitative', going on to suggest that 'the rhetoric of a new public sphere was (and still is to some extent) gratefully appropriated by businesses to salvage the virtues of the corporate sphere' (2013: 13). Christian Fuchs (2013) is concerned with the ways in which writings about the participatory nature of the internet fail to take into account issues of 'class, exploitation and surplus value' (2013: 215).

Against this backdrop of utopian versus dystopian discourse, it is easy to miss the point that participatory potential and corporate self-interest have been in tension in media landscapes since the invention of print. There are a number of approaches we can use to consider the role of networks and their value to the creative citizens as they seek to push the participatory needle a bit further along from the negative to the positive pole.

Milieu

In investigating the nature of networked environments in which often amateur creative practitioners engage in various forms of cultural production, the notion of milieu can offer a theoretical framework to understand the complex and situated nature of this activity. This approach draws on concepts and tools provided by Peter Webb's relational theorisation of the networked worlds of popular music (2007). Webb, whose work includes study of the development of Bristol music culture, rejects the term 'scene' in favour of 'milieu', on the grounds that the latter 'more fully illuminates the notion of a network that has a particular density in terms of connections, relevancies, typifications, commonalities and aesthetics' (2007: 30). Webb is drawn to Bourdieu's field theory (1992, 1993) as it allows him to drill down into the 'the small-scale production sub-field(s)' (2007: 34) that constitute the popular music scenes he seeks to study. Such fields have 'a high level of autonomy from the field of power and a high level of symbolic capital' (2007: 34). In essence, he can look up from the nuances of the Bristol 'trip hop' scene and make sense of its participants' relationship with global 'networks of information', examining the influence such networks exert (2007: 37).

Researchers in journalism studies (Couldry, 2003; Benson, 2004; 2006; Schulz, 2007; Postill, 2008; Willig, 2013) make use of field theory to examine the 'invisible structures of power and recognition' (Willig, 2013: 384) that shape fields of news production. Rodney Benson (2006) claims that field theory offers a 'new unit of analysis for media studies: between the individual news organisation and society as a whole, the "mezzo-level" interorganisational and professional environment of the field/institution' (2006: 199). These scholars see the ideas of Bourdieu as a route to 'looking up' and revealing the nefarious role of capital and power, but Simon Cottle (2007) is concerned that the researcher has enough to do in looking down and making sense of the shifting practices in increasingly complex news environments. Karin Wahl-Jorgensen agrees and claims there has been too much 'studying up' or engaging in 'elite research' (2009: 27) in traditional newsroom ethnographies. What's needed is a shift away from this 'newsroom-centricity' (2009: 22) with its methodological presumption that the practice of doing journalism only takes place in specific spaces (such as newsrooms), which are then bound by cultures, power relations and tacit rules. These sites of research sit in contrast to other spaces (such as the home) whose practices, culture and politics are therefore at risk of marginalisation.

Micro, meso, macro

Returning to Webb (2007), there is value in seeing our creative citizens' networked activities through the lens of the three levels of abstraction, which he argues enable a study of the complex factors associated with cultural production in specific localities (see also Dopfer et al, 2004 for a formal economic description of 'micro-meso-macro'). The first, at the *micro-level* of the community, deals with the social practices of individuals and their interactions with others in social spaces. It is interested in the particular histories, stocks of knowledge and sets of dispositions that are situated in our 'life worlds', a term he borrows from Erving Goffman (1971), defined as the social spaces in which we live and grow. The second, at the *meso-level*, locates these groupings within the relevant fields of cultural production that have their own evolving rules, regulations and habits. Here, interest is focused upon the impacts and influence of these groupings. The third looks more widely at a *macro-level*, at dialectical connections between individuals in social groupings and other milieux, such as local, national and global cultures, along with political and economic settings. Webb notes that new technologies increase linkages to information and communications, thereby offering an extended milieu:

> The extended milieu is one that is historically and technologically expanding. The extended nature of milieu is heightened in a period of technological development that links us to ever-increasing nodes of information that open our eyes and ears to understandings of a huge variety of milieux and new information about lifestyles, histories, technology, and culture. (Webb, 2007: 33)

Like Webb, Roberta Comunian (2011) wants us to look at the detail of the interactions in creative places in order to understand how they shape forces at the meso- and macro-levels. She makes the case that a 'creative city' is a 'complex adaptive system' (2011: 1158) and that it is the 'micro-level in the creation of networks between creative and cultural practitioners' (2011: 1170) that requires attention from both researchers and creative city policy makers. Such networks are organic yet almost intangible once one goes looking for them. She makes the case that looking to complexity theory offers a route to understand their behaviours:

> The value of Complexity Theory lies in the possibility of understanding the micro dynamics of the system. This allows us to identify the emergence of structures and organisational forms that support and facilitate the connectivity and growth of the system. (2011: 1163)

Steven Manson (2010) argues that we should not dismiss the potentially distant 'butterfly effect' of small variations at the micro level in complex systems. Their impact can indeed be significant and they mark the point where the micro can sometimes impact above and beyond the meso: 'local action may directly affect those at a larger scale without moving through intermediary scales' (2007: 408).

In both of the cases discussed in this chapter, we will shed light on the actions of a small number of very important connectors, along with the larger number of contributors and connectors that also play vital roles in the connected ecology of the creative citizen, revealing the rich complexity of their networked actions. Our intention is therefore to see value in the actions of our creative citizens at the micro-level of their immediate cultural and social environment, drawing attention to their participatory, networked media practices, so illuminating the complex nature of their cultural and social milieu.

Case study – South Blessed

First, we examine an informal creative network in Bristol. South Blessed, as noted elsewhere in this volume, showcases a diversity of young, creative talent from South West England in music, fashion, poetry, skateboarding, street art, graffiti, film, comics, media activism and journalism. At the time of the research, South Blessed had a small shop front studio in the heart of Bristol's St Pauls district but its main presence and identity was constructed around a video website. Southblessed.co.uk featured over 3,000 videos from different creators across the south west of England, and its YouTube channel had over 1,000 subscribers. Specialising in forms of visual media, South Blessed produced its own content, featured the content of others and offered informal studio-based training and collaborative production opportunities to young people. The material was mainly music-led, primarily hip-hop, though many different musical and cultural genres were represented. The site also included rudimentary documentary features, reportage and live streaming around local current affairs issues. South Blessed's wider functioning was supported through social media networks – mainly its Facebook page with approximately 386 members (at the time of writing, though many of its affiliates connect through its founder's own page, branded as South Blessed, with a friends network of several thousand) and its YouTube Channel (established in 2011).

South Blessed was founded in 2009 by Vince Baidoo, the most important 'node' in the network, when he was aged 21. Echoing the multilayered nature of Webb's (2007) approach, research began with a series of interviews with people from its core to its periphery. First with Vince, then six of his creative peers, people in the network he relied on, learnt from and worked with on a daily basis. They were primarily young people in their early 20s involved in a range of media production activities. These conversations aimed to establish the nature of their participation, along with relevant biographical information. Then, six outliers of the network were interviewed: the landlord, a community police officer, a local TV reporter, a community media practitioner and Vince's mum. These discussions sought to understand the nature of people's engagement with the network and to identify its wider impacts and influences. Other methods included content analysis, asset mapping (detailed in Chapter 8) of the resources used by the network and a study of Vince's relationship with his locality through walking and discussion. Finally, a co-creation project enabled Vince to engage in new creative collaborations to produce a print and digital comic book (graphic novel) based on a semi-biographical Bristol story of young creative citizens. Using these multilevel data and wider literature, the networked world of South Blessed has been examined in order to plot its contours and the factors that shape it. The following descriptions offer insight into its core milieu, the field in which it operates and ways in which it connects more broadly.

Milieu cultures

By examining the biographical narratives of Vince Baidoo, his key collaborators and other young creative producers and artists who engage in the South Blessed network, commonalities emerge in terms of their histories, viewpoints, knowledge and practices. These connect with place-based histories and scenes, which indicate particular relevancies and typifications of milieu culture.

Dispositional features of individuals operating in the milieu culture start with a shared sense of aspiration to maximise the potential of their creative talents, moving from informal towards more professionalised arenas of cultural production:

"The idea of South Blessed is that it exhorts people who have got talent within music and media." (Musical artist and media producer)

"It's hopeful for other people... They do want it to have a slightly legitimate stamp; they're not just a guy rapping for the sake of it ... there's an air of professionalism to it." (Poet and performer)

These talents tend to surface and grow in situations where family, friends, and communities provide sources of inspiration and support for emerging skills and interests:

"I was raised in the church so I still go to church. Just being in church is inspiring for me, especially on the music side. In my church there's quite a vibrant thing. There's a full band and loads of singers. Every time you're in church it's just, like, worshipping as well as a concert sort of thing." (Musical artist)

"I think my mum has a lot of respect for me so she respects if I want to do something ... my mum has been influential in forming my principles definitely." (Musical artist and media producer)

Second, we observed a socially enterprising disposition that combines community values and entrepreneurial ambitions. This is achieved through a willingness to operate in mutually beneficial ways such as freely creating, spreading and sharing content, skills, knowledge, connections and resources between peers. This occurs through face-to-face and online networking activity. It enables subjects and their peers to gain feedback, recognition and access to new opportunities through trusted relationships in order to develop their creative talents and work towards their aspirations and dreams on their own terms through a self-propelled process of 'becoming'. Crucially, this mutualism is interwoven with the actualisation of desires for individual and collective independence:

"We all benefit each other really. It's not 'oh, you help me out' and then 'goodbye'. Most things that we come to each other with benefit both parties, and because we work

together we all know what we're working with really."
(Media producer)

Vince himself is recognised as a facilitator and harbinger of alternative
media, creating a platform and means to represent voices and skills of
young people from the bottom up. This 'service' is seen to fill a gap
created by formal and professional media producers:

> "He's just always been a facilitator for creative people ...
> that person who gets them together." (Poet and performer)

> "I think he has got a strong commitment to democratic
> media, to creating opportunities for people to share
> information and a free speech ethic. I think he is
> demonstrating his commitment to it by what he is doing."
> (Community media practitioner)

Finally, there is a propensity for, and openness to developing knowledge
and skills through forms of self-directed and peer-to-peer informal
learning. These are augmented through online platforms, tools and
networks:

> "I learned it myself off the internet, watching YouTube and
> it all came from me. Obviously people around me know
> things, I learn from them." (Media producer).

> "When I first got a computer in my house, I used to
> download the most obscure-sounding documentaries
> possible. That's where a lot of the things that now I can
> say that I've researched for ten years, it's on that basis. I
> downloaded a documentary when I was 14 or 15 and then
> forever cross-referenced that information against what was
> being taught in school or then later on what other people
> were learning in universities." (Vince Baidoo)

Many of the values, principles, and framings for ways of knowing,
behaving, thinking and creating, find root in their geographic locale
of Bristol. According to a place-making and marketing strategy,
Bristol's 'personality' encompasses 'the spirit of innovation, creativity
and unorthodoxy. This refers on the one hand to an independence of
thought, a tendency to challenge convention and willingness to accept
a diversity of lifestyles, cultures and opinions' (Yellow Railroad, 2009:

8). Whilst this may sound contrived, there is no doubt that provincial Bristol's vibrant countercultural scene has long been in evidence, most prominently through music and graffiti. As Webb observed, the Bristol music milieu is 'infected with DIY ethics and independent bloody-mindedness' (2007: 4), which yields a culturally productive force:

> "Bristol is a very anti-establishment city. People like to feel this feeling of independence and that they determine their own existence and they're not caught up in the rat race." (Poet and performer)

The ley lines of the city, England's sixth most populous and one of the largest regional centres of culture, education and employment, reflect social reactions to an ambivalent history of transatlantic slavery, migration, trade, industrialisation and regeneration (Clement, 2012). The inner city area of St Pauls, the location for the original South Blessed studio, has a turbulent history of growth, migration, neglect, riot and regeneration (Burton, 2010). Culturally and ethnically, the area is most associated with the postwar African-Caribbean community. Its iconic St Pauls street carnival, started by the community in 1968, still runs annually involving local, national and international artists; it has attracted audiences in excess of 100,000 people.[1]

Using our asset mapping research approach, Bristol emerged as key to the vision of South Blessed, underlining the importance of place in creativity. The St Pauls studio location was seen as offering a central portal to connect people from across the city, geographically, socially, culturally and creatively. Its hybrid logo combines the British and Jamaican flag in a heart shape symbolising unity, representing the cultural antecedents and sentiments of many of those it attracts. Crucially, the branding and recognition of its principles and the strong local connections of South Blessed, and Vince Baidoo himself, have come to be seen as a networked resource of authentic and credible local knowledge with local up-to-date quality material reflecting the scene:

> "I regularly look at South Blessed. Obviously, I'm from Bristol so I like to see what everyone else is doing, so I'm up to scratch, up to the mark." (Media producer)

> "If you want to know the real Bristol ... what the people of Bristol are about, the youth of Bristol, everything of Bristol really, I would say go to South Blessed." (Media producer)

"A year ago when there were some riots in Bristol, Vince was out on the street getting footage. Other people were filming and bringing content to him. I think, certainly, local news was coming to him to get examples, to get footage of the events that happened." (Community media practitioner)

"He can provide a really valuable perspective, or a world-view, that to me is really, really important." (Bristol police community liaison officer)

Field

South Blessed operates in a number of fields of production. These include the grass roots creative scene in Bristol, participatory and youth media, alternative and community media, and the informal creative economy (itself a sub-field of the creative economy). These terms are characterised by intersecting values, philosophies and traditions, creating expectations which shape what people do and how. These produce a particular blend of discourses and habitual practices that characterise 'the field'. Culturally, key features include a do-it-yourself ethic and mode of making, where informal cultural producers orbit in and around communities of shared interest and practice. These create feathered edges where people may interact with more formal networks, involving cultural institutions or key players in the creative industries.

Politically, they are characterised by democratic ideals of access, inclusion and transparency where underrepresented voices find a foothold and means of expression, mediated by localised networks. However, the socialist politics of more traditional community media approaches are challenged by aspirations to make money, recognising that media access and public voice alone are no longer enough – that there are limitations and frustrations posed by working in the provincial milieu. Therefore, a shift towards social enterprise supports an aspiration to excel and positively exploit creative talent whilst generating civic benefits:

"Bristol does have a culture of triers, there are a lot of people trying but because there is a lack of accessibility so it is in turn just filled with triers... That feeds the notion of South Blessed, which is to exploit people who want to manifest, exploit triers. It gives them that accessible thing in inverted commas. It is an equivalent of whatever they are trying for." (Musical artist and media producer)

"It's just trying to get Bristol on the map and raise it up to the level of other cities." (Musical artist)

Economically, the field is marked by its enterprising spirit and its precariousness, a trait reflective of the wider creative economy (Gill and Pratt, 2008; Potts, 2011). A common paucity of income and material resource is juxtaposed with a rich seam of cultural capital that is generated by more free-flowing exchanges and interactions between people. For example, initial asset mapping of South Blessed had shown a lack of income and assets. However the affordances of new digital tools and platforms are opening up new opportunities with the potential to develop forms of social enterprise:

"I want a business in – I get off on the prospect of providing support and guidance for people who have got a talent but they don't necessarily know where and how to pursue it ... this is why I like the prospect and this is what I am doing at the moment. Building a website that facilitates the kind of pursuing of a talent or providing guidance ... because the one thing that all young people and people are familiar with this age – the one thing that is accessible to them is the internet." (Musical artist and media producer).

Extended milieux

There are other milieux that have a dialectical relationship with the South Blessed milieu, influencing and extending the way it operates in its field of practice and conversely impacting on those connected with it. Although its physical home is in Bristol, South Blessed digitally connects with others regionally, nationally and internationally, seeking out and interacting with a diverse range of potential affiliates, information and assets. Indeed we might argue that South Blessed acts both locally and globally at the same time. The participation of South Blessed in the research project has brought it into contact with an academic milieu, revealing ways in which the research team's networks intertwine with those of South Blessed.

One of the most salient aspects of that relationship was the action research project, which supported the creation of the graphic novel *Indigo Babies* (the co-creation of which is more fully described in Chapter 7), as a means to monetise its creativity, pursuing a business model in order to boost its long-term sustainability. Through the process of creating and publishing the book, Vince reoriented his practice to become a producer of 'transmedia', creating a new enterprise, Crown Root, to publish the outputs. This reconfiguration draws on his existing knowledge and connections whilst carving out new contours such as *anime* illustration, making new connections with graphic artists and producers locally, nationally and globally. Thus, he was able to plan expansion beyond the novel to create a transmedia cross-platform Indigo Babies storyworld and aspires to become a trailblazer in the production of his newfound genre:

> "The drive for the researchers to quantify what it is they were seeing and the use of the term transmedia has made me realise I've been a transmedia producer and storyteller since the age of four and that is one of the most profound insights of the project." (Vince Baidoo)

As Webb (2007) observes, the dynamics of such interactions can influence and transform the ways people operate in cultural scenes, affecting how they interpret and shape rules, regulations and habits in their fields of practice. However, it should be noted that new collaborations and connections also involve conflict and struggle as well as co-operation and consent. Commercialising creativity raises the stakes over issues such as ownership (for example, copyright and other intellectual property), which can stir up tensions with approaches reflecting traditional community values.

Networked civic participation

The South Blessed case study identified a number of civic benefits, starting with the motivations of individuals in the milieu that are then extended through the social grouping of the network. These processes have worked to boost engagement and social productivity, increase informal and formal learning opportunities, create training and employment in the creative economy and provide alternative information sources such as news for local media. In this kind of milieu culture, new technologies are being used to facilitate creative production, circulation of information and cultural products and discussion. These social circuits have the potential to fuel aspiration and provide affirmation, but importantly they can also work to challenge and change existing ideas and practices within networks.

New forms of media are also supporting new kinds of pedagogy that blend auto-didacticism, peer-to-peer and collaborative learning techniques through online educational sources and information; these things all help nurture critical dispositions through participatory culture. It has been argued that new technical resources and economic structures are making it easier to spread media texts and other content that appeal to communities of interest, notably via social media platforms and networks (Jenkins et al, 2013). Furthermore, in defence of more meaningful and democratic public participation, it is claimed that 'the spreading of media texts helps us articulate who we are, bolster our personal and professional relationships, strengthen our relationships with one another, and build community and awareness around the subjects we care about' (Jenkins et al, 2013: 304).

It has also been suggested, albeit in more qualified terms, that digital networks and platforms yield disruptive potential, offering a space where political positions might be played out (Loader and Mercea, 2011). Thus, use of the internet can help to create the conditions for democratic engagement, by facilitating new civic cultures and forms of civic expression (Dahlgren, 2004) across the continuum of citizenship. More pertinently for the case of South Blessed, an analysis of the civic and political significance of online participatory youth cultures suggests that youth engagement in non-political but interest-driven participatory cultures can 'serve as a gateway to participation in important aspects of civic and, at times, political life, including volunteering, community problem-solving, protest activities and political voice' (Kahne et al, 2011: 19–20).

Webb's relational framework helps explain the multilayered complexity of the networks and diverse milieu culture of South Blessed, by drawing close attention to its identity, social groupings, field of cultural production and wider areas of influence. Whilst the internet and the participatory media cultures it supports play an important role in facilitating the creative and communicative actions and potential of South Blessed, offline relationships and networks, linked to the physical place and space in Bristol, remain pivotal. Thus, whilst engaging young people's interests and passions can pave the way for social participation, this should be seen as a synchronous process that occurs both online and offline (Agusita, 2013).

Case study – Hyperlocal news

In our second case study we look at the network that has developed around one hyperlocal news media operation in south Birmingham. Networks that underpin the operational success of hyperlocal media – in this case and in the many other hyperlocal media operations we have researched – consist of contacts in public or private institutions that might provide news content along with the networks of citizens who act either as recipients of information or combine their role as audience with that of contributor. Such networks prove a rich resource for the hyperlocal producer and given the tendency to rely heavily on personal relationships on social media networks, they can even be more intricate and rich in nodes than that experienced by professional local journalists working their patch. These are networks that perhaps come into being as a consequence of technological changes which make 'everyone a journalist' (Hartley, 2009: 154, quoting Hargreaves). Such networks could be seen to form what Nick Couldry has called 'new networks of trust' (Couldry, 2004) – a recognition that there are 'new contexts of public communication and trust' (2004: 26), contexts that may redefine practices of both consumption and citizenship. We share Couldry's object of study in 'the productive and distributional potential of the internet' (2004: 26). His argument that we might find what he describes as the 'dispersed citizen' by examining 'websites or portals that collect information for consumption and civic activism on a relatively local scale' (2004: 25) rings true in this examination of a specific network in one UK city.

The other important network to consider in this context is that of similar operations. At the time of our study, the UK had over 600 hyperlocal websites (see analysis in Harte, 2013), covering small geographic areas from rural villages to urban housing estates with the majority run by non-professional journalists (Williams et al, 2014). The effect of this network, as loosely as it connects hyperlocals to each other, is significant. Lots of people separately undertaking roughly the same kind of practice inevitably gets noticed, whether or not there's a formally constituted network-level organisation playing an advocacy role. In the case of hyperlocal media, it gets noticed by those who agonise over the slow death of the ideal 'public sphere' (Habermas, 1989). Given the newspaper industry's worldwide trend towards closure and retrenchment of local and regional titles it is perhaps understandable that policy makers (Ofcom, 2009) and commentators (Greenslade, 2007) have scrutinised the role that the internet may play in supporting new forms of local news. In hyperlocal they find a new player in local media ecosystems offering a rich seam of community-orientated journalism that seems untarnished by the ailing reputation of the press. One that in some examples seems to create genuine value from the networked way in which it goes about its business of gathering and distributing information. Borrowing from Yochai Benkler (2003), we might think of the collective activity of hyperlocal as playing a role in a localised component of the 'networked public sphere'. For Benkler the networked public sphere is one where 'public inquiry, debate, and collective action … is fundamentally different from the structure of public inquiry and debate in the mass-media-dominated public sphere of the twentieth century' (2006: 414).

Participatory, networked journalism

This emerging narrative around hyperlocal news contains echoes of the technological optimism that we noted earlier as scholars writing about the emerging importance of the internet to journalism in the 1990s and early 2000s displayed a 'strong faith in the democratic potential of digital technologies' (Borger et al, 2012: 125). Borger et al offer a critique of the normative values of journalism studies, and in particular its positioning of 'public journalism' – now recognised as a short-lived phase of journalism practice in the mid 1990s (many examples in Rosen, 1999), that saw a concerted attempt by some newspapers in the USA actively to 'nurture the conversation that healthy public life requires'. (Merritt, 2009: 21). Scholarly positions on public journalism played a key role in shaping a utopian technological discourse around participatory journalism, offering 'a renewed chance to realise public journalism's goals … In the theoretical ideal underlying participatory journalism, the audience is explicitly approached as citizenry' (Borger et al, 2012: 126).

For Irene Costera Meijer (2012), the problem with mainstream journalism is that it focuses too much on problematic aspects of citizenry. Her detailed content and audience analysis showed the adverse effects on people of living in suburbs of Utrecht that were subject to press coverage focusing on the 'undesirable' aspects of living in these areas. What's needed, she argues, is a more participatory approach that eschews traditional journalistic approaches. She sees storytelling as a way for 'problem neighbourhoods' to 'ease the pain caused by mainstream news' (Costera Meijer, 2012: 14). In Utrecht the development of a community media project aimed at giving greater voice to residents resulted in a different set of stories emerging: 'everyday stories about everyday life by ordinary people living or working in the neighbourhoods' (Costera Meijer, 2012: 25). The intention was not to exclude the more problematic nature of these environments but to ensure that the 'ordinary' was also covered: 'residents valued items that visualised everyday personal, social and geographical landmarks' (2012: 22). John Postill's study of the 'vibrant internet scene' (2008: 422) in a suburb of Kuala Lumpur, Malaysia, has likewise noted the value of this focus on the everyday. He argues that this represents a kind 'banal activism' which academics too often ignore at the expense of a focus on '"serious" cyberactivism of the intelligentsia' (Postill, 2008: 420). Rather, the focus should be on the ways in which 'people, technologies and other cultural artefacts are co-producing new forms of residential sociality in unpredictable ways' (2008: 426).

Hyperlocal news in South Birmingham

It is to a 'banal' example of networked, local journalism that we now turn. Sas and Marty Taylor run a hyperlocal media operation in South Birmingham called B31 Voices (b31.org.uk). They gather and redistribute news and information for a series of suburbs inhabited mainly by working-class people. Their patch is dominated by the former Longbridge motor works, a vast former factory space employing 22,000 workers in its heyday and since its closure in 2005, the subject of extensive regeneration. We should not underestimate the role that such a factory played in maintaining social connections with most local people having a link of some description to the former Longbridge works.

The Taylors moved to Longbridge in 2003 and started blogging in 2010 out of concerns about the representation of their estate. It was not long before their blog became something else:

> "The area has got quite a bad reputation and we wanted to learn more about it really. So we just started with a little blog that covered the estate that we live on and it just snowballed from there really. I think as it grew and people started interacting with it more, peoples' expectations of it then changed so we started to deliver more to them… So the motivation was a little hobby about the small area we live in, and it's kind of developed into a feeling that you have to deliver a service to people now." (Sas Taylor)

In our study of this particular hyperlocal news operation we wanted to understand the online and offline production cultures and networks of B31 Voices. Because Sas and Marty operate from home, we had the opportunity to examine the role played by the everyday spaces in the production of content. The project drew on research methods by Pink (2012) and Gillárová et al (2014) in using visual ethnography to reveal the less visible dimensions of everyday life. Gillárová et al (2014) asked journalists to take photographs of the spaces in which they worked, which then formed the basis of photo-based interviews.

Their method allowed participants to reveal 'feelings' about work and working conditions and in particular the role played by technology. Whilst Gillárová's research revealed the ways in which professional journalists often escape to domestic spaces, the results for B31 Voices showed how they are bound by the same.

The photographs produced by Sas Taylor revealed the role of technology in the domestic setting as she chose to take her mobile devices on a tour of the places in which they are put to use in the course of updating B31 Voices' various online outputs. The results were images of the phone and tablet computer in the bedroom, the bathroom, the car and the living room (see Figure 6.1). Through this process the research immediately reveals how the 'habitus' of hyperlocal, whilst free from the hierarchies of traditional newsrooms and their working practices, might instead be subject to other, domestic, rules and social structures. Although the work of B31 Voices is informed by the textual norms of journalism (seen in the standard journalistic construction of stories on its website) the production culture is certainly very different. As was revealed in a subsequent interview, hyperlocal news-making practices for B31 Voices are bound up in the domestic lives of the publishers, lacking any resemblance to standardised industrial news-making structures of the type familiar in the routines of the 20th century news industry.

Whilst Sas and Marty rely on a small network of occasional writers to help them publish stories, the vast majority of the work they publish on their website is their own. Keeping this operation afloat seems to invade every aspect of their daily lives. As Marty says, "it's constant. We talk about B31, it's like 24/7 pretty much". Keeping up with the social media output takes up most of the time and it isn't unusual for the Taylors to find themselves waking in the middle of the night to make contributions to Facebook or Twitter: "We might have a missing

Figure 6.1: Photographs of domestic spaces taken by Sas Taylor to reflect where B31 Voices content is created and published

person or a missing pet that's touched everyone, and I will check in the middle of the night to see if there's any news," says Sas. Marty adds, "So when we're talking about a dog, it can be about four o'clock in the morning, we might wake up, has that dog been found? Yes, it's ridiculous, it really is, it's wrong."

Although Birmingham has well-established mainstream media in the guise of a daily newspaper (the *Birmingham Mail*) its decline in sales from 160,000 in the 1990s to nearer 40,000 in 2014 could be seen to have laid the foundations for B31 Voices' success. Yet Sas and Marty reject any comparison between their endeavour and mainstream journalism: "it's about bringing a community together and being a community. If you've got newspapers, they're just about money, that's all they're there for" (Marty Taylor). Instead of seeing their role as contributing to a mainstream local news culture, Sas and Marty instead cite Birmingham's thriving culture of place-based blogging as a key influence in getting them started. Other suburbs in the city have similar news blogs and there are citywide blogs covering politics, arts, environment and sport – indeed any topic you might expect the local press to cover. This network has veered in and out of formal organisation with occasional 'Birmingham blogger' meetings and with many, including Sas and Marty, participating in regular 'social media surgeries' (see Figure 6.2) to support charities and community groups wishing to increase their media impact. Such surgeries and the wider city blogging culture feel distinctly part of a more civic-orientated internet culture than a news one.

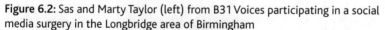

Figure 6.2: Sas and Marty Taylor (left) from B31 Voices participating in a social media surgery in the Longbridge area of Birmingham

Networked publics

The attention that comes with running a hyperlocal operation and being the centre of a network can be burdensome: "I'll be walking along the supermarket and I'll hear people saying, oh did you see about that on B31 Voices. And I'm like, oh that's us. You're aware that there are a lot of readers and they are relying on it" (Sas Taylor). The prospect of stopping always looms large but Sas Taylor sums up how many creative citizens feel when she says, "I'd feel bad if I gave up, I'd feel guilty... We're always interested in what people want to know about, but I think now it's got to a point where it has snowballed out of control in a way and people actually rely on it now."

So what does 'snowballing out of control' look like for B31 Voices? If we examine one month's worth of their output and engagement (Figure 6.3), we get a sense of the scale of an operation that is run from a modest house, on a newish estate, by a couple with children and much else to contend with in their lives.

Figure 6.3: B31 Voices' engagement across platforms during March 2014

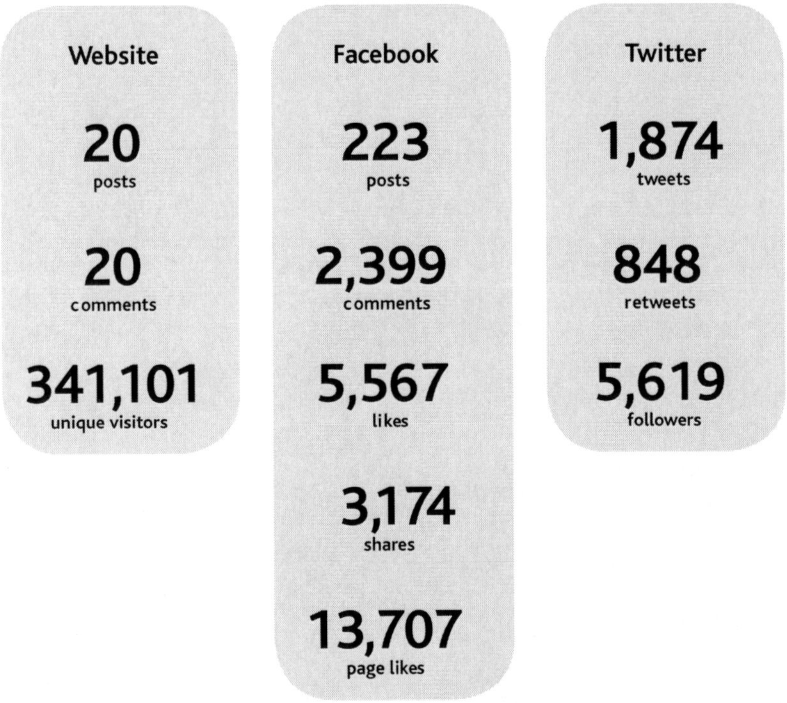

Website	Facebook	Twitter
20 posts	**223** posts	**1,874** tweets
20 comments	**2,399** comments	**848** retweets
341,101 unique visitors	**5,567** likes	**5,619** followers
	3,174 shares	
	13,707 page likes	

The statistics alone don't give a full view of the networked way in which B31 Voices operates. Whilst visitor traffic is high on the website, interaction is modest. Yet on Twitter and Facebook it explodes into a continuous noisy conversation about everyday living. It is here that the 'networked public' (boyd, 2008) is revealed in full flow with high levels of public participation, particularly on Facebook. Everything gets covered and brings people together online, from the trivial (a lost dog story gets 132 comments alone) to the more serious concerns of local governance and crime. Interactions are rich in everyday detail. A car prang has a narrative arc, as witnesses and participants emerge to offer their version of events. Indeed, it often seems that Sas and Marty themselves are redundant, given how 'the people formerly known as the audience' (Rosen, 2006) take control of their online space, contributing opinions, vivid detail and eyewitness accounts. And there are lots of people engaging: 1,144 people left comments on the B31 Facebook page during March 2014 but over 60% only left one comment, suggesting there's a long tail to online participation.

At points, Sas and Marty intervene to make sense of the networked conversation. So during the relative crisis of a heavy snowfall they use the same hashtag – #B31Snowwatch – across all their platforms, aggregating the networked impact of the B31 community. Updates from citizens on the ground paint a vivid picture of a suburb slowly grinding to a halt as buses stop running, schoolchildren are sent home and supermarket shelves empty as a result of panic buying. For Sas Taylor #B31Snowwatch was evidence of the value of their service:

> "The B31 snowwatch as well, I think was a big thing that sort of proved how much people relied on it and were interacting with it as well. So then you think, if B31 Voices hadn't done that, what would have happened. They'd have survived obviously, it wasn't like a major snowfall, but they really got a lot of benefit from it and so then you feel that you've got to keep that up, you've got to keep giving them that." (Sas Taylor)

The #B31Positive hashtag is a similar attempt to manage content but this time to promote good news stories and encourage good deeds in the community rather than simply gather news. It's not uncommon to see hyperlocals striving to represent their communities in a more positive, less controversial or sensational light, compared with mainstream commercial local media. The author of another Birmingham blog, 'Digbeth Is Good' is motivated by 'improving perceptions of Digbeth', a suburb of which they are 'very proud' and determined to act as a 'passionate advocate'.

Whilst there is plenty of evidence on B31's Facebook page of citizen engagement in important issues such as politics and crime, it is the banal that gets most attention. Any mention of pets – lost or found – received the bulk of likes, shares and comments. In March 2014 pet stories received three-quarters of the total shares for that month. By contrast, stories concerning local government were never shared. So in the suburbs of B31, people come together around everyday personal crises and in so doing show their networked potential. Such a focus on issues of seemingly little importance seems to be a rejection of journalism's traditional goal of holding local power to account, yet as Marty Taylor makes clear in his description, the intention is for B31 Voices to serve a more benign civic purpose:

> "I don't think it [the community] necessarily needs us. It needs something like B31, every area I think needs something like that to bring communities together, to bring people together, to share so you know what's about because otherwise you don't know what's actually going on in your area. So I think being able to do that is … well, it's all about being a community, isn't it, I guess." (Marty Taylor)

The value of everyday participation

Throughout our research with B31 Voices and other hyperlocal producers we saw evidence of the tensions between the goals of journalistic, civic-orientated, place-based blogging and professional mainstream journalism. Hudson and Temple argue that academics are 'stretching the concept of journalism to extremes' (2010: 66) by claiming that any 'user' that generates news content is therefore a journalist. This critique, however, does not deal with the significant scale of the news media gap in the suburbs of B31, which creates the opening for a hyperlocal to facilitate the emergence of its own 'networked public' (boyd, 2008). What once acted most strongly to hold the community together – the work-based ties engendered by the car factory and the social or work places associated with it – is now gone. Gone too is the controversial but vibrant political culture that went with the factory's 'lightning strikes' and mass union rallies. The local media pay the area attention as and when there's 'traditional' news to report and resource to deploy, but there is no dedicated local coverage other than that which originates from B31 Voices. So B31

Voices is a key element in this community's expression of itself and as a result Marty and Sas play an important part in reshaping the field of local journalism. It is too early to judge the sustainable strength of this hyperlocal news, but the 'weak ties' (Granovetter, 1973) made possible by B31 Voices, position each of those active in the network as potential activists, ready when needed to react in a networked way to more than just a lost kitten. The anthropologist Sarah Pink encourages us to see everyday activism, on and offline, as an established but evolving ecosystem. She states:

> Contemporary social media platforms and the technologies through which we access them make digital activism interweave with our everyday media practices and the environment in which we participate. (Pink, 2012: 131)

From one angle, hyperlocal is reasonably thought of as a citizen-led practice that disrupts the assumptions inherent in journalism's norms. But it is more than that. It offers a 'methodical confrontation of so-called "modern" life' (Lefebvre, 1991: 251).

Journalism's citizenship-focused future

Hyperlocal, as exemplified through the work of an operation like B31 Voices, offers a glimpse into a non-industrialised yet über-networked future, where citizens' concerns are foregrounded no matter how seemingly banal but where trust between reader and producer is built up as a result. This characterisation, naturally, invites a backlash. For Brian McNair, technology may offer the citizen a role in newsgathering but citizens should remain merely a source, leaving the act of 'critical, creative thinking' to trained journalists (2012: 87). Nothing less than the 'survival' of journalism is at stake. By contrast Manuel Castells (2012) gives scant attention to the role of professional journalism in discussing examples of the use of networked technologies by activists around the world. For him the 'networked space' 'enables the movement to relate to society at large beyond the control of the power holders over communication power' (Castells, 2012: 11).

Neither position adequately represents the ways in which hyperlocal news services are being practised in communities. Whether we think of the hyperlocalists as 'everyday activists' (Pink, 2012) or exploited 'precariats' (Gill and Pratt, 2008: 3) their emergence suggests that an evolving networked model for local news is what lies ahead. As such, this represents a category in which creative citizenship is establishing itself as pivotal to the wellbeing of communities. It is a clear example where the affordances of technology have played their part in reshaping the space for citizenship in the democratically important field of journalism.

Conclusion

These two case studies represent articulations of networks of creative citizenship in very different ways but both indicate the potential of creative citizens to create impact beyond the communities of place where they are situated. In Bristol we saw how a city's identity is negotiated and reshaped through the actions of a single creative citizen and his network. Whilst in the suburbs on the edge Birmingham we see how networks of bloggers operating in the field of the civic web influence the creative practices of a new breed of community journalists, who in turn play their part in reshaping the nature of journalism practice. Activity at the micro-level therefore has impact in the practices at the macro-level. Both case studies highlight the value of thinking beyond simplistic notions of networks and towards an examination of the details of the lived experience that sit behind them and the milieu they operate within. The personal narratives of Vince Baidoo and Sas and Marty Taylor reveal rich biographical details whereby the social and cultural histories of the places they operate from are crucial to our understanding of their potential as highly networked creative citizens.

The networks we have studied here at first glance seem geographically bounded and of initial importance primarily in their own places of emergence. Yet returning to the ideas of complexity theory, Martin and Sunley (2007), in their overview of this emerging field, have noted that, 'there are causal processes at work, but they operate through complex, distributed feedback and self-reinforcing mechanisms that are unlikely to be detected by standard measures of association (correlation) between assumed determinants and presumed effects' (2007: 579). Our intention here has been to see beyond the standard measures and argue instead for a fine-grained approach to studying the creative citizen within his or her milieu. From these studies of creative citizenship in practice, we can postulate the butterfly effect noted in complex systems and spontaneously evolving ecologies, so enhancing understanding of both the nature and potential of creative citizenship.

Note
[1]   See: www.stpaulscarnival.co.uk/about-us/history/

SEVEN

Conversations about co-production

Catherine Greene, Shawn Sobers, Theo Zamenopoulos,
Caroline Chapain and Jerome Turner with contributions from
Ingrid Abreu Scherer, Vince Baidoo, Ian Mellett,
Annette Naudin and James Skinner

Introduction

When we first gathered as a team to construct the Creative Citizen project proposal, the terms co-production, co-creation and co-design were new to several round the table. The team's designers, for whom this was a well-understood way of working in partnership with individuals and communities to design a new building, service or product, initially brought these concepts forward. Other team members were familiar with the approach from working on community arts and media projects. But for some the approach was new and while it raised questions about objectivity in research, along with some ethical issues, we agreed that co-production would be fundamental to the team's work.

An approach based upon co-production felt right because creative citizenship involves shared goals and collaborative methods. We wanted to understand the different forms, meanings and value of civic creativity, but we also wanted to test ways of growing the potential of creative citizens. Co-production allowed us to work in partnership with communities on creative projects useful to them, whilst also contributing to the research team's insights gained through other methods, including interviews, observation, textual analysis and surveys. This range of methods also had the merit of drawing upon the research traditions of a multidisciplinary group. By focusing on the mutual benefits of co-production, we were responding to 'a criticism that research conducted in communities often fails to meaningfully include communities in its design and undertaking' (Durose et al, 2007).

The literature in design has much to say about co-production, co-design and co-creation, but surprisingly little to say about the perspectives of participants and the communities themselves (Durham Community Research Team, 2011). In light of this, we present here a series of informal conversations, articulating the views of our community partners or 'creative citizens' in their role as co-producers of the project. These conversations highlight various methodological and practical factors that helped or hindered them through the creative process and point to ways in which academic researchers might better support their community partners in future.

Terms of engagement

During the research we used the terms co-creation, co-design and co-production interchangeably. In the literature, co-creation usually refers to collective creativity in general, co-design to collective creativity as applied to the design process (Sanders and Stappers, 2008) and co-production to citizens playing an active role in producing goods and services of consequence to them (Ostrom, 1996). Usage varies across different domains, so for instance, co-creation is fundamental to the study of interactive and participatory media, especially games studies (Banks, 2013), but all 'co-' approaches place an emphasis on stakeholders working in equal partnership towards a mutual goal. In this chapter, for the purposes of simplicity, we will refer to co-production because of its more explicit emphasis on the production elements of a project.

Our approach draws from three broad traditions of co-production – co-production of design or co-design, co-production in research and co-production in media.

Co-production in design (co-design) refers to the production of spaces, products, technologies or services through the formation of equal partnerships between professional designers and end users. This strand has a long history associated with two main schools of thought. The first sees 'end users' as a source of knowledge and skills for improving the quality of design (Sanders and Stappers, 2008). The second starts from an ethical or democratic standpoint that claims those affected by certain decisions have the right to participate in the design development and implementation of ideas. Examples include Scandinavian approaches to product design (for example, Gregory, 2003), participatory or democratic design approaches in architecture and urban planning (such as Blundell-Jones et al, 2005; Sanoff, 2006) and participatory approaches in service design (for example, Boyle and Harris, 2009).

Co-production in research refers to the production of knowledge through the formation of equal partnerships between academic researchers, practitioners and communities. It emerges out of two closely interrelated approaches. The first sees the formation of an equal partnership between academic researchers and community as a solution to the challenge of producing research that is more relevant and valuable to the community but also as a way of producing more 'democratic' and 'emancipatory' ways of knowing (for example, Durose et al., 2011). The second sees co-production more generally as a way of developing knowledge that is based on experiential learning, reflective practice (for example, Schön, 1983) or participatory action research (for example, Reason and Bradbury, 2008).

Co-production in media is exemplified in filmmaking, which has a strong tradition of participatory working and, in the work of the community media movement, carries a commitment to democratic participation and community engagement. Community media activities can be broadly categorised into these main areas:

- Communication platforms and educational activity (Sobers, 2010) are concerned with broadcasting productions and texts from those who may otherwise be voiceless, lacking access to mainstream media outlets. Community broadcast most emulates traditional media industry practice, albeit with a different voice. (Lewis and Jones, 2006; Howley, 2009). Media democracy or alternative media aim to disrupt traditional media, for example redressing the balance between reporters and the reported.
- Educational activity – comprising media education and media literacy – aims to inspire participants to become critical readers, creative media practitioners or more able users of media tools as a means of growing capacity (often by stealth) in communication skills, literacy, confidence, critical awareness, decision making and knowledge of subject (Nigg and Wade, 1980; Goldfarb, 2002; Rennie, 2006; Gidley and Slater, 2007; Sundar-Harris, 2008).

Over recent years co-production has become increasingly established beyond the media and design world and is now being advocated in sectors such as healthcare (Donnetto et al, 2014), social care (Social Care Institute for Excellence, 2013) and local government (Shafique, 2013). These changes have been made possible by the spread of access to the internet's generative culture (Zittrain, 2008). These do-it-yourself forces are also responsible for the burgeoning of the maker movement (Anderson, 2012), with its own implications and insights for creative citizenship (Ratto and Boler, 2014). Digital technologies have made it easier to access, connect, share and work within and between communities of users, leading to a growing recognition of their potential for the innovation process (exemplified by collaborative platforms such as Creative Commons, GitHub and Wikipedia) and enabling services designed with close knowledge of the needs and preferences of individuals and groups (Von Hippel, 2005).

But in common with other debates about the pros and cons of the online world, there is an opposing and negative view of co-creation, which says that collective creativity undermines individual intelligence, leading to a digital culture more fragmented and diminished than its analogue alternative (Sanger, 2007; Lanier, 2010). There are also economic counterarguments. Designer and researcher Von Busch (2012) questions the ethics of corporations which cite co-production principles to draw upon inputs from customers, harnessing what is seen, in effect, as unpaid and unrecognised labour. He also questions the loss of professional responsibility that may come with these approaches:

> In all its well-meaning, is not 'co-design' and 'participation' far too often used as an excuse for undesired outcomes where the co-designers are used as hostages or 'human shields,' covering up the mistakes of a badly organized and designed participatory process? 'The user wanted this design' the designers can say to avoid taking responsibility of a faulty and incompetent outcome. (Von Busch, 2012)

Whilst recognising these tensions and dangers, the team believed it right to pursue co-production for three main reasons. First, it improves our knowledge of action and is therefore pragmatically desirable; second, it makes some contribution to democratising society, workplace and research and is therefore ethically positive; and last, it enables people to take ownership of their environments, systems or products and therefore contributes to their resilience. Other explicit or implicit arguments for co-production, including claims for the benefits to individuals of self-actualisation, are set out elsewhere in this volume.

Overview

Our research asks what creative citizens do, why do they do it and what is the value of their activities? How are digital communications technologies, such as social media, enhancing their potential? To investigate these questions, we worked with eight different communities of creative citizens in London, Birmingham, Cannock and Bristol to co-produce media that aimed to address a particular need or ambition of each group. These media artefacts were then trialled with each community. Projects looked at how to engage with more people in the wider community, how to communicate better and tell stories using digital media and how to develop a more sustainable business model. Each co-production project ran differently, based on the specific interests and resources each community brought to the project, and the disciplinary background and expertise of the researchers involved. Hence the co-production activities involved a wide range of methods including asset mapping (explained in detail in Chapter 8), building workshops, photo walks and exhibitions. In this chapter we hear from key participants in five of these projects:

Ingrid Abreu Scherer – The Mill

The Mill is a community centre in Walthamstow, East London. An ex-library, it was saved from sale to a developer by the local residents who now run it, providing space and resources for local creative citizens to organise groups, events and activities for adults, children and families, ranging from art exhibitions to book clubs and language classes. Walking into The Mill is like walking into a communal living room – you feel welcome to sit and get on with whatever you want or just to watch as a myriad of activities take place and people, young and old, come and go around you.

Ingrid, a founding member of The Mill, played a critical role in our collaboration and it is probably fair to say that the researchers and designers learnt more from her than she and The Mill could learn from our research. During our first meeting, she explained that the point of The Mill was not to run activities, but to enable local people to set up their own activities or events – hence their slogan 'Making things happen'. Ingrid felt that this ethos was missing from their website and she was keen to use the opportunity of the Creative Citizen project to explore the potential for digital technology to address this point, through sharing activities and the stories that go with them among a wider community, and thereby also adding to evidence of The Mill's local impact. The resulting media project, 'The Story Machine', came about through a series of co-production events, including a digital storytelling event, 'Midsomer Murder at The Mill', and two prototyping workshops, which involved Mill members taking up pens and tools to create, prototype and build their ideas of what 'the Story Machine' should be. Now installed in The Mill, the Story Machine is used to photograph and film activities and events. These upload automatically to an ever-changing slide show in The Mill building and to The Mill's website, ensuring there is always an up-to-date representation of daily activity on show in both the online and physical spaces of The Mill.

With an academic background, and experience through Nesta's Neighbourhood Challenge (who supported The Mill's early development), Ingrid was already well versed in the language and methodologies of co-production – so too the researchers, who were mainly designers. This made it possible for the project to acquire a highly creative and collaborative approach from the start; the result was an outcome that emerged directly from the design development process (see Figure 7.1).

Figure 7.1: Left: The Mill community centre. Right: Prototyping workshop at The Mill

James Skinner – Wards Corner

James is a member of the Wards Corner Community Coalition (WCC), a grass roots group campaigning to stop the demolition of the market above Seven Sisters Station in North London and to deliver a community plan for the area which takes into consideration the needs and resources of local people.

Although not a local resident, James is an activist and has become a member of the coalition out of conviction for its cause. He is currently completing a degree in nursing, has also studied film and has a keen design eye. James was key to mediating communication between the academic team and the community group during the co-production process.

WCC has a very participative ethos and the co-production process involved multiple members of the WCC in a series of targeted workshops, along with other face-to-face meetings and informal conversations. These activities led to the creation of a 3D virtual tour of their community plan on Stickyworld, an online platform. WCC used the online site to engage more widely with local residents and businesses, explain the plans and invite comments and feedback, which, ultimately fed into the council's consultation process for the plan. The idea and the aims of this site were developed and agreed with the whole group. James and the architect of the community plan (Abigail Stevenson) were the main designers realising the site, with James using his self-taught graphic design and 3D modelling skills (see Figure 7.2).

Figure 7.2: Left: Members of WWC at a co-creation workshop. Right: The community plan as it appears on the Stickyworld platform

Ian Mellett – Connect Cannock

Connect Cannock is a hyperlocal news site based in Cannock, Birmingham. Ian and his partner Sarah run it. Ian does not have professional journalism training but works in IT, so is able to draw on these skills in developing the website and social media platforms. He started the website *Connect Cannock* against a landscape of receding local print media in the area, and talks about it as his 'hobby', typically updating the content in the evening after work. Ian explored with researchers the idea of a pilot printed newspaper as a vehicle to draw more people to the online platforms, as well as encouraging more participation, for example, in citizen-sourced stories.

Working together we co-produced the newspaper version of *Connect Cannock*. This was kicked off by a 'photo walk' around Cannock with local residents to discuss local issues and news they felt should be covered (whether in print or online). The project was highly collaborative from the design and production of the paper to the physical distribution of 1,000 newspapers to shops around Cannock (see Figure 7.3).

Figure 7.3: Distributing the newspaper version of *Connect Cannock*

Vince Baidoo – South Blessed

Founded in 2011 by Vince, South Blessed works with local talent such as rappers, music producers and upcoming television presenters, supporting them in providing an online platform for their skills. Vince grew up participating in community video workshops in Bristol, sometimes facilitated by members of the current research team working in previous jobs, and each member of the Bristol research team recalls being aware of Vince long before the project was conceived. For example, Shawn Sobers, research team co-investigator, first met Vince approximately in 2001 when Shawn was running a video workshop at the city's Kuumba Centre. At 13 years old, Vince was one of the youngest attendees and Shawn was struck by his intelligence and work ethic. Jon Dovey, lead investigator on the Bristol research team, remembers first seeing Vince in 2010 at a protest march in the city centre. Although at that time Jon did not know Vince, he was so taken by seeing a young black man with a video camera confidently confronting a policeman, that he was inspired to take a photograph. Jon took three frames of the moment, presented below in Figure 7.4.

Figure 7.4: Vince Baidoo confronting a policeman at a march, as photographed by researcher Jon Dovey in 2010

The boldness and professionalism of Vince's action and the agency of the presence of the video camera in this exchange stayed with Jon. It resonated to the extent that two years later when the Creative Citizen project started, and Vince's name was suggested as a possible case study, Jon immediately recalled these photographs. These stories make the point that Vince is someone who makes an impression. This was the dynamic that the Bristol research team were aiming to capture in their study – the bold DIY energy of Vince and the self-actualisation of his South Blessed network, and how they use media tools to carve their own paths and identities, and the motivations that drive these aspirations.

Responding to a query by Vince at the start of the Creative Citizen project about the nature of the research, Shawn was careful to stress to Vince that he was invited to take part, not as a participant young person, but as an equal (adult) partner with his own cultural capital, knowledge and skills to contribute. Vince certainly endeavoured to make the most out of this opportunity. His involvement in participatory video projects from a young age meant he was particularly confident with co-production, as were the research team working with him. The collaboration resulted in a graphic novel *Indigo Babies*, subsequently sold through South Blessed networks and spawning a self-publishing arm of South Blessed, Crown Root Publications, through which *Indigo Babies* sequels are planned.

Annette Naudin – Moseley Exchange

The Moseley Community Development Trust (MCDT) is located in a former telephone exchange close to the centre of Moseley in the south east part of Birmingham. MCDT was created in 2001 with the vision 'for Moseley to be a creative neighbourhood, valued and sustained by its community'. The way it operates is based on this vision, with activities ranging from support to regeneration and planning, street wardens, community school games, energy saving advice and support to the voluntary sector, along with more entrepreneurial aspects such as renting of meeting rooms, offices and the creation of the Moseley Exchange, a co-working space serving creative and knowledge workers living in the neighbourhood.

Annette was our initial point of contact with the MCDT, where she volunteered as one of the board members dealing with marketing strategy. A resident of Moseley at the time of our collaboration, Annette was also a senior lecturer in media and creative enterprise at Birmingham City University, where she was finishing her PhD on cultural entrepreneurship. Annette was dynamic and very involved in the creative and social media community within Moseley and Birmingham. Her enthusiasm for the research and the co-production project, along with her insights into both academic requirements and creative endeavours, helped create synergies throughout the project. Early on, she had identified that the MCDT and its activities suffered a lack of visibility within the neighbourhood and suggested that this could be an avenue for media intervention. Further interviews with other MCDT board members and staff, as well as a workshop bringing together various users of the building, confirmed this idea. Digital storytelling suggested itself as a good tool to bring the organisation together to address the issue. Annette, MCDT staff and the research team were trained and an online digital storytelling platform, Exchange Stories, was developed, bringing together stories from both MCDT users and the wider Moseley community (see Figure 7.5).

Participants and people coming into contact with the Exchange Stories platform have been very positive about the medium and many were enthusiastic about the new things they discovered about the MCDT and related activities. The MCDT aims to continue gathering stories to give place to more voices in order to reflect the community's diversity.

Figure 7.5: Left: Engaging Moseley residents for the digital storytelling project. Right: The exchange stories platform

Co-production from our partners' perspectives

We wanted to understand the community's experience of these collaborations and of co-production, so our conversations began by asking how they would describe the process of working on the Creative Citizen project. James, reflecting on the process at Wards Corner, provided an evocative description:

> "We are all in quite a dark room and there is you guys and there is me and then there is like the Wards Corner Campaign ... and there are all the things that we want in the dark room and maybe they are in the same place, maybe they are not. We are all kind of fumbling around trying to help each other get there to them and sometimes it has been difficult to ... navigate, some of the directions we are giving each other and then ultimately we have come out with really beneficial things."

Annette described the experience of doing the project as giving them the freedom to do something they wouldn't otherwise have done, contrasting with her own experience of other projects with council or agencies where the work tends to be much more focused on a particular outcome: "We started with a bit of a blank sheet; most projects and activities where you engage with other organisations don't tend to be a blank sheet."

For Ian, the collaboration was technical, with *Connect Cannock* creating the content and researcher Jerome Turner providing the graphic design know-how that they needed to produce the newspaper.

Vince was clear in defining the process of creating his graphic novel as co-production, which he simply and practically viewed as having more than one person involved. While *Indigo Babies* was very much his idea, it was co-produced with various people's expertise but with himself as director. Patrick, mentioned in the following quotation by Vince, is his long-term collaborator and confidant:

> "In terms of the co-production, it was my idea that [Patrick] helped me develop that I then took away and developed further and finished with others… So I think it comes down to ideas but specifying the intellectual property, so even if you are talking about a building, whose actual idea was it in the first place and are they leasing that idea to other people or are they directing that idea through the co-production?"

Vince's particular talent in relation to co-production and networking is that he is confident in pulling together new people along with others from his past, whilst still retaining ownership and creative control. Vince identifies a key moment in 2011 when he was taking part in Second Light, a British Film Institute intern scheme for young people, when he realised he needed to take a leadership role, otherwise his creative vision and voice would be lost. So whilst he is acutely aware of the openness needed in co-production settings, he also senses that it needs a leader to navigate the direction of the production in the interests of coherence and efficiency. The above quotation indicates that Vince has a sharp awareness of not only the ethics of these exchanges, but also the business issues arising from intellectual property rights.

From Ingrid's point of view the process behind co-production was valuable but the terminology superfluous. She questioned some 'buzzwords':

> "We were introduced to these words [co-creation, co-design], sort of buzzwords and often not very applicable. So we knew about them. But on a practical level we interpret it to mean working with experts on an equal basis to solve certain problems. Asset based community development techniques that we use involve working with architects, engineers and working alongside them as volunteers within the building or the space. I think we would be working that way anyway. We wouldn't distinguish between self-contained co-design projects and making stuff happen which is what we generally do."

Although each partner gives a very different response, they all recognise 'co-production' as a partnership where different stakeholders come together to make things happen and to achieve something that they wouldn't be able to do without each other. One subtle difference between the five is that Vince and Ian's viewpoints give more emphasis to the different skills and expertise that people bring within co-production while the others give more emphasis to the process of co-production enabling different groups to work together. It can be argued that this difference of viewpoints reflects on one side the predominant model of media production where the emphasis is placed on the intellectual property of individuals as opposed to grassroots civil action projects, where there is more emphasis on democratic participation and community engagement.

The role of the researcher and design practitioner

If, as Ingrid says, co-production is something she and her colleagues would be doing anyway, it may be asked – what was the role of the researchers and what difference have they made? From the researcher and designer perspective, what is our contribution as experts in the co-production process? Indeed what expertise do we bring within the emerging contexts of professional amateurism (Leadbeater and Miller, 2004), the new politics of knowledge (Sanger, 2007) and the do-it-yourself maker movement (Anderson, 2012). The internet has reduced barriers of access to expertise and knowledge through social forums, peer-to-peer networks, self-teaching and access to sophisticated tools thus making it easier for amateurs to participate in once purely professional fields (Von Hippel, 2005). James was, however, in no doubt as to the benefit of the researchers' contribution to the collaboration with Wards Corner:

> "You were driving the project theoretically and somehow pushing from a theoretical position … that was good because in a way that brings us out of thinking about the specifics and going back into it with new eyes. It has been nice to have this kind of pushing and pulling and these various interests and the different ways of presenting and different ways of working."

As well as this theoretical contribution, James highlights the value of the researchers' role as initiator of the collaboration and organisational and creative support. But he admits this resulted in a somewhat hierarchical relationship, although in his view a productive one. Annette found that the researchers helped Moseley CDT to be more exploratory, challenging them both creatively and intellectually and taking them out of their comfort zone. However, she also felt that the lead came from the researchers. Ingrid saw the role of the designers and researchers to "work with us to identify what we wanted and use your expertise to develop a tool that we could use". This too resulted in a slightly uneven relationship as the designers were then seen as leading and delivering on the design rather than it being a fully collaborative making activity with equal responsibility.

In the collaborative production of the *Connect Cannock* newspaper, once the working process had been agreed and the roles assigned (Ian and Sarah, content; Jerome, design and layout), it was Jerome who led. This was partly a reflection of the context of working situations, where Jerome was carrying out his tasks as a full-time researcher, and was therefore able to work on the newspaper in the day, whereas Ian could only answer and respond to increasingly demanding emails for 'more stories, more photos, more credits' in his time available after work.

In South Blessed, by contrast, it was Vince who took the lead on the *Indigo Babies* project. He described the researchers' role in this collaboration as more of a sounding board, valuing the conversations he had with them and the confidence they gave him: "Seeing that my answers are appreciated ... has made me realise, okay, so that's worth doing ... it's helped me in defining myself, it's helped me in what I plan on doing in the future." He also valued the fact that the researchers came with funding, which enabled him to produce his graphic novel to a high professional standard. It is interesting to note that throughout Vince's interview for this chapter he compartmentalised discussion of co-production in the realm of his network, and did not extend it to the university research team, which he placed in a context related to money, infrastructure and systems. The researchers themselves felt very much part of the co-production, working closely with Vince to develop the script, layout, design and other creative decisions and helping solve problems. As a result, they too learned a lot. The fact that Vince separated out the internal South Blessed network roles from that of the research team is, however, a point to be acknowledged and respected. Based on expectations, assumptions, motivations and positionality, exactly the same activities can be interpreted through different lenses. Co-production, as a form of action research, requires full participation, immersion and empathy by the research team (Meyer, 2000), though that might not always be how partners view it.

In these collaborations our roles as researchers and designers had a number of elements, from the functional – initiator, enabler and organiser – to something much more conceptually involved –

theoriser, designer, and expert. In action research these multilayered, complementary and contradictory roles can become confused and at any given time the definition of the space occupied by any of the stakeholders can be in flux. We took care on both sides to avoid hierarchies, but that does not mean that the dynamics shaping the relationship between researcher and respondent, university researcher and community partner, can be ignored. It would be foolish to say otherwise. As poetically put by Kushner (2002): 'Here was evidence of engagement, an intermingling of interests – but, ultimately, as in all good tangos, of final betrayal. I talked as a friend but slunk off to write as a scientist.'

While the starting intention for each project was for an equal partnership, the realities of running the projects dictated roles. Almost all of our community partners were volunteers and, on top of their normal volunteer responsibilities, they were often very busy and short on time. In contrast, we researchers were being paid to work on the project. This highlights not only the free labour provided by creative citizens in such enterprises as hyperlocal media, but also a mismatch in expectations, needs and everyday available time when researchers and communities work together. This meant that the projects began on an unequal footing, with the consequence that the motivation and drive to push the project forward often came from the researchers rather than from the communities themselves. This is not ideal and, as we discuss later in this chapter, has direct effects on the sustainability of projects. The case of South Blessed and the *Indigo Babies* project was a bit different. Vince Baidoo is very much the centre of the informal network of South Blessed and views himself and his associates as entrepreneurs rather than volunteers. Consequently he saw the project, *Indigo Babies*, as inextricably linked to his own future, motivating him to be the main driver and producer.

Our roles were also no doubt influenced by our sense of ourselves as experts. This can result in hierarchies, which can damage collaborative potential caused by redundant identifiers, as summed up in an education context by Paulo Freire:

> Through dialogue, the teacher-of-the-students and the students-of-the-teacher cease to exist and a new term emerges: teacher-student with student-teachers. The teacher is no longer merely the-one-who-teaches, but one who is himself taught in dialogue with the students, who in their turn while being taught also teach. They become jointly responsible for a process in which all grow. In this

process, arguments based on 'authority' are no longer valid. (1972: 53)

This was particularly highlighted in the work with Vince and South Blessed, as it was his idea to produce a graphic novel, and the research team agreed, even though none of them was expert in the graphic novel field, so together they had to learn and to draw on external expertise when required, resulting in the collapse of certain hierarchies between them. Vince was able to take the creative lead on the project and be supported by the research team. When expertise was needed, sometimes urgently, some production processes slowed down owing to the exploratory nature of the creative journey. This in turn created an embodied learning experience where the knowledge gained for those production processes was deep and lived through, not merely taught/learned and thus more robust (Matthews, 1998). In other collaborations the projects relied more directly on the specific expertise of individual researchers (product design, graphic design, interaction design, planning and storytelling) and hence lacked the depth and mutuality of the embodied learning experienced of the South Blessed collaboration.

The creative process

Prior to taking part in the Creative Citizen project, each of our co-production partners saw themselves as creative but in relation to different things, for example, Ian as a musician and writer, Ingrid as a problem solver in her work with the community and Vince as a filmmaker. In this project, together with other members of their community, each was being asked to direct this creativity towards developing a new idea, requiring some different skills and new ways of working. Different approaches were taken to supporting the development of these ideas, ranging from something quite structured, as was the case with the Mill and Wards Corner, to something much less structured, as with South Blessed, Moseley CDT and *Connect Cannock*. It is interesting then to understand how these creative processes differed and with what consequences.

South Blessed and *Connect Cannock* came to the project with an idea already partially formed and used the co-production process to develop it. Ian describes the specific moment when he came up with his idea to create a printed newspaper version of his blog. He was sitting in a council meeting listening to people lament the loss of their local paper and how this meant they could not let people know about the local fair. He realised that a lot of these people would not think to look at a blog but they would look at a printed newspaper. Later in conversations with the researchers, and encouraged by the potential of being involved in the Creative Citizen project, this idea emerged again but this time there were the financial and technical means to realise it.

In a similar way Vince describes the idea he brought to the project as "one of my core transmedia ideas waiting to bubble". Through "bouncing off and having conversations" with the researchers this idea was given shape and refined into something achievable. Vince explained that knowing he would have to complete the graphic novel within an agreed time period and that there would be support to help him gave him the drive to realise the idea.

With Moseley CDT the digital storytelling project emerged slowly. Numerous interviews with key exchange members highlighted a clear issue in relation to marketing and visibility of the exchange and a workshop showed that more needed to be done to represent the organisation within the wider community of Moseley. The idea came to the researchers after this and it appealed to Moseley CDT, who liked the idea of combining both traditional and online media in this way.

Wards Corner and The Mill were both involved in a more structured co-design process which began with key members identifying a problem and then running design workshops to help generate ideas in response. However, it is interesting that the ideas that they ended up developing emerged not during these organised ideation activities but in the more informal time around these activities, as Ingrid explains:

> "I think conversations were where the direction of the project was made clearer and it was the workshops where the detail was developed. I don't think the workshops were great in setting a direction. This happened during conversations, often one-to-one, often while we were doing something else."

So what can we learn from the experiences of each of these people about the creative process? If everyone has the potential to be a creative citizen, how can designers and researchers best support them in nurturing this creativity? Based on our conversations these factors emerged:

1. Flexibility

It is essential that designers and researchers (along with funders and initiators) are flexible. Both James and Ingrid described how this helped them to fit the project around the lives of their volunteers and the dynamics of their community. Ingrid said, "It was very positive that you were flexible, which fitted in with the way we work. It was good that you didn't make us stick to our original plan".

For Vince this flexible approach let him be creative: "Because there were no boundaries, and it's like, well this is about creative citizens and they actually let me be creative. Where I think there are other [projects that] allude to the fact that it's about creativity but they're actually scared of the creativity."

Annette found that the openness of the project led them to achieve something that they wouldn't have otherwise achieved and which ended up having an impact beyond the CDT and into the wider community of Moseley.

2. Provide a framework

It is easy to press a button on a camera and record an image. Less obvious is how to create an interesting film that people will want to watch and then know how to edit and upload it for public viewing. In this project we have experimented with how to create the conditions (digital and creative literacy) that enable creative citizens to use media and use them creatively. For example, in our work with The Mill and Kentish Town Neighbourhood Forum we went through a series of modifications, beginning with a basic installation of the media intervention, aimed at providing access to a much more involved process of upskilling community members, the creation of exemplary content, custom instruction manuals and simplification and limitation of technical functionality. These experiences showed us what we needed to provide for different levels of creative response. For many people, having a simple framework can help channel their creative response. This can be anything from providing a simple prompt to which partners can react, to more detailed step-by-step instructions that help to reduce the range of creative possibilities. The advantage of this came up in our conversations with both James and Vince:

> "When you give yourself parameters to work with you can be more creative. Sometimes if you can do anything you can't do anything. I think that as creative people we can sometimes get lost in the world of possibilities and what we might do, might do, might do... I'd say it's like the snake eating itself, constant cycle sort of thing."

Vince would have preferred more of a structure. For him, this was one of the key learning points on the project. But he goes on to question how you can create this structure in a way that does not at the same time suffocate creativity. In their work, Sanders and Stappers identify four levels of creativity: 'doing, adapting, making and creating', and identify the role of designer/researcher in facilitating each of these:

> When we acknowledge that different levels of creativity exist, it becomes evident that we need to learn how to offer relevant experiences to facilitate people's expressions of creativity at all levels. This means leading, guiding, and providing scaffolds as well as clean slates to encourage people at all levels of creativity. (Sanders and Stappers, 2008)

In some of our partnerships a memorandum of understanding was co-produced between the research team and the community, setting out expectations for the project as well as detailing ethical considerations. This was then reviewed periodically and updated where things had changed. As Ingrid noted: 'This was a really useful document to have to say every three months, "we are still going in the same direction"'. A framework could work in a similar way, for example, co-producing prompts or a project brief, which can then be updated as details become clearer and the project progresses. In this way, it becomes a working document for both parties and a mechanism to ensure shared understanding through the project.

3. Inclusivity

Currently there is a big move towards the use of 'non-text' tools (Beebeejaun et al, 2013) within the fields of research generally, and design research, aiming for a more inclusive approach. However, it is interesting to hear that it is also possible to err in the other direction; some people are more comfortable expressing their ideas through words and in non-group situations.

> "Some of the workshops were aimed at people who create in a certain way. The meetings we had with your team, almost everybody draws during meetings, which I am not used to and I don't draw. And the workshops themselves are very much about drawing your ideas whereas I tend to talk my ideas and there were fewer opportunities to do that." (Ingrid Abreu Scherer)

It is important to allow people to create and contribute in different ways and at different times. Co-production depends on getting together a group that represents the community, but this can be difficult. It is likely that you will reach those who already consider themselves to be creative and are available rather than those who either don't consider themselves to be creative or who have commitments that prevent them from attending meetings. Our participants questioned how co-production can move from something that happens 'when people who are likely to turn up' to something that allows for different types of contributions from participants that reflect the diversity of the community they represent. The effect of this could be seen in the aesthetic of The Story Machine (see Figure 7.6), which with a circus tent theme, was clearly designed and consequently appealed to young families rather than the wider community initially hoped for.

Figure 7.6: The Story Machine comprising left, the Story Chair, and right, the Story Wheel

Perhaps it was our responsibility as designers to intervene in the process and steer the design towards something that we considered more reflective of the community. However, this would have been our view on the community, not exactly in the spirit of co-production we sought. As researchers and designers we have to be reactive, we can't dictate who turns up to events but we can think about how to spread the net wider.

In hindsight, we should have used a more diverse range of co-production methodologies appropriate to different situations – methods not reliant on everyone coming together in one physical location. Suggested methods include low-level engagement tools such as postcards on which people can respond in whatever creative capacity they choose to high-level engagement methods such as smaller group workshops with specific groups and one-to-one 'walk shops' (see Figure 7.7). However, we must also acknowledge that the benefits of achieving higher participation in this way must be weighed against the creative benefit of bringing together a diverse group of people in direct dialogue.

Figure 7.7: Left: Postcards for people to fill in during an exhibition at The Mill. Right: 'Walkshop' with Vince Baidoo and Jon Dovey

Practicalities of co-production

Co-production is advocated as a way for researchers to work with communities. However, it is important to acknowledge the practical challenges that come with this approach. Many of these arise from the fact that co-production is about bringing different people and different organisations to work together. The two sides have to learn to work together and overcome differences such as working styles, language, and practical structures about matters such as contracts.

Time

In our conversations, participants were unanimous in saying the co-production took far more time than they anticipated. When asked what advice they would give to other communities embarking on a similar project all advised being more realistic about the time it takes:

> "There were times when I felt Mo and I were focusing much more on making sure the right people were in the room and we were doing things at the right time of

the year and right time of the day and it was more about administration and practical stuff, which meant by the time we got to the creative stuff we were a bit tired." (Ingrid Abreu Scherer)

The fact is that co-production relies on people with very different timetables and work styles working together. In the case of this project, researchers were working predominantly with volunteers, often only free during evenings or at weekends, and who, despite their dedication, sometimes had to prioritise job or family commitments. It therefore makes sense to try to reduce reliance on key people and to spread the load, as Ingrid suggested: "If I had known in hindsight I would have done a lot more work really early on, putting together a creative citizen project team who could have worked through the whole project." However, this would not have been practical for *Connect Cannock*, comprising just Ian and Sarah, both with full-time jobs and already spending evenings and weekends on their blog.

Structures

Vince at South Blessed owns the copyright to the *Indigo Babies* graphic novel, and thus any income arising from sales. This deal was agreed based on the core principle of the research strand – that the work produced would support the future sustainability of South Blessed. However, negotiating such a deal within the university and for contracts to be drawn up and agreed by all parties (including some key subcontractors) was a slow process, which on occasion caused tension, because there would be no return on its research investment, despite this commercial output.

A theme underpinning the project with South Blessed was that of talent development within the wider South Blessed networks. Vince is good at pulling people together. For this project he recruited the graffiti writer Silent Hobo as illustrator. Although very experienced, this was the first time Silent Hobo had worked in a graphic novel format, and here was a skill he wanted to acquire. Vince also brought on board a 15-year-old designer, Raees, to add colour to the black and white images produced by Silent Hobo. In Raees's words:

> "I chose to get involved in the project because it was a rather unique opportunity that came out of the blue. I am glad to have taken part in the project and would say overall it was a positive experience although stressful at times. As

for a benefit from the project, for me having my name on a published comic is an achievement. The positives of working on this project was the amount of freedom I had with what I did with most of the pages, as well as having a fast method of communication flow with the team to sort problems so that I could finish up on my end. Furthermore, as I was the second last process in production I had to report any quality issues in terms of format or line art, often also having to think and implement solutions. I enjoyed the experience."

Language

Another observation that emerged from these conversations was the barrier created by differences in the use of language. As James says:

"There was a lot of academic terminology which was quite new and defined by projects and talking about reproducing things or mapping things, all of these very abstract terms which people found very difficult to understand."

Terms like creative citizenship, co-design, co-production or asset mapping were used during introductory meetings but were perceived as abstract ideas. The engagement of communities with specific project activities and workshops (like the asset mapping exercise) was pivotal in order to give meaning to these terms. James felt that he became a translator between the researchers and the community. Annette felt that the community of Moseley CDT were not interested in concepts such as 'creative citizens' and questions being tackled by the research. She felt the community only became interested in the project when it became tangible to them while watching the digital stories of their friends and neighbours on the digital storytelling platform. Annette felt it was difficult for the researchers "to sort of helicopter in" and that, ideally, the researchers would have spent more time in the space getting to know the different co-workers and understand the surrounding area. She said, "The more immersed you could be, the more you could change the language you used when talking to people".

Communication is critical to co-production with all parties needing a clear mutual understanding. The development of the Story Machine proved quite a technical challenge, requiring the designers to make several different devices and software applications work together. The Mill felt that when it came to the technical development of the

Story Machine they were not able to understand what was being recommended to them and were therefore unable to engage creatively. This was further compounded by the fact that the designers often worked on the software development remotely, coming in to The Mill to get feedback on different solutions:

> "When it came to the digital stuff because there wasn't anyone in our team who was digitally literate enough to keep up with some of the digital tool development – I didn't feel that we had any ownership over the process at that point and I felt that a lot of the work that was happening was happening away from The Mill."

While it is understandable that The Mill felt like this we can also sympathise with the designers wanting to work from home and come in when they had something to show. For most designers, working on a client basis, this is normal working practice. What we learn is that co-production challenges normal working practices. In the case of both The Mill and Moseley CDT, they felt their projects would have benefitted more from increased presence of the researchers and designers. But at the same time co-production needs to be achieved within the realities of what is practical and feasible.

Ownership and sustainability

What about the argument that participatory projects result in outputs that are more sustainable, because they are created collaboratively with the people who will use them (Ramirez, 2008; Boyle et al, 2010)? The problem with this question is that it avoids the fact that important outputs occur outside the media interventions themselves. It can be argued that these side effects – learning, development of new skills, self-reflection, raised aspirations and perceptions – had more sustainable impacts than the media artefacts themselves. Thus, with South Blessed, the original goal of producing a graphic novel was added to by the formation of the new publishing company, Crown Root, via which it is intended that all future media productions will be produced, thus raising the bar in terms of professionalism and legacy. In Vince's words:

> "It helped refine the idea, first for me that I'm a transmedia storyteller, and then to refine what that actually is … and to strengthen that, and so I think that it strengthens the Indigo

Baby world itself, and then strengthened the possibilities of Crown Root as a transmedia production company."

Figure 7.8: Front cover of *Indigo Babies* graphic novel

While none of our community partners denied the benefits of being involved with researchers, it is fair to say that some said they would struggle to continue with it beyond the end of the project. Their reasons for this vary from not having the time and financial means to not having the technical confidence to continue. Ownership is key to the success of a project and its capacity to become sustainable (David et al, 2013). As researchers and design practitioners, our work on projects like these is for a set period of time. When this time ends the community's work on the project must continue. It is therefore important to create most impact within the time available but without creating a reliance on that support so that without it the project is unsustainable. The difficulty is getting the balance right – in the words of James: "taking the time to try and understand what is happening and engage in a meaningful way ... but not being so involved that you are indispensable to the campaign."

Or, as Ingrid and Annette say:

> "I think we expected too much from you in a sense we expected you to solve something rather than think we were solving it too, that we also had ownership over the process whereas we knew that we would have ownership of the solution."

> "I think that the nature of these projects, that you have somebody else leading on certain things, and it's how much and at what point you take ownership of it as an organisation, and what you do with it, how proactive you are with it. I think it's a two-way thing. It takes two to tango doesn't it?"

Conclusions

While overall experiences of co-production on the Creative Citizen project were positive, there were lessons for all, even those well versed in the methodologies of co-production. In particular, the project highlighted the difficulty in attaining equal partnerships between researchers and community partners when one party is being paid and the other not. Invariably this affects time commitments and synchronisation, resulting in 'ownership' issues on the part of the community. There are also challenges arising from differences in work style, language and practical structures. The South Blessed case study reveals potential insights arising in media production cultures based upon freelance structures.

There were also valuable insights to gain from the creative process of co-production and how best to support and facilitate it flexibly and inclusively. Creativity flourishes at the crossing of boundaries of knowledge and interests (Wilson, 2010). Co-production aims to create the conditions for this to happen through the purposeful bringing together of people with different frames of reference, different experiences and expertise.

In this respect some of the team felt they lacked skills to broker community engagement. In this instance, we can look towards the tradition of participatory and user-centred design where, over the past 40 years, designers have had to develop their skills as collaborators in order to bring together other stakeholders. This has influenced the development of design practice to focus on skills such as communication, interpretation and visualisation of ideas, facilitation and the creation of tools to nurture participant creativity.

While the experiences of this project have demonstrated that co-production is not an easy journey, we conclude that it is a journey worth taking, not least because of the strength of the relationships it produces. Too often we see big projects taking place which, while seeming positive, overlook the real needs of communities and undermine local expertise and relationships. So while there is a lot to learn about improving co-production, our faith in the concept and the approach is enhanced rather than shaken. Co-production has established itself in our minds as essential to the voluntaristic, bottom-up nature of creative citizenship. It follows that measures to 'propagate, grow and sustain' acts of creative citizenship must themselves be the result of co-production.

EIGHT

Asset mapping and civic creativity

Katerina Alexiou, Emma Agusita, Giota Alevizou,
Caroline Chapain, Catherine Greene, Dave Harte, Gail Ramster
and Theodore Zamenopoulos

Introduction

Throughout this book creative citizenship is explored theoretically and empirically as a concept that intrinsically leads to value generation. Acts of creative citizenship bring personal, cultural, economic, social and civic benefits, not only to individuals and communities directly involved in these acts, but also to the wider public. So, hyperlocal blogs may generate income for amateur journalists but also benefit local residents and businesses through communicating and raising awareness about issues that affect them, ranging from the weather and local services to political and planning issues (Nesta, 2013). Similarly, the benefits of community-led design enhance social value through civic participation, more democratic outcomes, creation of public goods, improved social capital and stronger community. In boosting qualities such as self-expression, confidence and skills, they also generate personal value. (Alexiou et al, 2013).

The Creative Citizen project is concerned not only with understanding and capturing current practice and its value, as enacted through the use of different media, but also exploring how this pursuit of value can be further supported and advanced.

One of the instruments we used to explore questions of value was asset mapping. In community engagement and community development theory and practice, the term 'asset' has long been used as an alternative for the term 'value'. Assets are tangible or intangible resources that have a potential – they can grow or be better used to achieve something new. Drawing from the strengths of different existing approaches, asset mapping was innovatively used in the Creative Citizen project both as an analytic research tool for capturing people's values and perceptions of value, and as a practical tool to support community engagement and co-creation.

The chapter reviews different asset mapping or asset-based development approaches and presents the approach developed and used in the Creative Citizen project, discussing theoretical and methodological insights. The chapter links to Chapter 4, which is focused on appraising and articulating the value of creative citizenship through the lens of cultural value.

Approaches to asset mapping

Asset mapping is a methodology used with community groups and organisations to help unearth, capture and visualise existing resources and capacities, which may otherwise lie undiscovered and underused. Rather than focusing on deficits or things that are missing, asset-based approaches suggest that community groups will be better equipped to develop their projects if they can identify and mobilise the assets they already have (Kretzmann et al, 2005). Assets can be:

- tangible, such as spaces, services and infrastructures
- intangible, such as creative talents, skills, knowledge, social and emotional capital.

O'Leary et al (2011) connect the idea of assets to a 'seven capitals' framework:

- financial
- built
- social
- human

- natural
- cultural
- political.

They emphasise the importance of intangible assets and their role in helping to strengthen and better use other types of assets, such as buildings or money. In contrast to tangible assets, which are more easily recognised and more likely to be already utilised effectively by communities, intangible assets often remain unrecognised and unrepresented. Thus, they can be identified as important carriers of untapped potential and value. As Alice Casey, a Nesta specialist in social and civic innovation, puts it:

> This approach isn't about ignoring needs, it is about finding strengths first. Most communities have considerable

unrecognised assets that can be used and built upon, given flexible, supportive investment. (Guardian Professional, 2 May 2012)

It is also worth noting that within the context of the creative economy, intangible assets now attract more investment in an advanced economy like the UK's than fixed assets, such as buildings and tools. This is all part of the burgeoning service economy, shaped by digital technology and communications (Hargreaves, 2011).

Asset-based approaches have been applied to all kinds of issues (for example, health, built environment, public services, IT). They deploy a variety of methodologies, such as questionnaires, inventories, collaborative workshops, and also a number of visual elicitation methods such as artist-generated representations, network maps or geographic maps. Digital and social media tools are also increasingly used to capture and visualise assets (for example, see Mapping for Change).[1]

Communities and organisations often have their own preferred ways of collecting and recording assets (for example, with regard to contacts, skills and local resources) but more systematic approaches provide better opportunities for *reflection* and *sharing*.

The ABCD institute (based at Northwestern University in the US and a pioneer of asset-based community development) has created a manual in order to help organisations identify their own assets, but also strengthen relationships with community assets (Kretzmann et al, 2005). The manual includes a series of questions to help organisations reflect on their development proposals and their relationships with five types of community assets:

- local residents (and their skills, experience, passions, capabilities and willingness to take part);
- local voluntary associations, clubs and networks;
- local institutions (public organisations, businesses and not-for-profits);
- physical assets (land, buildings, infrastructures);
- economic assets.

The resulting community map is effectively a list of the assets under different categories. The manual goes on to prompt organisations to identify and list their own assets and then think how to connect them to any given proposal. Organisational assets are defined under these categories:

- personnel, space and facilities
- materials and equipment
- expertise; constituents
- networks of connections
- economic power.

The manual also offers other tools for connecting assets, including an individual capacity inventory (gifts/abilities, skills and dreams), a master list of associations, and diagrams helping illustrate existing and potential partnerships with other organisations.

The ABCD approach is primarily targeted to community-based organisations to help them connect with their communities. As a result, the terminology and categories of assets used are quite domain-specific and do not translate easily for use with the wider spectrum of creative entities we encountered in the Creative Citizen project. These ranged from small two-person partnerships and loosely defined grass roots groups, to social enterprises and creative networks. In addition, the ABCD manual contains a lot of useful materials but all in the form of questionnaires and inventories, which lack the creative and engaging quality of other, more visual approaches, examples of which are included in Figure 8.1.

ABCD and related approaches take pains to ensure intangible assets are captured, with a particular focus upon 'people' assets, such as skills, knowledge, personal experiences and cultural traditions. The *Appreciating Assets* report (O'Leary et al, 2011) highlights the fact that intangible assets can be individual, collective ('held by multiple people in the community') or 'held in relationship' (2011: 12). Indeed what is of value for a community or a project may be the existence of a relationship between assets rather that the existence of individual or collective assets as such. This insight often remains unrepresented or merely implicit in applications of asset mapping techniques.

In the case of geographic asset mapping, approaches and tools (as for example, the community maps of Mapping for Change mentioned above), the focus tends to be on physical, tangible assets, such as buildings, parks and spaces, along with the organisations that occupy them. Although some applications accommodate recording of personal stories about a locale, people skills and resources cannot easily be mapped. The same is true of other types of intangible asset that are not geographically defined, such as media, infrastructures, personal networks and cultural events. Geographic maps also tend to be for a neighbourhood or community at large, encouraging everything in an area 'of generic value' within the neighbourhood to be mapped

Figure 8.1: Different asset mapping approaches. Top left: Laura Sorvala's emotional mapping; top right: Gail Ramster's mapping of asset relationships. Bottom left: Tessy Britton's mapping using physical props; bottom right: Catherine Greig's geographical asset mapping

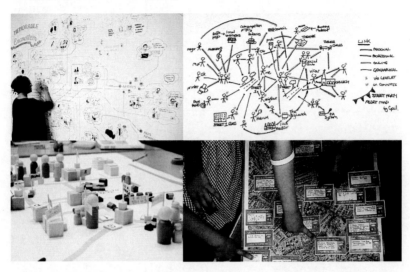

Sources: Memorable encounters by Laura Sorvala, www.auralab.co.uk; Nesta/NVCO Neighbourhood Challenge Workshop; Peckham by Tessy Britton, www.tessybritton.com; Townhill Park School Workshop by Catherine Greig, make:good, make-good.com

without establishing whether it is an asset for a particular purpose or project. In the geographical maps, there is also no distinction between existing and potential assets, thus limiting their application, for example, as instruments facilitating design and development.

A final dimension worth mentioning is how different methods approach the creation of asset maps. In the ABCD approach, people working individually and in groups identify assets through a reflective process. Other approaches may crowd source information (online or through surveys for example); while others rely on individual experts capturing or helping to describe assets on behalf of communities through diverse methods such as drawing, collage or model making.

Creative citizen asset mapping methodology

Principles

To develop our asset mapping method we took into consideration and built upon a number of existing approaches (Mathie and Cunningham, 2002; Kretzmann et al, 2005; Rowson et al, 2010; O'Leary et al, 2011; Guintoli et al, 2012). We also consulted experts and undertook a period of experimentation where various versions were tested with different groups. Amendments took into consideration the need for flexibility (so that the approach can be used in a variety of community settings), practicality (taking into consideration the needs and the time limitations of community participants) and observability (the need to be able to document observations and outcomes for further detailed analysis).

From ABCD we adopted the principle of using a specific project to focus and ground the process. We also took ideas about mapping existing and potential assets, as well as incorporating individual and group activities. Our ideas about intangible assets were informed by the *Appreciating Assets* report, as well as the RSA *Connected Communities* report (Rowson et al, 2010), which emphasised the notion of social capital (that is, connections between people) as an asset. Our approach, however, is distinctive in that it has a dual purpose (as a research and co-design tool), which is achieved through a combination of four elements:

1. capturing tangible and intangible assets
2. mapping relationships between assets
3. capturing the stories and rationale behind assets
4. engaging people creatively and in a playful way.

Following the project's literature review and a series of discussions, interviews and workshops with experts, we concluded that asset mapping would offer a useful tool for structuring the process of engagement and fertilising the co-design activities with our chosen creative citizen communities. Furthermore, we saw an opportunity to use asset mapping as a research tool for understanding the values that drive creative civic actions and the value generated from these actions. A map of a community's assets is a representation in time, so mapping assets before and after our co-production activities would help record any changes in the community's perception of its assets and any value added due to these activities (for example, new assets, or better connectivity between assets). Comparison between maps created by different types of community would also be useful for gaining a wider understanding of the things creative citizens value and towards which they contribute value. So, in this research, the asset mapping method had to be useful in two ways: as a research tool and as a co-design and co-production tool.

Our method in detail

The method captures various types of assets using six categories, each represented by a different three-dimensional object or prop:

1. spaces (built or open)
2. people (their roles, skills, capabilities)
3. infrastructures
4. groups and businesses (public, private and civil society organisations operating at local and national level, clubs, networks)
5. media (online or offline)
6. other – namely anything that doesn't fit in the other categories, picking up for example cultural events and concepts (see Figure 8.2).

The inclusion of the category 'media' is unique in asset-mapping practice to date and has a deliberately central role owing to the subject matter of this research. Participants are encouraged to think about social and other online media (for example, Facebook, blogs, Twitter, as well as websites and discussion forums), but also more traditional means of communication through newspapers, newsletters, face-to-face meetings and events.

The method uses a map that is organised into three concentric circles. Participants are invited to imagine that their project is at the centre of the map and to prioritise different assets at their disposal, according to how important they are to the project, or how easily they can be mobilised. Assets at the centre are more active or important; assets at the periphery can be seen as untapped or potential assets.

Participants are then invited to construct three types of map: a current assets group map, personal asset maps and a potential assets group map. A facilitator explains the process and helps participants construct the maps by reflecting on their assets and reasons for their value.

• Current assets group map: participants take turns to create a collective map of current assets by negotiating the value of each asset, its position and its relationship to other assets.
• Personal asset maps: individual maps are created to capture personal values and individual connections to different assets. Participants are asked to place themselves (rather than the project) at the centre of the map and consider their own roles and connections with assets on the collective map.
• Potential assets group map: a potential assets map is constructed collectively to identify missing or underused resources, and to kick-start the generation of a common vision and ideas for new projects and potential solutions.

While group maps are representations of consensual ideas about a community's assets, a personal asset map helps to explore individual

Figure 8.2: Types of assets used in the creative citizen asset mapping methodology

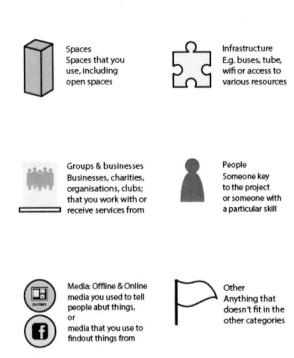

Asset Mapping
Key to assets

Spaces
Spaces that you
use, including
open spaces

Infrastructure
E.g. buses, tube,
wifi or access to
various resources

Groups & businesses
Businesses, charities,
organisations, clubs;
that you work with or
receive services from

People
Someone key
to the project
or someone with
a particular skill

Media: Offline & Online
media you used to tell
people abut things,
or
media that you use to
findout things from

Other
Anything that
doesn't fit in the
other categories

perceptions of value, which may or may not be shared among the whole group. It also provides a personal thinking space for individuals to understand their own role and potential contributions.

Asking people to rationalise why certain assets are considered to be valuable and to negotiate their relative importance is crucial for community building, helping the group to establish a shared understanding and a common vision. Giving everyone an equal opportunity to add an asset and rationalise it before opening it up to discussion creates a level playing field, avoiding dominance from those most central to the project or, perhaps, focused on the 'correct' or 'established' view, thus making innovative insights more likely. Individual perceptions are of value even if others in the group then challenge them. Capturing those narratives is also important for research purposes, helping to understand group dynamics and people's

Figure 8.3: The creative citizen asset mapping kit and examples of group and individual maps

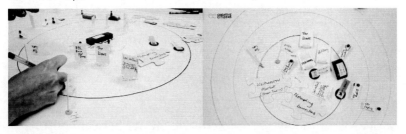

individual and shared values. Transcripts of the conversations help both the researchers and the participants to reflect on their underlying values, perceptions and motivations.

The use of physical props that can be moved around, redefined and repositioned is considered important for facilitating active, playful and creative engagement. Assets become more tangible as they are externalised and become literally graspable. At the same time they become more negotiable as they can be renamed, repositioned, combined and even discarded.

Relationships among assets are captured in different ways. Assets in the same circle are loosely related in terms of their importance, but participants are also encouraged to consider explicit relationships between assets by clustering them together, combining them, or moving them further apart. Relationships might include conceptual and geographical links, business or working relationships, personal connections and social bonds. Relationships are also captured through personal asset maps, where individuals reflect on their connections with assets identified on the collective map and the strength of those connections. Implicit relationships are also identified by aggregating information on the individual maps (where, for example, a person is found to be connected to an asset through another person).

Application across case studies

The asset mapping methodology was applied across all three strands of work of the Creative Citizen project: among hyperlocal journalists; creative networks; and community groups involved in place-making projects, making nine case studies in total. These cases were:

- three hyperlocals: *Tyburn Mail*, *Connect Cannock* and *Pobl Caerdydd*, in Birmingham, Cannock and Cardiff respectively;

- two creative networks in Bristol and Birmingham, namely South Blessed and the Moseley Community Development Trust;
- four place-making community groups in London: Goldsmiths Community Centre (GCC), Kentish Town Neighbourhood Forum (KTNF), The Mill community space, and Wards Corner Community Coalition (WCC).

The hyperlocals represented a range of organisational setups: from an individual running a website outside of his normal job (*Connect Cannock*), an established small community media company with a professional journalist creating a monthly newsletter (*Tyburn Mail*) and a small collective running a Welsh language blog (*Pobl Caerdydd* [Cardiff People]). South Blessed is an informal youth network which showcases talent from South West England in creative activities ranging from film, to music, street art and comics, while Moseley Community Development Trust (Moseley CDT) is a local development charity leading various social, economic and environmental projects as well as running a co-working space for creative entrepreneurs. The four place-making projects were chosen to be representative of a wide spectrum of communities and purposes. These were:

- a young community centre and social enterprise that was originally set up with funds from a public body with the aim to create innovative responses to local issues (The Mill);
- a grass roots organisation campaigning to save a local market from demolition and gentrification of the area and push forward with an alternative community plan (WCC);
- a long established not-for-profit community centre struggling with cuts in public funds and seeking to redefine its role and engagement in the local area (GCC);
- a neighbourhood forum established to shape development of its neighbourhood, taking advantage of the new rights and powers given to communities by the Localism Act (KTNF).

The number of participants in the asset mapping workshops varied from two to three individuals in the case of hyperlocal bloggers, four people each in South Blessed and Moseley CDT, and between eight and 15 people in the place-making communities. The same kit was used in each case, but adjustments were made according to individual conditions. For example, the exercise was carried out right at the beginning of the co-design process with the four place-making groups, but the timescales with other groups varied. Owing to time limitations and people's availability, individual maps were sometimes created at a different time, or using pen and paper instead of the physical props.

The maps were embedded in the co-creation process to different degrees and in different ways. In the community-led design strand, the group maps themselves were digitised/visualised and brought back to the groups to motivate further reflections (Figure 8.4).

Figure 8.4: Visualisations of the asset maps produced to share with community groups

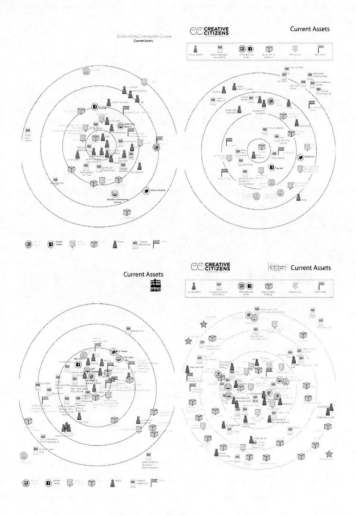

In some cases digitising and interlinking with personal maps helped to reveal how a group was connected and who held the relationships connecting assets. This had practical value, helping, for example, to understand the critical role of certain people as connectors and identifying 'weak ties'. It also helped reveal where some participants unknowingly had assets in common, such as varied connections to a park that was not currently playing a large role in the project (Figure 8.5).

Figure 8.5: A digital map incorporating group assets and personal connections to these assets

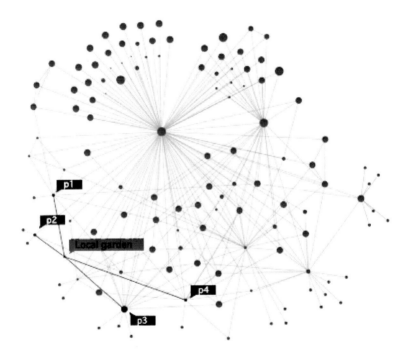

In two cases (KTNF and GCC), the identified assets were used as part of a brainstorming activity to support the generation of ideas for media projects (Figure 8.6). In this activity, participants were asked randomly to combine two assets to seed ideas for co-design projects and then think of how specific media assets might further help realise these projects. At the end, ideas were clustered together where appropriate and participants voted for their favourite projects. This shortlist became the basis for further co-creation activities.

Figure 8.6: Assets used to generate ideas for media projects with communities

Asset mapping was repeated at the end of the co-creation process with four out of nine projects. The repeat asset maps helped participants reflect on their journey and changes that had occurred, but also helped researchers understand the impact (the value generated) from the activities.

Insights across the case studies: what assets creative citizens hold and generate

The maps that were created involved different types of creative citizenship activity, different types of community and differing purposes. Those differences are reflected on the maps. For example, Bristol is placed prominently at the centre of the South Blessed map, revealing the importance of the local milieu in the shaping of the identity and opportunities of this creative network. The map of KTNF contains more spaces than any of the other maps (almost as many as among all of the other three maps of the place-making groups). These spaces are mainly at the periphery of the map, revealing the concern of the neighbourhood forum for better utilising and connecting those spaces. On the other hand, in the maps of the two community centres (The Mill and GCC), people such as community workers and volunteers take a very central place, as they are central to their operation. The maps of the hyperlocal bloggers are much more personal and focused around practice.

However there were also significant similarities across the maps.

People and groups and businesses

From a total of 360 assets identified in the maps, 53% fall under the category of people or groups and businesses (Figure 8.7). These two types of assets were also predominantly at the centre of the maps.

Figure 8.7: Percentages of the different types of assets identified in the maps. Over half of the assets identified were people or groups and businesses.

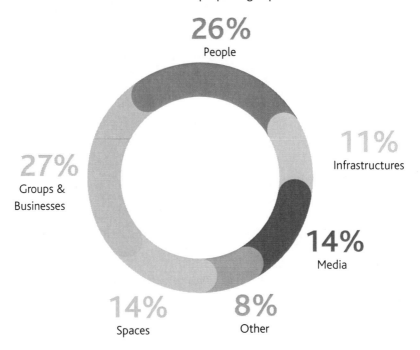

26% People
11% Infrastructures
27% Groups & Businesses
14% Media
14% Spaces
8% Other

This highlights the importance of intangible assets in creative citizenship activities and particularly the importance of human and social capital. For example, WCC explicitly identified social capital as one of its assets. Its social capital is created through connections with national and local groups (including housing associations and local businesses), but also through recognition and celebration of its cultural diversity:

> "Social Capital – Wards Corner as a space and as a coalition that represents the interests of the multicultural draw… If it wasn't for social capital nothing could happen: the reason even we are here is because of that. The social capital in Wards Corner, geographically, also is quite big, it is large. It is larger than any other place I think, not only in Tottenham but probably a few miles around… People travel

through that and they see each other and they know the space and everybody uses the space, and you see people as a consequence of that but it is also I suppose an ethos of always paying attention to personal relationships to build solidarity."

Moseley CDT participants also recognised the importance of social capital:

"It is the 'valuable network connections' that happen in this place. It is hard to put in concrete terms, but it is all the connections that Person 3, Person 1 and I have. They all come together under one roof here. That is something we probably need to harness more."

Similarly, The Mill's asset mapping participants added a lot of the different clubs and groups that run in The Mill's spaces – knitting group, chess club, guitar lessons, sewing machine lessons. This recording of tangible groups that use The Mill in a literal way led to a discussion about more intangible assets – the practical or trade skills of these individuals and networks that connect them – and how they can be called on both to do useful things for The Mill and be a route for The Mill to engage local young people to learn by bringing them into this network to learn about different professions or do apprenticeships.

The asset maps of South Blessed were also people-centric and discussions helped reveal the importance of the kind of collaborative currency that circulates in informal networks (sharing and non-monetary exchanges of 'gifts'/gift economy) and which leads to benefits such as self- and community-actualisation, credibility and recognition.

Crucially, the potential maps produced by the groups were also largely focused on other groups, organisations and spaces where more connections with other groups and people can be fostered and developed.

Media

Media were also quite central on these maps, and people valued both online and offline media. The maps contained an average of six media assets, with Facebook, Twitter and project websites being the three predominant assets.

Social media were universally considered to be important assets, becoming part of the practice of those communities. In the hyperlocal case studies it was clear that social media had become important both for connecting to community members but also in searching for content, for stories. For example, at *Tyburn Mail* they described Twitter as: "much more significant than it ever has been [...] It is something that I refer to several times per day." With *Connect Cannock* in particular there was a developed understanding of the way in which social media can collapse the boundaries between content producer, source and audience member. Those that might be largely positioned as general 'audience' also played their part in sourcing content and even in helping extend the reach of the hyperlocal:

> "Facebook readers or Twitter readers ... they're the ones who share posts and they retweet and push it outwards."

Similarly, in KTNF and The Mill, social media were universally considered to be important, despite most people in the room not engaging with them. This reinforced the reasons why these groups were involved in the creative citizen project to begin with. They respected and saw the potential in digital media, but they had not done much with it beyond 'having a Facebook', or their social media was reaching out but not engaging local people effectively.

Despite often tending to cluster social media under the same heading, the various groups recognised that different media serve or are better used for different purposes. For example, in South Blessed one of the participants commented about the use of social media for distribution of their work as well as wider communication and advertisement:

> "YouTube is your platform/product. Facebook/Twitter are your means to advertise."

There were also distinctions between the platforms with *Pobl Caerdydd* describing how some content suits one platform and not the other:

> "It's been a Facebook thing, because there's an image there and it's guaranteed it goes on there."

In GCC, the key community development worker managing social media outlets also commented about different purposes and audiences:

"Now the Goldsmiths website connects Goldsmiths to all of the outside world, not just Downham. Lewisham and [other boroughs]. The Facebook is one that I use to connect to generally with people within the centre who have Facebook accounts … I am a Twitterer as well … I have got people connected in the wider world."

Across the case studies the discussions also highlighted the importance of using multiple local and national media. WCC, for example, uses local newspapers as well as their website, Twitter and Facebook at different points in time:

"I suppose we use local newspapers pretty effectively at points in time. They come in and out but that is quite an important part of creating the culture of the campaign. I think they have been a contributory … with various points in the campaign."

"Twitter is important because it connects us with a different network, but also a wider network of people and not always locally. Especially like a lot of local journalists that don't come to the meetings."

However, the maps and discussions surrounding the value of media also revealed that social media work alongside more traditional avenues for communicating activities and achievements, raising awareness and inviting participation and support: printed media (posters, leaflets, newsletters), email lists and word of mouth being the most important. The comment below, for example, from one of the KTNF participants, resonates with what has been said by all the place-making communities:

"If you want to attract local people, then I'd say paper messaging is a lot better than the web, as that could reach someone on the other side of the world, whereas leaflets if you're walking around you see them."

While media proved to be a vital intangible asset for the groups we have worked with, it is important to note the often exclusive character of different types of media. So while social media may facilitate easy access to information and draw in more participation (especially as they are easily accessed from a person's mobile phone) they necessarily exclude certain types of people – for which more traditional means of communication might be more appropriate.

The WCC group also recorded challenges relating to language (as the market is host to a large Spanish speaking community) and digital literacy. Considering the role of media as an asset for creative citizens it is important to highlight the value of people who have the media and communication skills, and the time to use and maintain the various outlets.

Spaces

All case studies also had a strong emphasis on spaces (as they are geographically defined) and the maps showed that groups clearly valued their local spaces, particularly for their potential to generate social capital and a sense of identity and belonging.

In our hyperlocal strand, practitioners were inevitably tied to place and their services tied to their continued presence in the locality. *Pobl Caerdydd* practitioners were proud of being from Cardiff and cited the advantage it gave them in knowing the city well and being on the spot when news stories broke. *Pobl Caerdydd* also cited the value in playing to issues of Welsh national identity in drawing in audiences and creating connections. They talked of 'gaming' Facebook by asking readers to share patriotic messages:

> "We pepper what we do with 'Come on Wales', almost like little postcards that people can share on their timelines."

In Tyburn issues of place were acutely felt in relation to the area's reputational geography and the impact of local authority cuts that have resulted in a shift of focus away from the role of the council and towards the private sector:

> "In a way they are kind of withdrawing from the estate ... they have gone from being really important to us, in terms of news, what's happening. They will be almost irrelevant soon."

In this sense the hyperlocal has a role in documenting the changing economic and political landscape as volunteerism becomes more important in shoring up local amenities and the role of individual citizens, rather than organisations take centre stage and become key assets in localities.

Location was also very important for South Blessed and Moseley CDT. For South Blessed, being in Bristol provides both a cultural reference point but also connections to people and access to infrastructures:

> "South Blessed is meant to be a South West thing but Bristol is the capital of what I am doing ... central to everything."

> "Bristol feels balanced ... a creative graveyard but still offers potential/opportunity − the geography of Bristol makes things doable."

Similarly, being in the Moseley Village was crucial for the Community Development Trust's identity and operation:

> "It is just the location, the history, its reputation, and its facilities. I think it is an important asset that [the CDT] is located in this particular environment. It is one of our key selling points."

Place was obviously a key theme in the discussions among the various place-making communities. The asset mapping participants in GCC for example, discussed at length the value of their 70-year-old building and the potential as well as the difficulties and limitations it carries with it:

> "I would want to consider the building itself. Because that is our biggest asset I think, it is also the biggest noose around our neck because it costs a fortune to heat it, light it and maintain it. So I am struggling with where I should put it."

The Mill was initially a 'negative' asset for the local council, until members of the group took over the building as a community space. The Mill's rooms and space became positive assets through the activities and the relationships built between The Mill and the council and other organisations in the area:

> "So there were already assets here that attracted us as an organisation, so the first thing was social enterprises that already rent in this space, that it had really attractive training space as well, and we found out about it by talking to the councillors ... and people in the local authority said, 'You should go to The Mill, you should go to The Mill'; so many people said, 'You should go to The Mill'."

While other place-making projects are either campaigning about or operating from a single building, KTNF has a very wide area of interest (covering the whole of Kentish Town) and no base of their own. Their asset map therefore had more spaces marked than any other group and many of the spaces identified were local pubs, community centres and churches where they have or could hold meetings or community engagement activities.

A more detailed account of the relationships between creative citizens and their spaces, drawing on our case studies can be found in Chapter 9.

Overall, the asset maps themselves and the accompanying discussions exposed diverse motivations and standpoints for creative citizens, but also a huge underlying 'economy' which is founded on intangible assets. Creative citizens value their culture, their history, their connections to their place and to each other but they are also imaginative. They look forward and outwards and create new tools, services and spaces to promote social, cultural and civic purposes.

Evaluation and legacy

The asset mapping methodology was evaluated through discussions and questionnaires with participants, direct observations and through a reflective workshop with researchers and community partners.

In evaluation questionnaires (with 15 people), participants agreed that asset mapping helped unearth and visualise local assets but also that it helped articulate a vision about what is important for future actions. This supports our claim that the method is useful as a research tool as well as a co-design tool.

We have presented insights gained from the use of asset mapping as a research tool. Turning to the maps themselves and the discussions around them, we were able to elicit significant information about what our sample of creative citizens perceive as valuable resources, and what value they build through their activities. The method provided a structured way to do this in a group setting, whilst understanding collective perceptions. These things would not be easily achieved using interviews or focus group discussions. It also helped understand and negotiate relationships between individual and collective perceptions of assets.

Our original hypothesis was that we would be able to use asset mapping at different stages (at the beginning and at the end of the projects) to gauge the value generated from our co-design activities. Repetition of the asset mapping at the end of each project was challenging with some communities, owing to the changing dynamics of people involved (people coming and going or changing roles within a group), and changes in their immediate needs and objectives as the project progressed. The temporal aspect of community projects and of citizenship as a practice requires an adaptable methodology for capturing and mobilising people's assets. In the case of WCC for example, the repeat workshop was divided in two phases: one in which the group reflected back on the original maps and was encouraged to record changes; and a second phase where a new asset map was created, drawing from the original but with a new focus at the centre that was current at the time. This ensured that the workshop was useful both for reflecting back and for thinking forward. The repeat asset mapping revealed a few cases where new assets cropped up and old assets have disappeared (some organisations that ceased to exist) or changed place in terms of importance (people or organisations whose role or contribution changed in importance). The discussions also revealed that the group gained a greater appreciation of the value of media, directly linking to the co-design activities that took place. The main outcome however was that the group showed a better connection to and understanding of their assets as a whole. Asset mapping was therefore useful in helping the group reflect and externalise its assets, and served as a tool for directing future activities. In the questionnaire one of the participants commented:

> "[Initially] It felt a bit as if we were asked for info and then told back what we had said – I didn't think it was helpful at the time, but… [it has] been useful since then."

This also points to the fact that the most successful application of the methodology was when it was embedded in the co-creation process, rather than seen as a research add-on.

For example in Moseley CDT, the team had already completed interviews with staff and board members as well as a media workshop with board members and co-workers, so the asset mapping workshop didn't play a part in the generation of a vision and ideas for co-design as it did in the place-making groups. However, the workshop still proved to be useful not only for the researchers but also for the people who participated in it, as it helped increase communication, discussion and consensus building between them. The exercise brought people around the table who do not routinely meet and created the opportunity for some less dominant or divergent voices to be heard, enabling implicit issues to come to light and be negotiated.

The workshop had a similar function in KTNF. Here, asset mapping provided a welcome opportunity for information exchange between central figures and other members. The central figures shared details about all the work they had done to engage people in the forum, and the other members sometimes hit on a local asset that had not been tapped into, therefore giving ideas for future engagement. Respecting the rules of the game (turn taking and allowing assets to be equally considered and negotiated) was instrumental in achieving this outcome. Involving people who are not central in the operation of each group was generally beneficial, not only helping to build stronger relationships in the community, but also helping to provide innovative and 'fresh' thinking as well as validity to the groups' decisions and actions.

Considering the effectiveness of the method as a co-creation tool, we found that the exercise was more useful when the project at the centre of the map was well understood and the participants shared a common sense of purpose or a priority tied to a specific deadline (for example, a planning application). This might indicate that the methodology works best with communities who are already well formed, or when it is used at a more advanced stage of the co-design process, rather than the beginning. However, it was also found useful in helping create a common vision and ideas for new projects. Participants found the prioritisation element (deciding which assets to place more centrally) quite useful, helping to reflect on the relative value of different assets in terms of importance, accessibility and potential for development. In WCC, for example, the community plan was a priority at the time of the first asset mapping workshop. The subsequent co-design process with the research team was successful in that it helped to provide a focus for the work of the group around the community plan (focusing attention on a media intervention that would 'translate the community plan' for a wider audience), at the same time utilising and connecting to other assets identified at the workshop.

In the reflective conversations, participants and experts generally concluded that the methodology offered an engaging and playful way to elicit people's perceptions and narratives around what they value locally, and to stimulate thinking about how assets can be mobilised. The positive characteristics identified were:

- the physicality of the prompts and their playful character;
- the dialogical element;
- the prioritisation element;
- the element of thinking about relationships between assets;

- the variety of assets explored (both tangible and intangible);
- the link to purposeful action (a project).

These conversations were particularly encouraging as all these elements were programmatically considered and designed into the method. The discussions and comparative evaluation of other asset mapping approaches also unearthed various avenues for development. One area of potential development was around eliciting emotions as an important intangible asset, which helps to reveal people's perceptions of identity and belonging and to uncover connections to place, history and society. Opportunities were also identified for combining different approaches either by creating new hybrids, such as combinations of creative citizen asset mapping techniques with geographical mapping, or using different methods at various stages of the co-design process, where they can be more instrumental.

The methodology has been quite adaptable overall and has been successfully applied with variations to other research projects in UK and abroad (for example, the AHRC funded Unearthing Hidden Assets and Co-designing Asset Mapping projects).[2] These developments add weight to the understanding and value of asset mapping as a research tool. To be of further use to researchers, as well as to community groups and organisations, the asset mapping methodology has been made freely available online as a tool, containing the main asset categories and prompts and guidance for use in different contexts – through the *Seeing Things Differently* booklet,[3] produced as part of the co-design process with GCC.

Summary and conclusion

This chapter has introduced asset mapping as a tool for capturing and understanding the values that drive creative civic actions as well as the value generated from these actions. We reviewed different asset mapping or asset-based development approaches and presented an approach that was developed and used in the creative citizen project, with the dual purpose of supporting research and facilitating collaborative creation. In line with a growing body of investigations that draw attention to the need for capturing intangible aspects of value, the approach focuses on eliciting intangible assets such as knowledge, capabilities and skills, as well as social and cultural relationships and connections. Such intangible assets often remain unrecognised and unrepresented but are the main carriers of untapped potential and value for communities. The approach also places emphasis on creative engagement and provides a space for sharing narratives and rationale behind assets.

Insights were drawn together from the application of the methodology across nine case studies, covering different types of creative citizenship. There were many difficulties with using asset mapping in a systematic way across those studies, but the empirical evidence suggests that the methodology is useful for unearthing and capturing people's values and perceptions of value, and as a tool for community engagement and co-creation. More important, the insights drawn from the case studies substantiate the idea that creative citizens utilise and create a rich variety of assets for themselves and the world around them in their processes of collective action.

Notes

[1] www.mappingforchange.org.uk
[2] comparativeassetmapping.org
[3] creativecitizens.co.uk/files/2014/07/GCC_Booklet_Final.pdf

NINE

Civic cultures and modalities of place-making

*Giota Alevizou, Katerina Alexiou, Dave Harte, Shawn Sobers,
Theodore Zamenopoulos and Jerome Turner*

Introduction

Acts of creative citizenship require places, where challenges and tensions generate energy, inviting resolution through creative collaboration. In this chapter we aim to shed light on processes of place-making, whether they occur in physical, digital or hybrid spaces. We adopt a broad definition of place to explore what place and making mean within three urban settings of our action research. In all three of these locations, we encounter groups that share an interest in the relationship between artistic imagination and its political expression in projects of urban renewal. We pay particular attention to the ways in which communicative infrastructures may contribute to the construction of social relationships and civic agency, leading to dividends in the form of enhanced networks of affinity, trust and resilience.

Place and media making in a digital world

The emergence of web-based community news sites has provoked much discussion about the citizen voice in localities (Radcliffe, 2012; Goggin et al, 2015). Hyperlocal news services are usually discussed in relation to their value as a potential solution to the problem of news plurality in localities. However, hyperlocal news can also play a crucial role in place-making. Kirsty Hess (2012) has argued that the emergence of the term hyperlocal is evidence of 'a reinvigorated interest in geography, as media industry and entrepreneurs experiment with new business models in the changing technological landscape' (Hess, 2012: 53). Borrowing from Manuel Castells, she argues that small local newspapers act as nodes, holding 'a degree of symbolic power in constructing the idea of community and the local' (Hess, 2012: 56).

In a digitally networked world, geography is 'local and global at the same time' (Castells, 2012: 222).

The perspective of place is also fundamental within the broader landscape of participatory media/arts and community media. Goldfarb (2002) shows how participatory creative networks generate communities of interest, fostering civic engagement through their media making. As Couldry et al (2014: 1) write: 'digital media and digital infrastructures provide the means to recognise people in new ways as active narrators of their individual lives and the issues they share with others'. These affordances are said to be particularly important for young people, who through creative media acts acquire agency in civic debates (Günnel, 2006), offering a 'voice to the voiceless' (Lewis P., 2006). According to Phil Shepherd, former chair of the UK's Community Media Association, the practice of community media should be viewed as: '80% community and 20% media'.[1] Even where participants in community media think of themselves primarily as individual creators, their activities have implicit consequences for the communities of which they are members (Howley, 2005: 178; Rennie, 2006; Gidley and Slater, 2007: 57; Sobers, 2010). Place transcends geography, and presents itself as a crucible for ideology and values. Relevant notions of place extend from the smallest local community to the whole earth.

Citizen rooted place-making is a well established concept in the domain of urban studies and participatory design and planning. Contested neighbourhoods are seen as potentially transformable by citizens' creative agency (for example, Silberbergh et al, 2013). Several researchers and practitioners highlight the potent fusion of attachment, civic creativity and social capital (such as Alexiou et al, 2013; Laylard et al, 2013). In an era of instant communication, community media and social networking are also crucial (see Carvalho, 2011; Foth et al, 2011). Urban development literature includes a large body of work addressing the prevalence of culture-led urban governance and regeneration practice since the 1980s. According to Kloosterman (2014), a second wave of this work has emerged in response to the 2008 financial crisis and the resulting 'age of austerity'. Miles (2005) and Chapple and Jackson (2010) argue that the resulting top-down instrumentalisation of culture for urban development purposes may privilege certain cultural practices over others, promoting commercialisation and standardisation of urban cultures, along with property-led gentrification and displacement of low-income communities. Roberto Bedoya (2012) makes this point followed by a question:

Placemaking in city/neighbourhood spaces enacts identity and activities that allow personal memories, cultural histories, imagination and feelings to enliven the sense of 'belonging' through human and spatial relationships. But a political understanding of who is in and who is out is also central to civic vitality. How do current Creative Placemaking practices support this knowledge?

In approaching civic culture through a 'constructionist and materialist' framework, Dahlgren (2003: 104; 2009) pays close attention to the cultural patterns in which civic agency is embedded. Rooted in the sociology of collective action, he proposes a model of civic culture involving a 'circuit' of six interlocking dimensions of mutual reciprocity that condition processes of political participation: knowledge, values, affinity/trust, practices, identities and discussion/spaces.

Putnam's (2001) notion of 'social capital' views it as social connections within networks of reciprocal relations, tied in membership through formal organisations. Dahlgren's (2003) schema extends this to encompass the mobilisation of informal resources, supported by the role of digital media in a networked society, where one of the dimensions in play is that of place.

Creative citizenship brings to the fore a new emphasis on the creative process of groups and publics and the potential to drive social change. The circuit of civic culture highlights the many conditions within which these acts can materialise through the use of media and digital technologies (see also Gilchrist, 2009; Papacharissi, 2010a). A number of aspects are worth unpacking regarding these intersections.

First, space is conceived as a place for communicative exchange, through digital media and via physical civic encounters, which in turn 'make space' for democracy. The assumption here is that place can enable a communicative matrix – a terrain of media innovations residing alongside mass media, face-to-face encounters and word of mouth – and thereby facilitate new kinds of democratically accountable civic practice. Second, digital media facilitate storytelling, supporting the emergence of 'conversational media' (Lambert, 2006: 17) and 'story circles' (Hartley and McWilliam, 2009). These ideas are particularly pertinent to an urban civic culture embedded in the multicultural city (Georgiou, 2013). Third, for Dahlgren, 'civic skills and creativity can develop through practices, and in this process foster a sense of empowerment; the dimensions of practices and identities are closely intertwined' (2009: 118). Dahlgren stresses that these identities have a strong emotional content, inviting media researchers to analyse the effects of media on civic identity, taking account of the extent to which 'we-ness' can result nowadays from engagement with popular culture.

Activist planning: the Wards Corner Community Coalition

Our first case study relates to the activist and volunteer community group campaigning to halt the demolition of a city block, Wards Corner, in Tottenham, North London. This space hosted a richly multicultural indoor market, numerous independent businesses and residences. In February 2011 *Time Out*, a London publication devoted to listings and culture, described Tottenham's booming creative industries scene and convivial counterculture, conjuring up the spectre of imminent gentrification (Koch, 2011). Since the August 2011 riots, the area has been subject to stigmatising narratives (Wacquant et al, 2014), provoking, some have noted, an almost punitive regeneration of Tottenham (Peacock, 2014), involving large-scale public and private investments and a series of formal consultations (for example, London Plan; Tottenham Futures).

Rooted in principles of participatory planning and community-led design, the Wards Corner Community Coalition (WCC) predates these developments. Formed in 2007, WCC describes itself as a grass roots group of local residents, civic organisations and traders, who have worked to produce an alternative proposition for the Wards Corner heritage building and the adjacent commercial and residential block. Their plan was granted planning permission in April 2014. At the time of writing the group is seeking ways to achieve wider participation of local businesses and residents and gain funding through a Community Development Trust, which would make the plan a reality.

Our research team worked directly with WCC between 2012 and 2015, using techniques such as asset mapping to co-produce media interventions (see Chapters 7 and 8). Here we aim to shed light upon notions of civic creativity and creative agency, showing how valuable knowledge about the place is formed and shared by processes of mediated place-making.

The WCC logo (Figure 9.1) captures the ethos and practices of the group. The monochrome design makes a bold statement, popular in DIY activism; it playfully evokes a mission to advocate the heritage goal of restoring unique architectural features and the name of its formerly iconic department store, whilst also making a pun about contemporary urban planning: 'Restoration For *Wards*'.

The 'Plan for the Community' tag, says one WCC member, aims to capture the social, rather than the heritage or aesthetic aspects

Figure 9.1: Wards Corner Community Coalition Logos (courtesy WCC)

of the campaign and evokes substantive values within the group: representation and justice, caring and solidarity: "The building is about promoting a community-led plan for the wider area; a plan that … would respect the livelihoods of local residents and local business rather than displacing people."

The logo thus offers a multilayered story of heritage, affect and inclusiveness; an aspiration to galvanise values of social solidarity and local identity.

The differing goals of the campaign and its core media outputs reflect the range of those involved in WCC and their broad spread of identities. The charts in Figure 9.2 capture the range of working and voluntary work backgrounds of campaigners.

Figure 9.2: Wards Corner Community Coalition participant profiles

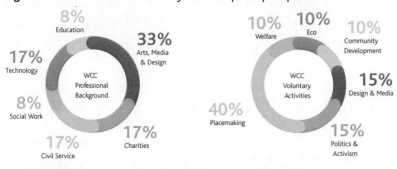

Note: n: 13 participants.
Source: Asset mapping workshop, February 2013

The group is strong in creative and technology backgrounds, but a range of other professional identities balances these. The group also includes those with longstanding expertise in civic matters, along with experienced local networkers – residents and traders, who also know from necessity the legal practicalities of planning and power relations. The fact that the group adopted the word 'coalition' in its title also indicates a readiness to combine diverse civil society networks:

- tenants and residents' associations
- cultural interest groups
- friends of parks
- business, shops, traders' associations
- other community-led planning groups.

Knowledge sharing about planning issues and a commitment to shared values are combined. For some members, motivation arises from a mix of professional expertise and personal political consciousness:

> "Something we haven't really exploited, we haven't really developed, is about how our approach to thinking about Wards Corner is linked to some wider social, health and economic issues really... I think we are being sold an idea of gentrification and regeneration [that] is going to make us healthier and wealthier and it won't, because actually it just adds more splits with people in society." (Group discussion, February 2013)

For WCC the desire to build connections through local associations (and in social media as we discuss below) is mobilised by the belief that using such networks would foster existing community ties and build a network of *representation* and *trust*. Knowledge sharing and creative mediation of issues around the place are paramount.

Many members of the group are intent upon adding to their knowledge about planning issues and the citizens' potential role in contesting or shaping them. Our fieldwork found many examples of informal learning and knowledge generation practices through creative participation. Several members of WCC have participated in workshops about community planning and have been in contact with relevant charities to seek advice. There is widespread use of the internet and social media to review cases of *success* and tensions surrounding grass roots approaches to community planning.

Knowledge sharing is seen as critical to the pursuit of an effective alternative vision for the Wards Corner site. Some are sceptical about formal local authority consultation processes. As one member reflects:

> "The Localism Act… It has a lot of interesting ideas … but then it kind of merged into very Big Society … a sort of community version of green-washing. None of it really gives any power beyond those that have the power to regulate and know what they can do, but it gives a lot of opportunity to think differently about the prospect of power and what you can do… So it requires a lot of creativity and thinking beyond, often obtuse plans and official policy documents … we are trying to use visual and social media wherever possible, we have taken part in numerous workshops and consultations sessions run by the council, yet most importantly we try to talk to people to learn what really matters to them."

Creative digital technologies have been used in exhibitions and local festivals throughout the campaign to enhance the aura of the market and stimulate discussion about the multicultural draw of the place. The group's website, designed as a wiki, aimed to offer a transparent and participatory approach to community engagement, whilst acting as an archive for planning documents, press releases, and the accumulated experiences of cooperation and mutual recognition. One member, who had managed the site almost exclusively, has described the impact of these online materials on other community groups:

> "The website has always been set up as an archive; an archive of campaigning material. It has acted as an important resource for other groups… It has put together all the materials and paperwork of the judicial review, the London Plan consultations … we get a fairly large amount of requests from other campaign groups, but it's difficult to answer and respond appropriately to all."

While WCC wishes to extend its profile of relevance across social media, there is a clear awareness of the challenging practicalities and tensions about inclusivity, lack of time, competition for attention and a commitment to promoting a consistent message that communicates the group's core values. Issues regarding the potential of digital technologies and social media to scale up accountability and transparency at the organisational level of the group are often set against lack of time and other resource. Other concerns relate to privacy, to issues arising from power relations, critical literacy and critical agency, with the result that solutions sometimes use simpler and more familiar techniques. With a network of almost 1,000 followers combined on Facebook and Twitter, these social media platforms are mostly used as digital noticeboards and tools for raising awareness around specific events at crucial points of the campaign:

> "Twitter is important because it connects us with a different network, but also a wider network of people and not always locally. Especially like a lot of local journalists that don't come to the meetings... But talking to a local audience that don't use social media is the most important aspect ... there's a community base that don't reach these channels; but there's a huge network through the emailing lists – both for internal communication and for coordination and for spreading the message across ... they exist in the context of already vibrant connected infrastructure ... the Haringey Solidarity group, the Haringey Federation ... and others."

The group considers its mailing lists crucial and its largest list has more than 600 members. It shares knowledge across a network of local civic groups, facilitating discussion and plans about events. The effect of these decisions is to strike a balance between public and private communication forums and between digital and physical encounters. The relationship with local newspapers and participation in hyperlocal forums has contributed to 'raising awareness and also creating the culture for the WCC actions at several moments' of the campaign. But there has also been a persistent aspiration to develop more trust in local networks through weekly meetings and regular exhibitions within the market and through participation in local festivals and other events.

> "It is not having an old brick building that would make this part of London interesting. It is not directly an asset, it is only an asset when people take an attitude towards it ... both the building and its adjacent market can be seen as important spaces of agency within this particular part of the city." (Group discussion, asset mapping workshop February 2013)

The affective connection with the 'corner' has also been expressed through the deployment of visual and digital storytelling in the group's public online media – principally the group's website[2] along with blogs. Image galleries – posted on the website and in social media – depict the human dimensions of the campaign and the immersion of the group in local activities. There are other aspects too, depicting the visual biography of the space. These include historical sketches of the Edwardian department store and others describing the contemporary reality of the market. Here the vividness of the market's life is evoked in panoramic views, along with the potential of unused spaces. An archive of short films from core members of the campaign sits with a media archive covering council debates and testimonies of local traders and residents. There is a strong sense of inclusivity. As one of the longest-standing members put it in one of our early discussions: "We have always been seeking out the quietest and least powerful, but equally relevant, voices in this story of potential urban change."

These mediated expressions have provided a sense of aspiration for the simultaneous recuperation of "a site for affordable business space and a cultural destination that puts the public realm at its heart".

The resulting community plan was supported by a set of scaled up drawings and computer generated images (CGIs) created, on a quasi pro bono basis, by an architectural designer who is also a core member of the group (Figure 9.3). CGIs have become commonplace as a means to market urban redevelopments (see Rose et al, 2014). Using digital technologies like Google Sketch Up, to design a projected vision of the future and communicate the aura of the building and its possibilities, this visual content was an attempt to professionalise an otherwise vernacular expression of creativity and so to assert its legitimacy.

Reflecting on the particularities of terrain composition and the use of people within these visual narratives, the architectural designer said

Figure 9.3: CGIs featuring in the community plan (Courtesy Abigail Stevenson; https://wardscornercommunityplan.wordpress.com/wards-corner-market/)

she wanted to add a professional edge to the plan, yet maintain the community's distinctiveness by sourcing human images from WCC community exhibitions and consultation events. In contrast to the developer, Grainger plc's CGIs, this was aimed at evoking 'real, flesh and blood life':

> "So the community plan had to visually come on the same level of Grainger... So that people had a fair chance at understanding what was there available ... because you need to have 'like for like' ... these images aren't as 'bling' as Grainger images... But they get the feeling across. [...] Some of them are people from the market, people from events, others are friends.... And I just wanted to look like ... from Tottenham... You know you've got the hoarding of the pictures for the Stadium ... and it doesn't look from Tottenham – it's all been done for the people that could move in... In these ones with the black silhouette and the real people it's like showing what it is to have fun... I want different people in there ... because so often friends of mine in the architectural school, cut out models from cat walks ... and this is not what this is about ..."

These 3D digital visualisations of the building and the street are more than an aesthetic manifestation of an aspirational future. They function as communicative media within wider cultural and official discourses and practices, made meaningful by the subjective attention of the viewer.

So far we have described a fluid, convergent civic culture where acts of communication surface a renewed impulse for the articulation and mediation of issues, values and tensions that may represent a community's affinity to place and its citizens' aspiration to make place. At the same time, these acts can be thought of as designed, because:

> Each one must be tailored by a reflexive, communicating agent to the specific context in which that communication is taking place: the context includes the communicator's interest, their understanding of their audience, the resources they have, and the mode of dissemination they will deploy. (Kress, 2010: 26)

On the visual level they represent composites from the network of aesthetic and affective modalities that we discussed above: the heritage and social aspects of the building and a layered provisionality in the *imagined* revival of the building; but also a dispersive vernacular creativity that is connected with a conscious act of citizenship, set alongside and against, official domains of digital urbanism.

This context is reflected in the decision to remediate the community plan using StickyWorld,[3] a digital tool where design and communication intersect creatively through several conversational layers. As our co-production workshops and subsequent discussions revealed, WCC needed a platform where the commitment to collaborative effort could be foregrounded through digital innovations and face-to-face encounters, using a show-and-tell tool that mutates and mobilises existing resources to offer a space for 'story-catching' and commentary.

StickyWorld offered a platform to remediate archival and current media produced by the group in a way that enabled WCC members, armed with laptops, tablets, leaflets and booklets, to engage with local people in multiple languages, and to invite comments on the planning application (Figure 9.4). The virtual tour experience, available through StickyWorld, was open to challenge and amendment from across the Wards Corner Coalition, thereby bringing the community together in an act of co-creation, which represented the community in a positive light and held the planning authorities to account. This campaign was a highly effective example of creative citizenship.

Almost 60% of the 226 comments on StickyWorld, received mostly through a three-week intensive engagement period in March 2014,

Figure 9.4: WCC Plan on Stickyworld featuring CGIs of the community plan

expressed an *affective* element with the space, along with a sense of aspiration for the site's future. Each individual offered new meanings by relating the images to his or her existing personal experience, knowledge and cultural discourses. The majority of comments were made on external views of the building, focused upon architectural and heritage features and the resurrection of the Wards Corner name. Comments on the atmosphere of the building from a user point of view reflect the social fabric of the place, citing multiethnic encounters, cultural mix and the opportunities for creative entrepreneurialism. Once it emerged, the strength of this grass roots civic culture was very clear. As one WCCer reflects:

> "I wish we had engaged in this process six months ago, and included comments in the plan itself... It makes me realise the weaknesses of the plan and how elitist and complex planning is. StickyWorld immerses people and makes them excited and confortable to comment."

The co-creation of the plan on StickyWorld, and the engagement practices feeding into the practices of the community development trust, provided an opportunity for linking producers and consumers, informal and formal civic activities. This played a crucial role for brokering differences, generating an opportunity to showcase place, not as an empty continuum, but as a location filled with people and actions. It highlighted lived cultural assets, ways of life, and visual raw materials, providing stimuli for civic creativity, inspiration, and a vivid sense of urban place.

Hyperlocal news: Castle Vale estate, Birmingham

In this case study we focus on the tensions around the representation of an urban environment through mainstream and community media, drawing on research undertaken at the Castle Vale estate in north east Birmingham. Through workshops with residents, interviews with the estate's community media organisation, and a co-creation project, we consider how assumptions about the democratically empowering function of community media meet tensions over positive and negative representation that exist between many media producers and their audiences.

When it was built in the 1960s, Castle Vale, or 'The Vale' as it is known locally, was the largest housing estate in Birmingham. Ali Madanipour's (2005) account of the estate's reputation is stark:

'the neighbourhood suffered from poor quality infrastructure and buildings, lack of services, fear of crime and vandalism, poor health, unemployment, low educational standards, and a poor image' (2005: 51). Veronica Coatham and Lisa Martinali outline how by the early 1990s, there was 'an identified need to develop a long-term strategy for Castle Vale, encompassing the key priorities of a regeneration initiative' (Coatham and Martinali, 2010: 91). Twenty years after the beginning of that regeneration process the estate's reputation still looms large in the minds of those who live and work there. In the words of the area's community media journalist: 'You live "on" The Vale. As though it's a ship... As though you have to take a step up to get towards it' (Clive Edwards, *Tyburn Mail,* 2012).

The Housing Action Trust set up in 1993 emphasised the 'redevelopment of the social infrastructure and combating social exclusion', (Evans and Long, 2000: 309), but it also supported the creation of a community radio station; Vale FM, which began broadcasting in 1995. This might initially have been developed to address public perceptions of the 'Vale', but it soon developed into a vehicle for the development of individuals with educational or creative potential. Its manager at the time, Neil Hollins, describes its early development:

> "Vale FM was born out of an idea by local residents who were maybe involved in pirate radio or who were maybe mobile DJs and believed that a community radio station would be good for Castle Vale [...] We then began running training courses under franchise. Contract radio courses for unemployed people to use it as a way of developing skills, confidence, employability. But of course those with talent and real dedication would be able to use this as a great opportunity to potentially get into the industry."

Like others trying to pitch for funds for community activities, Hollins had to become adept at expressing the value of Castle Vale as a place where funding agencies could see the potential to transform lives: "this is about putting out an image of Castle Vale as a vibrant creative place, where things are happening. It might not be the best place in the world but things are happening". Different funders might require different articulations of place but the desired outcomes were always the same: "the primary benefits were very much about the personal outcomes for beneficiaries. The secondary ones ... were about reputational aspects and challenging negative stigmas" (Hollins).

In 2001 an eight-page community newspaper was developed as an adjunct to the radio station, which was itself licensed to operate for 28 day periods under a Restricted Service Licence. Initially the newspaper's impartiality was questioned: "It was still under the control of the HAT (Housing Action Trust), so wasn't particularly trusted. It was seen as a bit of a propaganda sheet, and it was rather disorganised and didn't look very nice really" (Hollins). But problems with the radio station, as it attempted to transfer to a more permanent operation under a full radio licence from the regulator Ofcom, worked in the newspaper's favour. In Hollins' judgement, it became "the predominant form of communication in Castle Vale at the time". After 2011, the newspaper broadened the area it covered to surrounding suburbs. The *Tyburn Mail*, as it is now called, is a monthly, 24-page free newspaper, delivered directly to a population of 24,000 in the Castle Vale, Pype Hayes, Erdington Hall and Birches Green areas of Birmingham. It employs just one journalist who also runs an associated news blog, Facebook page and Twitter account. The journalist argues that the micro size of the operation results in constrained ambition:

> "The size of the organisation limits the extent to which we can do proper investigative journalism that would be helpful to the community in revealing to them what is actually happening. As opposed to what the organisations say is happening." (Clive Edwards, 2012)

Edwards points out that the newspaper's initial content was very much focused on the area's regeneration: "all the work that the Housing Action Trust did to regenerate Castle Vale in terms of its buildings and its organisations; they thought would be well served by a monthly newspaper" (2012). But since the separation of the community media operation and the Trust in 2005, the newspaper now acts more in the mode of traditional journalism. This change was not made comfortably:

> "We took the view that we would include bad news as well as good news. We still hold true to that for all of the downside that creates. It creates an uncomfortable relationship sometimes within what is a fairly small community. We can and we have alienated some organisations and some individuals as a result." (Edwards, 2012)

Although *Tyburn Mail*'s digital outlets are useful both for newsgathering and for gaining a sense of which content most interests its audience, the printed newspaper remains the focus of its service: "There are some stories that we leave out of the web, because we want the print version to have impact when it comes out […] I think the newspaper has got more status than the web output" (Edwards, 2012). In speaking to Edwards, a disconnect can be sensed between producer and audience. Although there are ample opportunities for feedback on matters of content, this is not always forthcoming:

> "The most frequent feedback we get is about delivery of the newspaper. In terms of either it hasn't been delivered to them, or they've had three delivered. The newspaper deliverer has left the flap open, so the draft is coming in. Things like that."

This account conveys a sense that Castle Vale citizens are not active players when it comes to contributing to their community media, beyond occasional individual involvement in the radio station. Mechanisms for input or for co-creation do not exist. Edwards says his contacts are largely formal (school, police, council, local politicians), although he recognises that digital media offer citizens the opportunity to express civic pride: "If you look at social media sites, such as people's Facebook pages, they are always referencing the community ethos around Castle Vale."

In our interviews with local citizens, we noted a degree of suspicion and distrust about the *Tyburn Mail*'s 'voice'. Some felt that it was still too closely linked to the Housing Association:

> "A lot of people's negative articles or opinions are being filtered out, especially if it's against the housing and social." (Resident)

Here, 'produsage' (Bruns, 2008) to 'build the capacities for active forms of cultural and democratic citizenship' was sparse and undeveloped.

In light of this disconnect, we proposed that the *Tyburn Mail* experiment with a piece of co-creation designed to offer citizens greater participation. As researchers we wanted to test the scope for more developed creative citizenship whilst enabling the journalist, Edwards, to explore the 'possibilities for citizen participation at various points along those chains of sense-making that shape news – not only new possibilities for citizens to 'break' news' (Goode, 2009).

The first element in our project was to create a blank space in the newspaper for citizens to insert their own news.[4] Readers were then asked to bring their contributions to a news café event organised in a local supermarket. The café was intended to bring readers into contact with the journalist and to enable them to discuss and co-create stories based on the sheets they filled in. Just three readers brought back completed blank pages (and one completed an online version) but their content drew attention to the ways in which they felt Castle Vale's image is contested. Respondents implored the journalist to 'tell it like it is' and worry about problems being 'swept under the carpet'. Yet at the same time, another voiced concern that there was 'too much focus on individual crime' – a recurring issue in our research. One resident argued that the coverage of crime on the estate was disproportionate: "The problem is it's no worse than others, but it gets reported more, so it makes it look worse." Though considered essential by the journalist, coverage of crime can be problematic in creating an informed citizenship: 'The focus on the spectacular rather than the typical – endemic in news coverage of crime, for example – rarely implicates citizenship in useful or informative ways' (Lewis J., 2006: 315).

Although the office of *Tyburn Mail* is located centrally on the Castle Vale estate in one of the few remaining tower blocks, the café helped make the organisation more accessible. After the pilot, the news café continued on a monthly basis and stories mentioned in the filled-in sheets were followed up. This encouraged Edwards to establish a regular feature of 'news from the café'. In a subsequent interview, the previously lone reporter and editor was persuaded of the change:

> "Clearly the News Café is a good idea. We feel that it has worked for us in terms of opening us out and saying we are after domestic stories... It may well be that we are now being perceived as a voice of the people, as opposed to a voice of the council... We've got to be realistic about what we expect from the News Café, but in terms of breaking the paradigm, it certainly has done that." (Edwards, 2012)

In this same period, Edwards also noted a growing value in digital media, with more story ideas coming in via Facebook:

> "Facebook is a means of feedback to us. So for example, if we put an article on our website, some people might comment upon the website, but on the whole the majority of people will comment on the Facebook site. I am not sure why that is. [...] So Facebook is a very good means of asking

for feedback to our stories. Are our stories interesting? We will find out via Facebook." (Edwards 2012)

Edwards goes on to describe how controversial stories about crime are more likely to receive anonymous comments on the blog,[5] rather than personal comments on Facebook. Indeed the Facebook page, with about a thousand likes, is relatively quiet in comparison to some hyperlocal news websites but Edwards recognises that, "we are slow on the uptake with it, but it has become important to us, yes. As a news source, particularly Twitter, and as a feedback mechanism particularly Facebook". Although we worked with *Tyburn Mail* at an early stage of its journey towards a more participatory approach, this modest co-creation exercise showed how a simple idea could prompt innovation and foster a more human interest approach, in Edwards' words, shifting the paper's voice away from the voice of officialdom.

The meaning of these changes in Castle Vale's community media activities is in line with perceptions of the place itself. The visitor to Castle Vale may be struck by the way it feels slightly cut off from the city, surrounded by big roads on all sides. In imitating traditional local news media, with their reporter diaries built around courts, crime and councils, the *Tyburn Mail* has encountered contested notions of how the 'Vale' should talk about itself when the outside world can listen. The early 21st century represents an important period in the estate's journey from public to community ownership of its core assets. The swimming pool and the sports pitches have recently come under threat of closure, with their long-term future in the possibly precarious hands of community organisations. This has necessitated a shift from paid to voluntary expertise in the management of these amenities, evidence to a degree that civic cultures are lively in Castle Vale, albeit in difficult circumstances.

A place called South Blessed

South Blessed is a community media network hub in Bristol. It addresses the notion of place through multiple lenses: through creative design, as geographic space, as designed environment, as online platforms and networks, as media content and as a galvaniser of identity formation.

In short, place-making is central to the ethos and practices of South Blessed, starting with the colours and design of its logo, which registers ideas of the Jamaican flag (the only country with this combination of colours), combined with the pattern of the Union Flag.

Figure 9.5: South Blessed logo

To see the colour logo please visit
http://www.southblessed.co.uk/

The colours relate directly to the parental heritage of Vince Baidoo, the English-born proprietor of South Blessed, though it is important to note that South Blessed is not self-identified as a 'black organisation' and (possibly ironically) deliberately eschews that label. Together the symbols of British and Jamaican identity speak of a notional combined experience, and shared cultural and historical heritages. As noted by Paul Gilroy, in his aptly named book, *There Ain't no Black in the Union Jack*:

> The assimilation of blacks is not a process of acculturation but of cultural syncretism. Accordingly, their self-definitions and cultural expressions draw on a plurality of black histories and politics. In the context of modern Britain this has produced a diaspora dimension to black life. Here, non-European traditional elements, mediated by the histories of Afro-America and the Caribbean, have contributed to the formation of new and distinct black cultures amidst the decadent peculiarities of the Welsh, Irish, Scots and English… An intricate web of cultural and political connections binds black here to black elsewhere. At the same time, they are linked to the social relations of this country. (Gilroy, 1987: 155–6)

If this logo tells the story of migration, the design suggests a British landscape of destination. The heart shape forces an optimistic reading of what the new narrative can become. In that sense the logo is postmodern, acknowledging history but proposing new experiences: building on the past and also indicating a radically optimistic departure from it for today's African-Caribbean diaspora. The elaborately scripted tag 'South Blessed' beneath the flag adds to this reading, with suggestions of history, identity and culture.

Based in Bristol, in the South West of England, the name plays on that geographic position whilst again evoking a Jamaican flavour, with the rhyming preference for the word 'Blessed' rather than 'West', playing on the diaspora's fondness for biblical terminology in everyday speech and salutations (Gilroy, 1999: 37). The inclusion of 'Blessed' also reinforces the sense of optimism, affection, and pride (Anderson, 1991: 142), indicating affection for the place of formerly imperialist rulers among formerly colonised peoples. Here is a place that is the hybrid product of the past, firmly rooted in the present. This hybrid logo offers multilayered stories of brand identity, without ever giving away the nature of the business – namely, media production. It prefers a big idea and set of narratives rather than a statement of business services. The logo presents values, and possibly even promotes a lifestyle and mind state, akin to a visual manifesto.

One member of the South Blessed network interviewed for this study offered this explanation:

> "In terms of his logo, he's incorporated so many things … obviously Vince has put the Jamaican flag colours, with the Union Jack there. On the Jamaican flag, the official tagline is "Out of one, many people", so it's perfect as far as Bristol. Every race lives here; people born and bred in Bristol, people not born and bred in Bristol. People from privileged backgrounds to non-privileged backgrounds and they all brush shoulders with each other. So mixing in that urban culture, antiestablishment aspect but also an idea of unity, that we're all one in this. In that, the idea that we reject mainstream and we're just creative, individualistic people. That identity, the logo itself, in one visual, just looking at it; all those ideas go into a person's head without them necessarily even processing it."

As is well known, a brand image does not always inform the working practices of an organisation (Klein, 2000). In the case of South Blessed, we must consider how the logo's rich evocation of space is reflected in South Blessed's practices and outputs, not least through their shop front studio premises in the St Pauls area of Bristol.

These premises started life as a South Blessed shop selling T-shirts and other self-branded items, before being adapted for use as a media production studio, live-streamed discussion shows, a film studio with green screen for music videos, and limited editing facilities. This is the physical hub of South Blessed's operations, and holds an affectionate place in the opinions of the wider network, as evidenced from interviews and asset mapping focus groups conducted with South Blessed stakeholders. For all of the participants in the asset mapping session, 'The Studio' was placed at the centre of the maps. As described by one member of the South Blessed network:

> "The fact that he has got a studio, and been working really hard to make that studio the best it can be. The first thing that I thought when I heard that he was building a studio was music, as usual. Because that is what everyone has, is a studio that is for music production. To find out that he is actually building a studio for media, so that you can record live shows, or maybe do your own little animations. I just think for myself that is really good, that is really out of the box, not everyone is doing that."

The studio is viewed as a safe space in the fullest sense of that term, with one respondent saying that, even though its location is in St Pauls, which has a very strong identity and reputation, the presence of the South Blessed studio on the edge of that area transcended rivalries, stating: "One of the things it gives is a place where the whole postcode stuff is just non-existent. So they come from wherever, they come from all over."

The principle of self-reliance is a driving force behind the business acumen of South Blessed. While equipment could be hired externally, South Blessed preferred where possible to buy and own it. Likewise, in an era when much media content is on demand, South Blessed chose to transmit its live streamed interviews with city leaders at set times, requiring an attentive, albeit remote, audience. South Blessed also chose to produce a physical graphic novel for the co-production element of this research project, again prioritising a tangible object over a virtual artefact. According to Vince, South Blessed's proprietor:

> "The studio gives people a space to physically have access to high quality equipment. The studio is a key resource. My Mac is a key resource, before my Mac my laptop was a key resource. My camera is a key resource; my microphone is a key resource. Yes I think the camera is one of the big ones. It was definitely worth more than the money that it cost."

It is important here to avoid simplistic binaries of physical/material versus virtual (Miller and Horst, 2012), and to acknowledge that South

Blessed's active online community of over half a million views on their YouTube channel and nearly 3,000 'friends' on their combined Facebook accounts interplay with offline material presences, each referencing and pointing to the other (Simon, 2012). On Facebook, South Blessed has two unique presences: the South Blessed community profile which anyone can join, and Vince's personal profile, which is taglined 'South Blessed', where you can only be accepted as a 'friend' of Vince. The community profile had (at the time of writing) nearly 400 followers, and the personal profile had 2,400 friends. According to our analysis, the South Blessed community profile is used (in order of frequency):

1. by followers advertising events and productions – predominantly music videos;
2. by South Blessed administrators to share productions from the South Blessed network and wider communities of interest;
3. by South Blessed administrators sharing relevant local interest or other stories; and
4. by South Blessed publicising its own productions.

It is seldom used as a place for debate or conversation. It is used primarily as a notice board, more for the purposes of knowledge transfer than knowledge exchange, with very little comment or interaction.

By contrast, Vince's personal page is used:

1. by Vince sharing local interest or other stories;
2. by Vince sharing productions from the South Blessed network and wider communities of interest;
3. by Vince updating friends on the business activities of South Blessed, occasionally asking for members' opinions on certain choices to be made;
4. by friends advertising events and their productions – predominantly music videos; and latterly
5. by Vince sharing his personal life experiences unrelated to South Blessed.

Besides the inclusion of #3 on Vince's personal Facebook profile, which is significant, the profile is also a site of much debate, conversation and interaction, in contrast to the community profile. More than a noticeboard, the private profile is a place of communication. These dual Facebook presences, which respectively could be termed 'public

public' and 'public private' (Crossley and Roberts, 2004: 13), speaks to Broadbent's (2013: 136) analysis that:

> Instead of thinking about any individual communicative medium, we have to consider each medium not only in terms of its specific affordances but also in terms of the wider media ecology, where it is defined relative to all the others that might have been chosen instead. Indeed most relationships now depend on using several channels for different aspects of the same relationship.

In the case of South Blessed's Facebook places, whilst Broadbent's analysis may describe the case in practice, it appears to be the product of circumstance, as Vince has spoken about how, in hindsight, he made a mistake when setting up the Facebook profiles and should have made his personal page the official South Blessed presence, and not had a community page at all.

In a small study of places in 25 of the 250 videos (dance, film, drama, fashion, documentary, music and sport) uploaded to the South Blessed YouTube channel, we found that Bristol was mentioned 94 times, ahead of second-placed London at 14. More surprising was that those same 25 videos mentioned 21 other places in the UK and 15 countries (see Figure 9.7).

Figure 9.6: South Blessed headquarters. Photograph courtesy of Rife Magazine - Ryan Francis

Figure 9.7: Mentions of place in 250 South Blessed videos

Areas across the UK places mentioned	Other countries mentioned
Bath (01)	Cuba (01)
*Bedfordshire (01)	Denmark (01)
*Birmingham (01)	Egypt (01)
Bournemouth (01)	France (03)
Bridgwater (01)	**Germany (03)**
Bristol (94)	Greece (03)
Cornwall (01)	Iceland (02)
*Derby (01)	Ireland (04)
Devon (01)	Lebanon (02)
Dorset (01)	Norway (01)
Exeter (01)	**Palestine (Israel) (04)**
Falmouth (01)	Russia (01)
Glastonbury (02)	Syria (01)
Gloucester (01)	Tunisia (01)
*London (14)	USA (04)
*Manchester (05)	Zimbabwe (02)
Newquay (01)	
Penzance (01)	
Taunton (01)	
Truro (01)	
Western Super Mare (01)	
Wiltshire (01)	

* Not in the South West region

These results show a local/global dimension of community media outputs, expressing in one online locus the phenomenon of community 'we-ness' (Dahlgren, 2009); 'communities expressing civic commonality and embodying group loyalty, based on the learning of shared skills' (Couldry et al, 2014: 8) and an outward-looking discourse of connectedness to places further afield, through a shared sense of ideology and politics (Anderson, 2006; Hall, 2013). In a South Blessed interview with the politically conscious rapper Lowkey, the rapper speaks about Palestine and accuses UK media institutions of complicity in oppression. In other videos there was a tendency to bring external references back to a Bristol narrative, such as the South Blessed documentary about the city's new local currency – the 'Bristol Pound' – compared with the troubled fortunes of the Euro. Such productions could be viewed as a community media version of globalisation discourse. According to Hall:

> Globalisation refers to those processes, operating on a global scale, which cuts across national boundaries, integrating and connecting communities and organisations in new space-time combinations, making the world in reality and in experience more interconnected. Globalisation implies a movement away from the classical sociological idea of a 'society' as a well bounded system, and its replacement by a perspective which concentrates on how social life is ordered across time and space. (Hall, 2013: 460)

That said, even with a nuanced, globalised positioning within the urban rhetoric of some of its content, the South Blessed network's pride in Bristol is unmistakable, and is a clear galvaniser of shared identities, experiences, and 'we-ness'. As articulated here by Vince himself, he positions Bristol's status within the wider south west area and globally, reaffirming a strong identity for the city:

> "Society, that is where the more Bristol element of it comes in. If you have a certain talent, and to some degree you are known as being able to execute that talent when you say that you will do it. Then you are going to get offers to do certain things, because as people are pulling together different stuff. Bristol is such a major player in the creative and alternative scientific communities, every aspect is going to come back to Bristol. Bristol is the capital of the South West, so if Bristol is not doing it, so you can't expect any of the other South West cities to do it. So that is the unique selling point."

Without the resources to make a feature length animation about Bristol, as part of this research project the academic team worked with Vince to support him making the graphic novel *Indigo Babies*. The graphic novel is scripted by Vince and illustrated by Silent Hobo, a well know local graffiti artist. The storyline of the novel is a fictionalised narrative based around the real world events of the Stokes Croft/Tesco riots that happened in Bristol in 2011. The narrative presents a series of streetwise, locally astute and globally aware urban teenagers, who may at times bend the rules to achieve wholesome end results. Without talking in the same language as Hall (2013), they are fully aware of the 'time-space interconnections' of globalised communications and networks. In the story they use the 'dark web' to mobilise a global force of internet hackers to effect change on the streets of Bristol (Baidoo,

2014). As with the rappers, interviewees and other contributors of the videos and commentators on Facebook, the characters in *Indigo Babies* are from diverse backgrounds and hold diverse views, underpinning the point that a multiplicity of notions of place permeates South Blessed's practices and outlook, a variety even broader than those reflected in the narrative of the South Blessed logo.

Conclusions

In this chapter we have highlighted three cases where mediated place-making, through the production of an alternative plan, a community newspaper and a community media production contributed to aspirations of urban renewal. We have gathered empirical evidence to explain how these groups' 'civic agency' – the power of community groups to change or influence their local environments – intersects with creativity to support the concept of creative citizenship. We have argued that place can be viewed as a focus for identity that spurs civic engagement and social activism. It results in articulations of civic value that both transcend and renew local geographies. Our fieldwork also gave us insights about the ways in which place becomes a locus for expressing affinity and trust – qualities crucially at stake in processes of 'mediation' and 'mediatisation' of place in local communities (Couldry, 2008).

At WCC, the strengths of a preexisting civic culture emerged clearly from our fieldwork and via the group's mediated presence. The expansion of the WCC community plan into the online realm illustrates that the physical and virtual in the urban context cannot be understood as separate spheres, but rather are conceptualised in relation to each other, enabling civic activism. *Tyburn Mail* built upon its practice in online journalism through engaging in a more direct and physical manner, in order to make stronger links with local people and associations. This allowed the tensions around how to represent the local area to be aired, and raised questions about the assumptions inherent in journalism practice.

South Blessed's videos highlight an under-researched aspect of community media discourse – looking beyond place as a galvaniser of identities and a platform for media engagement to the question of how place is talked about within media productions. Our work with South Blessed shows how place can be both an optimistic generator of networkable values and ideas and a means of making comparisons between the community's experiences and values and those from elsewhere. These projects of mutual recognition, belonging and creative participation may or may not be 'scalable' in response to public policy strategies, but that is not their purpose. The activities themselves are self-made and self-actualised, addressing the wider world directly rather than through external mediation. Rather than disaggregating agency into the hands of another, for example through participating in media literacy programmes, South Blessed declares its agency and uploads its network productions directly to the world. Fuelled by the energy of a young community, this 'glocal' creative citizenship is unapologetically optimistic.

In mediating place the local, hyperlocal, urban, national and global are strongly connected. We have demonstrated the ways in which the material affordances of digital media and social preconditions of civic creativity are connected with practices of cultural expression and political participation. Our analyses offer a fertile ground to rethink how these affordances have given rise to acts of creative citizenship, not simply as a digital era phenomenon, but as an experience that transcends the digital and physical understandings of place, and its local, national and global boundaries.

Notes

[1] Spoken at the Community Media Association Annual General Meeting – 23 February 2008, Sheffield, UK.

[2] wardscorner.wikispaces.com/ >> Media Section. And wardscornercommunityplan. wordpress.com/

[3] cc.stickyworld.com/room/presentation?roomid=11#page/about

[4] Chris Atton describes a similar project in a New York underground paper of the 1960s: "*Other Scenes* once offered an entirely blank set of pages for readers as a do-it-yourself publishing project" (Atton, 2002: 24).

[5] See tyburnmail.com/2014/03/06/jail-for-five-castle-vale-men-after-vicious-mailbox-brawl/

TEN

Technology and the creative citizen

Jerome Turner, Dan Lockton and Jon Dovey

The starting point for our Creative Citizen research project was a question asking whether and to what extent digital communications technologies afford new civic potential. We also invited ourselves to consider how this potential might be enhanced by digital media, thereby making an assumption that agency and significance might properly be ascribed to technology in its relation to creative citizenship.

As we have seen in the preceding chapters and their detailed accounts of creative citizenship in action, this assumption demands critical reflection. Technology itself is rarely addressed head on within communities of the kind we have worked with. The truly indispensable drivers of creative citizenship are motivated people who have built a shared commitment, usually through face-to-face relationships in specific real world places. Digital technologies are today a commonplace and important tool for such groups, in some cases even an operational necessity. How are we to understand the role of technology in these processes?

The definition, meaning and agency of technology has long been a key question in media and cultural studies, as we try to make sense of the 'changes in scale and pace of human affairs' (McLuhan, 1964) that are a characteristic of living in a permanent upgrade culture, where the impacts of technological innovation often seem to be accelerating. Raymond Williams (1974), in his analysis of television as a 'cultural form', argued that the technologies of photography, telegraphy, and radio were components in the invention of broadcast television, but that what drove technological invention were accelerated social processes, notably mobility and growth 'in a society characterised at its most general levels by a mobility and extension of the scale of organisations: forms of growth which brought with them immediate and longer-term problems of operative communications' (Williams, 1974: 18–19). In this reading, technologies of communication develop in relation to the communicative and organisational conditions of society. So for Williams the accelerated development of industrial-scale printing technologies in the 19th century was associated with the communicative needs of a newly urbanised population seeking democratic representation, rather than an inevitable result of coal, iron and steam driven technologies (1974: 21).

For Walter Benjamin (1936) and Marshall McLuhan (1964), technologies change the nature of our experience, whilst for Marx 'nature makes no machines' (1993: 693). Latour (for example, 2005) argues that human and nonhuman actors (things and machines) are potentially of equal significance in determining what happens when they combine in complex assemblage. Here cause and effect linearity is replaced by network and complexity, making the agency of technology difficult to read through the lens of methodological individualism or behaviourism. This approach to understanding technology has been extended in the work of media ecologists, who identify digitally connected communication systems akin to biological eco systems:

> Ecologists focus more on dynamic systems in which any one part is always multiply connected, acting by virtue of those connections, and always variable, such that it can be regarded as a pattern rather than simply an object. (Fuller, 2005: 4)

This systems approach has the benefit of helping us to understand the ways in which people, platforms, networks and actions connect. These patterns of technology networks provide context for the performance of creative citizenship.

However, what none of the approaches above offer quite as usefully as Williams is an analysis of motivation for the extravagant and unprecedented social and cultural effort involved in building the technological and cultural infrastructure of the internet. The development over more than a quarter of a century of the web and its associated applications, platforms and new economic models has been primarily driven by human desire to build technologies that enable people to communicate, share and express themselves in new and more direct ways. Tim Berners Lee is credited with 'inventing' the World Wide Web,[1] but what he actually did was to build a browser that made it easier for scientists to share information through already existing components of military/scientific information technologies. This breakthrough made it possible for human communicative capacities to be unleashed. Scholars of this early web observed an extraordinary investment of time and effort into *forming communities* online, essentially creating citizens or 'netizens' (as they are still known in China). The work of the journal *Computer Mediated Communication* and that of scholars like Steve Jones (1995; 1998) and Nancy Baym (1998) has demonstrated that the online users of the 1990s worked hard to participate in this new means of communication.

A good deal of research in this period was also devoted to asking the question, 'Can online users form communities?' For early computer visionaries, 'The Well', an online bulletin board network formed round San Francisco in the 1980s, became a prototypical online community:

> There's always another mind out there. It's like having a corner bar complete with old buddies and delightful newcomers and new tools waiting to take home and fresh graffiti and letters, except instead of putting on my coat, shutting down the computer and walking down to the corner, I just invoke my telecom programme and there they are. It's a place. (Rheingold, 1995: 62)

The value of such communities was promptly contested. John Perry Barlow, an early cyber-evangelist, famously argued that these burgeoning online communities lacked the diversity of 'real' communities, which had together faced material challenges (Barlow, 1995). This tension between the relative strengths of online and offline affiliations characterised the best of this early research into digitally mediated communities. Nancy Baym, for instance, concluded her study of online communities of TV fans:

> The research I have reviewed and the model I have proposed suggest that on-line groups are often woven into the fabric of off-line life rather than set in opposition to it. The evidence includes the pervasiveness of off-line contexts in on-line interaction and the movement of on-line relationships off-line. (1998: 63)

Nearly ten years later the first wave of research into social networking sites (SNS) observed their fluid connectivity between individuals and communities:

> The rise of SNSs indicates a shift in the organization of online communities. While websites dedicated to communities of interest still exist and prosper, SNS are primarily organized around people, not interests. Early

public online communities such as Usenet and public discussion forums were structured by topics or according to topical hierarchies, but social network sites are structured as personal (or 'egocentric') networks, with the individual at the center of their own community. (boyd & Ellison, 2007)

Moreover these public and private selves were intimately interwoven between online and offline communications and locations. In an early study of students' use of their own homepages in social media Kennedy (2006) concluded that:

> Online identities are often continuous with offline selves, not reconfigured versions of subjectivities in real life; for this reason it is necessary to go beyond Internet identities, to look at offline contexts of online selves, in order to comprehend virtual life fully.

This brief review illustrates that from the internet's earliest days, users have been creating new forms of community, association and affiliation, with a range of interwoven public and private benefits. Just as in Williams' analysis that the development of the 19th century press was driven by citizens' need for information, such that the extension of the franchise, of literacy and of the scale of the press and publishing industries went hand in hand across the long century (from the 1790s to the end of World War I), so the growth of the internet in the first 20 years after Berners Lee launched Mosaic has been driven by group formation, socialising, chatting, sharing, making (co-creating) and building platforms that enable users to connect with one another. Text messaging (as SMS) was invented to allow telephone engineers to communicate without using voice lines; its explosion as a super-convenient messaging system was unforeseen by Ericsson's engineers, but soon understood by teenagers. The modern internet was designed to allow scientists to share data but it was the passion of ordinary people to communicate that has shaped the meaning and value of Web 2.0 (and its successor forms) as we blog, Facebook, Tweet and Instagram our everyday lives.

Jenkins et al (2006) argue that this 'participatory culture' is characterised by:

- 'affiliation', elective group formation in online community around enthusiasms, issues or common cultures;

- 'expression', music, video, and design tools in the hands of far more users than ever before, used for every kind of human mode of communication;
- 'collaborative problem-solving' mobilising collective intelligence, crowdfunding, online petition making, alternate reality gaming, wiki-based shared knowledge practices;
- 'circulations' playing an active role in directing media dynamics through the new flows of viral media driven by Twitter, Facebook and YouTube.

This enthusiasm for the uses of social media technologies was also mirrored in a wave of technophiliac commentary appearing in the post Web 2.0 era. It was argued that the new affordances of digital media and social networking were creating new modes of capitalism (Tapscott and Williams, 2006), transformative levels of 'cognitive surplus' (Shirky, 2010) and new modes of collaborative innovation (Leadbeater, 2008). In 2010, political activists saw a wave of political unrest in North Africa and the Middle East as an 'Arab Spring' promising a socially mediated democratic summer – an over-optimistic assessment, as things turned out, in the short term at least.

Towards an economy of contribution

Since the 'Springs', digital passions have cooled, or at least been more heavily qualified. In the post WikiLeaks, post Snowden era, digital technologies of communication and media are understood as part of a darker landscape, driven, on one hand, by highly individuated consumer marketing and, on the other, by state and corporate surveillance associated with the burgeoning geopolitical insecurities of globalisation. Silicon Valley giants, such as Apple, Amazon, Google and Facebook, which helped build the global digital economy and its libertarian ethos, began to attract criticism for aspects of their corporate behaviour. The arguments of critical theorists of technology such as Terranova (2003) or Galloway (2001) appeared prescient. They argued that social media always had the potential to intensify exploitation and control. For the French philosopher of technology Bernard Stiegler (2010), the undoubted radical potential of collaborative and open source technologies is also a 'pharmakon', in so far as it can poison as well as cure, by conferring new kinds of power to those who exploit the data 'set into motion by actions and requests that network actors mostly produce without knowing it' (2010: 129). Nevertheless Stiegler is one of those critics of technology who are also committed to establishing the political, social and economic conditions that could obtain in order to produce what he calls the 'economy of contribution' in which the new collaborative potentials of our means of communication produce new kinds of value that can be held in common in particular places, including cities and regions.

Our own work in the Creative Citizen project indicates how this economy of contribution might start to form amid the grassroots dynamics at play when a range of social and technological actors come together in an attempt to produce value for people as citizens rather than people defined exclusively as subjects, consumers or mere individuals. Our analysis of these procedures and possibilities is informed by the wide range of domain disciplines involved in the project, including especially the thinking behind 'user-led' design, but also referring to journalism, economic geography, media and cultural studies. We turn to some insights from these knowledge domains before drawing lessons from specific case studies.

Affordance and the citizen as user

In everyday practice, debates and tensions about the role and scope of digital technologies may be addressed through the concept of affordance, which starts from the premise that as technologies develop they have many different potentials. These possibilities and their limits are as much a feature of the natural sciences – physics and materials – as they are of the human structures, agency and aspiration analysed in social science. Drawing on James Gibson's work on ecological psychology (1986), Donald Norman describes the perceived affordances required in an object in order for a person successfully to interact with it and accomplish a task (Norman, 1988). Building on this, William W. Gaver (1991) explored different ways in which people might perceive and understand the affordances of technologies around them. This work suggests that when considering technology's potential in the realm of civic engagement, we should focus upon social as well as technical affordance.

Social affordance requires attention to the circumstances of users, for example in their creative contexts as citizens, including their historical, social, cultural and class backgrounds, along with their technological skills. The Keeping in Touch project (Dovey et al, 2011) looked at '100 community based communication initiatives which appeared to have a goal of 'strengthening communities' and provides valuable findings as to the use of appropriate technology taking into account 'differences in age, gender, interest, literacy and affluence'.

This report also argues that the impulse toward relentless innovation needs to be recognised as a problem in some circumstances. Resistance to innovation is illustrated when well-established social media platforms, such as Facebook, continue to be widely used, for example in community journalism and community history, in preference to abundantly available and novel apps. The quest for innovation is understandable and its economic value well established, but too much novelty can make products and services confusing, unwieldy or even impossible for some users to operate. A design that builds on existing conventions and 'media ideologies' (Gershon, 2011) might be easier for a group to grasp. The *Keeping in Touch* report suggests that 'communication technologies [need] to connect into existing means of communication and across different networks. Thus, the simple and widely used technology of text messaging should not be overlooked even though more elaborate apps abound'.

Technology with high civic potential must also be affordable among the wider population of users. For the most part, software and social media services are free, on the basis that they are financed by advertising revenue, but hardware, and in the case of mobile phones, data contracts, can be expensive. Shakantula Banaji's study of young people and civic engagement (Banaji and Buckingham, 2013) finds that it is the financially disadvantaged who would welcome the opportunity to become involved in online civic participation but are frequently excluded by cost.

Technologies should also be time affordable. Consider video making, with the end result a YouTube video. Creating a short, good quality (professional standard) one-minute video can easily take an entire day, especially when we factor in digital transfer of footage and editing. With the advent of mobile phone cameras, such a video can now be shot, edited and distributed to YouTube entirely using a mobile phone. The erstwhile professional standards of camera work and lighting might have slipped in the process, but it could be argued that expectations and perceptions of 'quality' shift anyway when ad hoc technologies are used. David Gauntlett recognises that 'the online community are forgiving about formal quality issues', where quality might be measured in terms of content or immediacy rather than production polish. Overproduction, he argues, can even 'deaden' the human connection, because it is seen as unattainable or alienating (Gauntlett, 2013: 84–7). Implicit standards of 'quality' may also determine accessibility in terms of both time and creative capital.

Accessibility is a familiar challenge. This extends from the provision of basic infrastructure to the very challenging task of ensuring that publicly funded schools teach digital communications technologies well at primary and secondary level. For designers considering the needs of disabled users (Ellis and Kent, 2010; Ellis, 2015), for example, with impairments in motor skills, sight or hearing, accessibility is part of the design brief. As a matter of routine, designers must take into account diverse cognitive, numerical, language and social skills. Nor can accessibility be ignored when designing for the more usually abled – one treatment of colour or interactive behaviour in an animation will be judged as differently usable by individual members of any group. Taking into account differing user tastes and experience, there will usually be a 'better' way of approaching a design. The resulting 'inclusive design' (Eikhaug et al, 2010) aims to make products and services accessible to as broad a range of users as possible.

From user-led design to community-led design

Anyone introducing a technology to those who are unfamiliar with it needs a clear strategy. Simply providing a new technology to citizens will not in itself make them more 'creative', although it must be conceded that this was the business model of early YouTube (among others), provoking in turn the now prevalent phenomenon of user-created YouTube tutorials on all manner of subjects, eventually systematised by YouTube itself as specialist channels: YouTube Education, YouTube University and so forth (Burgess and Green, 2009). Taking such developments into account, what is more generally required for effective technology uptake is a process to discover how to enable the conditions of digital and creative literacy that allow communities to use technology to serve their particular needs. This process may involve modifications to the technology itself, iterated via tests with members of the community. It may involve upskilling some community members, the creation of exemplar content, meetings to co-curate content, custom instruction manuals and, in some cases, simplification and even limitation of technical functionality. In order to get the maximum benefit from new technology, most communities require expert support at the point at which they express the need for it. This kind of user-designed process is essential for the successful adoption of a user-designed or user-modified piece of equipment or procedure.

With community groups, the challenges of adopting a new technology rarely reflect lack of motivation – volunteers are almost by definition engaged in what they are doing. Nor, in an era where group members may regularly use a smart phone, is the problem chiefly that of a conventional 'digital divide'. From a design perspective, the challenge feels more like 'process friction', typified by the bumpy process of, say, encouraging people at a group event to upload images or videos for curation as an engaging combined story. The challenge of doing this well may arise as from the cultural issue of individual levels of comfort at 'broadcasting' themselves or different approaches to storytelling as much as from technical obstacles.

In the user-design world, the importance of reducing these frictions is well established (Cooper, 1999). But even among designers, there is a danger of focusing too much on the user as an individual rather than as a group. The result of this is to ignore complexities which cannot simply be set aside. Even in the academic field of computer-supported cooperative work, which focuses on interaction design for cooperation, most attention has been placed on inter-/intra-workplace collaboration, with a goal of scalability. Given the acknowledged and growing significance of community-level activity, or creative citizenship, in many domains, from the 'maker movement' and community-based social care to community journalism, there is an urgent need to respond in technology design terms to the needs and intricacies of community settings, where a group will likely contain very wide differences of age, background and skills, whilst enjoying high levels of affinity and motivation.

All of this points to the potential for community-led design, learning from the experience of user-led design, to address this process friction. It requires that communities themselves, facilitated by designers and researchers, frame problems and that co-developed solutions are then responsive to their use in practice among groups. People need to be 'actively and creatively' engaged in order to participate; it cannot be assumed that technology and access of themselves will create the conditions for creative citizenship (Tacchi, 2012: 230).

Technology in practice: community journalism

Technology can be defined very simply as tools used by people. So it is helpful to consider a pre-digital technology to identify some of the key concepts, methods and issues that may still apply to the technology needs of an online hyperlocal community media operation.

The village noticeboard offers a strong analogue image. It crops up constantly in discussions about contemporary hyperlocal media, especially when addressing someone unfamiliar with this latter term. The twin point is that the village noticeboard is both familiar to everyone and has a great deal in common with a blog-based hyperlocal news service (see also Li, 2009, for a Chinese version of this example).

The noticeboard, first, is usually placed somewhere central to the community, where it is likely to be seen: by a bus stop, on the village green, in a churchyard or outside a shop. The technologies used by hyperlocal communities are also similarly 'everyday' and therefore afford accessibility, without having to look to new or unexpected platforms outside a routine frame of reference. Roughly two-thirds of UK hyperlocal blog pages in our content analysis used WordPress, a long-established and standard platform; the remaining third were largely Blogger.com. Facebook, Twitter and email mailing lists are also used, sometimes as supporting roles to blogs offering additional audience participation and sometimes as a stand-alone service.

Second, the technology of the noticeboard is highly accessible and quite flexible. It is light enough to be mounted anywhere, has enough space for several A4 sheets to be displayed; these often protected from the elements and vandalism by a glass front. Similarly, platforms such as Twitter might be seen as 'light' and 'transparent', and widely used by hyperlocal editors, but also contributors, to offer firsthand experiences and news. Most of this news will be banal rather than sensational, less political drama or catastrophe, and more traffic and planning issues or recording visual evidence of dog mess.

Third, and perhaps most tellingly, noticeboards under glass demonstrate the pros and cons of mediated community media. A glass cover can be used to keep notices dry, but it also introduces a gatekeeper; that member (or those members) of the community who hold the key to unlock the doors and pin up a new notice or take one down. Even if the policy for putting up new material is relatively open, that individual must be contacted and faced in order for a new notice to be displayed and therefore broadcast (often with a request for response through contact details). If a policy of fair use is in place, this is another hurdle for the participatory citizen to overcome – the contents of the notice might not be in keeping with village community priorities, the notice may be too large, or the individual may have posted too many notices in a short period of time. Alternately, individuals may gain unfair access levels *because* they have posted frequently and developed a relationship with the keyholder. The same can be said of hyperlocal media, where it is one thing to provide a source or input for a story and publicly reference the hyperlocal platform (by mentioning them in a tweet, or posting to a Facebook page's wall), but this contribution only becomes visible to the wider audience if the 'editor' mediates to retweet, or reshare the content to their own 'stream'. Our research supports the argument that mediation (and certainly the setting up of hyperlocal operations) are necessary for effective civic engagement, but it is this mediation, and key relationships favouring certain community 'primary definers' (Atton and Wickenden, 2005), that must be considered in the interest of a healthy online public sphere and democracy. One solution to a problem of this kind in the online world, or the world of the village noticeboard, is for an under-represented group to establish its own community media platform in competition with existing outlets.

Technology in practice: co-design

Debates around the meanings of co-design, co-creation, participatory design and community-led design have featured in a number of places in this book. Our fieldwork took as given the requirement that 'people who will be using a product, service or environment, are involved in designing or planning it' (Sanders and Stappers, 2014).

Much social design work with communities is viewed as a kind of intervention, an attempt to influence behaviour, based upon assumptions about how people will act, what people are like and how to get them to do something new (Lockton et al, 2014). As Adam Greenfield (2013) notes: 'Every technology and every ensemble of technologies encodes a hypothesis about human behaviour'. The process of a design researcher actively involved in this context is thus one of continually questioning these assumptions and refining the hypothesis or model. The approach embraces complexity and shuns oversimplification: '... rather than create distancing caricatures, tell stories. Look for ways to represent what you've learned in a way that maintains the messiness of actual human beings' (Portigal, 2008).

Where a community is adapting or making use of existing technologies in new ways, this may comprise much of the design element. As with any technology, there are specialist skills involved in designing systems, and expectations that community groups will somehow immediately start designing entirely by themselves risk disappointment.

Relevant methodology questions in this type of research, therefore, centre upon the degree to which external design researchers are needed as part of the process, and how to negotiate this boundary in different projects with different groups. In the Story Machine case study below, we will see how a combination of design and facilitation from researchers – with insight, inspiration, and evolving articulation of needs by diverse members of a community group – led to the design and implementation of a technology system which fitted the community's style, yet also led to unexpected and novel forms of engagement.

Technology in practice: creative networks

A starting point for the community media aspect of the Creative Citizen project was to investigate the current state of community mediation and to discover how the newly available, everyday affordances of digital media production tools and social media were being used in the local media ecology.

Our research context included the relationship between the creative economy and communities. In 2013 the Nesta Creative Economy Manifesto put the size of the UK Creative Economy at 9.7% of Gross Value Added, employing 2.5m people (Bakhshi et al, 2013: 10). This made it a bigger segment of the economy than financial services at 9.4% (2011 calculations BIS, 2012: 10). Most of this creative economy consists in microbusinesses, that is to say businesses with zero to nine employees (Rhodes, 2012). In the Brighton Fuse report, 85.1% of the businesses surveyed in the region had fewer than ten employees, with 41.8% in the two to five range (Sapsed and Nightingale, 2013: 14).

Barriers to entry into the creative economy have been lowered by the availability of relatively inexpensive technologies of production, raising questions about the risks of a potential oversupply of creative talent in a period of coincidental economic austerity. Young people trying to make their way in this sector have been identified in critical cultural economics as typical of a newly 'precarious' creative class. Its workers are said to be characterised by:

> ... a preponderance of temporary, intermittent and precarious jobs; long hours and bulimic patterns of working; the collapse or erasure of boundaries between work and play; poor pay; high levels of mobility; passionate attachment to the work and identity of the creative labourer (for example, web designer, artist, fashion designer); an attitudinal mindset that is a blend of bohemianism and entrepreneurialism; informal work environments and distinctive forms of sociality; and profound experiences of insecurity and anxiety about finding work, earning enough money and 'keeping up' in rapidly changing fields. (Gill and Pratt, 2008: 14)

For McRobbie (2011), creative precarity 'has become the distinctively British way of dealing with structural and seemingly irreversible changes to the work society'. More recently, US researchers Kuehn and Corrigan (2013) have coined the term 'hope labour' to describe the work of online reputation-building by bloggers and reviewers aiming to build a portfolio that will lead to properly paid work.

In many ways, South Blessed, our informal creative economy case study, can be understood neatly within this framework. The economic and technological resources in the South Blessed network at the time of our research were negligible. We were struck by the way that 'the Mac' (desktop computer) was identified as a critical asset, along with the South Blessed video camera. Access to the digital means of production is not in fact universal; not all young people can afford the laptop that equips them for membership of the digital creative class. Other income came from street bucket collections aimed at raising funds for media training; paid jobs doing music promos at very low rates; a little corporate sponsorship for equipment and software; and the familiar mix of freelance, higher education student loans, training, internships and Jobseeker's Allowance that underpins the informal creative economy. The South Blessed studio building was made available as part of a 'live and work' sustainable regeneration scheme and depended on a great deal of flexibility on the part of the landlord. So access to technology and the South Blessed publishing platforms were a crucial motivation for being involved in a network that is resource poor but rich in aspiration.

The positive tone in which members of the network evaluated its impact belied its bleak financial base. The precarious economic mesh is sustained by all kinds of different affective dynamics, self-actualisation, branding, family ties and mutualism. We read this compelling contradiction as evidence of new forms of subjectivity, creativity and resistance that are the paradoxical counterparts of the 'precarity' described by Gill and Pratt:

> Precarity signifies both the multiplication of precarious, unstable, insecure, forms of living and, simultaneously, new forms of political struggle and solidarity that reach beyond the traditional models of the political party or trade union. This double meaning is central to understanding the idea and politics associated with precarity; the new moment of capitalism that engenders precariousness is seen not only as oppressive but also as offering the potential for new subjectivities, new socialities and new kinds of politics. (Gill and Pratt, 2008: 3)

In this case the paradoxical 'new subjectivities, new socialities and new kinds of politics' constitute a network that is neither creative economy start-up nor community media operation, but a newly possible mix of both. Access to the means of digital production and the ability though social media to market a brand are crucial effects of the technological affordances that have lowered barriers of entry to the cultural industries market. The South Blessed strategy was to create an open web platform to host music videos from their regional milieu, creating an open publishing platform that aggregated attention and built a brand. However, the motivation here was not to create intellectual property that could be exploited as a business development strategy; the culture of sharing that characterises the digital native generation was deployed to grow a network that sought creative, economic *and* social benefit. In this way, access to technology underpins the profile of a new kind of creative citizen, what might be termed the creative economy social entrepreneur.

Case study: the Story Machine, The Mill, Walthamstow, London

Figure 10.1: Images from the Story Machine project

The Mill, a community centre in Walthamstow, east London, provides space and resources for local creative citizens to organise groups, events and activities for adults, children and families, ranging from art exhibitions to book clubs and language classes. The Story Machine project at The Mill (Lockton et al, 2014) demonstrates how presenting digital technology (tablets, projectors, website and social media) in ways which fit with existing community activities and aesthetics, can lead to novel and significant forms of engagement.

Essentially a combination of mini-cinema, puppet booth, and video camera, with its own online presence, the Story Machine shows how community groups can adapt technology to their needs and circumstances using a process of community-led design where problems are addressed directly by community members and facilitated by designers and researchers.

Through a process of collaborative workshops involving volunteers and participants at The Mill, designers from the Royal College of Art's Helen Hamlyn Centre for Design, and local artist Michelle Reader, we arrived at a collaborative brief designed to enable The Mill community to distribute stories more widely and more easily, through a combination of digital and physical technology, incorporating low-tech artefacts and activities. These innovations needed to fit with, contribute to, and even extend the activities already taking place at The Mill, drawing in the wider community, and providing evidence of The Mill's impact on its local area (important for funding bodies).

The focus on storytelling, in one form or another, features in a number of elements of the Creative Citizen project. In every case, the activities and artefacts developed are 'one-offs'. In community-led design there is no one-size-fits-all. The Mill's brief led us in the direction of what became the Story Machine, built around a Story Chair (mini-cinema) wirelessly connected to the Story Wheel (an iPad Mini built into a steering wheel). The Mill can use the Story Wheel to film and photograph their activities. These then upload automatically to the Story Chair, where they can be viewed and shared, and to The Mill's website, ensuring an ever-changing kaleidoscope of images of activities which reflect day-to-day life at The Mill but in a way that is also visible to any online visitor.

Community activities were then built around the new affordances of the Story Machine – such as 'junior reporter' classes where young people learned journalistic techniques through interviewing each other and visitors to the centre, producing videos and then collectively critiquing them via the Story Chair. Novel usage patterns emerged; for example, younger children combined the ability for a projector to be used with homemade cardboard shadow puppets, with the real-time streaming video from elsewhere in the building. This led to a memorable production in which a local councillor, interviewed via the Story Wheel and projected on screen, is being 'attacked' by cardboard dinosaurs, oblivious to his predicament. This type of juxtaposition of technologies potentially affords many unexpected 'end user' innovations (von Hippel, 2005).

The Story Machine also enabled the exploration of questions about the creative potential of digital technology. Might it boost motivation and engagement within community groups? What might be judged to be the rewards for involvement? Can the opportunity to be creative, and show this off to other local people (or people further afield) be considered a sufficient motivator? Does this kind of creative work in a community context help generate a greater sense of belonging?

Case study: Facebook as a platform for hyperlocal media

Hyperlocal Facebook pages such as those set up in Wolverhampton (WV11.co.uk) and Cannock (ConnectCannock.co.uk) offer opportunities for discussion of local issues but, in many respects, are revealed to be mediated in the same ways as traditional media, partly a function of the structure and rules governing the technological platform (Bakardjieva, 2003).

Hyperlocal community websites are typically set up by citizens to service their neighbourhoods with news stories about local events, activism, and everyday concerns such as traffic problems. In the UK, a number of platforms have been launched by larger media corporations, often on a local franchise basis, but it is arguably the bottom-up, independent and non-commercial spaces that engage audiences more successfully. Citizens tend to use the blogging platforms Blogger or WordPress as they are free, adaptable and easily recognised by users. Even if the owner applies some creativity through a novel template, WordPress and Blogger productions are visually decodable as blogs, and this design affords an understanding of how the site should be used.

In addition, many of the same hyperlocals also use other social media, either to help promote the content they are blogging, or to use as a second output or mode of participation. Platforms such as Foursquare and YouTube are occasionally used, but more common are Twitter and Facebook. Here we focus upon the use of Facebook. There is a widespread expectation that Facebook is better at engaging an audience of everyday neighbourhood residents, reflecting the fact that it has been longer in the market and more widely adopted for personal and family usage, whereas Twitter followers and conversationalists are more likely to be other hyperlocal peers or organisations, such as the police or local authority councillors.

Hyperlocal media practitioners set up Facebook accounts because they see it as a way to situate their media within the everyday practices of residents – they are 'pushing' their content to people through the platform, rather than assuming users will regularly seek out ('pull') their content from their blog. In many cases, residents will start the day by checking Facebook (in general) before any other web service or page. New readers tend to find out about the hyperlocal's existence in the first place through existing networks of friends and family, discovering shared hyperlocal Facebook content, or by doing searches for local keywords on Facebook.

Practitioners also appreciate and understand that the norms of Facebook do not require them to write full-blown, perfectly eloquent stories, as they would in blog posts; rather, they can write shorter, more immediate and more frequent posts. This allows editors to address as it occurs everyday news such as power cuts, lost animals and school closures. Recognising the immediacy of this, hyperlocal editors will sometimes use Facebook as their primary platform, and blogging or Twitter as a secondary route.

In some cases, for hyperlocals wishing to engage new and larger audiences, using Facebook will seem like a simple case of adding another social media platform to their repertoire. It is simple enough, using free online tools such as *If This Then That*, to cascade content down a tree of media so that an initial blog post will then be automatically posted to Twitter, Facebook, and other platforms. In our research, two of the hyperlocals we worked with routinely did this, *Tyburn Mail* and *Connect Cannock*. At the time of our research, these Facebook pages had 1,158 likes and 1,843 likes respectively (January 2015). That gives an indication of their potential viewing audience on a daily basis, ignoring the fact that this may temporarily increase when their content is shared and keeping in mind that we do not always actively continue to read the things we sign up for via such things as mailing lists.

But even if we assume that only a small percentage of those 'likers' is seeing those posts, we might still assume there would be some level of interaction – likes, shares or comments. If we look at the following example from *Connect Cannock* (Figure 10.2, left), this turns out not to be the case.

Without being able to see restricted Facebook 'insights' statistics, it is impossible to gauge how many readers are clicking on the links that take them out of Facebook to the respective blog pages. This may reflect the difficulty that if someone does click and is temporarily removed from Facebook as a result, they will not necessarily return to 'like' or comment on that post. Some people may be reticent to click through because it removes them from their Facebook session. Regardless, there is no obviously visible interaction in the image – and this may also put off other potential participants: the Facebook equivalent of the busker's empty guitar case. There is no indication that the norm is for readers to participate.

Now consider the use of Facebook by another hyperlocal news provider: the Wolverhampton-based WV11 (Figure 10.2, right).

Figure 10.2: Left: Screenshot from *Connect Cannock*'s Facebook page. Right: Screenshot from WV11's Facebook page, a lost cat announcement showing replies.

This illustrates an audience approach involving reciprocal participation, leading to additional energy and content on the Facebook page. How is this achieved? First of all, not all the content on WV11's Facebook page drives users out of the platform via hyperlinks. When possible, the complete message, including images, is included in the Facebook post, making it easier for readers to interact and add to the conversation. In addition, the content is varied, from questions of council activity and events to banal concerns such as the weather. In these postings, the writer follows the novelist's advice: 'write what you would like to read'. The writers have an understanding of what is important to the community, including issues of local identity and pride; as a result they often tap into the community zeitgeist. Some posts are also very short and more or less marked as inconsequential; but, as a result, people feel they can commit on a similar level. Examples of stories with high levels of such interaction include asking readers whether they use gas or coal for their barbecue in the spell of good weather, and on Mother's Day, whether they call their mother 'mom' (local dialect) or 'mum'. Neither post can really be described as a news story, but both generated scores of responses. The effect of these banal stories is ongoing throughout their stream and softens the background against which harder-hitting content appears. It also explicitly aims to develop a sense of online community that is geo-specifically situated. As a result, everyone knows where they are, in a physical but also social and cultural sense.

The magic ingredient here is that the writers take the time to observe and understand what is working for their admittedly larger audience (over 6,000 likers). If they ever automate blog posts out to social media, they usually take the time to contextualise each with a few additional 'human' words, rather than relying upon the activities of a robot. It would not be safe on the basis of our research to declare a correlation between such automated posts and the lack of participation in the examples shown, but the traffic patterns on the different Facebook pages suggest that the 'human touch' of a citizen journalist or editor, who is resident in and knowledgeable about a community, is more likely to start helpful, participatory conversations in these online spaces and so to build the level of activity on the site.

Case study: South Blessed

South Blessed is a 'technologically determined' enterprise. By that we do not mean the technologies deployed are the sole determinant of its form and of its impact, but we do mean to stress that South Blessed would not exist without digital media production tools (video camera and editing software) or the social media means of distribution for video productions. The core activity for South Blessed is video production. It makes its limited video production kit available to trusted network members and offers documentation and music clip services for less than £100 per day. At the time of our research survey South Blessed called itself a 'community channel' centred on a website featuring 3,000 video clips, mostly music from local and regional artists, but also news reports, dance, fashion, graffiti exploits and live events, including experiments in live streaming opinion pieces from the studio. The network also hosts a YouTube channel with 1,400 subscribers and over half a million views; and two Facebook sites, one for South Blessed with (at the time of writing) 386 followers, and one for the proprietor Vince Baidoo with 2,397 friends. Additionally, Vince runs a South Blessed Twitter account with 380 followers. Hip hop and dubstep music videos are the core content, attracting a steady flow of YouTube views from 500–5,000 with a few at 20,000 plus views. (One of these is a five-minute feature on the Stokes Croft Tesco Riot that blew up near the South Blessed Studio in 2011.)

The South Blessed website proclaimed itself as open to all talent across the South West (of England) and the editors of the site would embed music clips and interviews from across the region, building a platform that created profile and connectivity for a range of users. Traffic was maintained through Facebook sites which announced and promoted new content and also became a noticeboard for network members to post news of live nights, or new music releases. The proprietor's Facebook site also discussed South Blessed's progress and was strikingly used to share decisions and difficulties; for instance, the request to be part of the local police liaison group was debated on Facebook, as were some of the decisions arising from our own co-production. For many users, Facebook is the first recourse when confronted with decisions or opportunities that need dialogue – these tactics of default openness also protect creative citizens like Vince Baidoo from the inevitable accusations of elitism or exclusion that their leadership roles attract. The enormous amount of work, enthusiasm and commitment in producing and promoting these assets underpinned the development and maintenance of the South Blessed brand, discussed in Chapter 9.

Technology, however, was also operative in this network at another level. Key members of the network are technology enthusiasts. The pleasure of learning the new tricks of cheap graphic software is palpable in the design styles of the many of their self-made music videos. Experiments in live streaming from the studio were led by a partnership with software developers who welcomed South Blessed as beta testers. For this network, the internet is a core learning environment, an infinite resource for opinion, theory (however untested) and information. The group works from the assumption that there is no task that cannot be learnt from the internet. This technological enthusiasm and web-based informal learning culture was profoundly influential in the co-production that the research team undertook.

Our ethical agreement with South Blessed was based on the principle that whatever we did we would try to ensure that our relationship left the network stronger and more sustainable than when we first encountered it. The first set of ideas for co-production centred on a manga-style film featuring a set of characters and a story that Vince had been developing with a collaborator for some time. Discarded on the grounds of cost, the film script eventually became the graphic novel *Indigo Babies*. The research team introduced the idea of transmedial storytelling, suggesting that the story and the characters could be launched in comic, online and video clip form, building an audience for a bigger production in the future.

This decision was driven at one level by the mutual recognition that the online assets and profile developed through digital video production and social media did not have the potential to produce a sustainable business model for the enterprise. The attention of a local audience numbering in the low thousands was insufficient for advertising or sponsorship revenue. The market in video services at £100 per day in the informal music production space was similarly inadequate as a means of sustaining the business. So the technological affordance that made the whole enterprise possible also appeared to undermine its sustainability. A physical product with a cover price and therefore a steady income stream presented itself as a low-tech but sustainable solution.

Technoculture is an active ingredient of the *Indigo Babies* comic. 'Indigo Children' is an internet meme that wants to recognise children's telepathic or magical powers as an alternative to the plethora of disabling diagnoses of dyslexia, ADHD, autism and Asperger's disorder that are also popularly read as a response to too much technology too soon. The Indigo Babies of the South Blessed comic are a group of young people with extraordinary technological powers, super hackers with special telepathic abilities and a commitment to social justice and greening the inner city.

The story can be understood as a creative response to the themes of the research: it portrays technologically adept young people trying to survive and build a community in a recognisable inner city Bristol. The group is challenged in a 'which side are you on?' crisis when a riot breaks out on their doorstep and they are forced to decide whether they will use their collective intelligence for violent or nonviolent ends. The comic is a physical and saleable creative property but it also dramatises the ethical dilemmas of the South Blessed community.

Conclusions

Finally then, we ask how is today's technology working in practice for creative citizens? And how can it work or be used better?

It is clear, first of all, that there is no set rule for how any technology should be used, as we observe in open internet standards, for example, where they are malleable, transformable and shift along with user requirements. When top-down platforms are designed, iterated and launched, such as Facebook, even if this design process has involved user experience research to deliver the best product, audiences and users will always surprise with their reappropriation, hacking or modification ('modding') of technologies. However, when platforms continually upgrade, redesign and change their terms of engagement without apparent benefit or explanation to the user, this causes unrest. The basic message to creative citizen networks is this: use those tools at your disposal that best match your own resources. If you want free and quick, that may mean Facebook. But also try to use tools creatively, exercising their full potential.

Everyone should recognise that high-tech, or the latest, highest tech, is not always suitable for all citizens. Many prefer old media such as print, or old communication forms such as face-to-face conversation and meeting at events. It may be better to start with print or a notice board and then move online, to social media and the use of apps; or it may (as we have shown) sometimes be necessary to reverse engineer from online platforms to physical media.

People develop different technological understandings and expectations within a community – this is one of the most important factors that a creative citizen looking to mobilise others in a neighbourhood can recognise. Building a new iPhone app to deliver news will appeal to a tranche of iPhone users; pushing leaflets through doors may get a message out to many more people. Don't seek to innovate at the expense of alienating everyday communities who don't want to be working hard for their media, or for methods to mould and co-design experiences. Go to them – don't expect them to come to you.

Digital technologies – their default setup, interface, password and security settings and storage mechanisms – are usually designed for use by an individual and not by a community. That is one reason why communities may struggle and often rely heavily on key creative citizens with the skills needed to act as champions, editors and even providers of server capacity on their behalf. For these people, usually volunteers, maintaining these digital activities can become a chore, so it is hardly surprising that such flows of communication or news become mediated spaces. In creating these spaces and platforms, editors, readers, audiences, participants, and a whole raft of other roles must be negotiated with care. On the one hand, mediated spaces become problematic if key participants exercise power over the rest of the network in an ill judged way. On the other, we recognise that such acts and projects of community creative citizenship would not be initiated at all if not for these key individuals. Leadership is necessary. The best we can hope for is understanding and transparency in such relationships, supported by the opportunities that technology offers in maintaining communication and collaboration in everyday life.

A group's reliance on its key people can mean that – for researchers – community-led design process often becomes based around the skills, abilities and interests of the key people rather than the wider community. In order to ensure that everyone has the opportunity to engage with evolving communication technologies, it is necessary to include the full range of community members in any co-creation process. Shifting reliance from working with a key person to working with a group of key people will also help to create shared ownership and responsibility, ultimately leading to a more sustainable technology project.

The co-creative case studies described in this chapter and elsewhere in this book were based in 'traditional' responses to the needs of creative citizen networks: a digital storytelling installation, a newspaper, a comic, an image sharing web planning platform, collectively used Facebook pages. Our emphasis on friction-free processes for community inclusion will become more urgent as the age of urban informatics intensifies. Already 'smart cities' of the future are imagined as places where data infrastructures will make the city more efficient, healthier or greener (de Waal, 2011). The future citizen is imagined as the producer of *and* the subject of urban information systems. The approach to technology that this chapter has described suggests the need for a radically new way to imagine the role of technology in the cities of the future; rather than relaying the top-down application of data systems to the everyday life of the city, our work makes the case for this to be balanced with smaller scale networks co-designed around the particular needs of identifiable user communities. Such networks would be designed to maximise trust so a level of participation that creates value is visible and available to the whole user network. We do not face a choice between big infrastructures, such as evenly spread broadband and mobile communications systems, and smaller systems designed by creative citizens for creative citizens. Big and small are both necessary. Without the latter, the former face an intensifying crisis of trust; without the former, creative citizenship will lack a resource critical to achieving its true potential scale.

Note

[1]   Story at: home.web.cern.ch/topics/birth-web

ELEVEN

A capacious approach to creative citizenship: implications for policy

Ian Hargreaves and John Hartley

In the first ten chapters of this book, we have explained how the concept of the creative citizen emerged within our research project and how it was subsequently explored, in conceptual and empirical fashion, through co-creative case studies. The concept, we believe, has shed timely light upon the important relationship between co-created civic activities of many kinds and a phalanx of digital communications technologies now in widespread use, but still rapidly evolving. Our central research question asked: how does creative citizenship generate value for communities within a changing media landscape and how can this pursuit of value be intensified, propagated and sustained? The question invites, among other things, some reflection on policy approaches relevant to creative citizenship open to governments and other bodies. This is the focus of what now follows.

One set of policy-relevant answers to the research question has already been captured in chapters one to ten, so first we summarise this chapter-by-chapter narrative, before moving on to more overarching points. Here we encounter the challenge that creative citizenship is such a wide-ranging concept that there is scarcely an area of mainstream political debate to which it is not relevant. We test the interface between our own work and mainstream political thinking by entering into conversation with four leading UK political think tanks; this discussion highlights commonalities and differences between our perspectives (academics and communities) and theirs (policy thinkers). We then provide some closing thoughts on some of the policy concerns, which have been prominent in the Creative Citizen project, namely economic wellbeing, education, city planning/urban development and journalism.

Summary

(Chapter 1) Politically, the idea of creative citizenship emerges through mainstream European and American 'communitarian thinking' in centre-left and centre-right politics around the turn of the millennium. It acquires urgency in the political circumstances that followed the 2008 banking crisis, which aggravated a much-diagnosed crisis of confidence in mainstream political participation and within other important civic and commercial institutions. We consider creative citizenship's many intersections with global digital media and other affordances of an increasingly mobile-accessed and globally accessible internet. We explain the title of this book with reference to the imaginative, poetic and politically charged epic work of Percy Bysshe Shelley: *Prometheus Unbound*. We describe the interdisciplinary research team's working methodology, structure and ethos, drawing particular attention to our co-creative working relationship with community partners. We note the relevance to our work of other academic projects that point towards a more 'porous' and impact-seeking approach to the work of universities. We express the hope that our thinking will be of interest beyond as well as within the academy.

(Chapter 2) A wide-ranging literature review establishes a conceptual framework for the idea of creative citizenship. It identifies 'methodological individualism' as a generic problem standing in its way, arguing that 'the place of citizenship in society and its connections with creativity needs a radical overhaul'. Having summarised three social science approaches to the concept of citizenship, we propose a fourth, namely 'a creative, cultural or DIY approach', made feasible by ubiquitous social media in a market environment. This approach arises from humanities thinking, rather than from social science, and embraces the tensions between citizenship as a source of obligations on the one hand, and as a resource of playfulness on the other. Creative citizenship reconciles these: 'brought together in one knowledge system though they remain apart from one another in scholarly traditions.' Creative citizenship, we say, can be 'scaled up in the digital age', but its dynamics are evolutionary and complex rather than subject to the linear momentum of classical economics. Creative citizenship's habitat is best understood as one of 'complex systems, interacting and shifting in relationship to one another at a planetary scale'. In this complexity, 'everyone, everywhere, across everything is a participant in the overall productivity of the system'. Policy settings need to shift from central control and 'picking winners' to distributed control (self-organising systems), trial and error and experimentation, with sustained investment in populations (education, connectivity and nurturing associations).

(Chapter 3) A creative economy perspective on creative citizenship offers a historical account of differing conceptual approaches, reflected in public policy and statistical reporting in many countries and via international agencies such as those of the United Nations. An account is given of the emergence of policies directed at the creative industries and the creative economy, judged by the UK government to account for over 8% of all UK employment. However, more than three times this number of people are known to be active as voluntary or amateur participants in arts and cultural activities. Adding to this, the unknown levels of participation in everyday creative citizenship activities, such as photography and fan networks, surely inflates these numbers further, but to an unknown extent. Studies show numerous benefits arising from these creative activities, from personal development to improved health and general wellbeing, contributing to enhanced social capital. Spillovers between these industrial, economic and cultural domains, formal and informal, are significant but inadequately quantified. For creative citizenship to achieve its potential, more careful study and statistical evaluation of these phenomena is required.

(Chapter 4) Non-economic forms of value arising from creative citizenship are argued to be significant and subject to examination here through the Creative Citizen project's co-creative case studies and media interventions. The characteristics of creative citizens include a strong drive toward self-actualisation and self-improvement; being good communicators and 'connectors'; and being invested in the values of self-determination within public democratic processes. Connectivity through social media constitutes a form of cultural capital that can lead to the ability to 'tell your stories' as well as to link up with other groups. This networked capital can be a social as well as a personal asset. Like other forms of cultural capital it may also yield financial returns. Our case studies show how networks give rise to commons assets as well as individual benefits. Creative citizenship practices predate the web, but they can be scaled and distributed at much lower cost in a global web environment. The challenge for research in the field is to develop methods that can evaluate these commons assets at regional, national and international scale. Future policy aimed at supporting vibrant, inclusive, healthy and productive communities would benefit from understanding better how creative citizens' commitment to local and regional representation produces value and how, through a carefully constructed and authentic process of co-creation, debate and negotiation can occur.

(Chapter 5) We seek to identify varieties of creative citizenship among our case studies as a step to differentiating their characteristics, including questions of motivation, purpose and context, and drawing a useful distinction between collective and connective acts of citizenship. Acts of creative citizenship make or produce something new and in parallel induce a critical reflection on political, social or cultural issues. These acts may occur in any type of community, whether of place or shared interest. From our case studies, we foreground everyday creativity, which is playing an increasingly active role in connecting the previously disconnected practices of citizenship and creativity. Creative acts release previously hidden potential in order to produce a critical change. We need to move beyond individualistic or psychological approaches towards creativity and citizenship in order to investigate the role and creative power of these connective and collective acts, not least as generators of social capital. Our observations support the proposition that the activities of an enhanced or 'unbound' creative citizen have the potential to make a substantial impact in civic life.

(Chapter 6) The social-media-rich landscape of the creative citizen gives rise to a rich and powerful set of network effects. We seek to understand, through in-depth exploration of two case studies, the salient characteristics of these networks, asking whether they have already acquired a depth, complexity and latency that invites insights from complexity theory to explain them. A relational framework is deployed to explain the existing multilayered milieu culture of South Blessed (Bristol), drawing attention to its identity, social groupings, field of cultural production and wider areas of influence. Whilst the internet and the participatory media cultures it supports play an important role in facilitating the creative and communicative activity and potential of South Blessed, offline relationships and networks, linked to the physical place and space in Bristol, remain pivotal. An examination of the B31 Voices hyperlocal news provider in Birmingham illustrates the emergence of an evolving networked model for local news. Here creative citizenship is pivotal to the wellbeing of communities: a clear example where the affordances of technology have played their part in reshaping the space for citizenship in the democratically important field of journalism.

(Chapter 7) In a series of 'conversations about co-production', we note feedback from the research team's community partners, reporting in-depth interviews with five key players. An overarching point is the diversity of circumstance of these community activists and the importance of researchers paying close attention to this aspect. The conversation offers insights into the use of language; the use of non-verbal communication techniques (such as drawing); the value and the limitations of theory; the role of expertise; the importance of thinking through the rhythm of different working circumstances (part-time volunteers versus full-time paid researchers); project structure and sustainability beyond the project. In some of the cases, strongly positive results were achieved, such as the collaboratively produced Wards Community Corner planning proposal. Leadership and working styles varied from place to place. Social media proved their value and their limitations. A mix of physical and virtual makes for the most effective communications system.

(Chapter 8) Asset mapping was the single most important methodological tool used in the Creative Citizen project. We set out to understand the history and best practice of this technique, then adapted asset mapping to the diverse and ambitious circumstances of our own work. Initially understood as a tool for capturing and understanding the values that drive creative civic actions as well as the value generated from these actions, we applied the technique for the dual purpose of supporting research and facilitating collaborative creation. We focused on eliciting intangible assets such as knowledge, capabilities and skills, as well as social and cultural relationships. Our work innovated by examining the value of media assets in community and personal asset maps. We concluded that intangible assets around people, groups and organisations are the main carriers of untapped potential. There were many difficulties using asset mapping in a systematic and linear way across very diverse types of community, but the empirical evidence suggests that the methodology is useful for unearthing and capturing people's values and perceptions of value, as a way of negotiating personal and group goals and as a tool for community engagement and co-creation.

(Chapter 9) Turning to issues of place, we explore the many ways in which physical and online places transcend geography, presenting a crucible for ideology and values. Social media offer a rich set of tools for place-making, exemplified in three case studies, where communities learn, adopt, reject and adapt numerous digital offers. At the Wards

Corner Coalition, activist community planners deployed an online visualisation tool, StickyWorld, to negotiate more effectively the group's ideas for an alternative planning vision. *Tyburn Mail,* an online community news provider, learned how to improve reader engagement by working from a physical News Café. South Blessed's logo presents an optimist reading: 'acknowledging history but proposing new experiences: building on the past and also indicating a radically optimistic departure for today's African-Caribbean diaspora.' These projects and the insights they provoke may or may not be 'scalable' in response to public policy strategies, but that is not their purpose. The activities themselves are self-made and self-actualised, addressing the wider world directly, rather than through external mediation. The material affordances of digital media and social preconditions of civic creativity are connected with practices of cultural expression and political participation. Our analyses offer a fertile ground to rethink how these affordances have given rise to acts of creative citizenship, not simply as a digital era phenomenon, but as an experience that transcends the digital and physical understandings of place, and its local, national and global boundaries.

(Chapter 10) The role of digital, social media technologies lies at the heart of the Creative Citizen project. We review arguments about the virtues and vices of these technologies, exposing the potential for approaches based upon community-led design. This requires that problems are framed by communities, facilitated by designers and researchers, and that the solutions co-developed are then responsive to their use in practice. Three case studies illustrate. The *Story Machine,* co-created with a community group in East London, adapts iPad technology in the context of a steering wheel and a circus-like platform, enabling stories to be displayed continuously both remotely and on public screens at the community centre, where they are reshaped by a 'live' audience. This hacking, modding or reappropriation of technologies is widespread, growing and important in creative citizenship. Communities naturally prefer established and easy-to-use technologies, illustrated by our study of the diverse usage of core social media such as Facebook and Twitter in a hyperlocal news operation in Wolverhampton. Here, much is learned from community usage of simple analogue media, such as the village notice board, indicating that mediated spaces become problematic if key participants exercise power over the rest of the network in an ill judged way. On the other hand, leadership is necessary. Our emphasis on friction-free processes for community inclusion will become more urgent as the age of urban informatics intensifies. In proliferating 'smart cities' we suggest balancing top-down data systems with smaller scale networks co-designed around the needs of identifiable user communities. Such networks would be designed to maximise trust and so sustain levels of participation. We need both big infrastructures, such as high-quality broadband, but also smaller systems designed by creative citizens for creative citizens. Without the latter, the former face an intensifying crisis of trust; without the former, creative citizenship lacks resource critical to achieving its potential.

The moment of the creative citizen

From our work, empirical and conceptual, we arrive at this central conclusion: we are indeed living in the time of the creative citizen. Important historical staging points from the last two decades are the invention of a business sector concept named creative industries (DCMS, 1998), accompanied by the emergence of the idea of the creative class (Florida, 2002), creative cities (Landry, 1994; 2005) and the creative economy (Howkins, 2001; Bakhshi et al, 2013). These developments way mark the impetus of digitally charged creativity on innovation, growth and productivity across the whole of the world's advanced economies, and most developing or emerging ones (Hartley et al, 2015), highlighting a deeply significant shift from economies dependent chiefly upon tangible assets, such as buildings and machines, to economies dependent upon intangible assets, such as brand, design and other creatively bestowed assets (Goodridge et al, 2002; Hargreaves, 2011; Dal Borgo et al, 2013; Haskel et al, 2014). Observed in this context, creative citizenship is a potently emergent next step. It is as if the creative citizen has been waiting in the wings, anticipating a now widely acknowledged crisis in industrial era structures of representative democracy, education and economic momentum, ready to be drafted into a reinvigoration or reinvention of public, civic and commercial/ economic life, whilst also playing an important part in ensuring that big tech and big data do not themselves fall into self-destructive pathways by breaching civic trust on such issues as privacy and honesty about taxation. The figure of the creative citizen thus simultaneously challenges and offers reassurance.

Our own thinking has been much affected by the sheer accumulation of stories of creative citizenship, whether by this or another name. These include groups working across the whole of public life and commerce, including health, public parks, social care, allotment gardening, reading-out-loud groups, libraries, food banks, sport, news services, fan networks and digital commons. Creative citizenship occurs in communities of place as well as in communities based on interest and which often have global reach. This is the domain of creative citizenship and its close cousin DIY citizenship (Ratto and Boler, 2014); namely that set of creative activities pursued by self-organised groups not usually, primarily, with only commercial goals in view, but committed to adding value to community wellbeing and to the wellbeing of individuals living in relationship with others.

During the life of the Creative Citizenship project, John Hartley, co-editor of this volume and co-author of this chapter, has driven the creative economy narrative further, arguing that the distribution of creative potential afforded by, inter alia, globalised digital communications media and their attendant social networks, entails nothing less than an epochal shift in culture, society and the economy, occasioned by the scale of possibilities now open to individuals within communities of all shapes and sizes across the whole planet, asking: 'Is it possible to have a creative economy based on the creativity of the *whole population*?' (Hartley et al, 2015: 45). Close-up studies of creative citizenship, such as have been reported throughout this book are, taken together, an attempt to answer that question of population-wide agency, at least to a first order of approximation.

Here, creativity is defined as 'the production of newness in complex, adaptive systems'. Newness or adaptive change can come from anywhere in the system; it is not confined to what economists currently recognise as innovation, nor is it confined to the firm. Anyone, anywhere, can make a contribution.

This means that models of agency based on representation and on a split between producers and consumers need to be revised. It is no longer the case that experts, elites or representatives act on behalf of relatively passive populations and this doesn't just apply to creative outputs, but to knowledge more generally and to civic representation. Nor can we continue to rely on an axiomatic model that assumes producers (trained, organised and capitalised in firms) to be quite separate from consumers (passively imagined, and often feminised or infantilised in the only expert discourse that cares about them – marketing). If anyone, anywhere, in concert with whom they please, can make something new that suits their circumstances, as is already clear from the dynamism and vibrancy of social media, crowdsourcing, crowdfunding, and innumerable instances of peer-to-peer problem solving (in other words, 'creative citizenship') using digital affordances, and if, in turn these new solutions are in principle accessible to others without costly restriction, then we need a new model of population-wide creativity to understand how such micro-level agency scales up (or is prevented from so doing) into large-scale productivity in 'complex systems' such as the economy, the polity or culture.

It follows from these arguments that theories of complexity and conceptual models derived from the study of evolutionary processes are valuable in understanding the scale, resilience and potential of what is now appropriately discussed as a creative 'ecology' (Hearn et al, 2007; Howkins, 2010). The notion of an ecology or ecosystem is itself productive in this context because it draws attention to the way that different forces interact, across boundaries that once confined attention to parochial horizons, such that creativity includes the way that different systems rub up against each other (sometimes cooperatively, sometimes in conflict) to produce 'newness' of which no one individual is the author or owner, but which impacts everyone, for good or ill. Just as attention to natural ecosystems has resulted in greater understanding of how local decisions and self-interest 'here' can result in disastrous outcomes 'there', so a new appreciation of 'creative ecology' can help researchers and citizens understand how creativity itself must be understood in relation to the actions and interactions of planetary systems, linked materially through globalised trade and markets and semiotically through globalised media and knowledge.

Using evolutionary and environmental approaches to creativity has the benefit of making context, connections and community just as important to the discussion as individual talent and intellectual property have been to date. Human creativity arises from sociality, relationships and common action, not simply from individual (and thus proprietorial) bright ideas. This is why the concept of creative citizenship is attractive to those who want to explain creativity at group level, and the larger the group the better. This concept of citizenship requires the prioritisation of association among strangers (Hartley, 2010) – of cooperation, common purpose, and decision-making in company. In such a context, creativity must also be understood as involving some element of 'common good' as well as cleverness. Using evolutionary or ecological approaches requires the analyst to attend to the potential productive energy of everyone, not just professionally trained elites or commercially contracted experts. Such a view chimes with emancipationist traditions of popular politics, popular culture and popular education, where 'more' does not mean 'worse', but rather it means extending the franchise, culture and knowledge to everyone, and receiving in turn the democratic, cultural and economic benefits of enormously scaled up inputs from much broader bases of popular participation that characterise post-Industrial Revolution societies

(Mokyr, 2009; McCloskey, 2010). Such a view requires that notions of politics, culture and knowledge change in the process – from aristocratic rule, high cultural taste and gentlemanly inquiry to mass politics, mass culture and mass education. Add to this set of extensions the affordances of industrial-scale business and the productivity of technologically connected social networks, especially now that these are digital, global and infinitely sharable, and we begin to see why a capacious approach to creative citizenship is worthy of consideration. If the vote and the classroom are good enough for all, why not also creative productivity? And if everyone is creative, how do they combine into associative groups for civic purposes? And what, in turn, does that activity tell us about creativity and about politics? A whole new storyline for citizenship beckons.

The implications of this storyline are significant. Creative citizenship in a digitally afforded environment requires breaching walls between academic disciplines; the arts and humanities become more data-driven; engineering, medicine and business become more creative. There are clear signs that universities and the organisations that fund them are getting the point, drawing not least upon analysis of the success of Silicon Valley, its institutions of higher education and innovations in mass online learning. Research funding councils in the UK and elsewhere have placed increasing emphasis in recent years on transdisciplinary reach and crossover funding between research funders. The Creative Citizen project and the UK Research Councils' Connected Communities programme, of which it is part, exemplify that trend. There remain, however, issues of scale and priority about these commitments.

What about government and the public sector? Here the picture is more mixed, but there are many signs of liveliness. President Lula da Silva of Brazil's appointment of an iconic black musician, Gilberto Gil, to the role of Minister of Culture (2003–08) provided one highly symbolic moment, not least as Gil declared a partnership with the Creative Commons movement (subsequently frustrated by corporate resistance). Barack Obama's periodic attempts at community-based, digitally enabled political organisation established new horizons and promised, for a time at least, elements of a co-created political project. Social media have also offered pivotally important affordances for insurgencies, such as Islamic State, as well as more western-rooted movements, such as Occupy and various anti-war movements. Establishment and support for 'creative hubs' has simultaneously become a globally competitive sport, with initiatives in places as different as Moscow, Vietnam, Nigeria, Indonesia, China, Korea, Iceland, Canada and Argentina (Hartley et al, 2015).

There are also issues about sustainability and consistency in pursuing these themes. So, having recognised the influential first mover claims of the UK government in establishing the 'creative industries' as an important and growing business sector in the late 1990s, it is also fair to note the subsequent hesitation of politicians in the early years of the new century to recognise the scale and depth of an emergent and wider creative economy. The result has been periodic policy thinking gaps around subjects such as the patchiness of digital infrastructure; the opportunities arising from mass availability of digital data; a fitful commitment to creativity in schools; and the need to reconsider legal and regulatory structures around intellectual property, privacy and the operating conditions of the internet. In the UK, the Conservative-Liberal Democrat coalition government formed following the outcome of a 'hung Parliament' in 2010 showed the considerable stamina necessary to initiate a useful level of reform of copyright (Hargreaves, 2011; Boyle, 2015). It also did a comparatively good job in responding to the demands of the global world of higher education for a more 'open access' approach to academic publishing and the dissemination of knowledge (Atkinson, 2015). Meanwhile the same administration's Government Digital Service pursued a 'digital by default' approach to open data and the delivery of services, such as motor vehicle licensing, tax and – with patchier success – in the hotly controversial field of healthcare. At the level of rhetoric, the 'Big Society' label upon which David Cameron's Conservative Party campaigned in 2010 was largely set aside in office, though it still got a mention in the party's 2015 general election manifesto.

This is not, however, to make an exaggerated claim for relative UK achievement. Within Europe, the laurels for digital innovation at the government level belong to small states like Estonia and Iceland. Finland has the continent's, if not the world's, most admired education system. And it was a Labor administration in Australia (as early as 1994), which pioneered the idea of a 'creative nation'. Meanwhile at the 'European level' (that is the level of the European Union, which provides important legal frameworks for member states, from human rights to regulation of trade) the context for creative citizenship (and much else) was rendered unfavourable as the EU slithered briskly from the global financial crisis of 2008 to a crisis of its own making: the eurozone crisis, which began in 2009 and which is still not over at the time of writing. This combination of forces also delivered the political and economic drama which engulfed Greece, where a left-wing alliance led by Syriza (a party named 'for the roots' and formed in 2004) provided political leadership first in a many faceted insurgency, which included recognisable creative citizenship concerns and elements, and then as the country's elected government. Syriza's style and ambitions found echoes in a number of other countries, including Spain, and in the global 'Occupy' movement, which eschewed specific political goals, but campaigned on issues of economic inequality. Against a background of relatively weak economic growth and stalled productivity, the EU was not best placed in these years to pursue bold policies with regard to the digital creative economy or creative citizenship, even though the European Commission appointed in 2014, under the leadership of Jean Claude Juncker, committed itself to the liberalisation of copyright and the ambitious pursuit of a 'digital single market,' modelled upon the borderless market upon which the EU built its post-war prosperity.

The London policy debate

The international Creative Citizens Conference held at the Royal College of Art in London in late 2014 has already been mentioned in the introduction to this book. A political debate took place there following a provocation paper written by Stephen Lee, Chief Executive of the liberal think tank, Centre Forum. In it, Lee expressed concern at the vagueness of creative citizenship as a concept, whilst acknowledging that this may not impede its appeal to politicians (Lee, 2015). On the other hand, he applauded the co-creative, bottom-up methodology of the Creative Citizenship project, arguing that this enabled it to identify a rich seam of knowledge, enabling everyone, politicians included, to see the value of authentic citizen engagement in specific zones of civic life, including service delivery in challenging territory such as social care and care for the mentally ill, as well as in the examples explored by ourselves in community journalism and neighbourhood planning.

The conference debate prompted by Lee's paper was a lively, illuminating affair and, for that reason, we offer a lightly edited transcript at pages 275–93. This captures a snapshot of the political debate in one country at one moment. What is audible is a closely overlapping range of views about creative citizenship from think tank leaders from widely differing party political perspectives.

Andrew Harrup, General Secretary of the left-leaning Fabian Society, argues that a 'trusted and empowered public service workforce' is a precondition for truly successful partnership between government and creative citizens. Without this, suspicion of the 'sharp elbows' and self-interested concerns of self-generated and minority creative citizenship formations will impede fruitful collaboration. Harrup, however, is in no doubt about the importance of creative citizenship, commenting that 'formal politics will die if it doesn't find a way of working in partnership with this world of creativity that we're seeing from individuals'. Lee himself dismisses the term creative citizenship as 'meaningless in public policy terms', but acknowledges its strengths in its clear engagement with technology; its understanding of the interplay between formal (professional) and informal (voluntary/ amateur) activities; and especially in its absolute commitment to co-creative working, based upon a clear understanding of the strengths of 'relational' networks upon which citizenship depends. Lee's own 'Manifesto for Creative Citizenship' adds to this by pointing out that creative citizenship harnesses the voice and experience of the user; builds upon the growth in 'portfolio' and freelance working and, by prioritising such voices, fosters innovation and alternative approaches to solving problems.

From the right, Eddie Copeland of Policy Exchange adapts Lincoln's Gettysburg Address to suggest creative citizenship as 'Government With the People,' where politicians and officials now harness 'the wisdom of the crowd'. Emran Mian, Director of the centre-left Social Market Foundation, draws on extensive experience inside government to report that in practice, government's view of citizenship-based initiatives is essentially instrumental, designed to enable government to accomplish what it is already minded to do and to 'create enough of a partnership' that government officials 'can ask for stuff'. Creative citizens, he suggests, are right to mistrust the motivations and culture of government in this regard. Mian advises creative citizens simply to get on with designing their own solutions.

Where does this leave us?

Conceptually, the idea of creative citizenship has, we believe, stood up pretty well to the critiques against which it has been tested during the research project. Thinkers in mainstream political parties can see its merits, whilst probing its limitations. Among community practitioners and activists, the term 'creative citizenship' is not in widespread use, but when raised, it usually provokes a thoughtful and engaged response, informed by the specifics of individual and community circumstance. For activists involved in pressing a community-informed planning alternative through the use of persuasive visualisation, creativity is self-evidently important in an explicit and collaborative act of citizenship. Among users of the co-working space of the Moseley Exchange in

Birmingham, co-workers mostly told us that they were not primarily concerned with either their creative or their civic role; their main concern was to make a success of their businesses. A number, however, acknowledged the importance of media and other creative inputs to their work and their 'business success'. Clearly this has civic value in its own right and, as such, represents a valid civic goal for the Moseley Exchange. The Exchange's co-created digital storytelling programme, designed to increase creative awareness among its co-workers, is an example of how creative citizenship draws upon researcher expertise, community storytelling and collaborative methods.

It is important, however, not to let the idea of creative citizenship be captured by existing interests such as volunteering on the one hand, or community arts and media on the other. Both of these worthy sets of activities may figure, but creative citizenship cannot be reduced to what we're already doing without losing innovative potential. Nor should it be captured by existing political discourse, which knows all too well what is on the right and the left, what calculus is required to send costs to the private or public sector respectively, and thence which tribal affiliations are being stroked. Policy talk that defaults straight away to a debate about 'government support' vs 'taxpayer subsidy' for the public sector or resisting/advancing the predations of neoliberalism is simply premature. Although the 'third way' is by now a broken political adventure – but still a relevant political idea, we argue (Giddens, 1998) – the creative citizen concept needs to be held *between* existing notions of creativity, citizenship, and thence politics, so as to identify a territory that looks liminal, even impure, when compared with established binaries, but which may open up new categories for the future. It is not enough to conclude with Lee that all is well if people just get on with creative citizenship by themselves, in that multitude of separately focused small-scale actions situated in some conveniently liminal space, neither private nor public. Doing so leaves out of account any possibility that policy makers and government agencies can *learn from* their own citizens' creativity when planning higher-level social action. Otherwise they will be confined to conceptual rigidities that will serve their interests poorly, leaving left/right, public/private, state/ commercial antinomies intact but sterile, when the really green grass is on the commons, along the path of that third way.

Although not intentionally addressed to creative citizenship as an idea, it is notable that the argument of *More Human* (Hilton, 2015) draws heavily on the author's experience of human-centred design practised at Stanford University's Design School, to lay out an eclectic programme of humanising political goals, which build upon the author's earlier work as lead architect of David Cameron's 'Big Society'. Noting an IBM study, which identifies creativity as the most crucial factor for success in business leadership, Hilton makes an extensive set of arguments about the importance of creativity in civic and commercial life, suggesting, inter alia, that, 'children need to be creative and collaborative to succeed in the 21st century economy' (Hilton, 2015: 70).

Removing constraints

How then might we encourage more creative citizenship and so, in the words of our research question, intensify, propagate and sustain its qualities? Or, returning to the language of this book's title, how do we make a move from creative citizenship *constrained* to the creative citizen *unbound*?

One answer to this question, as the London debaters agree, is that we need to study politics and contemporary civic settlements to identify and ease or remove constraints. These, to be sure, will include the full agenda of challenges faced by any given community at any given time and place. Some constraints will be rooted in poverty, ageing and physical and mental illness. Others will concern education, skills and opportunities for the young. Some will arise from problems of environmental sustainability, inadequate transport, ill-judged planning rules or neglected infrastructures. In previous generations, innovations such as public libraries, free access to museums, public service broadcasting and free education and health were bestowed from above and brought with them radical liberations for individuals and communities. Creative citizenship, by contrast, invites communities of any scale and in any place to use the communications tools accessible to them to identify problems and invent or reinvent solutions, whether of health, economic performance or cultural expression. The empirical evidence of our work indicates that well-judged, well-managed creative inputs to communities from groups of citizens well attuned to their own communities' needs and aspirations offer rich rewards, resulting in general benefits such as enhanced self-confidence and empowerment on top of the specific goals of any particular project. These are features picked up repeatedly in the case studies considered throughout this book.

For politicians, there are abundant opportunities to learn from citizen action in order to add to its scale or momentum. We can take as a working example the case of hyperlocal or community news, which the creative citizens project explored in some depth on a number of sites. Here we illustrate the readiness with which, at the time of writing in mid-2015, a set of ten credible policy demands can be assembled.

10 policies for hyperlocal news

At the time of writing, this is a slightly warm rather than a hot political topic, arising from a recognition of the severe decline in local newspaper circulations and staffing, and an arguably incommensurate spread of mostly volunteer hyperlocal bloggers and other online activists, sometimes known (though not all of them welcome the term) as 'citizen journalists'.

It is widely acknowledged that the biggest challenge facing hyperlocal news providers is sustainability. They mostly operate on a shoestring and, as we have seen from our case studies, approach financial questions as a side issue. Here, we list a set of interventions that might help UK hyperlocals grow, become more numerous and be stronger:

1. Direct public subsidy – not unusual in parts of Europe for local news, but regarded with suspicion in the UK where news providers are judged to need strong protection from undue political influence. A subsidy pot could resemble the Ofcom-administered community radio fund (Barnett and Townend, 2014: 13–15).
2. Supportive partnerships with the BBC, a publicly funded major news organisation, which might be asked to provide money, help in kind or simply to make its content available free on a Creative Commons BY open licence to hyperlocals. The 'BBC as a platform' figured strongly in the corporation's thinking in 2015 as it sought to negotiate a new financial settlement with the government.
3. A publicly supported hyperlocal agency, advocacy organisation or trade body, which could help hyperlocals with core needs, such as legal advice, training and technology. This could be a partnership with one or more journalism schools.
4. Prizes: possibly big ones, available perhaps through the Lottery Fund, as a reward for great ideas, performance and sticking at the task for hyperlocals and other bodies/people crucial to the irrigation of local democracy. The Media Standards Trust has proposed a version of the US Knight News Challenge.[1]
5. Exemption from VAT: already enjoyed by newspapers.
6. Admission to the ranks of those (mostly local newspapers) where local authorities are able to place (and pay for) statutory notices on such things as planning issues.

7. Funding support from corporate beneficiaries of a lively internet, such as Google, Facebook, Amazon and Twitter. This could be directed at policy 4 above, or some other well-judged support. Additionally, Google could advise on how to improve visibility of hyperlocals in searches. The BBC could also be asked to help with this.

8. Establish local news providers as 'community assets' under an amended Localism Act, forcing publishers planning to close a newspaper to offer it up for sale to their staff and/or the wider community. A commitment to developing collaborative, participatory local news hubs with ongoing training and skills provision by these new media community assets could be written into the conditions attached to this.

9. Encourage or require local authorities and other public bodies to engage more fully and openly with hyperlocals. Currently, hyperlocal news providers/journalists frequently encounter blockages to attending meetings, accessing documents and meeting officials. Government could ensure that, for example, full council meetings and planning committees are open to filming and social media reporting by observers.

10. A commitment from local authorities to publishing open and usable data. More funding could also be provided to support local authorities in responding to Freedom of Information requests from local journalists.

In our other case study areas, a comparable list of points could equally readily be assembled. There are various ways, for example, in which the coalition government's Localism Act (2011) could be built upon. This legislation aimed to 'break down the barriers that stop councils, localities, social enterprises and voluntary groups getting things done for themselves'.[2] It provided important context for the activities of the Wards Corner Coalition and the Kentish Town Neighborhood Forum. Arising from our own work, however, gaps in thinking and resourcing are clearly visible, including: resourcing community groups as part of empowering citizens; support for training; investment in partnership-building among citizen groups; inclusion of intangible assets in discussions about planning and built environment; encouragement and funding for university work with creative citizen communities on design and planning issues.

When it comes to the work we carried out with our partners at the Moseley Exchange and South Blessed, the most important factors on the political agenda may be the 'background issues' identified by Emran Mian in our debate, such as welfare, housing and social care, but there are also issues around education, skills, apprenticeships, buildings, digital access, contracting and supply chain rules, to name only a few of the problems which arise at the interface between public authorities and small or micro business organisations. The point is not that we need government departments to have a department of creative citizens or a programme for creative citizenship, because creative citizens are everywhere and they're involved in everything, but government at all levels does need to understand much better the nature and potential of creative citizenship as fundamental to the ways in which it understands citizen needs and engages in the design of solutions.

Education, economics and the broader policy agenda

If we shift our perspective from the detail of our own case studies, it is not difficult to imagine policy in most areas drafted in a way that takes account of the value offered by creative citizens. There is, for instance, a well-trodden track of thinking about the implications for approaches to education at all levels arising from the insights of DIY cultures concerning collaborative creativity. Waymarkers in the UK creativity in education debate include the work of Ken Robinson, whose 1999 report for the National Advisory Committee on Creative and Cultural Education staked out the creativity ground for schools, whilst accurately portending frustration in terms of real-life battles over curriculum and other contested aspects of education policy. Robinson's later remark that 'our only hope for the future is to adopt a new conception of human ecology, one in which we start to reconstitute our conception of the richness of human capacity' (Robinson, 2006) links directly to our own complex ecological understanding of creative citizenship. From here it is a feasible step to envisage 'learning as a distributed system' and 're-purposing education for innovation' (Hartley, 2009).

Equally, our research team's interventions in urban planning owe much to the work of Charles Landry, whose advocacy on behalf of creative cities has been prudently tempered by his awareness of the risk of over-statement. Landry's remark that creative cities rest upon an assumption 'that ordinary people can make the extraordinary happen if given the chance' (Landry, 2005) speaks directly to the potential of the creative citizen. Landry's own policy-focused work argued for improved hard and soft infrastructures (for example, digital communication platforms and investment in human capital through education). He also warns against the 'empire building tendencies of universities that are more like production factories', stressing the importance of allowing space for the maverick. A more recent overview of developments in

UK universities (Comunian and Gilmore, 2015) advocates four points of focus: urging universities to reach beyond their own boundaries; to invest in human capital in a way that supports both research and creative practice; to develop 'third spaces' beyond the walls of university where 'hybrid' academic/practitioners can thrive, collaborate and build enterprises; and to pursue an approach to the arts which balances the university's potentially conflicting roles of sponsor/patron and co-creative partner. This 'complex triple helix of relations and expertise' (Comunian and Gilmore, 2015: 17) lies at the heart of a thriving relationship between universities and the creative economy. An arguably more radical and technology-based view of these matters is offered by Sebastian Thrun, Professor of Artificial Intelligence at Stanford University and CEO of Udacity, a pioneer in online learning. Thrun, and Udacity, argue in the organisation's mission statement that higher education is 'a basic human right', raising questions about funding and business models in higher education. Our experience of the centrality of the internet as a tool of learning in resource-stressed communities such as South Blessed lends detail and weight to this aspiration.

If we turn to the creative economy, the terrain for further research and evolution of practice is emerging with sharp clarity. One source of intense debate among UK economists has been the UK's stagnant productivity (output per worker) since the 2008 financial crisis. (Haskel et al, 2010). According to Andy Haldane, Chief Economist of the Bank of England, productivity 'has not flat lined for that long in any period since the 1880s, other than following demobilization after the world wars'. It is also notable that this productivity blockage has been accompanied by a very significant growth in levels of self-employment, reasonable levels of output growth (as measured by gross domestic product) but (up until 2015) falls in real earnings. These apparently self-contradictory trends have not been authoritatively explained, but it appears reasonable to hypothesise that one dimension of the explanation, at least, is likely to be increased difficulties statisticians face in taking account of activities of the kind undertaken by creative citizens – most of which occur on an informal, possibly freelance basis, quite possibly beyond the scope of the statisticians or, in some cases, the tax collectors. To this 'grey economy' (or perhaps we should insist, this 'rainbow economy') phenomenon might be added another statistical explanation; that the measurement of economic output only using a GDP or GVA (gross value added) calculus is certain to miss forms of value identified as important by creative citizens and abundantly illustrated in our research project. There is an obvious overlap here with the concerns of 'wellbeing' economics, or 'happiness economics'

(Layard, 2011; O'Donnell et al, 2014) It is a truism that what goes uncounted by government statisticians goes unheeded by politicians, so creative citizens should take an interest in these questions if they wish politicians to take an interest in creative citizenship.

To these discussions around journalism, city planning, education and the economy could be added others focused upon health, transport, environment and almost any other topic. The debate about creative citizenship and the policy environment that would best motivate and sustain it is, to be sure, in its infancy.

The creative citizen unbound

What then, is the straight answer to our research question? How do we imagine that creative citizenship might generate more value for communities within a changing media landscape?

The answer does not chiefly lie in specific manifesto commitments linked to a 'creative citizenship programme'. Rather, it lies in the absorption of creative citizenship into the fabric of the way we think about problems, make decisions, innovate and get things done. Vibrant and stronger creative citizenship affects sport, health, medicine, shopping, art, business, universities, schools, government, energy, transport, prisons, immigration, justice and our sense of shared identity. It is important for our economy and our polity, for our society and for our culture.

To unbind the creative citizen is to tap into an incalculably large resource of energy, ideas, goodwill, purpose and pride, as well as to confront the reality of everyday conflicts and so-called 'wicked problems' – and how to resolve them – among an increasingly diverse and multivalent community. It involves thinking differently. Getting that right, from the perspective of government, requires a clear understanding of the importance of this resource for innovation and enhanced productivity, along with an equally clear understanding that this resource cannot be commanded, it can only be released. It can also, intentionally or unintentionally, be too easily blocked. That is the lesson Jupiter learned the hard way about Prometheus. But as Shelley told us: Creative citizens are many. The blockers are few.

Notes

[1]   See: mediastandardstrust.org/wp-content/uploads/2014/10/Positive-Plurality-policy-paper-9-10-14.pdf

[2]   See: www.gov.uk/government/uploads/system/uploads/attachment_data/file/5959/1896534.pdf

ANNEX

Creative Citizens:
the debate

This is an edited version of a debate that took place at the Creative Citizens Conference in London in September 2014. It is built around a discussion paper written by Stephen Lee, Chief Executive of Centre Forum, a politically liberal think tank, and Professor of Voluntary Sector Management at Cass Business School, London. He is joined in discussion with three other senior political think tank leaders. They are Eddie Copeland, Head of Technology Policy at Policy Exchange (a right of centre group), Andrew Harrup, General Secretary of the Fabian Society (left of centre) and Emran Mian, Director of the Social Market Foundation (centrist). Professor Ian Hargreaves chairs the debate. The debate took place on the same day as the independence vote in a referendum in Scotland.

Stephen Lee: I am by inclination very positive towards notions of citizenship, I'm very pro the notion of the active citizen, of citizens being enabled, and I work within a liberal think tank, which at its heart and at its core, would wish to promote the notion of pluralism. Here you see an expression of pluralism. My concern, though, and the brief given to me from Ian, was to what extent and how and in what way would policy makers wish to take on this concept of creative citizenship, is that rather like the lyrics in the song, creative citizenship has the ability and the potential to be loved at an ethereal, rhetorical level, but to be absolutely meaningless, actually, in a public policy context. Why? Well, I think for a number of reasons. First, you yourselves can find no consistent definition of the activity, and the activity is, itself, so broad to be both immensely important to the individuals engaged in it, but pretty much meaningless when you try to abstract it and think about it in a practical sense. It's also the case that in as much as it supports and promotes matters that the state would wish to itself promote, it is also there to act against the state, and is, in many senses, anti-statist. So, whilst it might be of immense interest and engagement to citizens, it's something that civil servants tend to want to shy away from, rather than actively promote. So, I think for many of these reasons, the notion of creative citizenship as the next

275

'big idea' is both dangerous and pretty much ill-conceived, although I'm sure others here will contend the other way.

Where I think creative citizenship may well be a force, and have a force for the future is firstly in its clear adoption of new technology, its clear adoption of the informal alongside the formal, its clear adoption of the importance of the non-professional alongside the professional, and I think most importantly its absolute adoption of two critical concepts. First the notion that it is inherently relational and local, it is always of immediate impact to people in their locality actively doing something with others, and interacting with others. Second, and building upon that, the notion that it engages in co-creation.

When you think about those things, then I think there is an opportunity to move the thing forward from a public policy context. I know others here will talk about public services. In my own organisation we've talked a lot recently about mental health, and about moving to an integrated sense of wellbeing and parity of esteem between physical and mental health, which involves at every stage the user in that process. If you wish to reach audiences that are not traditionally reached in the public policy process, creative citizenship offers great opportunities. So I think in each of these areas there is an opportunity, a manifesto, if you like, to take forward the notion of creative citizenship. The last thing I would say is, by allusion to both the third sector, the Big Society and to the open society, the liberal approach to these areas, in each and every one of those cases they were advocated for by academics or semi-academics.

Eddie Copeland: I'd like to start just by saying, a few years ago I was a politics teacher up in Cambridge, and I always resorted to the Gettysburg Address, which you'll all know well, with its principle of 'government of the people, by the people, for the people'. My take on creative citizenship is that basically we're adding a fourth option, and that's government with the people. It comes down to this very loose and fluffy concept of engagement, and it's a concept that politicians do, from all political colours, love. They've spoken about it in terms like 'the third way', the idea that it isn't just about government, and it shouldn't just be down to the market. The point is that we can triangulate and that gives us a different option.

The Liberal Democrats talk about 'open society'; I have no idea what that is, but maybe you'll be able to tell me. Conservatives have got this concept of the Big Society, much maligned and it's been relegated to – well, just not being used at all, you won't hear Conservatives talking about it. But I actually quite like the concept; I like the idea of thinking that government isn't the problem with everything. It's also not the solution to everything. There is an idea that government can work with businesses, that it can work with charities, that it can work with the individual to achieve a pragmatically chosen outcome that everyone cares about that makes everyone a bit better. So, politicians are really, really good at this whole vision thing. What they're not so good at is the how you do it. They do the what and the why, but not the how. Part of that I know because I've spent a lot of time talking to civil servants and to politicians. At least 80% of their work is just reacting to stuff. One of the developments of technology is with the pervasive Twittersphere, they're constantly on the back foot, reacting to information, reacting to news; there is very little time for reflection, for thought at how you do things in a radically different way. That's one of the ways that think tanks try and justify their existence, and why academics are so important, to have that time to reflect and to think. How do you do it?

New ideas in this sphere are really, really important. A journalist today was commenting on the Scottish Referendum and said this, which I thought was quite relevant: "The Westminster system", he said, "is broken, because it has been taken over by professional politicians who focus on their opposite numbers, rather than on the people that they're supposed to represent. That this has led to mass apathy and resentment did not trouble them at first. To a professional politician, those who don't vote might as well not exist. But now the abstainers have found new champions in the insurgent parties" – UKIP, SNP to some extent. "People are turning up to vote for the first time in years, a grumble has grown into a war cry. The question for us then is, how do you get people engaged in a way that's within the political system, part of the democratic process, as opposed to rejecting it, if they simply get fed up of the whole thing?"

Now, people talk about technology being the solution and this is an area that I spend my time looking at, technology in lots of different spheres, from the economy to public life, to the way that politicians work. It's an attractive option. We all know – you'll all be very conversant in the way that technology has revolutionised our lives, and engagement at its bottom is about communication; it's sharing ideas, thoughts, and visions about how we do things. With Twitter we can communicate with anyone, any time, anywhere. With Wikipedia we have a font of human knowledge that's greater, at least in quantity, than anything that ever existed before. With Google we can find the answer to any question we want. Amazing revelations in data, in collaboration.

Government, however, has singularly failed to take those massive benefits we've seen in every other aspect of our lives and apply them to the way that government works, to involve citizens. Let me just give you three brief examples. In policy making, how do we use technology? Well, it's online polls, it's e-petitions. Those things ask for our views on preset options. We're asked to express a preference between things that have already been decided for us by Whitehall. But good policy making, at the end of the day, relies on information; the fuel of government is information. Citizens out there have got incredible information, the wisdom of the crowd. At the moment, government is very good at trying to release data to citizens; there is no mechanism to bring it back up to inform policy making. That I see as a major flaw.

There is the Digital Democracy Commission at the moment, started by John Bercow, the Speaker of the House of Commons, trying to look at how technology could revolutionise democracy. We've heard about e-voting, we've heard about a Wiki group as part of the parliamentary process, a flash new website for parliament. To me, all of these things are starting in completely the wrong place. They start by the assumption that you can bolt on new technology to old ways of working. My view, and what I keep saying is, you have to start with the process. How does parliament work? How could it work differently? The problem with engagement is not a lack of websites, it's that people are disengaged with the political process. Get the process right, technology might enable a new way of working that delivers better engagement.

Finally, public services – some of you will be aware that a lot of public services are now moving online. The Government Digital Service creating online transactions is more convenient for citizens, but they haven't changed the substance of the interaction with the citizen. A paper form is now just a digital form. What I want to see governments doing is moving away substantively from the idea that it has to do everything, that government is something that it does to citizens, and starting to take on a role where it makes things happen, where it works. Perhaps you can call it the Big Society, call it whatever you want, but the idea that government can work with businesses, with charities, with citizens, to deliver an outcome, whereas at the moment it's just the public sector doing it to citizens. So, what would I advise? Well, we will always fail if we start this notion of creative citizenship by thinking about the technology, which is precisely the wrong place. My advice, talking to politicians, I would concur absolutely with the point raised, I wouldn't call it creative citizenship, I had no idea what that meant. Busy civil servants and politicians will not have time unless you can take the what and the why, which they understand, and turn it into a very tangible 'how'. Thank you.

Emran Mian: There is a part of me that wants to go along with most of that. I've worked on these issues a couple of times in government, and at least during that time I was trying to make some of this stuff happen. But I guess the role I'm going to play instead is the role that also goes well with having worked in government, which is the role of the hardened cynic. I suppose the other role is that I also write novels, and while I've been a civil servant, I've done it at the same time as being a civil servant, and it felt fine, and then when I left government I was quite surprised by how much of a difference it made to my writing. I didn't expect it to make any difference at all. I felt that I was free when I was writing, I felt that I was writing what I wanted to write, but it made a big difference. I left government about a year ago, and I guess I've also been trying to come to terms with that experience.

I think for me that leads to a set of thoughts about how I think the practice of the state and the practice of government probably is inimical to creative citizenship, at least in the current government that we have. I don't mean the current administration that we have, I mean the current mode of government that we have. I want to think about it more positively than that, and so the question I want to pose is: what are the things that would have to be true about our system of government for there to be a positive interaction with creative citizens? Well, I think the first thing that would have to be true is that our politics would have to be about something other than just maximising utility. I think that's really quite important. I think whenever you hear politicians talk about Big Society, open society, people power, public services, there is a range of different rubrics by which we talk about some of these same things, which is creating a more relational state.

No politician that I've come across perceives that as being something of intrinsic value, because the purpose of politics is instrumental, and so as soon as they'll have used the words Big Society or people power, public services, they'll talk about how that helps you make public services more effective or it helps you make public services cheaper, or it helps to get people more engaged.

You could redescribe it, you could talk about it differently. It could be about intrinsic value, but it seems to me it's pretty clearly the case that at least in our system that's all about instrumental value. There I can give examples from my time of government, where I think fundamentally we were just trying to create instrumental value, we were trying to get stuff done, basically, and every conversation that might purport to be a conversation about partnership, is fundamentally a conversation about what can you do for us. So, in my last role in the Cabinet Office I was heading up a team called the business partnerships team. Basically the way that those conversations would go is you would sit down with a business and they would tell you about their corporate responsibility strategy, and you'd listen very politely and take notes, and then 15 minutes later you'd say, "Okay, and the PM's office wants you to do this". That wasn't an exceptional thing about the conversation, that's what the conversation was about. It's about creating enough of a partnership that you can ask for stuff.

It seems to me that the nature of government's partnership with most civil society organisations is fundamentally that relationship, and I think that's because the model of politics that we have is a model of politics where the job of politicians is to maximise utility, it's what we expect them to do. Maybe it's not what we expect them to do, but that's the task that they've taken upon themselves. So I think our politics would have to be fundamentally different to that for there to be a good relationship with creative citizens. By the way, that's certainly possible, I think it's probably only the UK and the US that have such a model of politics that's focused on nothing other than maximising utility.

I think there are two other things there that would also have to be true about the nature of our government for there to be a good relationship. It would have to be long-termist. It would have to have a quite different time horizon. Actually the problem is deeper than that, because even when government purports to be long-termist, it tries to be long-termist with a plan, which sounds like a good thing, but actually if you're interacting with a wider range of civil society organisations, having a plan is sort of where the trouble starts. A government tries to have, let's say, a three-year spending plan, and it tries to have a set of objectives where it wants to get to by the end of the parliament. It seems to me that's fundamentally at odds with an act of creative citizenship where the possibility of dissent always has to be there, the possibility of destruction always has to be there, and you always have to be alert to the possibility that any event, any happening, any conversation, any interaction will itself reveal to you what the next thing should be. Whereas, if you go into that conversation knowing already what you want the next thing to be, and you have to steer that conversation and that event and that happening towards what the next one is supposed to be, then you're engaged in something different, you're engaged in public management, you're not engaged in creative citizenship.

So I'm taking quite a hardcore view, but I hope I explained why I'm taking that view at the beginning, it's because I've been involved a couple of times, under governments of completely different political complexions, to try to create a more fruitful relationship between government and citizenship, and it seems to me there are lots of things about our system of government and the way in which politicians behave and the way that we expect them to behave that makes that relationship go badly.

Then, the other thing that I think shapes my perspective is the much more personal one and the very unexpected one, which is that it kind of has made a big difference to how I write, the fact that I'm no longer a civil servant, which you might think, duh, but it was a really big surprise to me, because I thought there was no inconsistency between trying to look to the long term, as a civil servant might do, and trying to be that voice of impartiality within a system of public administration. I thought there was no inconsistency between that and being a creative artist, but actually there is – they're two very different mindsets.

Ian Hargreaves: I wasn't expecting to hear from a novelist, I didn't know that you were a writer of novels, but that's very interesting.

Andrew Harrup: What do you write about?

EM: So maybe it's partly because the novel that I'm writing at the moment, that I'm trying to finish at the moment, it sort of does go to the crux of some of these issues. I'm trying to finish a novel at the moment about two brothers, one of whom is a former diplomat and who loses his job as a consequence of some other choices that he makes. So I guess it's partly a function of what I'm choosing to write about that these issues are quite front of centre in my mind.

AH: Great. Hard act to follow. I was thinking about what are we talking about, first of all? I tried to sort of define it by negatives, you know, what would not being a creative citizen mean? The first thing I think we can all agree on is that really this is an extension of part of the active citizenship agenda, the idea that citizens are much more involved in everything about them. It might be their engagement with the public sector in one form or another, but it might be how they are leading their own lives, in their community, making some sort of contribution. That could go for everything from journalism through to helping run a public service, or being a good neighbour. Then there's the question of what's the creativity angle? What would an active citizen who isn't creative look like? I guess this is something about the interplay with arts or technology, or just innovation, doing things differently, doing things for the first time. I think that is quite a difficult bit of this debate, maybe you've talked about it all day, when is someone not being creative, if they are active, doing things for themselves?

Then I was thinking about, what should public services be doing to make this more real, as a phenomenon? I think that maybe a traditional liberal argument would be that really it's a bit about facilitation, but it's partly about getting out of the way, which is obviously not a traditional left argument, but there is some truth in this. If you think about the open data world view, partly it's just giving the data away, but actually there's a bit more to it than that, it's about making sure that it's available in the right sorts of formats, so it needs curating, it's not just about public services having no role. There are potential opportunities, if you like, you frame it – I'm using data as an example, but we've seen examples of great apps being developed by people, there is loads of creativity there, using public data in a way that the public sector had never even thought of. Or, the Eric Pickles vision of someone mining through data to hold account to a public service, as a citizen journalist, a lot less effective, as it turns out. The sort of resources that you need to really scrutinise and hold to account, actually tends to be someone paying you to do that. You might be an NGO and you might be a professional journalist, sometimes it's the bloggers who do this stuff, but I think the naïve version of citizens just mining through data for the sake of it, I think on examination, was always questionable.

So that's the sort of facilitation, 'get out of the way' view, and I'm not completely dismissing it, but what I want to suggest that, maybe from a left perspective, what we really need to be thinking about is how to create better partnerships, so that there is a role for active, creative citizens, but it is in the context of creative partnerships with public service professionals of one sort or another. We are publishing shortly a report on the future of public services, and we look at what is it that there isn't enough of in the public sector. We talk about several things, and one is, I'm afraid, very necessary but perhaps a bit dull, which is value for money and driving up performance and all the stuff that, in an age austerity, you can't entirely ignore. But the other two things that are important for this debate, one of them is the sense of what is the public mission, the ethos, the character of public services? The other, even more important for today's discussion, is the sense of deficits of trust and power throughout the way that we structure our public services. Maybe this is going to something that Emran's been talking about, that public services are very bad at trusting people and creating power for people. When I say 'people' I don't mean just, if you like, citizens, as in the users of services, I mean that throughout the way we structure government and public service. That means employees, it means the leaders of public services, it means not giving trust to elected politicians below national government.

So, when I think about partnership, I want us to try and think about how can we have active, creative citizens working together with trusted and empowered public service workers, public service leaders, elected councillors or whatever it might be, rather than trying to set the two against each other, which I think is sometimes the tone of the debate on co-production, co-creation. So there are a few examples where I think there is lots of potential, which is, for example the citizens design movement, where it's a facilitative process, it's not citizens coming up with the answers themselves, but it's an engagement where you have, if you like, the insights of the users of services, where people are working with a professional, it might be facilitated by a professional designer, but the employees, the users of the service, and some facilitation, where they are collectively creating a much better model. That is better in many cases than, if you like, throwing everything up in the air and citizens doing it for themselves. I think there is a real risk of a 'do it yourself' culture, which takes away professionalism and the ethos of public services that actually has a huge amount of embedded expertise and practice as well as sense of vocation.

So, for example, there is in health, and more particularly social care, there has been a big movement towards, instead of just having traditionally provided public services, just giving people the money to buy whatever it is they want to meet their health needs. Now, taken to extreme, actually that has significant concerns about the structuring of a public service. Does it still matter that we have professional social workers creating a sense of service and community, or should we just give people cash to bring in a home help for a few hours? Now, my argument is that you need to have that sort of structure of public service, rather than just, if you like, individual acts of creativity, about, how can I splice together the money in a slightly different way? Which is very much that personalised ethos.

Thinking about where does the left come on to this, the big concern you get when you talk to people on the left is about inequality in people's ability and interest to be active creative citizens. I think one of the challenges, and you'll get a wall of scepticism from people on the left if you don't engage with it, is how do you make sure this is something for everyone, rather than, if you like, sharpest elbows, people who want to shape their community to their own interest, but not necessarily to the interests of all. Now, how do you make sure that this is an agenda that really brings common good, rather than helps one group pitted against another? Actually, to some extent, it's just how do you make sure this goes to scale? If this is about interesting projects for a small minority that doesn't need to take off and become something that is actually having an impact on all our lives, then I think it's always going to be interesting but not political, if it's not having a big enough impact on lots of people's lives.

That, I think, is a nice bridge into the final set of comments I want to make, which is major concerns about the future of politics itself. I think that this creativity of citizen journalists and social media, but also grass roots campaigners, the sort of energy we've seen in the Scottish referendum, when you've got not only a lot more people involved in politics than have ever been before, but also involved in very different ways, so we're thinking about their futures but also a sort of process of engagement at a very grass roots, community level that frankly political parties fail to do. You also see it in the new generation of feminism, very much detached from the workings of political parties, often quite suspicious, but much more creative about the sorts of issues people want to work on, not normally seen as political issues, the ways they do it, the groupings. Formal politics is way behind on this, and I think formal politics will slowly die if it doesn't find a way of working in partnership with this wave of creativity that we're seeing from individuals.

The question is, how does that go if you like being isolated, slightly elite, shouting loud on the internet but actually not touching people's lives in a mass way? What is the role of a political party in making something that touches on everyone's lives? So you have this sense of how do you have political parties working in partnership in a community, but not crushing and owning everything themselves, and I think that that, culturally, is incredibly difficult for parties, they really haven't got their head around being facilitators and partners to individual effort. That needs to be brought back into the umbrella of a political movement, but not stymied by it, the culture of whips, which pervades politics.

IH: Thank you. We couldn't have wished for more interesting and subtly challenging. Basically, our think tank leaders say the idea of creative citizenship is a write-off, politically, but the thinking within the idea is striking all sorts of different chords. That would be my summary. Now, who would like to join in? Yes?

Q1: I think the other conclusion you could come to is that politics is a write-off.

IH: Well that has been said, once or twice, or in danger of being a write-off. Do you think that?

Q1: Well, listening to this really raises that question in my mind, because we do have plenty of evidence of a kind of growth of creative citizenry, and a hunger for a democracy that comes with that kind of alertness, and then we're hearing, 'It's not going to work, they can't do it. There's no space for it'. It was very nice to hear Emran recognising it as a systemic binary that we're seeing, and that actually what, in the panels I've been in today, the thing they have in common very often is a very systemic approach and an understanding of the connectedness of things, and the role of creativity in understanding and finding new connections, and the value of the things that spring out of that. Then I really see this binary between the anarchism of creativity against managerial utilitarianism is really problematic, but it does bring me back, it's a question I have in my mind all the time anyway.

EC: Could I respond to that? I'd just like to say, I'm not as pessimistic, I have to say. I take the point that you raised that we need long-term change, but if anyone here wants to get any of this stuff done, and I'm as excited about the potential for citizens to be involved as the next person, you have to work, frankly, in the realms of the politically possible. I think that right now there is a massive opportunity. By politically possible, I mean, local government for example has to save £12.4bn by 2020, it has to. The healthcare service, likewise, by the end of the decade will fall off a financial cliff if it continues with the current model, but there is not a zero sum game between trying to make services more efficient and maximising utility and embracing the kind of stuff that I understand you've all been talking about today. My view is that this is financially unsustainable because the current model is broken.

We need to tell politicians, "You need to fundamentally rethink the way that we deliver services. We need to stop the view that it has to be government taking everything into itself and then pushing it out. We need to work with the citizens; we need to work with other people to make stuff happen in a very different way.

Q2: I just wanted to say, all day we've been thinking positively. We've been hearing about how cities are being used differently, we've been hearing about how … consultation is changing, it's all been fantastic. I feel so depressed and let down, and it sort of feels like creative citizens, the ideas that are bubbling up, surely if you put them working with local governments, in a council, there must be some way of connecting all of these ideas to addressing this apathy that it seems like we're dealing with?

EM: But why do you need them working with government? I think one of my questions is, to what extent can the innovations that you're talking about, the developments that you can talk about, to what extent did they need government? Sometimes they do, I guess, for scale, they might need government for money.

Q2: No, I don't think that – money is an easy excuse to say, 'this can't happen'. I think we should stop talking about that, because we know the reality. I guess it's just a way of accessing, and a way of sharing the ideas, because it's easy to have an idea, but how do you actually get it implemented? So I think maybe I see government as a route to implementing those ideas. I don't know, maybe I'm thinking the wrong way around it. I think partnership is better than no government. I believe in government. I want to believe in it.

Q3: Most of this discussion was about building a partnership, about working with citizens, and in practical terms it's exactly as we just discussed. I'm an academic, but we are working with organisations, charities that work with communities, and in practical terms we do seek this collaboration. In some other cases there is this do-it-yourself culture. So, it sometimes is about building collaboration, but sometimes it's not, so I need to have the space and the freedom to be able to act independently, but I need to have the freedom and the space to collaborate. I don't know whether these two are conflicting or contradicting each other, or whether this is okay. It is possible to have the space of creating actions with communities independently, but also in collaboration in other cases, if there is this kind of freedom?

SL: I'm sorry that you're feeling not more buoyed up. I think there are actually some great opportunities if we can get the system of government to think differently, and actually I think there is a real opportunity that is emerging very, very quickly. I mean, I'm from the liberal side of this discussion; the liberals traditionally have been the peripheral idiots out there on the side of devolution and localism, and these sorts of issues.

One of the things I think about creative citizenship that I would absolutely applaud, is that it is always immediate and local to those people engaged in it, and it's often a micro response, a niche response. One of the dilemmas with government and with planning, is you immediately start to think about planning to scale, so you're looking for volume. Actually, creative citizenship should, I think, promote the notion of being idiosyncratically small, and growing in volume only where through happenstance it can do so, or wants to, or needs to, and whether it needs to partner with government, or with industry, or with other actors engaged in creative citizenship. It should be somewhat anarchic in that sense. I think people have talked a lot about trust and trust in the political system, and trust in society, I'm a really, really, really boring person because I've spent 12 years researching trust, and politicians actually are the worst people in thinking about trust, because they conflate two very different concepts, which are actually the alternatives of each other, it's a zero sum proposition in terms of people's behaviour and psychology. They put together the notions of trust and confidence. Governments and politicians are all about confidence, which is about having control. Trust is the opposite. Trust exists where you have no reason for confidence, it's a faith, it's an expression, an emotive expression of belief. Trust, therefore, is intensely local, it's intensely relational, it's always on the point of breach. You have to continually go back and earn it, which is why integrity is so important for trust, because it involves consistency over a long time in a normative construct, irrespective of which ideological perspective you come from. Now, what's really interesting in some of the research I did is that many of our national politicians are hated nationally. They are loved and trusted beyond belief in terms of their local constituencies. Many local councillors are trusted enormously and engage in an enormous range of trustful, creative behaviours. So, my point here is that the antidotes to your depression I think are in the activities of these people. I think they are there in our politicians. I think it's the national systemic problem that we face, and the way, frankly, in which the media supports that, and this notion of scale by plan, by volume.

Q4: That leads very nicely into my point, because we as a small national charity have really faced the challenge of partnership with government, because of the scale of our organisation, but also because of the disconnect that national policy seems to have with reality on the ground, and we've found actually the way we can influence, and I think this is something that we should think about with this creative citizens movement – and I think of it as a movement – it's not about what we can do to go and convince policy makers to inject a policy, it's about a change in culture that we can help move forward that will, in a sense, influence policy through a need for change and a change that is brought on by a movement of culture rather than just going to policy makers and saying, 'You need to do this because…' I don't think it works that way. I think there needs to be that movement of those small changes and local changes, and the stories that build, that change policy in the end.

Q5: Thank you, first of all, for the discussion. I'm not an anarchist either, and I came to the conclusion that government is a barrier in my life. I'm a citizen who doesn't feel the government is reflecting the engagement I want to have, and I start questioning if government is outdated, and probably around the idea of: is the process outdated? So my question is, is government ready for partnership?

Q6: Thanks. My question is about partnership as well. So my research has been around looking at the everyday experience of food bank volunteers and clients. Now, food banks are obviously a citizen-led, volunteer-led organisation, and there is something around that partnership, because obviously they're very embedded in the formal systems that are already in place, and how that partnership can exist and go forward with the work that they're doing that directly helps people within their local community, as a volunteer-led organisation working with professionals. But that's a terrible imbalance in lots of ways, because if they get drawn into the system, then as a volunteer they're doing something that they're not being paid for and are taking responsibility for. So I'm interested in how you see that partnership imbalance working out.

Q7: I think what I heard from the panel was that there is something broken about government in relation to a historic role of the state to protect citizens from the forces of the market, and my worry is that without the state in whatever political form it takes, defending the history of a kind of social democracy, then creative citizenship is simply going to be co-opted as an aspect of the neo-liberal market

Q8: Hi. Andrew mentioned Eric Pickles' naïve vision of the citizen journalist sifting through the council documents, and I used to agree with you, but I've been studying this stuff now for a couple of years, and I've found some quite convincing evidence that this is happening.

It's not on a huge scale but it's there, and in many communities, and it's to be celebrated, and I think it's to be fostered, too. But it's precarious, for the reasons you mentioned. It's hard, it's risky in many ways to do this kind of watchdog journalism without the back up of a newspaper institution, or your editor or the legal help that comes with that, and stuff like that. What do you think the prospects are for public subsidy for local news start-ups, given the importance of local media to democracy, and given the crisis of the local news industry in this country, which means that many newspapers are closing and many communities are underserved, not served at all in many cases, but where they are they're being served by community journalists who shouldn't be dismissed as easily as you did then, I think.

Q9: Yes, so I just had a question back on policy. So, we've been looking at the human rights convention, and the human rights of participation, specifically about environmental change. It strikes me in the concept of creative citizens, okay, that policy means we all have a right to participate in decision making, which is effectively consultation, which exists in our planning policy. Do you see a future where we might get to creative policy making? So a bit smarter, co-design, more creativity by citizens in what we're actually proposing, before we consult on changes?

Q10: My experience of trying to establish a neighbourhood forum and do neighbourhood planning, I've been around to several of the local assemblies in my area and spoken to them about our plans as a group of people to start taking on the powers that we've been given through localism to do that. People are actually very enthusiastic, and one of the main responses I get is in support of our local councillors, and this kind of reinforces this idea of trust. These people have actually got to the place that they're in through democratic means, and people have a lot of faith in that process at a local level, as you said, and that's my experience too. People always say, 'How do we know you're going to be transparent, how do we know you're going to be democratic as a group of citizens?' I think that's a really fair point; how do people know they can trust the few citizens that emerge as the leading forces in their communities?

IH: Thank you. We're nearly out of time. Pick up whichever of those questions you want to deal with, concisely, and then we'll ask Stephen to close.

AH: I think I alluded to that point as being sort of a key concern on the left, about the sharp-elbowed citizens. Partly it is when can this be about what we do together for everyone, rather than just being a sort of personalised take, which is hard. It's also about what's the role of public services, and one of the roles of public services should be to create capabilities for us all, partly through education of course, but if you take a long- term view on this, it is about endowment of creativity and a sense of citizenship and purpose. So it's not like the public sector is not in the picture in terms of what it is we can all expect to do. Very hard as it is to, through the education system particularly, create a sense of creativity and citizenship. The Eric Pickles point, you might slightly have misread what I was saying; I was empirically sceptical, rather than sceptical about it working. But actually your question about the funding of citizen journalism sort of shows the lack of resource point. If you're not getting there just through armchairs and volunteer-run websites, there is this deficit of good local journalism, and it's incredibly important, if you care about localism, to have strong media. This morning I was talking to a bunch of local government chief executives, and I talked to two in medium sized cities with really vibrant local media, and they were telling me how well things were going in their area. People can name the leader of their council, which is not true everywhere, and they were sort of saying, "Isn't that true everywhere?" And I was saying, "No, because there isn't good media everywhere", and that is the route, actually, to creative partnership. You've got to know who your responsible elected leader is, even if some of what you're doing is getting on and doing your own thing, you need to be able to rub along with the official public service offer as well. I think the previous question was sort of, is this all about markets, a neoliberal view of the world. I think, stepping back, starting with the definition problem again, is we're not very clear what the role of active citizens, civic society, the space between the market and public services is, but that's partly because we're not very clear about what the role of the market is, and what the role of public service is. Politics is partly there to channel and steer markets for the public good, and we need to recognise that. But it's also there to act outside of what the markets can possibly do, particularly where we need to act to benefit all of us, collectively, and where we need to provide us all with the things that a market transaction will never provide. So I think if we're clear about what the role of public service and politics is, maybe that's an easier grounding to then talk about where active citizens should do more than, if you like, the public service is there to do.

EM: So, having been quite cynical, I guess now I have to talk about something more positive, so let me offer two thoughts on how I think the conversation can get better. I think the question for creative citizens should be a question about, in terms of interacting with government, what are the capabilities and technologies the government has that would be useful to what we're trying to do. So flip the question from one where government is asking a question to one where citizens themselves are asking the question. There are some things that the government has never been particularly good at, there are some things the government has become less good at because of changes in society and technology. There are a whole bunch of things that the government is quite good at, and that it has, like it has lots of information, and government is able to coordinate public infrastructure in a way that other organisations are not, so let's look to government to provide the capabilities and technologies that it is uniquely well-suited to do. Then I guess, building on that, I guess there is a bigger point for me about what are the background conditions the government could create, against which more creative citizenship can take place, and I think this is the really big stuff. So, when you look at most European countries they have a much stronger social safety net than we do, or than the US does. So, if you're living in a system where, when you're unemployed your income might be as much as 80% of your income in work, I think that completely transforms what you can do as a citizen, because your activity as a citizen changes from being a struggle about how do you pay for housing yourself and how do you pay for food to being a much more creative struggle, as a citizen. Equally, a state that provided much more free childcare, a state that maybe limited the number of working hours in a week, those would be things that would just completely change the background conditions against which citizenship takes place, and you would then see much more creative citizenship. All this stuff to me about a bit of grant here, or a bit of grant there, or co-opting some local organisations into a plan for doing something else is all just noise, it ignores the big structural stuff the government can do to transform the way in which we behave as citizens.

EC: I guess if I can think about this concept of partnership and maybe even the creative policy making as well, I would honestly say don't wait for government, government is inherently full of inertia, understandably, any organisation that big is going to be very difficult. If you're waiting for them you'll be waiting forever. The most impressive civic action kind of initiatives I've seen have been where people have gone, 'Sod it, let's just build it'. I think of My Society, great app, set of interfaces that allow people to engage with local authorities better, from sheer frustration that no local authority would do it for themselves. Now that's becoming the norm; local authorities go to them and say, 'We'd love to work with you, because you've built it, it's there, it's easy for us'. It's not a hypothetical, it's something they can tangibly see we can engage with. Think of some of the apps we know and love in London, City Mapper, again, born out of a guy who got particularly frustrated that TFL (Transport for London) weren't doing it for themselves, so he built it, and it's great, better than they would have done it, but he didn't wait for the public sector to offer partnership. They come to you if you have created a model that works. That's from my pragmatic side, and I do urge you all to think about working – you have to work in the realms of the politically possible if you want things to get done. There is, like it or not, a financial reality that means that government does not have money – and it won't for the foreseeable future, whoever wins the next election – to be able to support new initiatives, you need to find ways where they are sustainable for themselves. My view, and maybe I'm playing the stereotype of the centre-right think tank, I wouldn't support local subsidies for local news, precisely because I worry that you build something great, and then the next government takes away the funding and what are you left with? I'd far rather we grasped that entrepreneurial attitude where people go, 'Let us find a way that we can actually make this work', and whatever business model, whatever social enterprise model makes it work, build something that's community driven and about the citizen.

SL: Well, my last word is I'm rather concerned because I agree with everything that pretty much everybody has said as we've gone down the line. I think that's really where I started from, with this notion of creative citizenship, that it's so intimately connected with motherhood and apple pie, that on the one hand it's much beloved, potentially, rhetorically, by politicians, but actually the articulation of it in public policy terms is really very, very difficult, and you have to get down, I think, into subsectors of actual functional policy activity, and then I think when you start to talk about areas of activity, such as journalism or architecture or labour planning, or where you start to talk about the impact it can have in driving access in supporting and improving democracy, social mobility, where it can help to transform – and I agree absolutely with what Andrew was saying about public services and a public service ethos, but where this can actually enable people to gain greater access into those services, into their design as well as into their delivery, I think you can have a real public policy impact. For me, that's the place of this embryonic manifesto for creative citizenship.

I think, ultimately, it isn't a one thing. Ralf Dahrendorf very famously talked about the voluntary sector as being completely anarchic, and it being important to let 1,000 flowers bloom and for many of them to die and to die in very different ways. Actually, it's probably not a movement, it's probably not a thing, it's probably not even a process. It certainly, I don't think, can work, in the main, as a scalable activity. But, when done well, it definitely drives trust and a sense of purpose, and it brings a strong normative element back into people's lives, which I think is very important.

IH: Thank you very much.

References

Agusita, E. (2013) 'Online influencers and advocates'. *Online Engagement, Offline Impact*. London: vInspired, 7-9. Available at: https://s3-eu-west-1.amazonaws.com/reports.vinspired.com/vInspired+OEOI+Report.pdf [accessed December 2015].

Alexiou, K. (2010) 'Coordination and emergence in design'. *CoDesign*, 6(2), 75–97.

Alexiou, K. and T. Zamenopoulos (2008) 'Design as a social process: a complex systems perspective'. *Futures*, 40(6), 586-95.

Alexiou, K., T. Zamenopoulos and G. Alevizou (2013) 'Valuing community-led Design'. *AHRC Discussion Paper*. Available at: http://valuing-community-led design.weebly.com/uploads/1/2/8/5/12856329/vcld_summary_report.pdf [accessed December 2015].

Ananny, M. (2014) 'Critical newsmaking and the paradox of "do-it-yourself news"'. In: M. Ratto and E. Boler (eds) *DIY Citizenship: Critical Making and Social Media*. Cambridge, MA: MIT Press, 359-71.

Anderson, B. (1991) *Imagined Communities*. 2nd edn. London: Verso.

Anderson, C. (2006) *The Long Tail: How Endless Choice Is Creating Unlimited Demand*. London: Random House Business Books.

Anderson, C. (2012) *Makers: The New Industrial Revolution*. New York: Crown Business; London: Random House Business.

Andrejevic, M. (2009) 'Exploiting YouTube: contradictions of user-generated labour'. In: P. Snickers and P. Vondereau (eds) *The YouTube Reader*. Stockholm: National Library of Sweden, 406-21.

Andres, L. and C. Chapain (2015) 'Creative systems: a new integrated approach to understanding the complexity of cultural and creative industries in Eastern and Western countries'. In: J. Bryson and P. Daniels (eds) *Handbook of Service Business*. Cheltenham: Edward Elgar, 349–70.

Arnstein, S. (1969) 'A ladder of citizen participation'. *American Institute of Planners Journal* 35, 215-24.

Arts Council (2008) *What People Want from the Arts*. London: Arts Council England.

Arvidsson, A. and E. Colleoni (2012) 'Value in informational capitalism and on the internet'. *The Information Society*, 28, 135-50.

Arvidsson, A. and N. Peitersen (2013) *The Ethical Economy: Rebuilding Value After the Crisis*. New York: Columbia University Press.

Arviddson A. and D. Tjader (2009) 'Laboratorium for spontankultur: slutraport Malmo: kulturforvaltningen'. In: A. Arvidsson and N. Peitersen (2009) *The Ethical Economy: Rebuilding Value After the Crisis*. New York: Columbia University Press, 93.

Atkinson R. (2015) 'Open data in the G8: a review of progress against the G8 Open Data Charter'. *Information Technology and Innovation Foundation*. Available at: www.itif.org/publications/open-data-g8-review-progress-open-data-charter [accessed December 2015].

Atton, C. (2002) *Alternative Media*. London: Sage.

Atton, C. and E. Wickenden (2005) 'Sourcing routines and representation in alternative journalism: a case study approach'. *Journalism Studies*, 6, 347-59.

Bachman, G., J. Dovey, J. Monaco and B. Sharpe (2012) *Cultural Value Networks*. Report for AHRC Connected Communities. Summary available at: www.dcrc.org.uk/publications/cultural-value-networks-summary-report [accessed December 2015].

Baidoo, V. (2014) *Indigo Babies*. Bristol: Crown Root Publishing.

Bakardjieva, M. (2003) 'Virtual togetherness: an everyday-life perspective'. *Media, Culture & Society*, 25, 291-313.

Bakhshi, H., I. Hargreaves and J. Mateos-Garcia (2013) *A Manifesto for the Creative Economy*. London: Nesta. Available at: www.nesta.org.uk/sites/default/files/a-manifesto-for-the-creative-economy-april13.pdf [accessed December 2015].

Bakhtin, M. (1984) *Problems of Dostoevsky's Poetics*. Minneapolis: University of Minnesota Press.

Banaji, S. and D. Buckingham (2013) *The Civic Web: Young people, the Internet and civic participation*. Cambridge, MA: MIT Press.

Banks, J. (2013) *Co-creating Videogames*. London: Bloomsbury.

Barbrook, R. (1999) 'The hi tech gift economy'. London: The Hypermedia Research Centre. Available at: www.hrc.wmin.ac.uk/theory-hightechgifteconomy.html [accessed December 2015].

Barnett, S. and J. Townend (2014) 'Plurality, policy and the local: can hyperlocals fill the gap?' *Journalism Practice,* 9 September.

Bathelt, H., A. Malmberg and P. Maskell (2004) 'Clusters and knowledge: local buzz, global pipelines and the process of knowledge creation'. *Progress in Human Geography*, 28(1), 31-56.

Baym, N. (1998) 'The emergence of online community'. In: S. Jones (ed) *Cybersociety 2.0*. Los Angeles: Sage.

Baym, N. (2010) *Personal Connections in a Digital Age*. Cambridge: Polity Press.

Barlow, J. (1995). 'A declaration of the independence from cyberspace'. *UTNE Reader*, 99, 53-6.

Bedoya, R. (2012) 'Creative placemaking and the politics of belonging and dis-belonging'. Available at: http://artsinachangingamerica. org/2012/09/01/creative-placemaking-and-the-politics-of-belonging-and-dis-belonging/ [accessed December 2015].

Beebeejaun, Y., C. Durose, J. Rees, J. Richardson and L. Richardson (2013) 'Beyond text: exploring ethos and method in co-producing research with communities'. *Community Development Journal*, 49(1), 37-53.

Beinhocker, E. (2006) *The Origin of Wealth: Evolution, Complexity and the Radical Remaking of Economics*. London: Random House.

Benamou, F. (2003) 'Artists' labour markets'. In: R. Towse (ed) *A Handbook of Cultural Economics.* Cheltenham: Edward Elgar.

Benjamin, W. (1936) 'The work of art in the age of mechanical reproduction'. In: *Illuminations.* New York: Harcourt, Brace & World (1968).

Benkler, Y. (2003) 'Freedom in the commons: toward a political economy of information'. *Duke Law Journal*, 52(6), 1245-76.

Benkler, Y. (2006) *The Wealth of Networks: How Social Production Transforms Markets and Freedom.* New Haven, CT: Yale University Press.

Bennett, L. (2008) 'Changing citizenship in the digital age'. In: L. Bennett (ed) *Civic Life Online: Learning How Digital Media Can Engage Youth.* Cambridge, MA: MIT Press, 1-24. Available at: http://mitpress.mit.edu/sites/default/files/titles/content/9780262524827_sch_0001.pdf [accessed December 2015].

Bennett, L. and A. Segerberg (2012) 'The logic of connective action'. *Information Communication and Society* 15(5), 739-68.

Benson, R. (2006) 'News media as a "journalistic field": what Bourdieu adds to new institutionalism, and vice versa'. *Political Communication,* 23(2), 187-202.

Bevelander, P. and D. DeVoretz (eds) (2008) *The Economics of Citizenship.* Malmo: University of Malmo Press. Available at: http://dspace.mah. se/handle/2043/7487 [accessed December 2015].

Bianchini, F. and M. Parkinson (eds) (1993) *Cultural Policy and Urban Regeneration: The West European Experience.* Manchester: Manchester University Press.

Bilton, C. (2007) *Management and Creativity: From Creative Industries to Creative Management.* Oxford: Blackwell.

Blundell-Jones, P., D. Petrescu and J. Till (eds) (2005) *Architecture and Participation.* London: Routledge.

Boden M. (2003) *The Creative Mind: Myths and Mechanisms.* London: Routledge.

Boix R., J-L. Hervas-Oliver and B. De Miguel-Molina (2014) 'Micro-geographies of creative industries clusters in Europe: from hot spots to assemblages'. *Papers in Regional Science*, 94(4), 753-72.

Bollier, D. (2008) *Viral spiral: How the Commoners Built a Digital Republic of Their Own*. New York: The New Press.

Borger, M., A. van Hoof, I. Costera Meijer and J. Sanders (2012) 'Constructing participatory journalism as a scholarly object'. *Digital Journalism,* 1(1), 117-34.

Bourdieu, P. (1993) *The Field of Cultural Production*. Cambridge: Polity Press.

Bourdieu, P. and L. Wacquant (eds) (1992) *An Invitation to Reflexive Sociology*. Cambridge: Polity Press.

boyd, d. (2008) *Taken Out of Context: American Teen Sociality in Networked Publics*. PhD dissertation. University of California, Berkeley. Available at: www.danah.org/papers/TakenOutOfContext.pdf [accessed December 2015].

boyd, d. and N. Ellison (2007) 'Social network sites: definition, history, and scholarship'. *Journal of Computer-Mediated Communication*, 13, 210-30.

Boyle, D. and M. Harris (2009) *The Challenge of Co-production*. London: New Economics Foundation.

Boyle J. (2015) '(When) is copyright reform possible?' [Blog] *The Public Domain*. Available at: www.thepublicdomain.org/wp-content/uploads/2015/02/Is-Copyright-Reform-Possible1.pdf [accessed December 2015].

Broadbent, S. (2013) 'Approaches to personal communication'. In: H. Horst and D. Miller (eds) *Digital Anthropology*. London: Bloomsbury, 127-45.

Bruns, A. (2008) *Blogs, Wikipedia, Second Life, and Beyond: From Production to Produsage*. New York: Peter Lang.

Burgess, C. and D. Pankratz (2008) 'Interrelations in the arts and creative sector'. In: J. Cherbo, R. Stewart and M. Wyszomirski (eds) *Understanding the Arts and the Creative Sector in the United States*. Rutgers, NJ: Rutgers University Press.

Burgess, J. (2006) 'Hearing ordinary voices'. *Continuum: Journal of Media & Culture* 20(2), 201-14.

Burgess J. (2010) 'Remediating vernacular creativity: photography and cultural citizenship in the Flickr photo-sharing network'. In: T. Edensor, D. Leslie, S. Millington and N. Rantisi (eds) *Spaces of Vernacular Creativity. Rethinking the Cultural Economy*. London: Routledge.

Burgess, J. and J. Green (2009) *YouTube: Online Video and Participatory Culture.* Cambridge: Polity.

Burton, C. (2010) *Carnival: St Pauls Carnival – Your Memories.* Bristol: St Pauls Carnival.

Carpentier, N. (2003) 'The BBC's Video Nation as a participatory media practice: signifying everyday life, cultural diversity and participation in an online community'. *International Journal of Cultural Studies,* 6(4), 425-47.

Carvalho, C. (2011) 'The creative citizen: citizenship building in urban areas'. Available at: http://education.unimelb.edu.au/__data/assets/pdf_file/0020/1106228/011_CARVALHO.pdf [accessed December 2015].

Castells, M. (2012) *Networks of Outrage and Hope: Social Movements in the Internet Age.* Cambridge: Polity.

Castells, M. and G. Cardoso (eds) (2005) *The Network Society: From Knowledge to Policy.* Washington, DC: Johns Hopkins Center for Transatlantic Relations. Available at: www.umass.edu/digitalcenter/research/pdfs/JF_NetworkSociety.pdf [accessed December 2015].

Caves, R. (2000) *Creative Industries: Contracts between Art and Commerce.* Cambridge, MA: Harvard University Press.

Cebr (2013) *The Contribution of the Arts and Culture to the National Economy.* London: Centre for Economics and Business Research. Available at: www.artscouncil.org.uk/media/uploads/pdf/CEBR_economic_report_web_version_0513.pdf [accessed December 2015].

Chamberlain, D. (2004) 'Publishing for the people: the foundations and fundamentals of blogging'. *Spectator,* 24(1), 30-41.

Chapain C. and R. Comunian (2009) 'Creative cities in England: researching realities and images'. In: 'Can we plan the creative knowledge city?' *Built Environment,* 35(2), 220-237.

Chapain, C. and R. Comunian (2010) 'Enabling or inhibiting the creative economy: the role of the local and regional dimensions in England'. *Regional Studies,* 44(6), 717-34.

Chapain, C. and R. Comunian (2011) 'Dynamics and differences across creative industries in the UK: exploring the case of Birmingham'. *REDIGE,* 2(2) Available at: www.cetiqt.senai.br/ead/redige/index.php/redige/article/view/115/170 [accessed December 2015].

Chapain, C., L. De Propris, P. Cooke, S. MacNeill and J. Mateos-Garcia (2010) *Creative Clusters and Innovation.* London: NESTA. Available at: www.nesta.org.uk/publications/reports/assets/features/creative_clusters_and_innovation_report [accessed December 2015].

Chapain, C. and P. Lee (2009) 'Can we plan the creative knowledge city? Perspectives from Western and Eastern Europe'. *Built Environment,* 35(2), 157-64.

Chapple, K. and S. Jackson (2010) 'Commentary: arts, neighborhoods, and social practices: towards an integrated epistemology of community arts'. *Journal of Planning Education and Research* 29(4), 478-90.

Chen, W. (ed) (2015) *The Internet, Social Networks and Civic Engagement in Chinese Societies.* London: Routledge. Wherein: Wu, J.C., 'Expanding civic engagement in China: Super Girl and entertainment-based online community'.

Cherbo, J. (2008) 'About artists'. In: J. Cherbo, R. Stewart and M. Wyszomirski (eds) *Understanding the Arts and the Creative Sector in the United States.* Rutgers, NJ: Rutgers University Press.

Cherbo, J., H. Vogel and M. Wyszomirski (2008) 'Towards an arts and creative sector'. In: J. Cherbo, R. Stewart and M. Wyszomirski (eds) *Understanding the Arts and the Creative Sector in the United States.* Rutgers, NJ: Rutgers University Press.

Cheshire, T. (2013) 'Talent tube: how Britain's new YouTube superstars built a global fanbase'. Available at: www.wired.co.uk/magazine/archive/2013/02/features/talent-tube [accessed December 2015].

Clement, M. (2012) 'Rage against the market: Bristol's Tesco riot'. *Race & Class* 53(3), 81-90.

Coatham, V. and L. Martinali (2010) 'The role of community-based organisations in sustaining community regeneration'. *International Journal of Sociology and Social Policy,* 30(1/2), 84-101.

Cohendet, P., D. Grandadam and L. Simon (2010) 'The anatomy of the creative city.' *Industry and Innovation* 17(1), 91-111.

Coleman, S. (2003) *A Tale of Two Houses: The House of Commons, the Big Brother House and the People at Home.* London: Hansard Society.

Coleman, S. (2005) *Direct Representation: Towards a Conversational Democracy.* London: Institute for Public Policy Research (ippr exchange). Available at: www.ippr.org.uk/ecomm/files/Stephen_Coleman_Pamphlet.pdf [accessed December 2015].

Comunian, R. (2011) 'Rethinking the creative city: the role of complexity, networks and interactions in the urban creative economy'. *Urban Studies,* 48(6), 1157-79.

Comunian R., K. Alexiou and C. Chapain (2012) *The Role of Complexity in the Creative Economy: Connecting People, Ideas and Practices.* Report presented to the AHRC Connected Communities Programme.

Comunian, R. and A. Gilmore (2015) *Beyond the Creative Campus: Reflections on the Evolving Relationship Between Higher Education and the Creative Economy*. London: King's College London.

Conway, K. (2004) 'Digital video, microcinema, and the rhetoric of media democratization'. *Spectator*, 24(1), 42-52.

Cooley, H. (2004) '"Identify"-ing. A new way of seeing. Amateurs, moblogs and practices in mobile imaging'. *Spectator*, 24(1), 65-79.

Cooper, A. (1999) *The Inmates are Running the Asylum*. Indianapolis, IN: Sams.

Cottle, S. (2007) 'Ethnography and news production: new(s) developments in the field'. *Sociology Compass,* 1(1), 1-16.

Couldry, N. (2003) 'Media meta-capital: extending the range of Bourdieu's field theory'. *Theory and Society,* 32(5-6), 653-77.

Couldry, N. (2004) 'The productive "consumer" and the dispersed "citizen"'. *International Journal of Cultural Studies,* 7(1), 21-32.

Couldry, N. (2008) 'Mediatization or mediation? Alternative understandings of the emergent space of digital storytelling'. *New Media & Society*, 10(3), 373-91.

Couldry, N., H. Stephansen, A. Fotopoulou, R. MacDonald, W. Clark and L. Dickens (2014) 'Digital citizenship? Narrative exchange and the changing terms of civic culture'. *Citizenship Studies*, 18(6/7), 615-29.

Coyne, R. (1997) 'Creativity as commonplace'. *Design Studies*, 18 (2), 135-41.

Craig, C. (2013) 'Creating cultural products: cities, context and technology'. *City, Culture and Society*, 4, 195-202.

Crossick, G. and P. Kaszysnka (2015) 'The cultural value project' [Blog] *Cultural Value Project*. Available at: https://culturalvalueproject. wordpress.com

Crossley, N. and J. Roberts (2004) *Beyond Habermas: New Perspectives on the Public Sphere*. Oxford: Blackwell.

Currid, E. (2007) *The Warhol Economy: How Fashion, Art, and Music Drive New York City*. Princeton, NJ: Princeton University Press.

Dahlgren, P. (2001) 'The public sphere and the net: structure, space, and communication'. In: L. Bennett and W Entman (eds) *Mediated Politics: Communication in the Future of Democracy*. Cambridge: Cambridge University Press, 33-55.

Dahlgren, P. (2003) 'Reconfiguring civic culture in the new media milieu'. In: J. Corner and D. Pels (eds) *Media and the Restyling of Politics*. London: Sage, 151-70.

Dahlgren, P. (2004) 'Civic cultures and net activism: modest hopes for the EU public sphere'. In: *One EU – Many Publics?* Conference presentation, Stirling: www.arena.uio.no/cidel/WorkshopStirling/PaperDahlgren.pdf [accessed December 2015].

Dahlgren, P. (2005) 'The Internet, public spheres, and political communication: dispersion and deliberation'. *Political Communication*, 22(2), 147-62.

Dahlgren, P. (2009) *Media and Political Engagement*. Cambridge: Cambridge University Press.

Dahlgren, P. (2013) *The Political Web: Media, Participation, and Alternative Democracy*. London: Palgrave Macmillan.

Dal Borgo, M., P. Goodridge, J. Haskel and A. Pesole (2013) 'Productivity and growth in UK industries: an intangible investment approach'. *Oxford Bulletin of Economics and Statistics*, 75, 806-34.

David, S., A. Sabiesca and L. Cantoni (2013) 'Co-design with communities. A reflection on the literature'. In: *New Media in Education Laboratory*. Lugano: Università della Svizzera Italiana.

Davidoff, P. (1995) 'Advocacy and pluralism in planning'. In: J. Stein (ed) *Classic Readings in Urban Planning*. London: McGraw-Hill.

DCMS (Department for Culture, Media and Sport) (1998) *Creative Industries Mapping Document*. London: DCMS.

DCMS (2004) *DCMS Evidence Toolkit – DET (formerly, The Regional Cultural Data Framework) Technical Report*. London: DCMS.

DCMS (2007) *The Creative Economy Programme: A Summary of Projects Commissioned in 2006/7*. London: DCMS.

DCMS (2008a) *Our Creative Talent: The Voluntary and Amateur Arts in England*. London: DCMS.

DCMS (2008b) *Creative Britain: New Talents for a New Economy*. London: DCMS.

DCMS (2009) *Creative Industries Economic Estimates. Statistical Bulletin*. January. London: DCMS.

DCMS (2010a) *Creative Industries Economic Estimates*. February. London: DCMS.

DCMS (2010b) *Creative Industries Economic Estimates. Experimental Statistics*. December. London: DCMS.

DCMS (2011) *Creative Industries Economic Estimates. Full Statistical Release*. December. London: DCMS.

DCMS (2012) *Taking Part 2011/12 Adult and Child Report. Statistical Release*. London: DCMS.

DCMS (2014) *Creative Industries Economic Estimates. Statistical Release*. January. London: DCMS.

De Cindio, F. and C. Peraboni (2011) 'Building digital participation hives: toward a local public sphere'. In: M. Foth et al (eds) *From Social Butterfly to Engaged Citizen: Urban Informatics, Social Media, Ubiquitous Computing, and Mobile Technology to Support Citizen Engagement.* Cambridge, MA: MIT Press.

De Propris, L., C. Chapain, P. Cooke, S. MacNeill and J. Mateos-Garcia (2009) *The Geography of Creativity.* London: Nesta.

Devlin, P. (2009) *Restoring the Balance. The Effects of Arts Participation on Well-being and Health.* Newcastle-upon-Tyne: Voluntary Arts.

de Waal, M. (2011) 'The Ideas and Ideals in Urban Media'. In: M. Foth, L. Forlano, C. Satchell and M. Gibbs (eds) *From Social Butterfly to Engaged Citizen: Urban Informatics, Social Media, Ubiquitous Computing, and Mobile Technology to Support Citizen Engagement.* Cambridge, MA: MIT Press, 5-20.

Dissanayake, E. (2008) 'The universality of the arts in human life'. In: J. Cherbo, R. Stewart and M. Wyszomirski (eds) *Understanding the Arts and the Creative Sector in the United States.* Rutgers, NJ: Rutgers University Press.

Donetto, S., V. Tsianakas and G. Robert (2014) Using Experience-based Co-design to Improve the Quality of Healthcare: Mapping Where We Are Now and Establishing Future Directions'. London: King's College London. Available at: www.kcl.ac.uk/nursing/research/nnru/publications/Reports/EBCD-Where-are-we-now-Report.pdf [accessed December 2015].

Dopfer, K., J. Foster and J. Potts (2004) 'Micro-meso-macro'. *Journal of Evolutionary Economics*, 14(3), 263-79.

Dovey, J., C. Fleuriot and C .Miskelly (2011) *Keeping in Touch.* Bristol: Digital Cultures Research Centre. Available at: www.dcrc.org.uk/research/keeping-in-touch-final-report [accessed December 2015].

Drake, G. (2003) '"This place gives me space": place and creativity in the creative industries'. *Geoforum*, 34, 511-24.

Durose, C., Y. Beebeejaun, J. Rees, J. Richardson and L. Richardson (2011) *Towards Co-production in Research with Communities.* London: AHRC Connected Communities Programme Scoping Studies.

Durham Community Research Team (2011) *Community-based Participatory Research: Ethical Challenges.* London: AHRC Connected Communities Programme Scoping Studies.

Edensor, T., D. Leslie, S. Millington and N. Rantisi (eds) (2010) *Spaces of Vernacular Creativity: Rethinking the Cultural Economy.* London: Routledge.

Eikhaug, O., R. Gheerawo, C. Plumbe, M. Berg and M. Kunur (2010) *Innovating with People – The Business of Inclusive Design.* Oslo: Norsk Designråd.

Ellis, K. (2015) *Disability and Popular Culture: Focusing Passion, Creating Community and Expressing Defiance.* Farnham: Ashgate.

Ellis, K. and M. Kent (2010) *Disability and New Media.* London: Routledge.

Evans, G. (2001) *Cultural Planning: An Urban Renaissance?* London: Routledge.

Evans, G. (2009) 'Creative cities, ceative spaces and urban policy'. *Urban Studies,* 46, 1003-40.

Evans, G. (2010) 'Creative spaces and the art in urban living'. In: T. Edensor, D. Leslie, S. Millington and N. Rantisi (eds) *Spaces of Vernacular Creativity: Rethinking the Cultural Economy.* London: Routledge.

Evans, R. and D. Long (2000) 'Estate-based Regeneration in England: Lessons from Housing Action Trusts'. *Housing Studies,* 15(2), 301-317.

Evans, G. and P. Shaw (2004) *The Contribution of Culture Regeneration in the UK: A Review of Evidence.* London: London Metropolitan University, for DCMS.

Finnegan, R. (1989) *The Hidden Musicians: Music-making in an English Town.* Cambridge: Cambridge University Press.

Flew, T. (2014) 'Six theories of neoliberalism'. *Thesis Eleven,* 122(1), 49-71.

Flew, T. and S. Cunningham (2010) 'Creative industries after the first decade of debate'. *The Information Society,* 26, 113-23.

Florida, R. (2002) *The Rise of the Creative Class: And How It's Transforming Work, Leisure, Community and Everyday Life.* New York: Basic Books.

Flowers, S. (2008) *The New Inventors: How Users are Changing the Rules of Innovation.* London: Nesta.

Foth, M., L. Forlano, C. Satchell C. and M. Gibbs (2011) *From Social Butterfly to Engaged Citizen: Urban Informatics, Social Media, Ubiquitous Computing and Mobile Technology to Support Citizen Engagement.* Cambridge, MA: MIT Press.

Fox, B. (2004) 'Rethinking the amateur: acts of media production in the digital age'. *Spectator,* 24(1), 5-16.

Fraser, N. (1989) *Unruly Practices: Power, Discourse and Gender in Contemporary Social Theory.* Minneapolis, MN: University of Minnesota Press.

Frey, B. (2003) *Arts and Economics: Analysis and Cultural Policy.* 2nd edn. Berlin: Springer-Verlag.

Frey, B. and A. Stutzer (eds) (2013) *Recent Developments in the Economics of Happiness*. Cheltenham: Edward Elgar.

Friedmann, J. (1987) *Planning in the Public Domain: From Knowledge to Action*. Princeton, NJ: Princeton University Press.

Friedmann, J. (2011) *Insurgencies: Essays in Planning Theory*, London: Routledge.

Freire, P. (1972) *Pedagogy of the Oppressed*. Harmondsworth: Penguin.

Frontier Economics (2006) *Comparative Analysis of the UK Creative Industries*. London: Frontier Economics for DCMS.

Fuchs, C. (2010) 'Class, knowledge and new media'. *Media, Culture & Society*, 32(1), 141-50.

Fuchs, C. (2013) 'Class and exploitation on the internet'. In: T. Scholz (ed) *Digital Labor*. New York: Routledge, 211-24.

Fuller, M. (2005) *Media Ecologies: Materialist Energies in Art and Technoculture*. Cambridge, MA, MIT Press.

Gallent, N. and D. Ciaffi (eds) (2014) *Community Action and Planning: Contexts, Drivers and Outcomes*. Bristol: Policy Press.

Galligan, A. (2008) 'The evolution of arts and cultural districts'. In: J. Cherbo, R. Stewart and M. Wyszomirski (eds) *Understanding the Arts and the Creative Sector in the United States*. Rutgers, NJ: Rutgers University Press.

Galloway, A. (2001) 'Protocol, or, how control exists after decentralization'. *Rethinking Marxism* 13(3/4).

Gans, J. (2012) *Information Wants to be Shared*. Boston, MA: Harvard Business Review Press.

Garnham, N. (2005) 'From cultural to creative industries'. *International Journal of Cultural Policy*, 11(1), 15-29.

Gauntlett, D. (2013) *Making is Connecting*, Malden, MA and Oxford: Wiley.

Gaver, W. (1991) 'Technology affordances'. In: *Proceedings of the SIGCHI Conference on Human Factors in Computing Systems*. ACM, 79-84.

Georgiou, M. (2013) *Media and the City: Cosmopolitanism and Difference*. Cambridge: Polity.

Gershon, I. (2011) *The Breakup 2.0: Disconnecting Over New Media*. Ithaca, NY: Cornell University Press.

Gibbs, L. (2004) 'Looking to the future from the beginning'. *Ofcomwatch*, 20 February. Available at: www.ofcomwatch.co.uk/2004_02_15_blogarchive [accessed December 2015].

Gibson, J. (1986) *The Ecological Approach to Visual Perception*. Hillsdale, NJ: Lawrence Erlbaum Associates.

Giddens, A. (1994) *Beyond Left and Right: The Future of Radical Politics*. Cambridge: Polity Press.

Giddens, A. (1998) *The Third Way: The Renewal of Social Democracy*. Cambridge: Polity Press.

Gidley, B. and I. Slater (2007) *Beyond the Numbers Game: Inclusion Through Media*. London: Centre for Urban and Community Research, Goldsmiths University of London. Available at: http://inclusionthroughmedia.org/ITM%20Evaluation/BTNG_Report.pdf [accessed December 2015].

Gilchrist, A. (2009) *The Well-connected Community: A Networking Approach to Community Development*, 2nd edn. Bristol: The Policy Press.

Gill, R. and A. Pratt (2008) 'In the social factory? Immaterial labour, precariousness and cultural work'. *Theory, Culture & Society*, 25(7-8), 1-30.

Gillmor, D. (2004) *We the Media: Grassroots Journalism by the People, for the People*. Sebastopol, CA: O'Reilly Media.

Gillárová, K., A. Tejkalová and F. Láb (2014) 'The undressed newsroom'. *Journalism Practice*, 8(5), 607-618.

Gilroy, P. (1987) *There Ain't No Black In The Union Jack*. London: Hutchinson.

Gilroy, P. (1999) *The Black Atlantic: Modernity and Double Consciousness*. London: Verso.

Goffman, E. (1971) *Relations in Public*. Harmondsworth: Penguin.

Goggin, G. (2008) 'Regulating mobile content: convergences, commons, citizenship'. *International Journal of Communications Law and Policy*, 12.

Goggin, G. and J. Clark (2009) 'Mobile phones and community development: a contact zone between media and citizenship'. *Development in Practice*, 19(4-5), 585-97.

Goggin, G., F. Martin and T. Dwyer (2015) 'Locative news: mobile media, place informatics, and digital news'. *Journalism Studies*, 16(1), 41-59.

Goldfarb, B. (2002) *Visual Pedagogy: Media Cultures in and Beyond the Classroom*. Durham, NC: Duke University Press.

Goode, L. (2009) 'Social news, citizen journalism and democracy'. *New Media & Society,* 11(8), 1287-1305.

Goodridge, M. (2002) *Screencraft: Directing*. Brighton: Rotovision.

Goodridge, P., J. Haskel and G. Wallis (2002) *UK Investment in Intangible Assets: Report for Nesta*. London: Nesta. Available at: www.nesta.org.uk/publications/uk-investment-intangible-assets [accessed December 2015].

Granovetter, M.S. (1973) 'The strength of weak ties'. *American Journal of Sociology*, 78(6), 1360-80. Available at: https://sociology.stanford.edu/sites/default/files/publications/the_strength_of_weak_ties_and_exch_w-gans.pdf [accessed December 2015].

Gray, C. (2003) 'Participation'. In: R. Towse (ed) *A Handbook of Cultural Economics*. Cheltenham: Edward Elgar.

Gray, J., J. Jones and E. Thompson (eds) (2009) *Satire TV*. New York: NYU Press.

Greene, C. and S. Lindsey (2015) 'Creative citizens: a photo collection'. *Cultural Science Journal*, 8(1), 3-29.

Greenfield, A. (2013) *Against the Smart City*. New York: Do Projects.

Greenslade, R. (2007) 'The peoples' papers? A new view of hyperlocal media'. *The Guardian Online*. Available at: www.guardian.co.uk/media/greenslade/2007/jul/12/thepeoplespapersanewview [accessed December 2015].

Gregory, J. (2003) 'Scandinavian approaches to participatory design'. *International Journal of Engineering Education*, 19(1), 62-74.

Günnel, T. (2006) 'Action-orientated media pedagogy: theory and practice'. In: P. Lewis and S. Jones (eds) *From the Margins to the Cutting Edge: Community Media and Empowerment*. Catskill, NJ: Hampton Press.

Habermas, J. (1989) *The Structural Transformation of the Public Sphere: An Inquiry into a Category of Bourgeois Society*. Cambridge: Polity.

Habermas, J. (1998) *The Inclusion of the Other: Studies in Political Theory*. Cambridge, MA: MIT Press.

Habermas, J. (2001) *The Postnational Constellation. Political Essays*. Cambridge, MA: MIT Press.

Hall, P. (2004) 'Creativity, culture, knowledge and the city'. *Built Environment*, 30, 256-58.

Hall, S. (1996) 'The global, the local, and the return of ethnicity'. In: C. Lemert (ed) *Social Theory: The Multicultural, Global and Classical Readings*, 5th edn. Philadelphia, PA: Westview Press, 459-63.

Harari, Y. (2014) *Sapiens: A Brief History of Humankind*. New York: Random House.

Hargreaves, I. (1998) 'A step beyond morris dancing: the third sector revival'. In: I. Hargreaves and I. Christie (eds) *Tomorrow's Politics: The Third Way and Beyond*. London: Demos.

Hargreaves, I. (2011) *Digital Opportunity: A Review of Intellectual Property and Growth*. London: Intellectual Property Office. Available at: www.ipo.gov.uk/ipreview-finalreport.pdf [accessed December 2015].

Hargreaves I. and J. Hartley (2015) 'Creative citizenship: two journeys, one destination'. *Cultural Science Journal,* 8(1), 100-129. Available at: http://cultural-science.org/journal/index.php/culturalscience/article/view/109 [accessed December 2015].

Hargreaves, I., L. Guibault, C. Handke, P. Valcke and B. Martens (2015) *Text and Data Mining: Report from the Expert Group.* Brussels: European Commission. Available at: http://ec.europa.eu/research/innovation-union/pdf/TDM-report_from_the_expert_group-042014.pdf [accessed December 2015].

Harris, A., J. Wyn and S. Younes (2010) 'Beyond apathetic or activist youth: "ordinary" young people and contemporary forms of participation'. *Young: Nordic Journal of Youth Research,* 18(1), 9-32.

Harte, D. (2013) '"One every two minutes": assessing the scale of hyperlocal publishing in the UK. *JOMEC Journal.* Available at: www.cardiff.ac.uk/jomec/research/journalsandpublications/jomecjournal/3-june2013/index.html [accessed December 2015].

Hartley, J. (1999) *Uses of Television,* London: Routledge.

Hartley, J. (ed) (2005) *Creative Industries.* Malden, MA and Oxford: Wiley-Blackwell.

Hartley, J. (2008) 'Journalism as a human right: the cultural approach to journalism'. In: M. Loffelholz and D. Weaver (eds) *Global Journalism Research: Theories, Methods, Findings, Future.* Malden, MA and Oxford: Wiley Blackwell, 39-51.

Hartley, J. (2009) *The Uses of Digital Literacy.* St. Lucia: University of Queensland Press. Republished by Transaction, New Brunswick, NJ (2010).

Hartley, J. (2010) 'Silly citizenship'. *Critical Discourse Studies,* 7(4), 233-48.

Hartley, J. (2012) 'Interaction design, mass communication and the challenge of distributed expertise'. In: E. Felton, O. Zelenko and S. Vaughan (eds) *Design and Ethics: Reflections on Practice.* London: Routledge, 111-25.

Hartley, J., J. Burgess and A. Bruns (eds) (2013) *A Companion to New Media Dynamics.* Malden, MA and Oxford: Wiley-Blackwell.

Hartley, J. and K. McWilliam (eds) (2009) *Story Circle: Digital Storytelling Around the World.* Malden, MA and Oxford: Wiley-Blackwell.

Hartley, J. and J. Potts (2014) *Cultural Science: A Natural History of Stories, Demes, Knowledge and Innovation.* London: Bloomsbury.

Hartley, J., J. Potts, S. Cunningham, T. Flew, M. Keane and J. Banks (2013) *Key Concepts in Creative Industries.* London: Sage.

Hartley, J., J. Potts and T. MacDonald, with C. Erkunt and C. Kufleitner (2012) 'Creative City Index'. *Cultural Science Journal*, 5(1) (whole issue).

Hartley, J., W. Wen and H.S. Li (2015) *Creative Economy and Culture: Challenges, Changes and Futures for the Creative Industries*. London: Sage Publications.

Haskel, J., T. Clayton, P. Goodridge, A. Pesole, D. Barnett, G. Chamberlain, R. Jones, K. Khan and A. Turvey (2010) *Innovation, Knowledge Spending and Productivity Growth in the UK: Interim Report for NESTA 'Innovation Index' Project. Discussion Paper*. London: Imperial College London. Available at: https://spiral.imperial.ac.uk:8443/bitstream/10044/1/5279/1/Haskel%202010-02.pdf [accessed December 2015].

Hearn, G., S. Roodhouse and J. Blakey (2007) 'From value chain to value creating ecology: implications for creative industries development policy'. *International Journal of Cultural Policy*, 13(4), 419-36.

Henaff, M. (2014) 'The Humanities the arts and the market: total social fact and the question of meaning'. In: J. Brouwer and S. van Tuinen (eds) *Giving & Taking: Antidotes to a Culture of Greed*. Rotterdam: V2, 27-40.

Hesmondhalgh, D. (2007) *The Cultural Industries,* 2nd edn. London: Sage.

Hesmondhalgh, D. (2010) 'User-generated content, free labour and the cultural industries'. *Ephemera: Theory and Politics in Organization*, 10(3-4), 267-84.

Hess, K. (2012) 'Breaking boundaries'. *Digital Journalism,* 1(1), 48-63.

Hewison, R. (2014) *Cultural Capital: The Rise and Fall of Creative Britain*. London: Verso.

Higgs, P., S. Cunningham and H. Bakshi (2008) *Beyond the Creative Industries. Mapping the Creative Economy in the United Kingdom*. London: Nesta.

Hilton, S., S. Bade and J. Bade (2015) *More Human: Designing a World Where People Come First*. London: W.H. Allen.

H.M. Treasury (2005) *The Cox Review of Creativity and Business*. London: HM Treasury.

Hogan, S. and L. Warren (2013) 'Women's inequality: a global problem: explored in participatory arts'. *UNESCO Observatory Multi-Disciplinary Journal in the Arts*, 3(3), 1-27.

Holston, J. and A. Appadurai (1996) 'Cities and citizenship'. *Public Culture*, 8(2), 187-204.

Hoskins, B., D. Kerr, H. Abs, J.G. Janmaat, J. Morrison, R. Ridley and J. Sizmur (2012) *Analytic Report: Participatory Citizenship in the European Union*. Southampton: Institute of Education. Available at: http://ec.europa.eu/citizenship/pdf/report2_analytic_report.pdf [accessed December 2015].

Howkins, J. (2001) *The Creative Economy: How People Make Money from Ideas*. London: Penguin (new edn, 2013).

Howkins, J. (2010) *Creative Ecologies: Where Thinking Is a Proper Job*. St. Lucia: UQP; New Brunswick, NJ: Transaction (2010).

Howley, K. (2005) *Community Media: People, Places and Communication Technologies*. Cambridge: Cambridge University Press.

Howley, K. (ed) (2009) *Understanding Community Media*. Los Angeles, CA: Sage.

Hudson, G. and M. Temple (2010) 'We are not all journalists now'. In: G. Monaghan and S. Tunney (eds) *Web Journalism: A New Form of Citizenship?* Eastbourne: Sussex Academic Press, 63-76.

Hyde, L. (2007) 'On being good ancestors'. In: L. Hyde, *The Gift: Creativity and the Artist in the Modern World*, 2nd edn. New York: Vintage Books, 369–85 (Afterword).

Inglis D. (2005) *Culture and Everyday Life*. London: Routledge.

Innes, J. and D. Booher (2010) *Planning with Complexity: An Introduction to Collaborative Rationality for Public Policy*. London: Routledge.

Isin, E. and G. Nielsen (eds) (2008) *Acts of Citizenship*. London: Zed Books.

Isin, E. and B. Turner (eds) (2002) *Handbook of Citizenship Studies*. London: Sage.

Jackson M. (2008) 'Art and cultural participation at the heart of community life'. In: J. Cherbo, R. Stewart and M. Wyszomirski (eds) *Understanding the Arts and the Creative Sector in the United States*. Rutgers, NJ: Rutgers University Press.

Jackson M. and J. Herranz (2003) *Culture Counts in Community: A Framework for Measurement*. Washington, D.C.: The Urban Institute.

Jackson M., F. Kwabasa-Green and J. Herranz (2006) *Cultural Vitality in Community: Interpretations and Indicators*. Washington, D.C.: The Urban Institute.

Jacobs, J. (1969) *The Economy of Cities*. New York: Random House.

Jenkins, H. (2006) *Fans, Bloggers and Gamers: Exploring Participatory Culture*. New York: NYU Press.

Jenkins, H., S. Ford and J. Green (2013) *Spreadable Media: Creating Value and Meaning in a Networked Culture*. New York: NYU Press.

Jenkins, H., R. Purushotma, K. Clinton, M. Weigel and A. Robison (2006) *Confronting the Challenges of Participatory Culture: Media Education for the 21st Century.* Available at: www.newmedialiteracies. org/files/working/NMLWhitePaper.pdf

Jones, S. (ed) (1995) *Cybersociety.* Los Angeles, CA: Sage.

Jones, S. (ed) (1998) *Cybersociety 2.0.* Los Angeles, CA: Sage.

Kahne, J., L. N-J. Lee and J. Feezell (2011) 'The civic and political significance of online participatory cultures among youth transitioning to adulthood'. *The Journal of Information Technology & Politics*, 10(1), 1-20.

Katelle, A. (2004) 'Once, there was film... Looking back at amateur motion picture technologies'. *Spectator*, 24(1), 53-64.

Kay, A. (2000). 'Art and community development: the role the arts have in regenerating communities'. *Community Development Journal*, 35(4), 414-24.

KEA (2006) *The Economy of Culture in Europe.* Brussels, Belgium: KEA European Affairs, European Commission.

Keane, J. (2010) *The Life and Death of Democracy.* London: Simon and Schuster.

Keane, M. (2006) 'From made in China to created in China'. *International Journal of Cultural Studies*, 9(3), 285-96.

Kellner, D. (2001) 'Techno-politics, new technologies, and the new public spheres'. *Illuminations*, January. Available at: http://pages.gseis. ucla.edu/faculty/kellner/essays/technopoliticsnewtechnologies.pdf [accessed December 2015].

Kennedy, H. (2006) 'Beyond anonymity, or future directions for Internet identity research'. *New Media & Society,* 8(6), 859-76.

Kimlicka, W. (1995) *Multicultural Citizenship: A Liberal Theory of Minority Rights.* Oxford: Oxford University Press.

King, G., J. Pan and M. Roberts (2013) 'How Censorship in China Allows Government Criticism but Silences Collective Expression'. *American Political Science Review*, 107(2), 326-43.

Klein, N. (2000) *No Logo.* London: Flamingo.

Kloosterman, R. (2014) 'Cultural amenities: large and small, mainstream and niche – a conceptual framework for cultural planning in an age of austerity'. *European Planning Studies*, 22(12), 2510-25.

Koch, C. (2011) 'Why Tottenham is so trendy'. *Evening Standard*, 21 February. Available at: www.standard.co.uk/lifestyle/why-tottenham-is-so-trendy-6569312.html [accessed December 2015].

Kress, G. (2010) *Multimodality: A Social Semiotic Approach to Contemporary Communication* London: Routledge.

Kretzmann, J., J. McKnight, S. Dobrowolski and D. Puntenney (2005) *Discovering Community Power: A Guide to Mobilizing Local Assets and Your Organization's Capacity*. Evanston, IL: Asset Based Community Development Institute.

Kuehn, K. and T. Corrigan (2013) 'Hope labor: the role of employment prospects in online social production'. *The Political Economy of Communication* 1(1), 9–25.

Kushner, S. (2002) 'The object of one's passion: engagement and community in democratic evaluation'. *Evaluation Journal of Australasia*, 2(2) (new series), 16–35.

Laclau, E. and C. Mouffe (1985) *Hegemony and Socialist Strategy: Towards a Radical Democratic Politics*. London: New Left Books, 2nd edn, Verso (2001).

Ladd, E. (2000) *The Ladd Report: Startling New Research Shows How an Explosion of Voluntary Groups, Activities, and Charitable Donations is Transforming Our Towns and Cities*. New York: Free Press.

Lambert, J. (2006) *Digital Storytelling: Capturing Lives, Creating Community*, 2nd edn. Berkeley, CA: Digital Diner Press.

Landry, C. (2000) *The Creative City*. London: Comedia.

Landry, C. (2005) *Lineages of the Creative City*. London: Comedia.

Lanier, J. (2010) *You are Not a Gadget: A Manifesto*. New York: Alfred A. Knopf.

Lanier, J. (2013) *Who Owns the Future?* New York: Simon & Schuster.

Lantis, M. (1960) 'Vernacular culture'. *American Anthropologist*, 62(2), 202–16.

Latour, B. (2005) *Reassembling the Social: An Introduction to Actor Network Theory*. Oxford: Oxford University Press.

Layard, R. (2006) 'Happiness and public policy: a challenge to the profession'. *The Economic Journal*, 116: C24–C33.

Laylard, A., J. Milling and T. Wakeford (2013) *Creative Participation in Place-making. A Connected Communities Report*. London: AHRC.

Leadbeater, C. (2008) *We Think – The Power of Mass Creativity*. London: Profile Books.

Leadbeater, C. (2014) *The Frugal Innovator*. London: Palgrave.

Leadbeater, C. and P. Miller (2004) *The Pro-Am Revolution*. London: Demos.

Leadbeater, C. and K. Oakley (1999) *The Independents: Britain's New Cultural Entrepreneurs*. London: Demos.

Leavis, F.R. and D. Thompson (1933) *Culture and Environment: The Training of Critical Awareness*. London: Chatto & Windus/Penguin Books.

Lee, D., K. Oakley and R. Naylor (2011) 'The public gets what the public wants? The uses and abuses of "public value" in contemporary British cultural policy'. *International Journal of Cultural Policy*, 17(3) 289-300.

Lee, S. (2015) 'Creative Citizenship and the public policy process: A flibbertigibbet, a will-o-the-wisp, a clown?' *Cultural Science Journal*, 8(1), 82-7.

Lefebvre, H. (1991) *Critique of Everyday Life Volume 1*. London: Verso.

Legnér, M. and D. Ponzini (eds) (2009) *Cultural Quarters and Urban Transformation: International Perspectives*. Sweden: Gotlandica.

Li, H.S. (2009) 'The turn to the self: from "big character posters" to YouTube videos'. *Chinese Journal of Communication*, 2(1), 50-60.

Lievrouw, L.A. (2011) *Alternative and Activist New Media*. Cambridge: Polity.

Lessig, L. (2001) *The Future of Ideas: The Fate of the Commons in a Connected World*. New York: Random House.

Lessig, L. (2008) *Remix: Making Art and Commerce Thrive in the Hybrid Economy*. London: Bloomsbury Collections. Available at: https://www.bloomsburycollections.com/book/remix-making-art-and-commerce-thrive-in-the-hybrid-economy/ [accessed December 2015].

Levy, P. (1997) *Collective Intelligence: Mankind's Emerging World in Cyberspace*. Cambridge, MA: Perseus.

Lewis, J. (2006) 'News and the empowerment of citizens'. *European Journal of Cultural Studies*, 9(3), 303-319.

Lewis, P. (2006) 'Community Media: Giving "a voice to the voiceless"'. In: P. Lewis and S. Jones (eds) *From the Margins to the Cutting Edge: Community Media and Empowerment*. Catskill, NJ: Hampton Press, 13-39.

Leydet, D. (2011) 'Citizenship'. In: E. Zalta (ed) *The Stanford Encyclopedia of Philosophy*. Available at: http://plato.stanford.edu/archives/fall2011/entries/citizenship/ [accessed December 2015].

Livingstone, S. and P. Lunt (2007) 'Representing citizens and consumers in media and communication regulation'. *The Annals of the American Academy of Political and Social Science*, 611, 51-65.

Lloyds, R. (2002) 'Neo-bohemia: art and neighborhood redevelopment in Chicago'. *Journal of Urban Affairs*, 24(5), 517-32.

Loader, B. and D. Mercea (2011) 'Networking Democracy'. *Information, Communication & Society*, 14(6), 757-69.

Lockton, D., C. Greene, G. Ramster, A. Outten, and E. Raby (2014) 'The Story Machine'. In: D. Lockton and others (eds) *Creative Citizens' Variety Pack: Inspiring Digital Ideas From Community Projects*. London: Royal College of Art.

Lowe, S. (2000) 'Creating community: art for community development'. *Journal of Contemporary Ethnography*, 29(3), 357-86.

Macconville, R. (2007) *Looking at Inclusion – Listening to the Voices of Young People*. London: Sage Publications.

Madanipour, A. (2005) 'Value of place: Can physical capital be a driver for urban change?' In: CABE (ed) *Physical Capital: How Great Places Boost Public Value*. London: Commission for Architecture and the Built Environment, 48-71.

Maiden, N. (2013) 'Creativity workshops for urban design'. [Blog] *Centre for Creativity at City University London*. Available at: http://centre4creativity.wordpress.com/author/cc559/ [accessed December 2015].

Mandela, N. (1995) *Long Walk to Freedom*. London: Abacus.

Markusen, A. (2010a) 'Organisational complexity in the regional cultural economy'. *Regional Studies*, 44(7), 813-28.

Markusen, A. (2010b) 'Challenge, change and space in vernacular cultural practice.' In: Edensor T., D. Leslie, S. Millington and N. Rantisi (eds) *Spaces of Vernacular Creativity. Rethinking the Cultural Economy*. London: Routledge.

Marshall, T.H. (1963) *Sociology at the Crossroads and Other Essays*. London: Heinemann.

Martin, R. and P. Sunley (2007) 'Complexity thinking and evolutionary economic geography'. *Journal of Economic Geography*, 7, 573-601.

Manson, S.M. (2001) 'Simplifying complexity: a review of complexity theory'. *Geoforum*, 32(3), 405-414.

Matarosso, F. (1997) *Use or Ornament? The Social Impact of Participation in the Arts*. London: Comedia.

Matthews, J.C. (1998) 'Somatic knowing and education'. *The Educational Forum*, 62(3), 236-42.

Mauss, M. (1925) *The Gift: Forms and Functions of Exchange in Archaic Societies*. Trans: I. Gunnison. New York: Norton & Co (1967).

Marx, K. (1993) *Grundrisse*. Trans. and ed. M. Nicoloaus. Harmondsworth: Penguin.

Mathie, A. and C. Cunningham (2002) *From Clients to Citizens: Asset-based Community Development as a Strategy for Community-driven Development*. Antigonish, Canada: The Coady International Institute.

McCloskey, D. (2010) *Bourgeois Dignity: Why Economics Can't Explain the Modern World*. Chicago: University of Chicago Press.

McLuhan, M. (1964) *Understanding Media: The Extensions of Man*. New York: McGraw Hill.

McNair, B. (2012) 'Trust, truth and objectivity: sustaining quality journalism in the era of the content-generating user'. In: C. Peters and M. Broesma (eds) *Rethinking Journalism: Trust and Participation in a Transformed News Landscape*. London: Routledge, 75-88.

McRobbie A. (2011) 'Re-thinking creative economy as radical social enterprise'. *Variant*, 41, Spring.

Meadows, D. and J. Kidd (2009) 'Capture Wales: the BBC Digital Storytelling Project'. In: J. Hartley and K. McWilliam (eds) *Story Circle: Digital Storytelling Around the World*. Malden, MA and Oxford: Wiley-Blackwell, 91-117.

Meyer, J. (2000) 'What is action research'. In: C. Seale (ed) (2004) *Social Research Methods: A Reader*. London and New York: Routledge, 453-55.

Meyer, M. (2008) 'On the boundaries and partial connections between amateurs and professionals'. *Museum and Society*, 6(1), 38-53.

Miles, M. (2005) 'Interruptions: testing the rhetoric of culturally led urban development'. *Urban Studies*, 42(5/6), 889-911.

Miller, D. and H. Horst (2012) 'The digital and the human: a prospectus for digital anthropology'. In: H. Horst and D. Miller (eds) *Digital Anthropology*. London: Bloomsbury.

Miller, T. (2006) *Cultural Citizenship: Cosmopolitanism, Consumerism and Television in a Neo-Liberal Age*. Philadelphia, PA: Temple University Press.

Miranda, C. (2014) 'The art of social practice is changing the world one row house at a time'. *Art News*, July.

Mitchell, W.J. (1999) *E-topia: Urban Life, Jim – But Not As We Know It*. Cambridge, MA: MIT Press.

Mokyr, J. (2009) *The Enlightened Economy. An Economic History of Britain 1700–1850*. New Haven, CT: Yale University Press.

Moore, I. (2014) 'Cultural and creative industries concept – a historical perspective'. *Procedia – Social and Behavioral Sciences*, 110(0), 738-46.

Morozov, E. (2011) *The Net Delusion: The Dark Side of Internet Freedom*. New York: Perseus PublicAffairs.

Morozov, E. (2013) *To Save Everything, Click Here: The Folly of Technological Solutionism*. New York: Perseus PublicAffairs.

MTM London (2010) *Digital Audiences: Engagement with Arts and Culture Online. UK Data Archive Study No. 6842*. Available at: www.artscouncil.org.uk/publication_archive/digital-audiences-engagement-arts-and-culture-online/ [accessed December 2015].

Mulgan, G. (2005) 'Reshaping the state and its relationship with citizens: the short, medium and long-term potential of ICTs'. In: M. Castells and G. Cardoso (eds) *The Network Society: From Knowledge to Policy*, 225-40.

Musterd S. and A. Murie (eds) (2010) *Making Competitive Cities*. Malden, MA and Oxford: Wiley-Blackwell.

Nesta (2013) *UK Demand for Hyperlocal Media*. London: Nesta. Available at: www.nesta.org.uk/sites/default/files/uk_demand_for_hyperlocal_media.pdf [accessed December 2015].

Nigg, H. and G. Wade (1980) *Community Media: Community Communication in the UK: Video, Local TV, Film and Photography*. Zurich: Regenbogen Verlag.

Norman, D. (1988) *The Psychology of Everyday Things*. New York: Basic Books.

Normann, R. and R. Ramirez (1993) 'From value chain to value constellation: designing interactive strategy'. *Harvard Business Review*, 71, 65-65.

Nowak J. (2007) *Creativity and Neighbourhood Development*. Washington, D.C.: The Reinvestment Fund.

Oakeshott, M. (1975) *On Human Conduct*. Oxford: Clarendon Press.

Oakley, K. (2009) 'The disappearing arts: creativity and innovation after the creative industries'. *International Journal of Cultural Policy*, 15(4), 403-413.

Oakley, K. (2011) 'In its own image: New Labour and the cultural workforce'. *Cultural Trends*, 20(3-4), 281-289.

O'Connor, J. (2010) *The Cultural and Creative Industries: A Literature Review*, 2nd edn. Newcastle: Creativity, Culture and Education. Available at: www.creativitycultureeducation.org/the-cultural-and-creative-industries-a-literature-review [accessed December 2015].

O'Donnell G., Deaton A., Durand M., Halpern D. and Layard R. (2014) *Wellbeing and Policy*. London: Legatum Institute.

OECD (1996) *The Knowledge Based Economy*. Paris: OECD.

OECD (2005) *The Measurement of Scientific and Technological Activities: Guidelines for Collecting and Interpreting Innovation Data. Oslo Manual, Third Edition*. Paris: OECD.

OECD (2009) *Applications of Complexity Science for Public Policy. New Tools for Finding Unanticipated Consequences and Unrealised Opportunities*. Paris: OECD Global Science Forum. Available at: www.oecd.org/science/sci-tech/43891980.pdf [accessed December 2015].

Ofcom (2009) *Local and Regional Media in the UK*. Available at: http://stakeholders.ofcom.org.uk/binaries/research/tv-research/lrmuk.pdf [accessed December 2015].

O'Leary T., I. Burkett and K. Braithwaite (2011) *Appreciating Assets*. Fife: IACD and Carnegie UK Trust.

Ong, A. (1999) *Flexible Citizenship*. Durham, NC: Duke University Press.

Ostrom, E. (1990) *Governing the Commons: The Evolution of Institutions for Collective Action*. Cambridge: Cambridge University Press.

Ostrom, E. (1996) 'Crossing the great divide: coproduction, synergy, and development'. *World Development*, 24(6), 1073-87.

Papacharissi, Z. (2010a) *A Private Sphere: Democracy in a Digital Age*. Cambridge: Polity.

Papacharissi, Z. (ed) (2010b) *A Networked Self: Identity, Community, and Culture on Social Network Sites*. New York: Routledge.

Papacharissi, Z. (2015) *Affective Publics: Sentiment, Technology, and Politics*. Oxford: Oxford University Press.

Parker, D. and C. Karner (2011) 'Remembering the alum rock road: reputational geographies and spatial biographies'. *Midland History*, 36(2), 292-309.

Peacock, C. (2014) 'Territorial stigma and regeneration in Tottenham'. *Open Democracy*, 18 February. Available at: www.opendemocracy.net/opensecurity/chloe-peacock/territorial-stigma-and-regeneration-in-tottenham [accessed December 2015].

Peters, M. and J. Cherbo (1998) 'The missing sector: the unincorporated arts'. *The Journal of Management, Law and Society*, 28(2), 115-28.

Pew Research Center (2012) How the Presidential Candidates Use the Web and Social Media. Available at: www.journalism.org/2012/08/15/how-presidential-candidates-use-web-and-social-media/ [accessed December 2015].

Pink, S. (2012) *Situating Everyday Life: Practices and Places*. London: Sage.

Pollard, J. (2004) 'From industrial district to "urban village"? Manufacturing, money and consumption in Birmingham's jewellery quarter'. *Urban Studies*, 41, 173-93.

Portigal, S. (2008) 'Persona Non Grata'. *Interactions* 15(1), 72-3.

Poster, M. (1997) 'Cyberdemocracy: the internet and the public sphere'. In: D. Porter (ed) *Internet Culture*. New York: Routledge.

Postill, J. (2008) 'Localizing the internet beyond communities and networks'. *New Media & Society,* 10(3), 413-31.

Postill, J. (2011) *Localizing the Internet: An Anthropological Account*. New York and London: Berghahn Books.

Potts, J. (2009) 'Why creative industries matter to economic evolution'. *Economics of Innovation and New Technology*, 18(7), 663-73.

Potts, J. (2011) *Creative Industries and Economic Evolution*. Cheltenham: Edward Elgar Publishing.

Potts, J. and S. Cunningham (2008) 'Four models of the creative industries'. *International Journal of Cultural Policy*, 14(3): 233-49.

Potts, J., S. Cunningham, J. Hartley and P. Ormerod (2008) 'Social network markets: a new definition of the creative industries'. *Journal of Cultural Economics*, 32(3), 166-85.

Power, D. (2011) *Priority Sector Report: Creative and Cultural Industries. European Cluster Observatory, Europa Innova Paper N.16*. Brussels: European Commission.

Pratt, A. (2002) 'Hot jobs in cool places. The material cultures of new media product spaces: the case of the south of market, San Francisco'. *Information, Communication and Society*, 5, 27-50.

Putnam, R. (2001) *Bowling Alone: The Collapse and Revival of American Community*. New York: Simon & Schuster.

Putnam, R. (2001) 'Social Capital: Measurement and Consequences'. *Isuma: Canadian Journal of Policy Research*, Spring, 41-51.

Qiu, J.L. (1999/2000) 'Virtual censorship in China: keeping the gate between the cyberspaces'. *International Journal of Communications Law and Policy*, 4, 1-25.

Radcliffe, D. (2012) *Here and Now: UK Hyperlocal Media Today*. London: Nesta.

Ramirez, R. (1999) 'Value co-production: intellectual origins and implications for practice and research'. *Strategic Management Journal*, 20(1), 49-65.

Ramirez, R. (2008) 'A "meditation" on meaningful participation'. *The Journal of Community Informatics*, 4(3). Available at: http://ci-journal. net/index.php/ciej/article/view/390/424 [accessed December 2015].

Ramsden, H. (2013) *A Skeleton Overview of the State of the Amateur Arts in Europe*. Cardiff: Voluntary Arts.

Ramsden, H., J. Milling, J. Phillimore, A. McCabe, H. Fyfe and R. Simpson (2011) *The Role of Grassroots Arts Activities in Communities: A Scoping Study. Working Paper 68*. Birmingham, UK: Third Sector Research Centre.

Ratto, M. and M. Boler (2014) *DIY Citizenship: Critical Making and Social Media*. Cambridge, MA: MIT Press.

Reason P. and H. Bradbury (eds) (2008) *The Sage Handbook of Action Research*. London: Sage.

Reeves, M. (2002) *Measuring the Economic and Social Impacts of the Arts: A review*. London: Arts Council England.

Rennie, E. (2006) *Community Media: A Global Introduction*, Lanham, MD: Rowman & Littlefield.

Rheingold, H. (1995) 'Cyberhood vs neighbourhood'. *UTNE Reader*, March-April.

Rhodes, C. (2012) *Small Businesses and the UK Economy.* House of Commons Standard Note: SN/EP/6078, 19 Dec.

Richards, R. (ed) (2007) *Everyday Creativity and New Views of Human Nature.* Washington, DC: American Psychological Association.

Robinson, K. (1999) *All Our Futures: Creativity, Culture and Education.* London: HMG. Available at: http://sirkenrobinson.com/pdf/allourfutures.pdf [accessed December 2015].

Rogers, N. (2002) *Halloween: From Pagan Ritual to Party Night.* Oxford: Oxford University Press.

Rose, F. (2012) *The Art of Immersion. How the Digital Generation Is Remaking Hollywood, Madison Avenue, and the Way We Tell Stories.* New York, NY: W.W. Norton.

Rose, G., M. Degen and C. Melhuish (2014) 'Networks, interfaces, and computer-generated images: learning from digital visualisations of urban redevelopment projects'. *Environment and Planning D: Society and Space*, 32(3), 386-403.

Rosen, J. (1999) *What Are Journalists For?.* New Haven, CT: Yale University Press.

Rosen, J. (2006) 'The People Formerly Known as the Audience'. [Blog] PressThink. Available at: http://archive.pressthink.org/2006/06/27/ppl_frmr.html [accessed December 2015].

Rowson, J., S. Broome and A. Jones (2010) *Connected Communities. How Social Networks Power and Sustain Big Society.* London: Royal Society of Arts.

Ruskin, J. (1862) *Unto This Last: Four Essays on the First Principles of Political Economy.* Available at: http://web.archive.org/web/20081025033653/http://etext.lib.virginia.edu/toc/modeng/public/RusLast.html [accessed December 2015].

Rydin, Y. (2014) 'Communities, networks and social capital'. In: N. Gallent and D. Ciaffi (eds) *Community Action and Planning: Contexts, Drivers and Outcomes.* Bristol: Policy Press, 21-39.

Saada, E. (2012) *Empire's Children: Race, Filiation, and Citizenship in the French Colonies.* Chicago: University of Chicago Press.

Sanders, E. and P. Stappers (2008) 'Co-creation and the new landscapes of design'. *CoDesign,* 4(1), 5-18.

Sanders, E. and P. Stappers (2014) 'From designing to co-designing to collective dreaming: three slices in time'. *Interactions*, 21(6), 24-33.

Sanger, L. (2007) 'Who says we know: on the politics of knowledge'. *The Edge.* Available at: http://edge.org/3rd_culture/sanger07/sanger07_index.html [accessed December 2015].

Sanoff, H. (2006) 'Multiple views of participatory design'. *METU JFA*, 23(2), 131-43.

Sapsed, J. and P. Nightingale (2013) *The Brighton Fuse Report*. Available at: www.brightonfuse.com/wp-content/uploads/2013/10/The-Brighton-Fuse-Final-Report.pdf [accessed December 2015].

Sayer, A. (2003) *Valuing Culture and Economy*. Available at: www.lancaster.ac.uk/fass/sociology/research/publications/papers/sayer-valuing-culture-and-economy.pdf [accessed December 2015].

Saxenian, A. (1994) *Regional Advantage*. Boston, MA: MIT Press.

Scammell, M. (2000) 'The internet and civic engagement: the age of the citizen consumer'. *Political Communication*, 17, 351-55.

Schön, D. (1983) *The Reflective Practitioner. How Professionals Think in Action*. New York: Basic Books.

Schudson, M. (1999) *The Good Citizen: A History of American Civic Life*. Cambridge, MA: Harvard University Press.

Schultz, I. (2007) 'The journalistic gut feeling'. *Journalism Practice*, 1(2), 190-207.

Scott, A. (1999) 'The cultural economy: geography and the creative field'. *Media, Culture and Society*, 21(6), 807-17.

Scott, A. (2005) *On Holllywood: The Place, the Industry*. Princeton, NJ: Princeton University Press.

Shafique, A. (2013) *Enterprise Solutions, New Approaches to Commissioning and Public Services Mutual: Lessons from Cooperative Councils*. London: RSA. Available at: www.thersa.org/__data/assets/pdf_file/0011/1523495/Enterprise-Solutions_Lessons-from-Cooperative-Councils_Final.pdf [accessed December 2015].

Shand, R. (2008) 'Theorizing amateur cinema: limitations and possibilities'. *The Moving Image*, 8(2), 36-60.

Sharpe, B. (2010) *Economies of Life: Patterns of Health and Wealth*. Available at: www.internationalfuturesforum.com [accessed December 2015].

Shirky, C. (2010) *Cognitive Surplus: Creativity and Generosity in a Connected Age*. London: Penguin.

Silberberg, S., K. Lorah, R. Disbrow and A. Muessig (2013) *Places in the Making: How Placemaking Builds Places and Communities*. Maldon, MA: MIT, Department of Urban Studies and Planning. Available at: http://danley.rutgers.edu/files/2014/02/Places-in-the-Making-MIT-DUSP-2013.pdf [accessed December 2015].

Simon, R. (2012) 'Remembering together: social media and the formation of the historical present'. In: E. Giaccardi (ed) *Heritage and Social Media: Understanding Heritage in a Participatory Culture*. London: Routledge.

References

Smith, R. and K. Warfield (2008) 'The creative city: A matter of values'. In: P. Cooke and L. Lazzeretti (eds) *Creative Cities, Cultural Clusters and Local Economic Development*. Cheltenham: Edward Elgar, 287–312.

Sobers, S. (2008) 'Consequences and coincidences: a case study of experimental play in media literacy'. *Journal of Media Practice*, 9(1), 53–66.

Sobers, S. (2010) 'Positioning education within community media'. In: K. Howley (ed) *Understanding Community Media*. Los Angeles, CA: Sage, 188–99.

Social Care Institute for Excellence (2013) *Co-production in Social Care: What It Is and How To Do It*. Available at: http://www.scie.org.uk/publications/guides/guide51/ [accessed December 2015].

Soysal, Y. (1994) *Limits of Citizenship: Migrants and Postnational Membership in Europe*. Chicago: University of Chicago Press.

Stebbins, R. (1977) 'The amateur: two sociological definitions'. *The Pacific Sociological Review* 20(4), 582–606.

Stebbins, R. (1992) *Amateurs, Professionals, and Serious Leisure*. Montreal and Kingston: McGill-Queen's University Press.

Steenbergen, B. van (1994) 'Towards a global ecological citizen'. In: B. van Steenbergen (ed) *The Condition of Citizenship*. London: Sage, 141–52.

Stern, M. and S. Seifert (2007) *From Creative Economy to Creative Society*. Available at: www.trfund.com/tag/creative-economy [accessed December 2015].

Stern, M. and S. Seifert (2010) 'Cultural clusters: the implications of cultural assets agglomeration for neighborhood revitalization'. *Journal of Planning Education and Research*, 29(3), 262–79.

Sternberg, R. (ed) (1999) *Handbook of Creativity*. New York: Cambridge University Press.

Stephenson, W. (1967) *The Play Theory of Mass Communication*. Chicago: Chicago University Press. New edition, Transaction Publishers, 1988.

Stewart, M. (2013) 'Mysteries reside in the humblest, everyday things: collaborative anthropology in the digital age'. *Social Anthropology*, 21(3), 305–21.

Stewart, R. (2008) 'The arts and artist in urban revitalization'. In: J. Cherbo, R. Stewart and M. Wyszomirski (eds) *Understanding the Arts and the Creative Sector in the United States*. Rutgers, NJ: Rutgers University Press.

Stiegler, B. (2010) *For a New Critique of Political Economy*. Cambridge: Polity.

Sundar-Harris, U. (2008) 'Video for empowerment and social change: a case for rural women in Fiji'. In: E. Papoutsaki and U. Sundar-Harris (eds) *South Pacific Islands Communication: Regional Perspectives, Local Issues*. Singapore and New Zealand: Asian Media Information and Communication Centre.

Tacchi, J. (2012) 'Digital engagement'. In: D. Miller (ed) *Digital Anthropology*. London: Bloomsbury.

Tallon, A. (2010) *Urban Regeneration in the UK*. London: Routledge.

Tapscott, D. and A. Williams (2006) *How Mass Collaboration Changed Everything*. London: Penguin.

Taylor, G. (2006) *More Than a Pastime: Informal Arts Improve Communities and Increase Formal Arts Participation*. Chicago: Metro Chicago Information Centre.

Taylor, G. (2008) *Magnetising Neighborhoods Through Amateur Arts Performance*. Chicago: Metro Chicago Information Centre.

Terranova, T. (2003) *Free Labour: Producing Culture for the Digital Economy*. Available at: www.electronicbookreview.com/thread/technocapitalism/voluntary [accessed December 2015].

Tether, B. (2009) *Design in Innovation. Coming Out from the Shadow of R&D. An Analysis of the UK Innovation Survey of 2005*. London: Department for Innovation, University and Skills.

Toker, Z. (2007) 'Recent trends in community design: the eminence of participation'. *Design Studies* 28(3), 309-23.

Towse, R. (ed) (2003) *A Handbook of Cultural Economics*. Cheltenham: Edward Elgar.

Throsby, D. (2003) 'Cultural capital.' In: R. Towse (ed) *A Handbook of Cultural Economics*. Cheltenham: Edward Elgar.

Turner, B. (ed) (1993) *Citizenship and Social Theory*. London: Sage.

Turner, J. (1976) *Housing by People*. London: Marion Boyars.

UNCTAD (2008) *Creative Economy Report 2008. The Challenges of Assessing the Creative Economy: Towards Informed Policy Making*. Geneva and New York: United Nations Conference on Trade and Development.

UNCTAD (2010) *Creative Economy Report 2010. Creative Economy: A Feasible Development Option*. Geneva and New York: United Nations Conference on Trade and Development.

UNESCO (2013) *Creative Economy Report 2013. Widening Local Development Pathways*. Geneva and New York: United Nations Educational, Scientific and Cultural Organisation.

Urry, J. (1998) 'Globalisation and citizenship'. *World Congress of Sociology*. Montreal.

Van Biezen, I., P. Mair and T. Poguntke (2012) 'Going, going ... gone? The decline of party membership in contemporary Europe'. *European Journal of Political Research*, 51, 24-56.

Van Dijck, J. (2013) *The Culture of Connectivity: A Critical History of Social Media.* Oxford: Oxford University Press.

Vickery, J. (2007) *The Emergence of Culture-led Regeneration: A Policy Concept and its Disctontent. Research Paper No 9, Centre for Cultural Policy Studies.* Coventry: University of Warwick.

von Hippel, E. (2005) *Democratizing Innovation.* Cambridge, MA: MIT Press.

von Busch, O. (2012) 'Generation open: contested creativity and capabilities'. *The Design Journal*, 15(4), 443-59.

Wacquant, L., T. Slater and V. Pereira (2014). 'Territorial stigmatization in action'. *Environment and Planning A*, 46(6), 1270-80.

Wahl-Jorgensen, K. (2009) 'On the newsroom-centricity of journalism ethnography'. In: S.E. Bird (ed) *The Anthropology of News and Journalism.* Bloomington, IN: Indiana University Press, 21-35.

Wali, A., R. Severson and M. Longoni (2002) *Informal Arts. Finding Cohesion, Capacity and Other Cultural Benefits in Unexpected Place. Research report.* Chicago: The Chicago Centre for Arts Policy at Columbia College.

Ward, C. (1976) *Housing: An Anarchist Approach.* London: Freedom Press.

Warwick Commission (2015) *Enriching Britain: Culture, Creativity and Growth: The 2015 Report by the Warwick Commission on the Future of Cultural Value.* Coventry: University of Warwick. Available at: www2.warwick.ac.uk/research/warwickcommission/futureculture/finalreport/ [accessed December 2015].

Webb, P. (2007) *Exploring the Networked Worlds of Popular Music: Milieu Cultures.* New York: Routledge.

Webster, F. (2006) *Theories of the Information Society,* 3rd edn. London: Routledge.

White, M. (2008) 'Can an act of citizenship be creative?' In: E. Isin and G. Nielsen (eds) *Acts of Citizenship.* London: Zed Books, 44-56.

Williams, A., S. Barnett, D. Harte and J. Townend (2014) *The State of UK Hyperlocal Community News: Findings From a Survey of Practitioners.* Available at: https://hyperlocalsurvey.wordpress.com/download-the-report/ [accessed December 2015].

Williams, A., D. Harte, and J. Turner (2015) 'The value of UK hyperlocal community news: findings from content analysis, an online survey and interviews with producers'. *Digital Journalism*, 3(5), 680-703.

Wilson, N. (2010) 'Social creativity: re-qualifying the creative economy'. *International Journal of Cultural Policy*, 6(3), 367-81.

Williams, R. (1958) 'Culture is ordinary'. In: A. Gray and J. McGuigan (eds) *Studies in Culture: An Introductory Reader*. London: Arnold (2002).

Williams, R. (1974) *Television: Technology and Cultural Form*. London: Fontana.

Williams, R. (1977) *Marxism and Literature*. Oxford: Oxford University Press.

Willig, I. (2013) 'Newsroom ethnography in a field perspective'. *Journalism*, 14(3), 372-87.

Wittel, A. (2001) 'Toward a network sociality'. *Theory, Culture & Society*, 18(6), 51-76.

Work Foundation (2007) *Staying Ahead: The Economic Performance of the UK's Creative Industries*. London: DCMS.

Wright, N., R. Davis and S. Bucolo (2013) 'The creative citizen: understanding the value of design education programs in the knowledge economy'. In: *Design Learning for Tomorrow – Design Education from Kindergarten to PhD*. Oslo: DRS//Cumulus. Available at: http://eprints.qut.edu.au/56343/1/WRIGHT_Davis_Bucolo.pdf [accessed December 2015].

Wulz, F. (1986) 'The concept of participation'. In: H. Sanoff (ed) *Participatory Design, Theory and Techniques*. Raleigh, NC: Bookmasters, 39-48.

Yellow Railroad (2009) *Bristol Place Making and Marketing Plan 'Competing for Talent, Tourism and Trade'*. Bristol: Bristol City Council.

Young, I. (1989) 'Polity and group difference: a critique of the ideal of universal citizenship'. *Ethics*, 99(2), 250-74.

Zamenopoulos, T. and K. Alexiou (2005) 'Linking design and complexity: a review'. *In ECCS'05 Satellite Workshop Proceedings: Embracing Complexity in Design*. UK: Open University, 91-102.

Zimmerman, P. (1986) 'The amateur, the avant-garde and ideologies of art'. *Journal of Film and Video*, 38(3/4), 63-85.

Zittrain, J. (2006) 'The generative internet'. *University of Oxford Faculty of Law Legal Studies Research Paper Series. Working Paper No 28*. Oxford: Oxford University.

Zittrain, J. (2008) *The Future of the Internet – and How to Stop It*. New Haven, CT: Yale University Press.

Index

Note: page number in *italic* type refer to Figures.

Birmingham, UK:
  Castle Vale estate 216–21
  jewellery quarter 70
    see also B31 Voices;
    BournevilleVillage.com; Moseley
    Exchange/Moseley Community
    Development Trust (CDT); Tyburn
    Mail
Blair, Tony 10
Blogger.com 240, 246
blogging:
  and publishing industry 62
    see also hyperlocal journalism/news
Borger, M. 144
Bourdieu, P. 132
BournevilleVillage.com 115, *116*
boyd, danah 130
Brighton Fuse 242
Bristol 199
  in asset mapping 193
  culture of 137–8, 139–40
  and place-making 226, 227, 228
    see also South Blessed
Britain's Got Talent 65
Britton, Tessy *185*
Broadbent, S. 226
Broughton Spurtle 86, 87
Brown, Gordon 77
Bruns, A. 62
Buckingham, D. 130
Burgess, J. 106
butterfly effect 134

C

Cameron, David 10, 265, 269
Capture Wales programme (BBC) 62
Cardiff University 19, 109
carnival 33
Carvalho, C. 39
Casey, Alice 182–3
Castells, Manuel 31–2, 151, 205, 206
Castle Vale estate, Birmingham 216–21
  see also Tyburn Mail
Cebr (Centre for Economic and
  Business Research) 68, *69*
Centre for Community Journalism,
  Cardiff University 19
Centre for Creative Industries and
  Innovation, Queensland University
  of Technology, Australia 12
Centre Forum 7, 266, 275
  see also Lee, Stephen
CGIs (computer generated images)
  213, 213–14

Chapain, Caroline 49–74, 103–28,
  153–79, 181–204
Chapple, K. 206
Charlie Hebdo 29
Cherbo, J. 60
Chicago, USA 68
China 12, 17
Ciaffi, D. 105
citizen benefits 82–97
citizen journalism *see* hyperlocal
  journalism/news
citizenship:
  and creative acts 106–7
  economics of 25
    see also creative citizenship
citizenship of rights 30
citizenship studies 26
  communication and media studies
    approaches 35–6
  historical approaches 27, 30–1
  humanities approaches 29, 32–5
  social sciences approaches 26–30
  technological and economic
    approaches 36–7
  theoretical approaches 31–2
City Mapper 292
Civic Informatics Laboratory,
  University of Milan 80–1
civic rights 30
class:
  and culture 58
  and participation 41
    see also creative class
clusters 69–71, 264–5
co-creation 3, 7, 22, 153, 154, 219
  see also co-production
co-design 153, 154, 241–2
  see also co-production
Co-designing Asset Mapping project
  (AHRC) 203
co-production 153–6, 259
  creative process 168–73, *172, 173*
  in design 154
  in media 155
  overview of projects 156–62, *158,
    159, 160, 161, 163*
  partners' perspectives on 163–5
  practicalities of 173–8, *177*
  in research 155
  role of researcher/design practitioner
    165–8
Coalition government (Conservative/
  Liberal Democrat), UK 9–10, 28,
  55, 265
Coatham, Veronica 217